International Relations and World Images

A Study of Norwegian Foreign Policy Elites

By
Helge Hveem

Universitetsforlaget

Oslo – Bergen – Tromsö

PRIO MONOGRAPHS FROM THE INTERNATIONAL PEACE RESEARCH INSTITUTE, OSLO

No. 1. Arne Martin Klausen: Kerala Fishermen and the Indo-Norwegian Pilot Project. 1968

No. 2. Johan Galtung: Members of Two Worlds. A Development Study of Three Villages in Western Sicily. 1971

No. 3. Helge Hveem: International Relations and World Images. A Study of Norwegian Foreign Policy Elites. 1972

ISBN 8200 08842 1

Preface

This report is based on a survey undertaken in 1967 when the author was a final-year student of political science at the University of Oslo, and a Research Assistant at the International Peace Research Institute, Oslo. A preliminary report on part of the survey was submitted as a thesis for the *magister* degree. The present work includes the whole survey and is therefore both an extension of and a completely rewritten version of that first report.

Many persons have contributed immensely to the study reported here. I am particularly indebted to Johan Galtung of the International Peace Research Institute, Oslo, who has been of great help and much inspiration at all stages of the study. I am also indebted to Nils Ørvik and Henry Valen for advice during the writing of the first report.

Further thanks are extended to my colleagues at the International Peace Research Institute who individually and through the stimulating milieu they have created, gave invaluable support at various stages and in various ways. In particular I mention Steinar Wigtil, Anne Lisa Frostad, and Åke Hartmann, for invaluable help in data processing. I am also indebted to my fellow students Margot Kolberg, Jon Eivind Kolberg, and Bjørn Johannessen, who assisted in data collection, and to all those persons from whom data were collected.

The report could not have been written without the help, the understanding and the stimulance of my wife, Kari Hveem.

None of the persons or institutions mentioned, however, should bear any responsibility for the report in itself, nor the points on which it may be criticized. That responsibility rests of course entirely with the author.

Contents

Introduction

This study has both a general and a specific purpose. The general one is to contribute to the development of theories in international relations and foreign policy making. The specific purpose is to present data on international images and foreign policy attitudes of Norwegian foreign policy elites.

The unit of analysis chosen for the purposes of the study is the individual, and the focus will be on his images or cognitions of the world around him, and his attitudes towards various phenomena of that world. While the approach might be seen as social-psychological, behavioralistic, or structural, it is my intention that the study not be subsumed under any of these or other headings or 'schools'. It is more an attempt at combining several approaches than at advocating any specific one.

One of the main problems to be dealt with is the general question of what factors determine people's images and attitudes. Another question then is what determines the foreign policy of a given nation-state, in casu Norway. This is largely one and the same question, since we shall be dealing with elite people, on the assumption of a relatively strong correlation between the foreign policy of a state and the corresponding attitudes and images of its elite. Many such factors – from the idiosyncratic or individual to the systematic or international level – have been proposed, analyzed, and advocated. In its search for decisive factors, this study tends toward the systemic or international end of the continuum. The reason is two-fold: that international relations and foreign policy making theories do not discriminate sufficiently between different actors as to their relative independence of other actors and their possibilities of acting on their own; and that Norway is an actor which is relatively dependent on the international system or specific parts of it.

It is generally recognized that the international system is stratified according to the power or capacity of an actor to enact a given policy toward other actors: to impose its will upon them. Far less recognized is that this fact may have important consequences for the policies of the 'imposed upon' actors and for the images and attitudes of the foreign policy elite of those actors.

This is not to say that systemic factors are *the* determining or the most determining factors in the case of a small, not resourceful, not powerful actor, as Norway. The word 'determine' should be used with care, since causal relationships are hard to establish in our field. And the possibility that factors on the idiosyncratic or individual end of the continuum, contribute rather decisively to the formation of policies, attitudes, and images, is present even in the case of the tiny mini-state actor. This is then why we study elites.

Studying elites is important since it is their perception or cognition of the world – factors part of the environment, or non-idiosyncratic factors (or perhaps even those factors) – which largely shape their attitudes and determine their international behavior. We distinguish between objective and subjective parts of the environment. Objective are concrete, observable factors like the outbreak of a war, the implementation of economic sanctions, etc. The subjective parts are the world in the minds of men: how they believe the environment to be, their subjective knowledge of it.

Whereas the objective parts of the environment are not altogether decisive in shaping events and determining behavior, the subjective ones are what matters. Then the important thing is not how the world actually *is*, but how it is *perceived* as being.

The study of elites is no new field within social research. In foreign policy making and international relations, however, such studies have been few. For several reasons, survey studies have been more used on nationally selected samples, for the study of public opinion in general. Such studies are of course important, but they cannot and should not replace elite studies, especially not if the purpose is to gain insight about the background on which the foreign policy of a state actor is founded. There can hardly be any doubt that in that respect, elite studies are more important than studies of the general public, although one basic question here is the possible consequences and importance of great variances as well as similarities in the images and attitudes between elites and public. We shall have something to say of this. But first, we shall have to deal rather extensively with the question how much and what kind of variance there *is* among the Norwegian elite samples. This is *one* of the basic problems on which this investigation is built: the problem of consensus.

PART I

Design and Theory

1. Design

1.1. *Definitions and distinctions: the concepts*

There is, as Rokeach argues, an apparent lack of consensus among social scientists on the question of defining even basic concepts in social research theory[1]. This is true of the concepts of *image* and *attitude*. There is also dissensus on to what extent and in what way these and related concepts should be distinguished from each other.

We shall not make any original contributions to these problems in this context. There is now another, probably equally important contribution to be made: using definitions and distinctions already at hand, and with some degree of support in the literature. That is, we should work toward reducing the conflict over definitions by using the 'established' ones when they still seem suitable and valid, and by applying definitions which now appear in the series of relatively recent encyclopedian literature (for instance the *International Encyclopedia of the Social Sciences*).

According to the scheme used by Parsons and Shils, human beings relate themselves to their environment through *perception* (cognition), *preferences* (cathexis or affect), and *evaluation*.[2] *Perception* is the process of attaining knowledge of and discriminating objects, events, actions, issues. *Preference* is the investment of objects, events, actions, or issues with emotional significance or affect. *Evaluation* is the process by which individuals organize and select their perceptions, preferences, and values in establishing a position from which political action can be initiated.

A definition of cognition perhaps more precise and at the same time broader, is offered by Festinger when he argues that the concept covers

> any knowledge, opinion, or belief about the environment, about oneself, or about one's behavior.[3]

This definition will be applied here, although we shall have to use the concept of opinion in another context or for other purposes.

Out of these processes (but not only from them), attitudes and images are then formed. These concepts are among the most used, but at the same time among the most ambiguous. Blumer advocates abandoning the concept 'attitude' because its ambiguity makes it useless in research.[4] Most authors still keep it, but among them there are at least two schools of thought.

The one considers an attitude as an organized set of preferences: emphasis is put on the affective aspect of an individual's orientations. The other defines attitude as composed of both affective and cognitive properties and formed by the interactions of these properties. Both agree that an attitude is a relatively enduring feature in the individual's orientation, and that it has a relatively high generality.

Choosing between the schools is unnecessary here. We take it that cognitive properties may have an impact on the formation of attitudes. It must be decided empirically to what extent this is true and what form such an impact generally has. In so doing, we must also take account of the possible impact on the formation of attitudes of other factors or properties – human, social, cultural – such as personality and experience.[5]

Ambiguity and differences in approach are also the case with 'image'. Boulding, although stressing the importance of value scales in 'determining the effect of the messages it (the individual) receives on its image of the world'[6], seems to think of images as basically cognitive properties. Krech and Crutchfield are more explicitly on the side of the cognitive predominance when they say that images or

> beliefs have only a cognitive element while attitudes have both cognitive and affective components.[7]

Kelman, on the other hand, advocates the both-and approach in saying that the concept image should not be defined in a restrictive sense

> that would differentiate it very sharply from such related concepts as attitude and opinion. Rather, the concept is meant to be broadly representative of the whole family of attitudinal variables.[8]

A similar line is taken by Scott when he says that all the three aspects of orientation already mentioned – cognitive, affective, and evaluative – are 'probably closely intertwined in the typical image structure'[9].

Thus, we find a convergence of conceptual definitions: discriminating between 'attitude' and 'image' becomes semantic if we follow the approaches of Rokeach and Kelman as the advocates of the both-and-approach for attitude and image, respectively. Not only for analytical reasons does it seem most appropriate to take the line of Krech and Crutchfield, and even to see attitudes as *predominantly* affective or preferential constructions. This does not mean, however, discarding the possibility of an impact on attitudes of cognitive elements. On the contrary, such an impact is assumed and will be tested.

'Opinion' is defined as the concrete response an individual gives on a specific item, 'picked out of' the environment by himself, or presented to him as a stimulus. A set of opinions may present a basis for infering an attitude or an image, depending on whether the items used are representing affective or cognitive properties, respectively.

1.2. *The foreign policy elite*

A basic question in elite theory is whether in a society there is *one general elite* (or a very small number of social groups acting as such) or *a number of different elites*. The problem in other words is elite singularity versus elite pluralism.

Suzanne Keller differentiates between strategic and segmental elites, the strategic being 'those which have the largest, most comprehensive scope and impact'.[10] Making use of the Parsonian pattern variables, she designates four categories of elites, the first of which – the 'goal attainment elite' – she calls 'the current political elite'.

The pluralism model is also advocated by Deutsch, Edinger, Macridis, and Merritt when they in a recent empirical study distinguish between 'special' and 'general' elites:

> Special (or 'functional') elites comprise those who represent their own individual spheres of public life: decision-makers in politics, government, business, the military, communications, religion, and so forth. General elites are those who dominate the life of the society as a whole.[11]

These concepts of general and special elites seem to have very much in common with the Keller concepts of strategic and segmental elites, respectively.

The pluralism model, however, has not been commonly accepted among contemporary scholars. Wright Mills uses the concept 'power elite' to describe a social stratum, consisting of the corporations, political institutions, and military services and based on 'the many interconnections and points of coinciding interests' among these groups.[12] This elite, which seems to comprise the pluralistic general or strategic elite *and* the political (special) elite, (the two are more or less interchangeable, because economic and military

15

power or prestige, either automatically or due to the social structure, *is* political power) in Mills' theory has an especially strong and undisputed influence over foreign policy making.

Contrary to Wright Mills, Riesman presents 'an amorphous power structure which reflects a diversity of interests' by introducing the concept of 'veto group'.[13] And Dahl, in his study of local community (1961), raised support for the pluralistic elite thesis although on a basis and with an outcome somewhat different from that of Riesman.[14] Using the 'event analysis', Dahl searched for evidence of specific influentials or decision-makers on particular issues and found that power followed issues and was not generalized in the sense that one single group decided all issues.

Floyd Hunter, on the other hand, utilizes the 'reputational' form of investigation (which will be commented upon later) to find a relatively pyramidal, generalized elite structure.[15] This study, which also refers to local communities, would support the singularity thesis.

Spinrad, however, criticizes the extrapolation of such findings to a higher social level, i.e. from the local community to the national society level.[16] And Rose, in opposition to what he calls the 'economic-elite-dominance' hypothesis of Mills and Hunter, proposes the 'multi-influence' hypothesis which is not rigidly pluralistic, but which clearly tends in that direction.[17]

Over time and with the development of social science, theory seems to have tended form the singularity to the pluralism conception of elites,[18] a development which partly mirrors the development of society itself. With the modernization of society (and it is predominantly the modern, developed society we shall be talking about in this study) has followed a specialization of task or function performance. In a traditional society with little or no specialization, we might conceive of a single, general elite based on ascribed, formal and/or socio-economic status which performs most of or all the leadership functions of the society. In a modern, highly specialized society, there will be groups of individuals who through achievement criteria have reached a pre-eminent status or competence on a special field of activity. These individuals do not necessarily have the highest socio-economic status or the highest social prestige in the society as a whole, although some of them may. Nor need they be members of other elites, although some of them usually or even by necessity are: a modern society cannot preserve a minimum of homogeneity and cohesion without a certain overlapping of elite memberships. The extent and the role of such elite overlapping – a notion that makes us abandon Riesman's fragmentation conception – will decide whether a given society at any given time has an elite structure closer to the singularity or the pluralism model.

16

Torgersen maintains that Norway from an international view point represents 'a system where the elite groupings are extraordinarily tightly interwoven –'. He finds the explanation for this partly in the relatively small size (population) of the country. And he makes the hypothesis that Norway presently finds herself at a very interesting stage of her 'numerical development'.[19] We believe that Torgersen's observations are basically correct.

The foreign policy elite then is mostly composed of individuals who are members of other elites. There may be some important exceptions, notably in the case of the foreign policy specialist – the diplomat or the international relations professor. As a general rule, however, recruitment to the foreign policy elite is through other elite channels.

Which elites, which social groups the foreign policy elite is composed of will vary from one country to another. A number of recent elite surveys have been based on much the same design or sampling criteria.[20] The elite categories included have been the political or parliamentarian, the administrative, the business or interest group elites, and – varying somewhat from one study to another – the mass media, military, and professional (or intellectual) elites.

Not all members of such elites are members of the foreign policy elite. Most often only a minority is, but this may vary over time and from one issue-area to another. The boundary between those who are 'in' and those who are 'out' is in principle set by the activity, status, and functional tasks of the specific elite roles. In practice we should think of this boundary as rather loose, penetrated as it is by communication channels and by a certain mobility.

By 'activity' we are thinking mainly of participation in producing and transmitting information on international politics and foreign policy, primarily for 'home consumption' in the society. By 'functional tasks' we are particularly referring to policy-making.[21] By status we are thinking of both formal and informal status.

We shall not confine our study to those individuals or roles who may be found directly involved in the policy-making, as some scholars do. We stress the importance, actual or potential, of those individuals or roles which outside the policy-making roles contribute to the formation of images and attitudes through advice or information. We do stress, with Deutsch[22], the importance of the control of information and of communication channels. Focus should be less on policy-making, more on the process of steering, on the substance of thinking: i.e. elite images and attitudes, and on the probabilities that this steering process and the content of the communicated message will result in a given policy.

What we understand as the foreign policy elite are those individuals in a society who actually contribute, by their own minds and activities, or as agents of others, to steering or formulating the foreign policy of a national state actor, and of the extra-national orientations of the general public of that actor. This second aspect of the role of elite member, the socialization or education of the public, is not just part of the policy-making function, but primarily an important sphere of the activity in itself.

Being an elite member means that the public listens to what one communicates and even – or at least for parts of the public – engages in communicating to one. If an individual scores high both as a sender and as receiver of communication, he may be said to be at least potentially member of the elite. To what extent his position in the communication structure corresponds to a formal role in the policy-making institutions is an interesting problem but not decisive for the question of elite membership. We have to operate with a combination of the two roles or membership qualifications. An active communicator may not have formal status and still be policy-maker de facto, because his contributions carry the substance of policies, attitudes, or images into the policy process. A formal 'decision-maker' may not be active in communication, but still retain some influence over policies because he has the power to legitimate them.

Thus, what we have called policy-making activity is not to be seen as *the* decisive indicator of elite membership: the passive individual, whether temporarily or even more permanently passive, is a *potential* activist, a person in the 'elite reserves'. He may be the person who enters the policy-making process in times of crisis, on specific issues, or to back particular policies.

The distinction between 'in's' and 'out's' should not be seen as parallel to that between 'establishment' – those who support and carry through the official policy of a state at any time, and the 'non-establishment' – those who oppose that policy: the 'establishment' is not identical to the elite, as for instance Mills seems to mean. The opposition as members of the elite, or as policy-makers, is not a *contradictio in absurdum*, but is based on the two functions the opposition-within-the-elite performs. The one is its role as an alternative policy-maker, with alternative policies. The other is its role as a negative reference group for those in position.

1.3. *Foreign policy and social communication: the opinion-makers*

Behind the notion of a stratified society is a large body of theory. Parts of this theory or these theories of particular interest and relevance for our

18

purposes deal with stratification according to status and according to position in the communication structure.

In the first category, we may cite Aron, who reserves the term 'elite' for 'those who in diverse activities are high in the hierarchy, who occupy any important privileged positions, whether in terms of wealth or of prestige'. Defining the elite category rather broadly, Aron finds above this category 'the political class' "who actually exercise the functions of government"; between this class and the elite is 'the ruling class', a category of people who "influence those who govern and those who obey."[23]

In the second category, we find Katz and Lazarsfeld, Deutsch, although the model is only indicated on the general theoretical level, and Almond on the specific field of foreign policy[24]. Almond classifies society from top to bottom in three or rather four categories or levels. On top he finds 'the legal or official policy leadership,' a group of people within a category which he names 'the policy and opinion elites, the articulate policy-bearing stratum of the population which gives structure to the public, and which provides the effective means of access to the various groupings'. Beyond this level is the 'attentive public – informed and interested in foreign policy problems, and which constitutes the audience for the foreign policy discussions among the elites.' At the bottom of this continuum, Almond finds the 'general public', uninformed, non-interested, non-auditive.

Almond's conceptualization of the policy- and opinion-making structure has been applied by Rosenau and others.[25] Aron's scheme differs from that of Almond in the criteria it choses for definition of position, but the broad definition of elite seems to coincide somewhat with the latter. Our reason for applying Almond's model in this study is threefold: first, it follows the line we have taken in the choice between a pluralistic or a general or singular elite model (Aron evidently follows the latter); secondly, it puts main emphasis on the communication structure of society, not on socio-economic status hierarchies (which should not, however, be altogether abandoned in this context); and thirdly, it is more refined than most other conceptual schemes in the classification of the foreign policy- and opinion-making structure beyond the elite level.

The Katz and Lazarsfeld model of the 'two-step flow of communication' is both one of the most important theoretical contributions and one of the very few to be backed up empirically. It has to be included somehow in our design. However, it has not been our intention nor has it been technically possible due to research resources at hand, to make the nation-wide survey needed to tap the real content of the Katz–Lazarsfeld 'opinion-leader' category. Instead, we settled upon a sample which would represent an opinion-elite in Almond's sense, but at the same time take care of at least some of the opinion-leading function in the Katz–Lazarsfeld sense, although we would not be able to cover the small-group, informal kind of opinion-leader they found.

A scheme of the kind discussed here is a crude instrument which in important respect does not reflect reality. We are particularly thinking of the delimitation of boundaries between the categories: where to refer individuals who are not unequivocally members of one particular category or group. A more general problem is that several dimensions are variously used in theoretical discussions.

Three dimensions have to be considered in constructing a hierarchical model of society with respect to politics or in particular foreign policy:

> the social *status* of an individual in terms of reputation (prestige), economic wealth, and formal roles; the exposure of an individual, that is the degree to which he is (permanently) exposed to political affairs and responsive or attentive towards them; and the *participation* or activity of an individual in the process of policy- and opinion-making.

This list should cover some of the content of the status or prestige approach while also drawing primarily on the Almond model. In a way it might also be said to cover the basic idea of Galtung's center-periphery model based on the theory of social position.[26] In fact, Galtung's theory is in important respects a very useful combination of the two approaches for the study of society and stratification in general, but it is probably not specific enough for the study of the polity – the 'nerves of government' – of a society.

Our own idea (we shall not call it a model) is by combining the three dimensions mentioned, to arrive at a basis for both theoretical considera-

Table 1.3.1. *Dimensions for differentiating between structure levels*

	status	*exposure*	*participation*
High	high socio-economic status/high prestige ('upper class')	the attentive or exposed	the 'policy-makers'
Structural position			the 'opinion-makers'
Low	low socio-economic status/low prestige ('lower class')	the partially exposed or unexposed *or* the inattentive	the public audience: the 'opinion leaders' *and* the 'receptors' or mass public

tions and for sampling. This is not done by a strict combination in the sense of an index, but rather tentatively and on an a priori basis (which will be explained later). Table 1.3.1. visualizes the dimensional picture.

The dimensions go very much in the same direction: those with high socio-economic status are the most attentive or exposed and are the most probable influentials, the policy-makers and the opinion-makers. But there is no one-to-one correspondence between the dimensions: many with high status are among the politically inattentive and are non-participants in the political process. Conversely, there may be policy-makers who are relatively low on socio-economic status, and highly attentive or exposed individuals who are neither high-status people nor very influential in the policy- and opinion-making processes.

The participation dimension needs some further elaboration. While the two main aspects of this dimension – policy-making (in the broad sense referred to above) and opinion-making – are closely connected, they do at the same time differentiate, not only between the top-participators or highly active and the inactives or receptors, but also between the active. What we think of as policy-makers are in fact mostly *also* active opinion-makers, while the category we shall call *the opinion-makers* are primarily opinion-making and only temporarily, indirectly, or marginally participating in the policy-making itself.[27]

What we have said about the non-necessity of a connection between high socio-economic status and elite membership does not mean that socio-economic status is without importance in differentiating elite members from other groups of individuals. On the contrary, the category of people who score relatively high on these two criteria *and* at the same time are relatively active policy- and opinion-makers, we shall call the 'elite'.

Keller is perhaps right when she argues that

> From a long-range perspective ... it is clear that the link between high social class and strategic elite status has, in many modern societies, become indirect and informal.[28]

The opinion-makers are to a greater or lesser degree linked with the elite through a network of communication. They discuss with the elite people, they criticize their policies: in short, they constitute another reference group for the elite. But to a large extent the opinion-makers also constitute the *reservoir* of the elite, from which new elite members are recruited. Conversely, the opinion-maker category may also serve as a reserve group for fallen elite members – individuals who permanently or temporarily have lost their status or their formal role as an elite member.

21

These dynamic relationships between the two categories make the boundaries between them obscure and fluctuating. The same may be true of the relationship between the opinion-makers and the rest of the public.

The in-between position of the opinion-makers makes them suitable *intermediaries* between the elite and the general public. Another function they perform, already mentioned by Almond (see above) is that of 'giving structure and content to the public'. How this is done, whether directly or through a stratum of opinion-leaders, and to what extent it is done for instance compared to the extent the same is done by the elite, are questions to be explored.

1.4. *The samples*

Theoretically, the foreign policy elite and the foreign policy opinion-makers constitute concrete universes which could be studied *in toto* provided we knew who were members of these universes. However, it is now quite evident that such a research design is impossible. We have to make a selection of units for study.

This selection is problematic because the universe is problematic. A sampling in the often-used and rather narrow sense of the word is out of question. Consequently, there were already at the outset of the study some problems as to what purposes it could meet. One of these is the purpose of generalization.

While we shall be able to test substantive hypotheses, i.e. propositions about variables on the very sample we draw, it may be questioned to what extent we may generalize our findings, drawing conclusions from the samples to the universes. We are not able to draw a probability sample.[29]

This is not to say that non-probability samples may not be used for generalizing purposes: only that one should be careful in drawing conclusions where the findings are not sufficiently unambiguous or the trend in the quantitative results not clearly going in one direction.

This study has in many respects an explorative character. We feel, however, that at least our more basic conclusions are relatively good descriptions or predictions about the universes we are focusing on. What might be said to be the aim of this study besides that of exploring into unknown or little known areas, is to focus on a stratum which we believe to be *sufficiently representative* of the elite and opinion-makers, and to describe and explain those images and attitudes (of individuals in this stratum) which are reasonably *indicative* of the ones that go into the processes of foreign policy and opinion making.

22

As to *sampling,* we were faced with the choice between several different procedures. We chose a two-stage sampling, and a combination of the 'formal-institutional' and the 'judges' sampling method.[30] In the first stage, we selected several social categories to draw the units of analysis from. Four such categories were selected: parliamentarians or politicians, civil servants, mass media leaders, and interest group leaders. This selection corresponds fairly well with that made by Almond. On the other hand, it leaves out a category like the military leadership, included by Deutsch et al.[31]

One important reason for this kind of selection is that we intended to make a comparative inter-group study on the sub-national or sub-elite level. Consequently, the sampling was strictly purposive in the first stage, and partially so in the second stage.

Sampling procedure are explained in more detail in Appendix A, as is the choice of *m* or total number of units to be included in the samples for analysis. Response rates for the two samples and for the different sample categories are given in Appendix B. Comparing the ideal and the actual *m*'s (i.e. the number of units we decided to include and the number we actually got), in the case of the elite there was practically no difference, while the difference was rather great in the case of the opinion-maker sample.[32] This variance is largely due to the difference in data collection methods.

The sampling raises the problem of validity, first of all of the validity of the differentiation between the elite and the opinion-maker sample. We may validate this differentiation, or more specifically the notion that they constitute two relatively distinct groups or categories, by using the three dimensions of stratification and communication proposed in the scheme above (cf. Fig. 1). The result of this analysis, shown in more detail in Appendix C, gives satisfactory support to such a differentiation.

Another aspect of the problem of validity, however, is perhaps more important. This is the question of the degree of heterogeneity, representativity, and possible bias in the samples.[33] These questions may be answered by comparing our actual samples with the respective universes – to the extent they are known – and with similar samples from other universes. The comparisons are made according to several key background variables, as shown in Appendix D.

Heterogeneity does not seem to create any problem, while representativity and bias do. According to sex, education, and occupation the two samples are satisfactorily representative. By age, they are probably somewhat young, especially so with the opinion-maker sample, although we should bear in mind the role of the opinion-maker stratum as a 'pool' or re-cruits to the elite and thus necessarily somewhat younger than it. By party preference, the opinion-maker sample probably leans too much toward the left within both the 'socialist' and the 'bourgeois' groupings, but mostly so in the former.

In general, however, we may conclude that the sampling has produced sufficiently valid results, given reasonable demands for validity as the basis of evaluation.

1.5. *Data collection: the choice of instrument*

The choice of a data-collection method is a multi-level choice or a continuum of choices. Basically, it implies how one wants to present the stimuli – the *setting* – and how one wants to collect the responses – the *form*. It may be made from several different view-points: the more or less defined purpose of the research task undertaken; the range and the types variables to be explored; the research facilities available; and of course the types of units under study.

As said before, we intend to do both an explorative and a more strictly empirical study. This both-and purpose or starting-point has largely neces-sitated a similar both-and attitude toward the choice of forms of data collection.[34]

This is particularly true with our use of both an unstructured and a structured setting. Further, we used both oral and written responses. In the case of the elite, we employed an interview guide plus a small questionnaire for a limited number of questions. From the opinion-maker sample, we had only written responses, obtained through a mailed questionnaire. The basis for these choices is given in Appendix E. The same appendix also gives a brief review of how the instruments were tested and applied.

This part of the study raises the question of the validity and the reliability of the methods employed. One particular problem is the validity of a com-parison between the two samples of this study when they have been tested by different methods or data collecting instruments.

One way to test the validity of this kind of comparison is to compare responses on items which were presented in much the same form and context in both the schedule and the questionnaire used on the elite sample, and on the other hand, compare responses the elite sample gave on interview and the opinion-makers on questionnaire stimuli. This combined approach was used in another context, with the result that no variation amounting to what might reasonably be called a bias was found.[35] Relatively strong correspondence in the distribution of the two samples on a range of variables, particularly those of a cognitive content, seems to confirm this conclusion.

Other questions related to the problem of validity and reliability are discussed in Appendix E. On the whole we would say that our study, both as to data collection and as to data processing, responds positively to reasonable standards of validity and reliability.

1.6. *The scope of the study*

Considering the fact that empirical research on the problems we deal with has been rather modest, not the least as for Norway, [36] we chose large *scope* rather than solid depth. That is: we want to focus on a large scale of dimensions instead of concentrating on a few.

Given that choice, some methodological and practical problems arise. In a number of studies, one highly important question has been what period of time one may expect the respondent to occupy himself with the schedule or questionnaire. This practical question has been thought of as involving important methodological considerations. It has been thought that the period should not exceed one and a half hours, preferably less. There are reports of both negative and positive experiences.[37] We feel, on the basis of our study, that fears of a too long schedule or questionnaire have been exaggerated. There were some complaints about the length, but the great majority had nothing to complain on this point. In fact, it seems that those who complain about the length do this more often out of a *general* mistrust or dislike of social research or survey studies.

Such fears, however, made themselves felt in the initial design of the study on the range of dimensions or rather sub-dimensions selected, and on the choice of items representing the given dimension. As pointed out in 1.5, on the problem of validity, we needed several such items on each dimension we wanted to explore. Only in some cases, where one single or a couple of indicators with little or no doubt may represent a single dimension, may this problem be overlooked, but such cases are probably rare.

Thus there is an evident problem of how to compromise between the different requirements. But there are certain other compromises to be considered. One is that between what dimensions the respondents would find it interesting or relevant to deal with, and what the researcher on his part would prefer. Given the preference for a formal setting (1.5) the answer would necessary have to be in favor of the researcher: a genuine compromise was left out.

25

The interests of the respondent may, however, be represented by going for saliency of issues and opinions, i.e. by constructing the list of dimensions such as to give a picture of what is considered important and what is not by the respondent. Another crucial aspect of the respondent's orientation is the intensity of his attitudes or opinions. While we have much opportunity to say something of the former, the latter aspect is more problematic because of the lack of rigorous rating instruments in this study, and because panel analysis had to be left out due to lack of research facilities.

In general, we are focusing on present issues and trends on perception and evaluation and on the future: predictions and hopes. Given the limits of the study in time and space (it is synchronic, while it at least attempts to be nomothetic) this might be said to improve its lot, as far as the time dimension is concerned. Another attempt to improve the research strategy was the comparative perspective attached to it: the study aims at comparison both intra-nationally and extra-nationally. That so few empirical studies were available to us at the time of the preparation of this study made a comparative design which extensively built on the same variables or items, impossible.[38] Much of the inter-national comparison we shall make will thus be based on studies reported well after the data collection of this study was carried out. In some instances this necessarily leads to problems as to what extent the items or indicators in fact are comparable.

We shall mainly focus on attitudes (and images) as *dependent* variable in the framework of this study. In a larger setting – that of Norwegian foreign political behavior – attitudes are, however, more of an intervening variable.

A number of independent, so called 'background' variables, were included, as already indicated (see 1.4). The selection of the dependent variables was of course strictly purposive. In the first stage, a number of dimensions were singled out as 'focal points' We were not only interested in a broad scope, but even in an extensive domain. Or to put it simply: we were interested in *world* images and attitudes toward world phenomena, both those which the respondents found salient and those which *we* chose to focus on. At the same time, sub-system phenomena would also be singled out, by both parts.

There is no need of going into detail on the dimensions and variables selected for the study, as all variables are mentioned in the presentation of the schedule and the questionnaire in Appendix F. Let us therefore only briefly mention the main fields of interest and the major issue-areas included.

This study relates to three broad issue-areas: the international system, Norway's relations to the system, and the respondents' relations to it. The latter two areas overlap each other, because the elite really 'is' the nation.

We shall focus on the perceptions of the structure, main patterns, and on the future of the system. We will see what attitude our respondents have toward different actors in the system, and find out their preferences for Norway's relationship with different parts of and actors in the system, and for their own position within both the national and the wider, international system.

We will focus on their attitudes toward different international problems and their solution, e. g. the war-peace problems, and problems related to the developing countries. On the whole, we believe we have been able to cover most of the issue-areas which actually have importance in Norwegian politics, as well as in the world at large.[39] A basis for more deep-going analysis of particular issue-areas, as well as more inter-state comparative research, should then have been made.

2. Foreign Policy Opinion
as a Function of International Position

2.1. *Determinants of images and attitudes: the relative influence of factors*

There is a large body of theory on what factors determine the foreign policy of national actors. Much may be adapted for our purpose of describing and evaluating what factors determine or shape the images and attitudes of our units of analysis. The basis for doing so we find in what has been stated before: the assumption of a relatively strong positive correlation between the policy or behavior of a given national actor and the international images and foreign policy attitudes of the leading strata or foreign policy milieu of that actor.

Images and attitudes, studied here as dependent variables, are used by many authors *as* determinants of policy and thus as independent variables of the type we shall now explore. This, however, should not confuse anyone as long as the choice we have made and which is quite 'legitimate' theoretically and methodologically, is kept in mind by the reader and adhered to by the author.

The 'level-of-analysis problem', in particular raised by Singer,[1] is a question of how many levels of foreign policy determinating factors – one should distinguish between. Singer roughly introduces two levels: the intra-(domestic) and the extra-national (or international, foreign); North et al. present six levels of analysis, ranging from the individual to the supranational; while Galtung employs an even more refined scheme.[2] Others, putting less emphasis on the individual-to-international continuum, utilize a classification of determinants following other dimensions or no specific classification system at all.[3]

There are two inter-related problems to which different solutions have been offered. One is whether the list of causal variables should be 'inclusive' or all-encompassing (include a whole lot of possible variables on each level or within each category, a detailed catalogue) or more 'exclusive' or selective. The other is which factors should be considered of greatest causal importance – *one single* group of variables, or a whole *range* of variables in a certain ranking order. This is the problem which will occupy us here. Let us, however, first state our preference for the *exclusive* approach: the detailed list of Snyder et al. in our opinion is quite inapplicable. The kind of research we are attempting needs a map of factors accurate and concise enough to guide the researcher to the important points, not a map over-crowded with details, unsystematic, and largely untheoretical.[4]

The problem of the relative influence of factors is, however, the most important. The map may very well be detailed *as long as* we know reasonably well what factors are important (causally) and which are not. Theory has up to now been extremely reluctant to take this challenge seriously, and we quite agree with Rosenau's criticism of this state of affairs.[5]

As indicated in the Introduction, we might analyze our problems in the light of a set of different variables, ranging from the idiosyncratic to the systemic level. Singer emphasizes the importance of integrating this whole set of variables in a single theoretical framework.[6] We fully agree with the argument that no *category* or *level* of variables should be left out of consideration, neither in a general theory nor in the specific case study. Much research so far has not adhered to this rule, but instead advocated a single-level approach. Such an advocacy in many cases is based on an evaluation of the importance or causal relevance of different categories or levels, and a choice of or preference for one specific category.[7] In fact, such a choice is sometimes necessary; the question is on what basis it is made. We have the impression that very often preference for causal relationships are held on an intuitive basis, because of the research school or tradition of the individual researcher (psychologists take the idiosyncratic or personality approach to foreign policy attitudes, at least some political scientists the 'national interest' approach, etc.) or because of the personality or political preferences of the researcher.[8]

Several arguments can be raised against these research traditions. One is that they leave a number of possibly important variables out of discussion a priori. Another is that, as already indicated, there is really *no theory* behind the assumptions of causal relationships and the choice of variables. A third argument is that they do not *discriminate*.

By this we mean that there is no attempt at seeing the actors or units under study in the light of actual or possible differences between them. There is an a priori rule – a convention which has not been questioned or discussed according to empirical observations – that all actors may be studied with the use of the same instruments, categories, and concepts. One of the few to criticize this state of affairs is Rosenau. While we share his critical observations, we shall have some objections against the research scheme he proposes.[9] At the end we shall present our own alternative scheme.

Rosenau's 'pre-theory' of foreign policy-making distinguishes between influences at five levels or categories of variables:[10] the *idiosyncratic, role, governmental, societal*, and *systemic*.[11] He then constructs a tentative classificatory scheme for various types of states or national actors. This scheme is built on three – with an elaboration, four – dichotomies: *great vs. small* actors; *developed vs. underdeveloped* economies; *open vs. closed* polities; and *penetrated vs. non-penetrated* societies.

This scheme yields eight (sixteen) different types of actors. Rosenau goes on to present a number of hypotheses about the relative potency of each of the five categories of variables for each class of actor. Although the rationale behind these hypotheses is not very much elaborated, the hypotheses are relatively concrete and may be subjected to empirical testing.[12] They are, briefly:

systemic:	varies inversely with the size of a state (the larger states, having greater resources, are less dependent on the international system than are the smaller ones)
societal:	more potent in open than in closed polities (there is less need for the officials in the latter to heed non-governmental demands than in the former)
governmental:	more potent than societal variables in closed polities than in open ones (for the same reason as mentioned under societal)
role:	more potent than idiosyncratic variables in developed economies (because the bureaucracy and the large-scale organizations impose more restraints in the developed than in the less developed economies)
idiosyncratic:	more potent in less developed economies than role variables (for the same reason as mentioned above)

Rosenau develops this list into a quite exhaustive list of hypotheses.[13] While we believe that the list could be made more fruitful by more systematic reasoning behind it and some changes in the hypotheses proposed, there is no doubt that testing of the classificatory scheme and of the concrete hypotheses would be of considerable interest to foreign policy-making theory.[14] On the other hand, the fruitfulness of such work could be much enlarged if some of the concepts employed and the exemplifications used, e.g. the cases chosen for study, were improved.[15]

30

The fourth dichotomy introduced by Rosenau is in many respects the most important: the penetrated vs. nonpenetrated dichotomy. A penetrated political system is according to Rosenau

> one in which nonmembers of a national society participate directly
> and authoritatively, through actions taken jointly with the society's
> members, in either the allocation of its values or the mobilization
> of support on behalf of its goals.[16]

From this it should follow that systemic variables are particularly influential within penetrated, small, less developed, and 'open' systems. We return to this problem later on.

The concept of issue-area, important in Rosenau's theory, suggests that foreign policy behavior and policy-making structures are different and should be differently analyzed.[17]. While it seems well substantiated (although Rosenau and others use impressionistic data on this point) that *some* such differences do make themselves felt, we do not think that they deserve any prominent place in theory-building. In the first place, the issue-area approach is based very much on the findings of Dahl,[18] and these should not uncritically be adapted to the inter-national system. Secondly, even if there is a good point for the approach in general theory, in the case of a small, homogeneous national actor like Norway, the foreign policy elite or milieu is not *that* specialized or pluralistic.

Brecher et al. have employed Rosenau's issue-area approach in a content analysis study of elite images in situations of foreign policy decision-making.[19] Employing only his developed vs. developing economies dichotomy for actor classification, they arrive at findings which, however interesting, will be of limited value to a broader theory construction; some of them will, however, be kept in mind throughout this report.

Following Rosenau's scheme, Norway would fall into the class of a small, developed, and open-polity actor. The relative potency of the five categories of variables will, according to the theory for this class, be: (1) role,(2) systemic, (3) societal, (4) governmental, and (5) idiosyncratic.[20] Then the question is whether that actor constitutes a penetrated or non-penetrated system. If penetrated, the systemic variables move to the top of the ranking list and role variables to the second place; if non-penetrated, the ranking remains the same. Rosenau himself gives no indications toward an exemplification of actors after this fourth dichotomy is introduced. We shall leave the question open in order to present an alternative, partial theory, which will include parts of the Rosenau pre-theory in modified form.[21]

2.2. *World perspective*: *the case for a center-periphery theory of international relations*

The world perspective of the foreign policy milieu is a combination of the fundamental images and attitudes, the main values or wants of the totality of the members of the milieu. It is a rough, single-concept description of how the foreign policy milieu of an actor relates itself, and consequently the national actor it represents, to the environing world.

This perspective is the focus of analysis in the pages to follow. What will occupy us here is what makes, what is the basis of, the perspective. We feel this is largely *the international social position* of the national actor, the foreign policy milieu of which is under study.

The theory of foreign policy opinion as a function of social position is now well known from the study of national societies. It is based mainly on socio-economic and communication structure variables. In the index constructed by Galtung, there are altogether eight variables.[22] For our purpose, we have constructed an additive index comprising eight variables, a number of which may be said to correspond fairly closely to those employed in the 'national index'.

This procedure raises the very important question whether or to what extent one may assume a certain degree of *isomorphism* between the international and the national community (or between parts of them). Another question is the validity of the variables (or the whole index) we have chosen for the assignment of an actor's position in the community of nations.[23]

The isomorphism question is particularly important in the cases where micro-sociological theory is used as a *reservoir* for theory construction at the international system level. Many of the attempts in this direction no doubt should be subject to criticism. Some others evidently stand on safer ground, particularly as they have received backing from empirical data.[24]

Galtung, who has used small group theory as a basis for elaborations on international relations theory, stresses the importance of the former as a reservoir of fruitful hypotheses to be tested at the level of the latter. At the same time, he emphasizes the danger of making too easy inferences from one level to another.[25]

While these questions also are relevant to our study, our problem in this context is not the same since we are not dealing with units (nations) *interacting* with each other, but with one unit (Norway represented by its foreign policy milieu) *looking at* other units and the relations between those units and itself, and with the different sub-units (groups, categories and individuals within the two milieu samples) in varying support of this 'looking at' other units. The problems mentioned certainly apply to our general theory, but as we are not in a position to test it thoroughly here, the more thorough-going discussion may be left out. What we shall have to address ourselves to, however, is the validation of the index employed for assigning international social positions.

An obvious question in the construction of the index is to what extent the variables in the national social position index should be transferred to the international index. The national index consists of three types of variables: both 'ascriptive' and 'achievement' variables as to social background, and communication structure variables. We chose not to transform the variables used in this index directly, but to pick out variables representative of the three types at the international level.

The three types of variables in our context may be termed *attributive – 'ascriptive', attributive – 'achievement'*, and *relational* or interactional variables. Obviously, international center or periphery are not only character-ized by the latter type, which more or less would correspond to depicting positions only horizontally. Neither is international social position deter-mined only in terms of the former two types, as it would have if we were investigating stratification or ranking systems within the world community. Studies of this latter type are now becoming quite numerous.[26]

Another major problem is the relative weight to attach to these three types of variables. Our choice here parallels the one made in the case of the national index, as the three types mentioned above in the order they appear, are given the weight 3/8, 3/8, and 2/8 respectively. One may argue that this weighting is arbitrary: we must admit that we have no theoretical defense for it other than that given for the national index.[27]

As to variables to be used as indicators in the index, *power* or size vari-ables obviously are the best measure of the attributive 'ascriptive' cluster, while *development* level indicators would best indicate the attributive-achievement one. The variables selected are thus the following (with the national index variables to which they most closely would correspond listed in parenthesis):[28]

Attributive-ascriptive:	*Age*	(Age)
	GDP	(Income)
	Population	(none)
Attributive-achievement:	*Industrialization*	(Sector of occupation)
	Literacy level	(Education level)
	GDP per capita	(none)

Relational:	*Geographical*	(Place of residence:
	centrality	geographical)
	Memberships in	(none)
	international	
	organizations	

Objections may be made e.g. as to the classification of variables: GDP is very much an 'achievement' indicator, whereas memberships in international organizations may be seen as indication of both ascriptive and achievement attributes, being highly correlated with rank or power.[29] Distinctions between the variables in terms of proper classification should not be seen as particularly rigid.

The index was validated by a variable indicative of the international behavior of national actors: their tendency to be absent from voting in the UN General Assembly, in 1962 and 1963.[30] According to our theory, center actors would tend to be present, while the periphery ones would tend to be absent.[31]

This measure offered a Spearman's rank correlation between rank on the international social position index and absence scores of. 65 for the 1962 and 1963 data. This coefficient was obtained from index scores and absence data for 110 countries, i.e. the then member states of the world organization. That the index data and information on voting absence are not wholly synchronic should not make any great difference.

In three of the total 110 cases, international position and absence ranks differed widely: South Africa, Portugal (both high on the index, low on presence), and Mongolia (low on the index, but very high on presence). If these three 'odd' cases are excluded, rank correlation is obtained for the remaining 107 cases only of .71. This means that some cases of low presence are due to factors other than international position; in the cases mentioned, the explanation seems obvious. On the whole, we find that the index has been given at least sufficient validation.

What are then the implications of the center-periphery structure of the international system *to* the system itself? What makes it relevant and not only a theoretical construct?

By this structural approach we focus on *how the foreign policy milieu of national actors* – the representatives of these actors – *perceive, feel, or generally behave, as a function of the position of the national actor they represent in the international system.*

This implies, for one thing, that what Rosenau calls systemic and idiosyncratic variables act together: the international position of the actor is consequential or influential insofar as it is cognitively present to the persons constituting the milieu, through their own perception *or* as it is perceived and taught them by others (other milieus). However, this systemic-idiosyncratic combination is not the same for all actors under all circumstances. Its strength relative to other variables may vary, and the strength of either of the two variables relative to the other will change from one actor to another, both because of varying international position, and because of e.g. variations in the stability of the values on the variables.

That Rosenau's concept of penetration is useful is true only with some important modifications. First of all, its usefulness lies in the strong attack it makes possible against the prevailing tradition of distinguishing sharply between the international and the national system.[32] As Rosenau says, the two go very much over in each other. What he fails to emphasize is that this will most probably vary from one part of the system to another, and from one type of actor to another. More importantly, the content, direction of, and the consequence of the penetration or internationalization of national polities will vary from one set of actors to another.

One important aspect of the internationalization is the built-in *asymmetry* in the relationship between two or more national actors. This asymmetry may exist between center and periphery, between the big power and the small power, between geographical neighbors, between dominant and dominated within specific groups of actors, etc. *Domination* is one aspect of the internationalization: one actor penetrates another, but not vice versa. Another aspect is what Russett calls *responsiveness*.[33] A third factor would be whether and to what extent the internationalization is accepted or rejected – whether it is *legitimate* in the penetrated system.

Domination *may* be seen as legitimate for varying reasons: the dominated may, while losing policy-making sovereignty, benefit from the domination in other respects. And in the case of asymmetric responsiveness, one actor tends to respond favorably to demands or wishes from the other and thus lend himself to the other actor's penetration into his own policies. An actor may be responsive toward another for ideological, strategic, or economic reasons.

That internationalization or penetration may take different forms has great potential importance when influence stemming from the systemic level is considered. It is not enough to discriminate between penetrated and nonpenetrated, but between *degrees* and *forms* of penetration and non-penetration.

Indications of the form or the content of penetration are given by variables like state ideology ('communist' versus 'capitalistic-liberal'), culture (language family, religion) military alliance, economic dependency (aid, investments).

The last theoretical problem we shall take up relates to the concept of *rank disequilibrium*.[34] An actor who ranks high on some variables or sub-dimensions but low on others is rank-disequilibrated, while an actor who ranks almost equally high on most or all variables is said to be rank-equili-brated. The types of and the consequence of rank-disequilibrium are different. China is an example of the big (measured by power criteria), but less developed and not centrally located actor. Another example of the dis-equilibrated type of actor is Luxembourg: small but developed, and centrally located. These are extreme cases. Between them is a whole range of more or less disequilibrated actors.

2.3. *International position and the images and attitudes of the milieu: a theoretical model*

Our task now is to present a model or a theoretical framework which inte-grates the dimensions presented and discussed in the foregoing: the inter-national position or the center v.s. periphery dimension; the penetrated vs. nonpenetrated dichotomy; the open vs. closed dichotomy; and the rank-disequilibrium factor.

Our general proposition is that the international position of an actor determines the main tendency in the world perspective of its milieu.

Russett contends that

> if we imagine a pair of curves for the distribution of political attitudes in a nation and in the entire international system, that for the world has both a wider range and a less-pronounced central tendency – the curve is flatter.[35]

In terms of our center vs. periphery dichotomy, explorations of the dichot-omy within national societies seem to indicate that there are at least less pronounced central tendencies in the periphery than in the center; the range of images and attitudes found, on the other hand, will tend to be greater than in the periphery. These trends would probably be found even in the international community, between center and periphery nations.

Dimensions or factors mentioned other than international position provide variations on the main tendency created by international position. In some cases, however, such factors may even outweigh the international position factor in importance; in others, they will tend to modify its influence. Instead of presenting a complete and exhaustive theory at this stage, we shall attempt to specify how and why these different factors or dimensions relate to the influencing of the image-building and attitude-formation of different national actor milieus.

The penetration dimension has relevance as to whether the relationship between two actors is *asymmetric* or *symmetric*. In the relationship between two actors who are both center nations, the penetration – *if* any – will by definition be symmetric; this will generally also be true in a periphery-periphery relationship.[37] There may, however, be rather strongly asymmetric penetration even in such cases, as when one of the center (periphery) nations is big (in terms of size), while the other is small. However, asymmetry *ceteris paribus* should be greatest in the center (big) – periphery (small) relationship.

The center nation is comparatively better off than the periphery nation in avoiding strong asymmetric penetration. It is more centrally located in the communication structure and can 'make its voice better heard'. It can interact more on an equal footing with other actors. At the same time, however, the center nations will penetrate *each other* (i.e. penetration takes place within the center category of nations) more than the periphery generally will as its single units will be more isolated. But again the important question is the form and the content of the penetrative activity: is it *legitimate* or not, and to what extent is there consensus on fundamental values between the penetrator and the penetrated?

The center nation has more values to defend than the periphery nation. It is 'aware' of being a center nation, and this awareness creates a feeling of 'responsibility' as well as 'we-ness', a feeling of *community* with other center nations. This 'we-ness' may make the center nation view the periphery nations as an out-group, possibly a *negative* reference group. And it may make it especially responsive to other center nations.

Responsiveness may stem from other factors as well. Russett has shown that for instance extensive trade relations make traders (especially those whose trade amounts to an important part of their total economy, or GNP) more responsive toward each other.[38] Furthermore, common culture, ideological links, geographical proximity, etc. may create greater responsiveness.

However, even when responsiveness is discussed, differences in international position, particularly on power, make for important distinctions between actors. In a relationship between two actors, the reactions of the one toward the other will depend on the relative position and/or power between them, and on the degree of responsiveness. This is illustrated in Table 2.3.1., which attempts to present a typology of penetration where the three dimensions discussed so far under this heading, are included. It may seem an unnecessary doubling of dimensions to include both symmetric vs. asymmetric and dominance versus non-dominance. But there may be asymmetric relationships between two actors which are penetrated into each other where there is no dominance by the one over the other.[39]

The cases chosen to exemplify the different types of relationships are somewhat arbitrary and might be discussed. The types of reactions proposed could also be discussed or modified. Important, however, is that there is a basis in 'the real world' for a classification of relationships between different actors according to the principles introduced here.

Table 2.3.1. *A typology of international penetration relationships:*
B's reactions to actor A

	Symmetric		Asymmetric	
Actor A:	Non-dominance	Dominance	Non-dominance	Dominance
Actor B: Responsive	Cooperative Respectful (mutually) (Norway toward Denmark)	Dependent: domination accepted out of expediency (UK toward USA)	Following: Respectful (Norway toward Western Germ.)	Servile: (Small/peripher. allies toward USA; developing countr. toward France, USA)
Non-responsive	'Strictly formal' (mutual interests) or Antagonistic (USSR toward US in East-West relations during the Cold War)	Retreating: trying to isolate from or cut off domination (China toward USSR in early '60-ies; France toward USA in middle of '60-ies)	Avoiding (non-aligned tow. blocs) or Antagonistic (Cuba toward USA; Yugo-slavia toward USSR)	Protesting Revolting Reacting or Tacitly adhering to (CSSR toward USSR)

To be responsive toward (the elite or milieu of) another national actor or a group of such actors means that one perceives this or these actors as a positive reference group. To be non-responsive does not necessarily mean that one is antagonistic and perceives the other as a negative reference group: one may also be more or less affectively neutral or indifferent.

Generally, we believe that the responsiveness is potentially higher among center actors than among periphery ones, and clearly higher between center actors than in a periphery actor *toward* the center one. There are exceptions, probably quite numerous (cf. Table 2.3.1.) At the same time, there is evi-

38

dently a large amount of non-responsiveness among center actors where ideological and strategic differences come in. But in the concrete case of East-West relations we believe that responsiveness on the whole has increased on both sides toward the other in recent years, despite evident setbacks.[40] And what has created this greater responsiveness is not only (in a negative sense) the *détente* itself, but the growing feeling on both sides of 'we-ness': that both East and West have power over the rest of the world (despite the fact that they also compete for dominance), that they are more developed, constituting the rich countries' club (despite quite clear differences in attitudes and approaches, for instance in UNCTAD), that they are technologically superior, etc.

What then are the world perspectives characteristic of center and of periphery nations, respectively? A list of hypotheses on what constitutes the typical center and periphery perspectives is given in Table 2.3.2.

To a large extent, hypotheses are adapted from the national center-periphe-

Table 2.3.2. *Differences in perspective, modes of thought and system activities between center and periphery nations: a list of hypotheses*

	Center	Periphery
System activity:		
H1.1: Participation	High	Low
H1.1: Opinion-holding	High	Low
H1.3: Communication	Sender, initiator	Receiver, imitator
Modes of thought:		
H1.4: Attitude-formation	Differential evaluation: both-and	Total evaluation: either-or
H1.5: Style	Pragmatic, means-oriented	Moralistic, ends-oriented
H1.6: Consistency	High	Low
H1.7: Stability of perspective	High	Low
Perspective:		
H1.8: Attitude to existing world order	Partial acceptance or rejection, revisionism: change within existing framework	Total acceptance or rejection: status quo *or* discontinuous, apocalyptic change
H1.9: Change should be	Gradualistic	Absolutistic
H1.10: Attitude to system structure	Moderately authoritarian, 'oligarchic'	Egalitarian, 'democratic' or strong authoritarian

Table 2.3.2. (*cont.*)

	Center	*Periphery*
H1.11: Vertical mobility aspirations	Moderate: 'achiever', maintain present position	High: 'non-achiever', improve present position
H1.12: 'We vs. other':	'We-ness': center solidarity, periphery negative reference group	'Other-ness': weak periphery solidarity, center positive reference group

ry theory; some of these have already received empirical backing and are thus put forth as propositions.[41] On *system activity*, we see from the fact that the center is better placed in the communication network, that it also should be participating more in international affairs generally, and be more active in sending information (i.e. its perspective and policies) than is the periphery nation.

The *modes of thought* of the center nation milieus is believed to be characterized – in much the same way as is the center individual or small group – by the both-and type of evaluation, a pragmatic more than a moralistic way of looking at problems, high consistency and high stability in their perspective. Now, the proposed differential or both-and way of evaluating questions seems incompatible with the indication made above that we should find a stronger tendency toward consensus in the center than in the periphery. However, the two hypotheses are not necessarily or logically incompatible, as the both-and approach may be working over several items or issues, not only one single: the milieus may pick one value on one item, another on the second, etc., and thus on each single item still maintain high consensus scores. This may in turn be incompatible with the hypothesis that the center shows more consistency in its perspective than the periphery, but not necessarily so.

On the *perspective* itself – our main concern in the following – the proposed differences in attitude towards existing world order and towards change, are due to the fact that the center nations are the 'have's' and that nations as well as individuals strive to preserve what they have. The center nation perspective is very much the modern conservative 'change in order to *preserve*' approach, while that of the periphery nation either is stressing 'preserve' only, i.e. complete acceptance, or takes the 'change in order to *change*' approach, a more truly radical approach.

40

In other words, the center perspective on the international system is that present trends of development merely should be extrapolated into the future. It will accept deviations from these trends and from the behavior found compatible with them only insofar as these deviations do not threaten the values or the position of the center nation.

Clearly there should be strong positive correlations between the perspectives of center and periphery actors on a range of different issues which do not primarily stem from penetration of the two (or one of the other) creating correspondence in perspectives between them. Some values would be common to all or most actors: 'peace', 'development' socio-economically, self-preservation, etc. But in a number of concrete relationships we believe that such correspondence, particularly on the dimensions listed in Table 2.3.2, is primarily due to penetration (by center nations of periphery ones, mostly) as would be the case e.g. with the former French colonies in Africa in their present relationship to France under the common heading of *la francophonie*: here it is exactly the milieus of the African periphery actors which have been penetrated by the French elite.[42]

And in the cases where perspectives are largely shared between a center and a periphery actor, the correlation between their actual behavior – their foreign policies – may tend to be negative due to other factors (geographical context, strategic location, etc.). On the other hand, negative correlations between world perspectives would not exclude positive correlations between the policies of two given actors. Due to the domination of the one by the other, the dominating part may be able to make the other behave like himself, but the latter may still uphold a different world perspective (possibly as an underlying protest against the political domination). Thus, the positive correlation between policy and perspective which is assumed in the case of Norway does not imply that such a correlation *generally* or most often exists. Moreover, it has to be explained (cf. Chapt. 3) and tested (cf. Chapt.4).

2.4. *The potency of 'intra-national' factors*

The open-closed polity dimension as most commonly used, is conceived of as unproblematic: Western democracies or regimes defined by Western scholars as democratic are open polities; other polities (Communist states, certain 'radical' and/or socialist states in the 'Third World') are closed ones. These conceptions are not only scientifically uncorrect and often politically misleading: they also fail to consider certain basic problems.

First of all, polity may be 'open' in the sense that there are working channels of communication and formal rights of free speech; it may still be 'undemocratic' in the sense that most communication goes one way only – from top and downwards; and the right of speech is used by a small group only – those at the top: the elite and the milieu. The main question then is not whether or not open channels of communication exist (in most present societies they do, to some extent) but the *patterns* of communication which exist and direct the content of the communication.

Oligarchic tendencies within the Western democracies have been stressed by several authors.[43] They seem particularly predominant in the field of foreign policy, although recent developments seem to modify this situation.[44] To the extent that such a situation exists, however, the potency of societal factors is reduced, while the two remaining classes of variables – role and governmental – are made, to the same extent, more potent.

The potency of societal factors on foreign policy making – interest groups, public opinion generally, etc. – is very much determined by the extent to which society or public opinion is mobilized for foreign policy activity or activism.[45] When this activism is relatively high, polity will become more open vertically (provided the activism does not lead to breakdown of the communication structure). When communication about foreign policy matters goes mainly or almost exclusively between the units within the milieu or the elite, polity is truly open only at the top level of the society: it is horizontal 'openness' within an oligarchic structure. Then we have to look for the potential influence of role and governmental variables.

Rosenau assigns a relatively high potency to role variables, without really saying why.[46] It is evident that being foreign minister of a national actor entails some extra 'burdens' not attached to most other roles. The question is, however, whether the fact of being foreign minister (or foreign policy-maker) in the Netherlands (Rosenau's) is more important than the fact that the Netherlands are part of the 'Western community' (within the group of center nations) and that the images, attitudes and behavior of the foreign minister of that country will to a very large extent be a function of this position. We shall propose that the latter is the more important.[47]

It should be added that role variables probably are more potent in policy-making than in image-building and attitude-formation. One important consequence of this is that the occupation of a specific role may make the occupying individual carry out policies which he does not really prefer. As we have said before, to what extent this is true depends among other things on the type of actor that individual represents, on the issue concerned, and on the probability that the individual will reduce the dissonance or discrepancy between behavior and preferences (cf. Chapt. 7).

The potency of governmental variables is a function of the formal and informal structure of the elite, and the relationship between those in position and those in opposition *vis à vis* official policy at any given time. When differences in images and attitudes between different parts of the structure, within the elite, milieu, or within the whole polity are great, and when the differences between position and opposition are great, then the potency of governmental variables is great.

The potency of all these categories of intra-national variables – to be treated in detail in the following – is strongly dependent on the relative potency of other factors. We propose that *the potency or influence of such intra-national factors is greatest on the whole in a center/big, non-penetrated, and open/upwards-communicating actor, while it probably is at a minimum in the periphery/small, dominated, and closed actor.*

This holds as long as we are talking of the top levels of the polity structure.

The perception or cognitive awareness of the international position of 'one's actor' is most strongly held at the elite level or within the milieu, and the penetration from outside is also most strongly felt at these levels. The potency of extra-national factors then is less within the public opinion in general, although parts of it may be strongly penetrated.[48]

This means that the milieu of an actor where both extra- and intra-national factors make themselves felt, will be exposed to opposite or at least different tendencies or influences – to a situation of *cross-pressure*. Where there is much upward communication in an open polity *and* penetration is high, cross-pressure is potentially greatest. Here the elite or the policy-makers will compromise between the two, chose the one of them, or escape into a situation of no choice.

But this cross-pressure situation of course will not materialize and make itself felt to the same degree where the *consensus* of the penetrating elite of a foreign actor and the public opinion (or the whole polity) of the actor concerned is high. In this situation of external-internal harmony, the elite or the policy-makers of the actor concerned will not be faced with great difficulties either in shaping its images and attitudes *nor* in making its policy, i. e. if other factors may be held constant.

Where this consensus is not predominant and the elite of the actor concerned is exposed to some cross-pressure, in a situation of relatively high penetration (especially asymmetric) the elite will incline toward sharing images and attitudes with the foreign elite. International demands (e. g. towards supra-nationalization of decision-making), strategic necessities, or dominance from outside will thus tend to create a *unity of elites* – a perspective shared by elites which is contrary to or different from that of the respective public opinions. The very structure of the international society, dominated by the interaction of elites in a variety of ways, makes this even more likely. The elites are more exposed to each other than the respective public opinions are exposed to each other or to elites of actors other than their 'own'. In this respect we should stress, as Deutsch and Kelman do, the importance of international communication structures.[49]

The functions of rank disequilibrium may be quite numerous, as shown by studies on the micro- and the macro-level.[50] Generally, it is assumed that a disequilibrated actor will tend to equilibrate his position, that is: achieve equal ranks on the dimensions he himself or the system of actors deems important.

As will be evident, some ranks are givens – ascriptive statuses – as for instance the rank on dimensions as geographical space (size), geographical position, etc. These ranks cannot be changed unless by occupation or annexation. But most other rank dimensions may be changed, as they are achievement statuses.

The equilibrating of ranks naturally will aim at a higher rank on the dimensions on which the rank profile is 'dipping' low. When such striving is unsuccessful, this may result in frustration which again may produce reactions like aggression, isolation, compensation, etc. – depending on the type of actor and its position.

We believe that the position of rank disequilibrium makes the disequilibrated (e.g. the one large on power criteria, but undeveloped or vice versa) more mobility-oriented than the equilibrated, even the actor ranking low on the relevant dimensions (small, undeveloped). The idea is that the state of disequilibrium is creating equilibrating activity.

However, the rank-disequilibrated actor may also 'satisfize' itself with its position. This will be the case especially when it is low on ascriptive criteria (with which it can do very little) and relatively high on achievement criteria. Indeed, the latter is the kind of status one *can* do something about. The small but centrist (developed, white, and relatively old) actor then may be satisfied with the fact that it has achieved quite a lot – has reached the position it can hope to obtain – and may consequently *play out* its high statuses (and play down, or repress its low ones). An example of such an actor may be Norway.

2.5. *Norway's world perspective: determinants and hypotheses*

In this section, we shall present some hypotheses on the images and attitudes of the Norwegian foreign policy milieu. From what has been said in 2.1–2.4, this will be done on the basis of Norway's international position and on the extent to which it is penetrated. In addition, we shall present a rather sketchy overview of Norwegian foreign policy in the last decades. Since we are not doing – nor do we presently have the possibility of doing – a diachronic analysis on this topic to relate it to the theory of international position, we shall have to view Norway's past behavior as part of the background of present images and attitudes. Such an approach seems legitimate, since the past largely determines the present and the future. When people's cognitions and preferences are not exposed to very discontinuous changes, they tend to remain relatively stable as measured by some starting-point – in the case of Norway, a strongly discontinuous change represented by World War II and its aftermath. As Russett has shown on the basis of UN voting patterns a general trend for most nations in the 1950's and the early 1960's is that they

> did not readily change their basic strategies and their elites, whether from preference or because internal and external systemic pressures, did not quickly alter their international alignments.[51]

a. Past experiences: the historical burden .[51] Going back to World War I, we may divide official Norwegian foreign policy into *three periods.* The first, 1919 to 1939–40, is the period of neutrality and 'small power policy' within the framework of the League of Nations most of the time.[52] Norwegian policy in this period was heavily based on cooperation with the other Scandinavian states, with the smaller Continental states (Poland, the Netherlands) and with Great Britain, a relationship stemming very much from traditional anglophilian ties from the pre-war period which were further developed and strengthened during the first World War.[53]

The second period – from Norway's involvement in World War II in April 1940 up to joining NATO in 1949 – is the period of changed images and attitudes, and at the end, of changed policies.[54] These changes took place not as an abrupt switch from one set of orientations to another (although some individual elite members did switch that abruptly) but more in the form of a growing oppositional fraction within the elite, making manifest attitudes held even from before the outbreak of the war or the occupation of Norway. Taking over the policy-making as the war developed and structural changes took place,[55] the fraction made these attitudes the leading principles of Norwegian foreign policy.[56]

At the end of the war, these principles, which first of all established Norway's alignment and orientation preferences to the greater Western powers, were not manifested strongly as the United Nations was founded, and the policy of neutrality in a way (at least at the manifest policy level) was continued. Adherence to and support of the world organization became the primary aim of official Norwegian policy.

Formally, this primacy has been maintained during the third (and present) period.[57] There is hardly doubt, however, that the very basic shift in regional orientation and alignment preferences – the shift in foci of *responsiveness* – which was made in the minds and declarations of leading policy-makers as early as in 1940–42, but which did not become manifest policy until 1948–49[58] indicates where the policy-making basis and thus the perspective really lie. The shift was, among other things, a change from a philosophy of 'small power politics' to that of 'alignment with the great powers politics'. The trust in primordial friendship with other actors changed from a modest, but rather important 'trade union of small powers'[59] on an equal basis, to the rather hierarchical, inequal 'community of Atlantic powers', dominated by the Anglo-American 'special relationship'. This shift was completed when the above-mentioned images and attitudes, which had largely been shaped during the war or the first part of this period, but had lain latent under the cover of UN positivism, were manifested with the 1948 Prague *coup d'etat* and with what was perceived as a possible Soviet Russian entrance into Western Europe.[60]

Norwegian foreign policy in the third period then is, roughly speaking, a follow-up of these fundamental changes and the new perspective and policy basis laid down, with the addition of certain new issues and the milieu's orientations towards them. An exact description of these changes or the chronology of events and issues is not the task of this study. Such descriptions, almost all in the historical tradition, are already at hand. In fact, what has been written so far on modern Norwegian foreign policy is largely descriptive and – to the extent it may be said to be 'research' – ideographic (or singularizing). The lack of analytical works of a more nomothetic (or generalizing) character seems apparent.[61]

The effect of such discontinuous changes on image-building and attitude-formation may be quite dramatic and in important respects more decisive than the effect of such other factors as e. g. international position of a given actor. Our theory of world perspectives as a function of international position then has to be based on certain preconditions, or at least has a *limited application in periods of major discontinuities in international politics.* This observation fits quite well in with the findings of Russett, quoted above, since the international system has been relatively stable in structure and main issues in the last two decades.

b. Present position: dependency and responsiveness. For Norway, the basic shift in orientation in the 1940s has had an effect in two respects: first, that of a relatively strong *penetration* of its milieu (and much of its polity) by 'the Atlantic community'; secondly, the creation of specific 'Western versions' of the center values.[62]

Western or Atlantic penetration of Norway's polity has been based on increasing and extensive dependency on the great Atlantic powers for security (military) and welfare.[63] But it has to a great extent also been based on strong and increasing responsiveness, at least during most of the post-WWII period, in the Norwegian milieu towards these powers. From this we may infer that systemic and idiosyncratic factors have worked hand in hand. Systematic influence has been *internalized*[64] and *legitimized* through increasing responsiveness at the idiosyncratic level. Or possibly – as causal relationships may be disputed at this point – responsiveness is a function of the internalization and legitimization of systemic (= Atlantic, Anglo-American) influence.

Important here is that idiosyncratic variables, while without much significance in making for much of the variance found, are vital in that they act as a *constant* and thus as a prerequisite of lasting and consistent systemic influence. If the idiosyncratic, individual factor were removed, major changes *might* occur, even if the case of Norway is probably not a good case in point, because other constants such as 'external realities' may be of as much importance.

Concerning trade relationships, Norway is relatively dependent upon this kind of interaction with other states: the total value of its trade amounts to about 50% of its total GNP.[65] Great Britain until recently was its single most important trading partner, with the US ranking number four.[66] Moreover, Norway's trade balance with the US as measured by the relationship between imports and exports, is strongly unfavorable, more unfavorable than that with any other country.[67]

Norway's dependency upon Atlantic countries is further reflected by several other indicators; e.g. more than 60% of its total trade is with NATO countries.[68] Indicators of responsiveness show a similar trend. Several such indicators establish the US and Great Britain as a positive reference group for Norwegians.[69]

There exists, however, another positive reference group for the Norwegian public: the Scandinavian countries. Although responsiveness towards these actors probably has declined during the post-WWII period, it is still considerable and in the last few years seems to have increased again.[70] This points to the fact that Scandinavistic feelings – partly remnants of last century ideologies and the cooperative between-the-wars neutralism – still live as 'remnants of the past' or as actively supported alternatives to present policies. This again leaves the polity in a position of underlying, latent conflict.

Such a conflict was quite manifest, at the elite as well as at the public opinion level, in 1948–49 when the choice for considerable parts of the milieu stood between a Nordic defense pact and NATO.[71] It was manifested later on when plans for a Nordic common market have been confronted with extra-Nordic market schemes.[72]

As an alternative to this conflict interpretation of Norwegian foreign policy, it has been argued that this policy in general may be seen as a *'concentric field'* where different political aims are integrated in a non-conflict setting.[73] According to this line of thought, UN policy, NATO membership, the more strictly European aims and the relations to the Scandinavian states all fall within the same field of thought and are easily reconciled. Although the perception of such a reconciliation probably is most easily achieved at the top elite level – one of the main tasks of the elite *is* reconciliation of conflicting policies – it is our hypothesis that conflict still prevails and will at least be found latent in the attitude set of the milieu.

On two system dimensions – often referred to as the main conflict dimensions of the present-day world system – the East–West and the so-called North–South dimensions, Norway's position on the Western and the Northern sides, respectively, is convincingly shown by Jacobsen.[74] Of the different causus groups Norway may be referred to, Norway most often votes with the Scandinavian countries, and is at the same time more Western (i.e. votes with the US) and Northern than are the non-NATO Nordic states Sweden and Finland. On the other hand, Denmark – another Nordic NATO member – is according to UN voting patterns the very closest associate of Norway. As measured by voting agreement, Norway, besides being part of the 'Western', NATO, and Nordic groupings (increasingly in that order), tends to take a place among the Commonwealth nations – which further indicates the relatively strong Norwegian anglophilia.[75]

Turning now to our center-periphery index, Norway's international position is not in the *top* center group, but in the next-to-the top group: it is a *moderate center nation*. Measured by scores on the additive index (top score 16), Norway has a total score of 13, placing it among four countries receiving international position rank of 23.5. As shown in Appendix G, it ranks in the same position as Argentina, Bulgaria, and Finland, while the positions of some of Norway's closest associates is *one* step higher in the case of Denmark (14 on the index), *two* steps in the case of Sweden and the US (scoring 15), and *three* steps or positions higher in the case of Great Britain and Western Germany (scoring the top 16 score).[76]

From this we may hypothesize that the world perspective of the Norwegian foreign policy milieu is also of the moderately centrist type. We hesitate to do so because Norway is extremely rank-disequilibrated both when the index variables and particularly when many attribute variables are taken into consideration.[77] From what has been said above on the possible consequences of rank disequilibrium, we assume that the question of compensation is relevant in the case of Norway. Although the Norwegian public ranks relatively high on degree of aggressiveness, in *certain* aspects of the concept,[78] this has little relevance to our problem as Norway lacks the resources with which to *act* aggressively toward other nations.

More relevance should probably be attached to the fact that Norway may suffer from a certain 'partial inferiority' complex, the feeling of being a periphery nation *within the center*. Comparing her international position with that of her NATO colleagues, we see that she ranks lower than nine (out of fourteen), higher than only five. *And* these five are Iceland and Luxembourg, extremely low on size, and Greece, Portugal, and Turkey, all low on development. Norway then receives the lowest rank among the not too small and developed NATO countries.

What is left then is a basis for *compensation*. Three hypotheses may be put forth here. One is that the Norwegian milieu is playing down its lack of power – that it is a medium size country – and playing up its high rank on development. The second hypothesis would be that Norway actively tries to intermix as much as possible with those actors with which she shares a number of high ranks (on e.g. development) *or* with a higher total international position rank than Norway (e.g. the nine NATO countries) These countries may 'lend' some of their high-ranking status to Norway through a network of interaction which associates Norway to them.[79]

The third and last hypothesis on this point will be simply that Norway *because* she receives a somewhat lower international position than her positive reference group, i.e. her closest associates, will tend to be 'over-centrist': she will be more centrist in her perspective than the objective center actors, at least on some issues being 'more Catholic than the Pope'. The perspective of Norway's foreign policy milieu is made more 'truly centrist' as an effect of her rank disequilibrium.

The compensation-by-intermingling hypothesis also means that the Norwegian milieu will put a great value in international cooperation or organization *as such*, or as a means of achieving national goals. According to

Terhune, this is exactly the defination of 'internationalism', one of the most confused concepts in international relations theory.[80]

It seems necessary to distinguish between at least three different types of 'internationalism': *supra-nationalism, cross-nationalism,* and *trans-nationalism.*[81] We shall relate these concepts to our data later on. Let us here say something of the dimension *globalism versus regionalism,* which is related to the concepts mentioned.

Globalistic attitudes are shown by a preference for cooperation on the global level and for a global foreign policy in general; regionalistic attitudes are preferences for cooperation with or a foreign policy directed toward a limited number of national or multinational actors (limited primarily by geographic criteria). We would say that globalism means a willingness to tackle problems or phenomena at the global level, *or* in the (geographical or functional) areas outside the closest and those most naturally preoccupying oneself, into one's perspective, becoming internalized and essential to one's attitudes on relevant issues and the policy one is making.

Generally, 'internationalism' means willingness to take the interests of *other* actors and their perspectives into account; and, in situations where the interests (perspectives) of one's 'own' actor and those of others are in conflict, not necessarily and *a priori* place own interests before those of others. Moreover, the concept is related to responsiveness.

Regionalism logically means a tendency to identify oneself first of all with those areas which are close. This raises one important question: in the case of a small or medium small actor with limited *capacity* in terms of resources, and *capability* in terms of power, does such an actor really *have* any choice? Whether it wants it or not – will it not simply have to limit itself to activities within and thus identification toward the closer areas, i.e. to regionalistic perspectives and policies?

This is the problem of *domain versus scope.* And the problem posed before particularly the small actor is whether it can afford to participate as a full member of the society of national actors in *both* domain and scope. Instead of trying to match both these demands, it may be more rewarding to try to concentrate on one of them, thus maximizing one's output and possibly one's influence there. Or, the question may even be whether to choose both limited domain (regionalism) and limited scope (e.g. only functional cooperation).

Although we may find examples of small state influence on global politics (where great powers are involved), the general hypothesis would be that the small state will usually choose regional policies. This does not mean, however, that there may not be strong globalistic feeling within the foreign policy

50

milieu or elite of that actor, or that it necessarily has to make this choice on the policy side. On scope, the small state – at least if it is a relatively centrist one, and not a 'mini-state' (like Andorra) – will in a sense have no real choice. Because the different fields of activity are so intermingled and overlapping, participation in one field leads to or presupposes participation in another or several others. There is a 'partout' ticket which all actors have to buy if they want to be an accepted member of the international society. Thus the small state has to divide its resources, its capacity on a number of different fields of activity.

In the case of Norway, however, at least one major factor might be expected to make the perspective and 'internationalism' of her milieu more globalistic: her global shipping business, which is considerable, both in absolute and in relative terms.[82] This fact together with the 'special' Norwegian affiliations toward the UN point to a large degree of globalistic orientation within the milieu, although the practical policy – the behavioral side – is supposed to lean toward regionalism.

Going back to the center-periphery dimension, one might argue that an actor like Norway, which on the basis of scarce resources not only plays up the importance of development variables, but also objectively has maximized or 'over-achieved' on these variables, will be most eager to maintain what it has, which means that it will demand stability, peace, and security from the international society.

At this point, we must distinguish between achievement in the *past* and achievement in the *present*. The former, the already *achieved* actor, will in particular tend to take the attitude just mentioned: it was upward mobile in the past; at present when its rates of growth are not particularly high, it first of all wants to maintain what is achieved.

The *achieving* actor will tend to take an attitude more favorable toward change, mobility, even toward taking risks. Its position is not settled yet, it is still on the move because of high rates of growth. Its attitude or acts may even take the form of aggression.

Another distinction which may be useful when it comes to potential aggressiveness and risk-taking, is that between resourceful and non-resourceful actors. The former is believed to be more apt to take an aggressive attitude: it may be able to replace what it possibly loses from risk-taking by using own resources. This holds for both the achieved and/or achieving as well as the non-achieved resourceful actor: the former may be able to recapture its losses in position relatively rapidly – post-WWII Japan and Western Germany may well be examples of this; the latter may feel that it has little to lose from taking risks as what it may achieve is still potential.

Now, measured by economic growth rates, Norway in the post-WWII period seems to take the position of a still 'achieving achieved': she has a higher growth rate than many of her center or moderate center companions, although the rate is not among the highest.[83] It is probably correct to put most emphasis on her past or up-to-the-present performances: she *has* achieved.[84]

Another example of the risk-taking achieved or achieving center actor may perhaps be found in the question of attitudes toward the nuclear non-proliferation treaty: some of the strongest opposition against it has come from states which are achieved and resourceful, while many of the strongest protagonists are the achieved but non-resourceful e. g. Norway. Moreover, opponents are also found among the non-achieved, resourceful actors, e. g. China and India.[85]

In this chapter, we have presented the case for a structural approach to the study of images and attitudes among foreign policy elites. The thesis was put forward that these images and attitudes are a function of the international position of the actor which the foreign policy milieu members represent. In the following chapter, we shall carry our theory further, partially modifying it, by looking at the impact of factors internal to the actor concerned – the intra-national structure and its relevance to the formation of images and attitudes.

3. Consensus or Cleavage:
The Case of the Intra-national Factors

In the preceding chapter we established a basis for making hypotheses about the main tendency in the general world perspective of the milieu. In the case of Norway, this basis was first of all found to be her international position and the degree to which the Norwegian polity is penetrated from outside. Now we shall present a theoretical framework for hypothesizing about possible *reinforcements of or deviations from the general tendency*. The reservoir now is the intra-national variables, the broadly societal ones as well as those connected with role and governmental factors. Since idiosyncratic variables have been discussed in connection with responsiveness theory and the potency of systemic variables, they will for the most part be left out here.

First, we shall look at the general problem. Then we will focus on our case – the Norwegian polity.

3.1. *Concepts and definitions*

The concept of *consensus* is commonly used in the sense of a set of beliefs about the fundamental aspects of society, such as distribution of power, distribution of wealth, moral and social norms, fundamental human rights, etc.[1] In our terminology, it has a much less fundamental 'socio-political' content and is simply understood as *the degree to which a certain social group* (or category) *shares an opinion, an attitude or an image on some specific issue or set of issues*. Correspondingly, the word 'dissensus'[2] means the degree to which there is *different* opinion etc. on an issue.

We distinguish between *consensus within* and *consensus between* social groups or categories. In order to avoid confusion, we shall call the latter *agreement* (between), while the former will be referred to as *consensus*.

When the images or attitudes of an individual are under the control of or shaped by a group norm, we talk of *conformity*.[3] When there between two or more social groups is strong *disagreement*, there is a latent conflict of attitudes between them, which under certain circumstances may become manifest, i.e. through behavior.

Consensus is measured by the percentage of the members of a given social group which shares any specific opinion. Operationally, consensus has been defined as 90%[4] or 75%[5] sharing the same opinion. The exact delimitation of the minimum level of consensus will often be somewhat arbitrary. As we have stretched the concept of consensus to not only the fundamental, live-or-die questions of a society but *any* international or foreign policy issue, the latter limit seems more appropriate.

Actually, we shall in general set a 70% sharing or *modal value* as the lower limit of consensus. This we do in order to account for responses of 'Not ascertained' or 'Don't know' which most often occur and very often at the rate of 5–15% of the respondents. If all respondents expressed an opinion on an issue, then 75% or $\frac{3}{4}$ of the group – a degree of sharing opinions which seems high enough to deserve the term consensus – would have been the choice. As this is not the case, consensus will be said to occur when $\frac{3}{4}$ of those who respond to an item with a specific opinion on it, express the same opinion.[6] This means that *ratios* often may be a better measure of consensus than modal value.

Agreement (or consensus between groups) is best measured by the *percentage difference* or distance between the groups in question, when the difference taken is that between consensus scores of the groups. The operationalization of agreement seems even more problematic than in the case of consensus. One may conceive of a 20 or 30% difference as the agreement threshold. However, we must take into consideration at least two other factors. One is the number of respondents: when the number is relatively low, great differences – i.e. disagreement – may occur rather randomly. The other factor is the degree of consensus in the groups in question. If, for example, the relationship between them is a 90% against 55% consensus for the respective groups, this 35% disagreement, at least in some respect, is different from e.g. a 70% against 35% relationship. Such problems have to be further considered under the impact of concrete data and by analyzing the issues concerned.

In the case of strong disagreement, e.g. of 40% or more disagreement, conflict is probable. But even the concept of conflict is problematic. One thing is what will make the conflict manifest; that is not a problem to be taken up in this context.[8] However, in the case where one group presents an

80% support of a given position ('In favor of x') and the other group at the same time is 80% *rejecting* that same position – the situation then in the latter group reveals what Shils calls 'the paradox of a dissensual consensus'[9] – conflict is highly potent. But whether it will manifest itself in destructive behavior and will carry any serious effects on the polity or the policy, depends on the *intensity* with which attitudes are held in this particular issue, on the *importance* attached to the disputed issue by the parties or by the polity as a whole, and on the number of individuals in both (or in one of the) groups who maintain an attitude of political unconsciousness, indifference or neutrality toward the issue.

Level of analysis is again important. 'Dissensual consensus' indicates that disagreement on one level corresponds to consensus on another (and lower) level. A social group may in some cases purposely create disagreement with other groups *in order to* obtain consensus within itself.[10] The multi-level analysis of the consensus-dissensus dimension is thus crucial because it may show variations or patterns of dissensus (= (our) disagreement) 'hidden' if one only focuses on the level above that where dissensus exists. As the most obvious illustration of this, focussing on the national level only (through national opinion surveys) without at the same time focussing on important social groups within the nation (as the elite, minorities, etc.) is a serious shortcoming too often experienced in social research.

We shall be focussing on agreement, interchangeably, at four (or five) levels of analysis: the *national* where we look for agreement between different national actor elites; the *intra-national* where we analyze the general public opinion in relation to the elite and the opinion-makers; the *milieu* level where we focus on elite – opinion-maker relations; and the *elite* level where the focus is on intra-elite agreement (the possible fifth level indicated being what may be called the policy-maker level). At most of these levels, we shall be analyzing even consensus within the relevant groups or categories.

Further, this study will analyze *multi-dimensional, one-dimensional,* and *single-item* consensus and agreement. That is: consensus as measured through an aggregate of *several dimensions,* on *one dimension* (through several items), and as a percentage score on *one single item.* These operations will be explained in more detail later on.

3.2. *The bases of consensus*

Several variables may be used to explain the position of Norway or of any other actor of the same class of (moderate) center actors, on the consensus-dissensus dichotomy. We shall concentrate on three fundamental factors:

the homogeneity-heterogeneity, the pluralism-monism, and the congruency-incongruency dichotomies.

Norway is a very homogeneous country, according to race, language, religion, etc.[11] At the same time she is relatively monistic in the sense that school, religion, radio, etc. are monopolized by the states, also, a large number of institutions or organizations like the trade union movement, are nation-wide and 'monopolistic' in their respective spheres.[12] The relative homogeneity in the fundamental social life then is further strengthened by institutionalization of monistic or monopolistic tendencies.

This institutionalization of monism is no new trend in Norwegian history. In fact, it goes back to the period when Norway was a colony of its neighbor states and under a strong central government, which was more or less taken over by the Norwegians when they got independence; the history of Norway thus very much resembles that of the developing countries. The strength of the central institutional system is a factor which not only helps to create consensus, but also results in a considerable tenacity of it.[13]

The third dimension is that introduced by Eckstein in his study of Norway.[14] He argues that the stability or ultra-stability of the Norwegian system is not primarily due to the homogeneity of the country or the institutional monism of the system. The primary factor is the congruency of the system which creates stability: the way authority is exercised in the central institutions is mirrored in other social structures or authority relations – in the organizations, in school, in the family. There are, according to Eckstein, important social and political cleavages in Norway, but they are bridged over by the congruency in the system.

Although his theory may be challenged on certain points and perhaps even more so his description of Norwegian society as relatively dissensual,[15] his congruency hypothesis seems very much to the point and may extend the basis of consensus explanation sought here.

The dimensions of multi-dimensional consensus and the boundaries of the structure of it may vary within any given society, over a longer trend, but also from one situation to another, from one issue to another. Such variations, however, are assumed relatively rare and small in the case of Norway. Some dimensions have been part of foreign policy consensus for a considerable period of time (cf. Chapt. 2). Others have been adapted to new realities (as perceived by the opinion-making strata). In an ultra-stable system as that of Norway, very few dimensions of the multi-dimensional consensus will be discarded or disappear over time as long as the international system itself is not radically changed.[16]

New items or dimensions are usually included in the consensus through a process of consensus-building. This process starts with a given value on the dimension being accepted by some social group, develops through increasing support of the value by growing groups of adherents until it reaches the consensus 'threshold'. Thereafter, it is upheld by a large, but somewhat fluctuating public with more or less intensity. Usually this public support has to include the major part of the elite and the milieu particularly when it is a question of *national* consensus.

Social structure is crucial in this context. It is the main vehicle in consensus-building, as well as in its failure. As Merton has pointed out, deviant behavior, or dissensus, is just as much a product of social structures as is conformism – or consensus.[17]

Consensus may be initiated and established by groups or individuals outside the central parts of the social structure – the elite or the social center. But in most important cases, these groups are if not initiators, the ones producing consensus. To produce consensus is in fact one of their main functions in the society.

While instruments of consensus-building are many and varied, the most important ones are probably *communication* and *socialization*. It follows from what we have said above on the structure of opinion-making in international affairs and the foreign policy field, that communication here is very much the upper strata communicating *to* the lower and thus socializing them into the attitudes and images they have come to accept themselves. It also follows from what is known about the degree of foreign policy attentiveness and knowledge in particular, and about the degree to which the messages sent from the socializing strata really reach the lower or periphery strata, that the effect of consensus-building is different on different levels within the structure.[18]

We hypothesize that consensus generally increases with increasing social position. On the whole, consensus is higher in the elite (or center) than in the opinion-maker (middle or next-to-center) category. And the opinion-maker consensus is generally higher than the public opinion (middle or periphery) one. Socialization is more effective, and communicated messages 'go through' more often, the higher up in the social structure one gets.

If socialization is relatively intense and effective, consensus will increase over time. As a general rule, consensus is more rapidly reached, the higher the average social position of the group or level in question.

Consensus build-up may take the form of a continuous movement, or it may go in discontinuous 'leaps'. *Outside stimuli*, like an international crisis affecting the actor in question, may create sudden consensus *or* dissensus. An example would be the case where an actor, dissenting within itself over some major foreign policy issues, is attacked by another and runs together on the very basic consensus over the need to defend itself.[19] The above mentioned purposive use of conflict with another actor just to get one's own dissenting public together is another example of a consensus-building instrument. The other case – that of dissensus-development – is the steady growth of a national dissensus (and even dissensus within the elite) within e. g. the US over Vietnam policy during the 1966–68 period.

In the case of Norway, the Communist *coup d'état* in Prague 1948 had the immediate effect of backing up (within some groups, indeed creating it) consensus over the policy of an alliance with the Western great powers.[20] The effect was most immediate and important on the elite or milieu levels; the build-up of a national consensus was a task for the years to come. Subsequent events – Hungary 1956 and Czechoslovakia 1968 – has as evidenced by public opinion polls, bolstered the consensus on this issue, for some parts of the public only *ad hoc* so that it became more of a sudden blow-up. On the milieu and especially elite level, however, the effect was more that of reinforcing already existing attitudes or making them somewhat more manifest (this latter perhaps on an ad hoc basis).

Communication and socialization are more effective the higher up in the social structure one gets. In addition, specific patterns of *recruitment* to high positions provide extra pressure or incentive toward consensus. The task of the elite or the policy-makers is to administer consensus and get support for it. To make sure that this task is performed, the elite sees to it that consensus-accepting people are recruited to elite positions. Conversely, individuals who aspire to elite or high positions within a stable consensus will fit themselves, their attitudes and images, into the consensus in order to obtain those positions.

Communications do not flow with the same ease between all individuals or groups within the polity. Groups holding different perspectives socialize recruits to these perspectives. There are separate channels of recruitment up to the roles holding them. These channels are to a large extent protected against intrusion by different perspectives.

Within these separate channels – which are vertical structures – there is a steady consensus-building. But between them, dissensus is likely, at least on some issues. One channel leads to the 'establishment', another to an 'outsider' group. We may distinguish three such groups: the Establishment, the Left outsiders, and the Right outsiders. The Establishment is – when we take the polity, the milieu and the elite as a whole (but separately) – consensus-maintaining; the outsider groups are consensus-destroying, or more correctly, *partially* consensus-destroying. The logical fourth group – the

Anti-establishment – which is *generally* consensus-destroying, is not likely to be represented within the elite or the milieu, but will be so in lower or more periphery strata where protest or revolution against *any* major policyline is widespread.[21]

A final consensus-promoting factor to be mentioned here is the importance of *consensus as a goal in itself*. Adherence to this dictum and thus its effect is also positively correlated with high social position: the value of a 'cross-political' or 'cross-party' consensus on foreign policy is often stressed by elite members. This is frequently connected with the argument that a small country like Norway cannot afford to stay dissensual with itself in important international or foreign policy questions, because this will weaken its position and its power.[22]

The Establishment is naturally a multi-dimensional consensus. The question then is what it contains, which dimensions are included in it. Not all dimensions within the perspective are part of the Establishment, because only a limited number of dimensions really matter. A range of questions, issues, or dimensions is left out as unimportant or indifferent to the question of consensus. There *may* be a nearly 100 percent disagreement on an issue without this creating any problems to the policy or the polity: this issue is seen as unimportant by most groups.

On the other hand, when an issue is subject to intense and lasting public *debate* and when there is a relatively strong *polarization* of the public on that issue, this indicates that the issue is an establishment-outsider item. In addition to this one there are two more indicators of such items. The first is the '*age*' of the issue: whether it is old or young, has been discussed for a long time, or has been recently introduced. The second is whether or not the issue has been subject to an intense and lasting *socialization*, of the general public by the opinion-making strata. What the elite sets out intensely socializing public opinion about, is establishment items because it is up to the elite to define what the Establishment is at any time.

The idea of a relatively strong polarization as an indicator of establishment items may perhaps seem somewhat contradictory to the very meaning of consensus, which excludes polarization. The idea does not presuppose, however, that the poles are equally strong, but rather that there is a dissenting minority and a consenting or conformist majority opposed to each other. The idea further presupposes that the strength of the dissenting pole is gradually reduced due to the effect of the two other factors mentioned: time and socialization. Of course there is the possibility of the initial dissenting minority in the longer run and through socialization of the public at large becoming a majority, finally taking over policy-making power or forcing the policy-maker minority to adopt their own attitudes and policies. But in a stable political system, this is clearly the exception and not the rule.[23]

An issue which is intensely debated, has been so for a relatively long time, and is subject to intense socialization is thus likely to attract high consensus, while items which score low on all three dimensions are likely to score lower on consensus. However, certain factors may modify this trend. For instance, an item which is not disputed over, and which at the same time is old and subject to socialization, will attract a higher consensus. An issue's perceived *importance* – whether or not it is related to the very life of the national actor or some of its major values – will be highly influential on the degree of consensus. That is: 'survival of the actor' is hardly subject to less than a 99 % consensus, *but* the ways and means of securing survival may be much disputed.

On the other hand, that an issue is part of an aggregate of issues like the Establishment, may reduce degree or rigidity of consensus on that issue. The Establishment, or any other multi-dimensional consensus, is very much a *compromise,* made up through a process of give-and-take between different interest groups. In this process, one group gets support for the issues it is enthusiastic about itself by lending some support for issues it is merely willing to tolerate. Thus, within certain parts of the Establishment, there will always be a tendency toward either of the outsider positions, which may fluctuate in strength according to the changing impact of different consensus- or dissensus-creating factors.

This will first of all be true with the affective parts of the perspective, but it may also concern what Boulding calls the 'public image' of the social group in question.[24] Another aspect of 'consensual belief patterns' is their pluralism in the sense that

> they espouse a number of beliefs which are not wholly consistent
> with each other and which are able to coexist quite easily as long as
> no one of them are carried out in full.[25]

With these modifications and this emphasis on pluralistic aspects of consensus items, we appear to be back in the so-called concentric theory of Norwegian foreign policy discussed and partially discarded above. The validity of this theory, which presupposes a conflict-free multi-dimensional consensus or establishment, will have to be tested; but our hypothesis still is that it does not hold, and that this is the more true the more one goes below the elite level.

3.3. *Intra-national consensus: elite – public opinion relations*

We have made some hypotheses on elite versus public opinion relations, and we shall present some more. This part of the study will have to be limited in scope because of the lack of comparable data. Such data in fact are available on only a limited number of dimensions.[26]

In another study on the same material we analyzed elite-public opinion relations on peace and war, on 'crucial' foreign policy, and on disarmament issues.[27] The study related itself to the intra-national or micro-level theory of foreign policy opinion as a function of social position; and the hypothesis that as expressed by opinion position on an index of a number of items, the elite constituted an *ultra-center* was relatively well confirmed. More generally, the hypothesis – which we called the *projection hypothesis* – was that we may project the opinion on an issue or cluster of issues, of a given social group from other social groups in the same universe *if* we know the exact opinion of these latter groups, the social position of all the groups in question (both the group whose opinion we want to know, and the groups whose opinion we know) and their position relative to each other. This hypothesis was partially confirmed.

We shall not be dealing with the micro-level theory of social position in this context, except for testing some hypotheses on intra-group or intra-sample variances. Our concern is with relations between the three levels: elite, opinion-makers, and public opinion. To some extent, this is the same problem; it was maintained above that the elite – public opinion stratification correlates positively with the center-periphery index: the elite is more centrist than the opinion-makers. This does not mean, however, that the elite *is* the same as the center.

The difference is that the center is a social *category*, the elite very much a social *group*. Some of the factors which make the elite differ from other social strata also make the center differ from the more periphery categories. But the amount and content of communication, socialization, recruitment, and role performance is more purposive, specific, and has far more effect in the elite than in the center. The foreign policy elite is a group of specialists, and the efficiency demands placed on it necessitate its being as closely 'knit together' as possible – structurally, preferably by social background, but at least in the attitudes and images of its members.

But then the question must be asked: *are* there any systematic differences over foreign policy issues between the elite and other social groups or strata? While not many universal generalizations can be drawn from the modest research done so far on elite-public opinion relations, Singer points out evidence of certain regular 'mass-versus-elite' discrepancies.[28] On the other hand, cross-national opinion polls summarized by Eckhardt and Lentz indicate that elite opinion generally parallels public opinion.[29]

In fact, these observations based on empirical data from two different sources do not necessarily contradict each other. The last-mentioned authors base their observations on questions of peace and war, while the former is based more on a diversity of issues. This seems to support the hypothesis that elite-public opinion differences will exist only on *some* dimensions or issue-clusters. In our opinion, these dimensions or clusters are primarily those which are part of or related to the foreign policy establishment.[30]

But there are still other differences within the relationship mentioned. Scott for instance, from an empirical study on psychological and social correlates of international images, concludes that higher socio-economic status is associated with more friendly attitudes toward foreign nations, and optimism concerning the course of international relations.[31] Several studies indicate that elites are more 'internationalistic' and 'supranationalistic' than the public at large. Such indications – although there is often a lack of precision as to *what* is really indicated – seem convincing enough. This is even more so when we recall the contention made above that the elite or the milieu at large are the groups which interact most closely and often with foreign elites or milieus.

To the extent to which such elite versus public discrepancies exist, they may be rather consequential to the society at large. Particularly if they are prominent on Establishment issues and on other issues to which larger parts of the society attach importance, elite-public relations may be decisive as to what kind of political system the actor in question will have, and to the degree of *legitimacy* of the system.

According to elite-public relationships on important foreign policy issues, we may distinguish between at least *four different types* of foreign policy systems:

a. the *'autocratic'* system: the difference between the elite and the public opinion is large, amounting to an overall disagreement on images and attitudes; the elite forms its perspective and makes its policy independently of the public, or 'over its heads'.
b. the 'guided democracy' or the *'oligarcic'* system: the elite clearly differs from the public in perspective, but stands closer to it on all or most important issues; disagreement is thus only partial.
c. the *'democratic'* system: the elite has a perspective close to that of the public; agreement between them is large.
d. the *'dictatorship of the proletariat'* system: in this system the public evidently are the masters, imposing their perspective on the rest of the society.

The elite-public relationship, however, is not the only factor which determines the shape and the content of the foreign policy system. The relations of the opinion-makers, *and* even those of the center category (i.e. the social elites according to socio-economic status in general) with both the elite and the public opinion are also of great importance. Among other things, the position of the opinion-makers vis-a-vis that of the others will largely determine the degree of *stability* in the system. As was shown above, the opinion-makers have a dual role to play: both that of opinion-making as such and that of constituting a reservoir or possibly an alternative to the elite, since it may not only contain persons willing to be recruited to elite positions, but also persons who actively seek to capture those positions.

If the elite has the backing of the opinion-makers and even the center, then the system should be rather stable. The position of public opinion is then of relatively minor importance, although a 'revolutionary' lower strata movement of course may make itself felt and approach the type d. mentioned above. If the opinion-makers on the other hand, possibly with the support of the center, are strongly opposed to the elite, the system is at least potentially unstable. In this case the opinion-makers will probably seek to take over the policy-making power held by the elite. In particular, the situation will be 'revolutionary' when the position of the opinion-makers is close to that of the public, *and* the relationship between the elite and the public is dominated by a great difference between them.

Table 3.3.1. *The relationship between elite-public opinion differences and the position of opinion-makers*

| Elite-public difference | Opinion-makers position | | | |
	Close to public (1)	Between elite and public (2)	Close to elite (3)	Above/below elite (4)
Great (a)	Strongly autocratic: strong polarization	Moderately autocratic: communication moderate	Autocratic: the apathetic public or revolutionary	Ultra-autocratic: opinion-makers isolated
Moderately large (b)	Autocratic: polarization	Moderately oligarchic: communication high	Oligarchic: the guided public	Autocratic: opinion-makers avant garde
Practically none (c)	'The great harmony': communication high, tension low, mobilization wide			Opinion-makers apathetic or avant garde

Let us systematize the implications of these different situations schematically by looking at the interaction between the two variables mentioned so far: the difference between the elite and the public opinion, and the position of the opinion-makers relative to both of them. This is done in Table 3.3.1.[33] Which of the systems indicated in the Table is the most unstable and potentially revolutionary in the sense that the elite is threatened? This may differ from one system to another depending on the form and content of the social and political system at large of the given actor, and depending on the degree to which different social groups or strata, in particular public opinion, is mobilized and active in the foreign policy system. But it may also depend on the role the elite plays or is supposed to play in that system: whether its role is to initiate, to take a strong lead or guidance of the public (and thus differ from it in perspective), or to go only as fast and as far as public opinion allows (and thus stress elite-public consensus). This again may change somewhat our preliminary propositions about which system is the most legitimate.

The most unstable system is believed to be the one where the opinion-makers (and possibly the center) are very close to the public and the elite is at a great distance from the public (type $a1$). This is the situation where the opinion-makers can mobilize the public against the elite; to some extent this holds even for type $b1$. Another potentially unstable system is $c4$. Here we might expect that the opinion-makers (especially if followed by the center) will produce opposition against the perspective of the elite because it is lagging behind their own, and stand out as an alternative elite, challenging the existing one.

In the case of an actor like Norway, we would hypothesize that types $b2$ or $b3$ are the most stable systems. They fit well into a relatively educated and foreign policy interested polity, and avoid challenges from the opinion-makers to the elite. And especially $b2$ seems to provide the communication and the bridge building necessary to avoid an opinion gap. The position of the opinion-makers somewhere in-between the elite and the public seems important, guaranteeing that the system will not move towards the type $a3$, which could be the result of a close elite-opinion-maker alliance.

Types $c1$–$c3$ are believed to be restricted to a limited scope, while $c4$ could be generally found in some non-initiating, inactive, 'closed' i.e. extremely periphery actor.

What is then the real position of the opinion-makers in the Norwegian system? We believe that there is no *overall* position: sometimes or more correctly, on some dimensions it may be of the type $b2$, on others of the type $b3$, $a3$, or $b4$. Above, the projection hypothesis was presented in connection

64

with the theory of social position and it should now also be applicable to the public-opinion-maker-elite relationship. We thus hypothesize that the positions of these categories on Establishment dimensions constitute the type $b2$ system.

As has been said already, the opinion-makers basically have two functions to fulfil: to educate the public and socialize them into the opinions of the elite; and to represent public opinion, often not very articulate itself, toward the elite. But there is a third role which the opinion-makers will play: that of representing images and attitudes *of their own*.

When and on what issues they play out some *specific* role more than the others, is a complicated question which can be answered only by extensive data. It seems relatively safe to assume that when they take positions 1 or 2, they are first of all performing the public-representative function. In position 3 they are socializing for the elite, while in position 4 they naturally are acting primarily for their own sake (cf. Table 3.3.1).

Relating the problem to the theory of international position, we believe that the international position of 'one's own actor' is most strongly felt within the elite and least so in the public. Thus we make the projection hypothesis again which means that the opinion-makers are somewhere in-between (type $b2$). The elite is more penetrated, is more responsive to outside actors; the opinion-makers are more likely to be influenced by societal factors (which follows from their representative function). Or, to state the hypothesis more correctly: the elite is more responsive to outside factors working toward the centrist perspective, while the opinion-makers on the one hand are more responsive to societal and to outside factors which are *not* particularly center-directed. To take one example: we believe that regionalistic feelings in Norway are more prominent in the elite than in the opinion-maker category, which is supposed to be more globalistic. The rationale behind this is mainly that the perspective of the elite for structural reasons is more geared to the priority policies of the given actor – *in casu* Norway, the Western regional alliance policy.

The opinion-makers may also perform a *fourth* function: that of initiating, of taking new issues and certain opinions on them into the polity. The elite, entrenched in policy-making and in keeping established images and attitudes for the sake of continuity and predictability of action (on which other actors may put a high value), will generally not be free or indeed willing to introduce new issues and opinions to the same degree as the less 'responsible' opinion-makers. An example would probably be the policy toward less developed countries.

For the same reason – that the elite has the policy-making responsibilities and the opinion-makers not – the opinion-makers may be ahead of the elite in several issues where the elite feels the 'pressure of realities' and tends to relax in their affections about certain opinions because of the problem of their implementation. Here the opinion-makers may see to it that consensus and intensity of that opinion is kept high. An example would be disarmament.

3.4. *Harmony or polarization: intra-sample variances*

In the preceding sections, we focussed on the vertical structure of the system of image-building and attitude-formation. We now turn to its *horizontal* aspects. Different sub-groupings within the samples drawn will be compared on a number of dimensions, mostly at the elite level, but in some cases even at the level of opinion-makers.

The question then is what sub-groupings and what dimensions. According to the variables used in the study, the samples may be divided into a whole range of sub-groupings, but not all of them will be equally interesting and worth studying. Neither would all the different dimensions or variables, which may present variance or non-variance when the sub-groupings are compared, offer equally fruitful and important theoretical problems. These arguments, plus limitations in space, force us to make a choice.

Then the question is: what is interesting, fruitful, worth studying? When it comes to sub-groupings, or *independent* variables, the answer is not, 'those variables which show the greatest amount of variance on a number of dependent variables'. Too much emphasis is placed, by many researchers, on analyzing and explaining variance to the neglect of non-variance, which in many cases may be quite as interesting and demand as much explanatory work. In this study, we shall try to work on both problems, as we have been doing already in elaborating on the consensus (non-variance) versus dissensus (variance) dimension.

The lack of hard data again means that we do not stand on very safe ground in these questions. Two independent studies, however, show that socio-economic variables or the so-called 'background variables', which in general public opinion studies do explain much of the attitudes and behavior of individuals, at the elite level have a very limited explanatory capability.[34] This is not only so because social background within this category is far more equal than in the society as a whole, but primarily because several structural factors 'neutralize' the socio-economic ones and become more important: extensive communication, socialization, recruitment according to achievement criteria (such as knowledge, basic attitudes, etc.).

Robinson and Snyder argue that 'the social background of decision-makers is becoming increasingly democratic', i.e. less strictly egalitarian, more varied according to socio-economic criteria, with the consequence that 'more varied images and perspectives are being considered in foreign and international policy-making'.[35] While the first part of their argument is reasonable, we would like to challenge the latter part which runs contrary to what we proposed above on the effects of socio-economic variables. Robinson and Snyder fail to take into account exactly these variables which have or may have a counter-effect on 'democratization,' and whose effect probably increases more over time than the 'democracy-effect' does.

In order to test our propositions on this point, we include *social position*, as measured by the Galtung center-periphery index of eight social background variables, as an independent variable.

The four categories from which the samples were drawn naturally constitute another important sub-grouping variable. *Sample category* membership is thus one of the independent variables we shall focus on. A third one is *party affiliation*, one of the more important behavior indicators in the study. We have already stated that party affiliation in public debate on Norwegian foreign policy has accounted for some of the greatest differences and most serious polarizations, since the Socialist People's Party was founded, based on opposition against the foreign policy Establishment. Between the political parties to the right of this party, the very widespread opinion exists that there are no significant differences in attitudes and images. We challenge even this opinion, proposing that the alleged polarization between the Socialist People's Party on the one hand and the other parties, apart from some of the issues going into the Establishment, is not so clear-cut as in the opinion of some commentators. That consensus, even inter-party agreement between the remaining parties is a goal in itself does not mean that there *is* such consensus.

The *Establishment-outsider* dimension gives a basis for the fourth independent variable we shall study. This dimension was operationalized with the use of four indicators representing two basic dimensions in Norwegian foreign policy. These two dimensions in turn were established as basic through the evaluations of the respondents themselves. They were asked to state on what issues they found themselves in *most* disagreement with their foreign policy protagonists. This variant of the socio-metric method produced then the four indicators which were adapted in the Establishment-outsider index. These dimensions were 'Western cooperation' or what may be called 'Westwardness' and 'globalism'. The index clearly reflects the pluralistic content of the Establishment; it combines regionalism and globalism, the distinction between which was proposed and emphasized above, but puts most emphasis on regionalism.[36]

Recently it has become very common to talk about 'the gap between the generations', both in their world images and in their foreign policy attitudes. This together with some interesting hypotheses on age differences produced by earlier research, give us reason to focus on *age* as an independent variable. Lastly, we shall have something to say on the relations between the elite 'nucleus' of *policy-makers* and the rest of the elite.

This leaves us with three categories of independent variables to be investigated: one is the sample category variable, which is primarily constructed for the sampling purpose; another category is what is usually referred to as background variables, i.e. social position and age; the third would then be the class of attitudinal variables represented by party affiliation and the Establishment-outsider index. The policy-maker variable probably will also fall into this class, as it is a result of the self-evaluation of the respondents.

The variables will in the following be dealt with in the order in which they appeared in this attempt at classification.

A. *The sampling groups.* Two factors are of particular importance to differences between the four sampling groups or categories: the pattern of *recruitment*, and the intensity of socializing *communication*. When it comes to recruitment, we may distinguish between the Administration (AD) on the one hand and the Politicians (PO), Mass media (MM) and the Interest organizations (IO) on the other. The recruitment to the Administration is narrower, more controlled than in the case of the three others. It is made according to the fundamental sets of norms of the foreign policy conducted. Its task is to choose the administrators of consensus, to secure continuity in and maintenance of the Establishment.

The Politicians, recruited according to party affiliation and the relative strength of parties in the Parliament, have a double and potentially contradictory function to perform. On the one hand, they shall reflect the dissensus-representing role of the Parliament; on the other hand, their constitutional role is to make the foreign policy legitimate on the basis of the largest possible consensus. As the Politicians are almost identical with the Extended Foreign Relations Commitee in the Storting, most emphasis is placed on the consensus-legitimizing role; such a recruitment pattern has been evidenced by Hellevik.[37]

Communication intensity is, on the within-group level, believed to be highest within the Administration. This group has a centralized structure

68

and is full-time employed with foreign policy matters. The Politicians also have a relatively close-knit structure, but are far from full-time foreign policy specialists. Table 3.4.1 gives a more detailed picture of this.

Table 3.4.1. *Difference between the sampling groups*

Variable	Characteristics	PO	AD	MM	IO
recruitment	narrow/close	×	×		
	wide/open	×		×	×
role performance	high		×	×	
specialization	low	×			×
structure	centralized	×	×		
	non-centralized			×	×
within-group communication	high	×	×		
	low	×		×	×

Another or fifth factor is what we may call the *opinion-impact,* i.e. the tendency in a group to be influenced by public opinion and to hold attitudes and opinions as close as possible to those of public opinion. It is believed that the Politicians are more subject to such an impact than the other groups and that the Administration is the least.[38] Where the opinion impact is greatest it will contribute most to intra-elite dissensus, but at the same time contribute most to national consensus by shortening the distance to the public opinion.

After this we may propose the hypothesis that intra-group consensus is greatest within the Administration; between the other groups it is difficult to hypothesize any clear differences, although we may reasonably assume that the Politicians are more Establishmentarian than the two remaining groups, but less than the Administration, given its Establishment-legiti-mizing role.

On the inter-group level, communication is crucial. We maintained above that the Norwegian elite is comparatively close-knit. This implies high inter-group communication, although other factors (social homogeneity, intense socialization, etc.) will to some extent make high communication 'superfluous'. This communication consists largely of the exchange of information, which may be value-loaded and thus contain messages of affective form (preferences which others are invited to share).

Not all groups communicate equally much with the others. That is: there are initiators and receivers, sellers and buyers. Which group then most typically perform each of these functions? In particular, we wish to know who is the initiator or the seller.

In our opinion that is the Administration and the Mass media. The latter is a self-evident case; the role of the former has to be explained. In a formal interpretation of the structure of the foreign policy elite, it is the task of the administration to provide and prepare the material on which policy-making (by government and parliament) is based. It is also its task to implement policies. The process of preparation and implementation, however, means that the Administration has control (if not absolute) of both the input and the output sides of the policy- and opinion-making. It provides information, possibly feedback from outside reactions to implemented policies, from the international system through diplomatic channels. By definition then this group is the most influential.[39]

The key position of the Administration in the communication structure together with its consensus-maintaining primacy, means that it will be both an active seller *and* a determined guider (i.e. presenting information where value-derivations is at least implicit). Its information will tend to be singularistic, that of the Mass media more pluralistic. The singularism of the Administration will not necessarily be found *within* the group: the information it *receives* is more pluralistic than what it *sends out*. The former is stored and may be used inside; the latter is filtered and arranged for outside use.

B. *Social position.* The general hypothesis is, as indicated already, that social position within upper strata samples does not account for much of the variance within the samples. That these individuals and groups are performing a specialized function in society in common is of greater importance than what social background they have in different respects.

In studies based on national surveys, several trends of center-periphery variance have been found. These findings should clearly not be directly taken over as hypotheses for our purpose; our center-periphery index is quite different from the one used in these studies, and our samples far from reflect society as a whole.[40] Some of these findings may, however, be adapted for the purpose of making hypotheses. The question which would interset us then is whether variances found in society as a whole even make themselves felt, although to a lesser extent, within a social group which spans only a small segment of that society. Another problem would be whether the center-periphery dimension within elite samples creates differences *other* than those found within national survey samples.

70

Galtung presents a list of concrete hypotheses about the relationship between the *form* ('tough' vs. 'soft' policies) of a person's foreign policy orientation and his social position.[41] They are based among other things on the proposition that the center is gradualistic and the periphery more absolutistic.

But this proposition is part of our theory on centrism, and we should be able to extend the hypothesis to include other aspects of that theory as well: the hypothesis then is that the social center (within the milieu) has a more centrist outlook when it comes to international perspectives than has the periphery.

Relating our elite analysis to general social position theories (i.e. the studies using the nation as the universe) we found elsewhere that the elite constitutes a kind of 'ultra-center' within the society.[42] We shall have another look at this problem in this context.

A third rather evident hypothesis would be that the center is the most Establishmentarian of the social position categories. Another finding from a study made by Halle and which refers particularly to Norway, is that the items (among a great number of different items) on which social position shows greatest impact are three items included in or related to our Establishment-outsider dimension.[43]

C. *Age.* There is much talk about differences or divergences between generations – the age categories – in present political life throughout the world. *Are* such differences felt in the fields of foreign policy and international politics, and *to what extent*?

We believe they *are* felt, but not to the extent that one may talk of a 'generation gap'. Recruitment and socialization patterns secure continuity and consensus. The elder, when recruiting younger people to elite positions, will naturally see to it that the latter share their own images and attitudes as much as possible. *Below* the elite level, these tendencies will probably be less prominent; thus, on the opinion-maker level, age will probably account for more of the variance than on the elite level. This downward trend, however, is not necessarily uni-directional or linear; public opinion surveys show that the age variable is not especially important on the public opinion level.[44]

Some variances in the perspectives of milieu members will be due to age. Our first hypothesis here may be called *the hypothesis of the basic socialization period*. It proposes that an individual's perspective is at least partly a result of the socialization he went through in the formative years between the age of 15 and 25 or so.

Some of the basic structure of the perspective of course is laid down in childhood. It is therefore relevant to study the image-building and attitude-formation of children even for studies that focus on individuals in 'adult' policy- or opinion-making positions.[45] Our hypothesis relates itself to the impact on individuals of the period when they are 'maturing' and, most of them, being politically mobilized or 'politicized', i.e. the age of 20 to 30.[46] It argues that the prominent issues, the major international problems of that age influence the individual's perspective.

Operationally, this means that *the aged* (more than 55–60 years old) are relatively more concerned with cooperation, integration, etc. than the other groups, both cognitively in the sense that these features are cues in the cognitive structure of the aged, and affectively in the sense that they are more preferred and positively responded to. This category, whose socialization took place in the first of the three periods of Norwegian foreign policy (cf. 2.3) will be particularly positive to the NATO alliance, as the security arrangements they believed in – the League of Nations and neutrality – were destroyed by WWII. Its message is in a way: 'Cooperation was and *is* right, but the way we practiced it was a mistake, so don't make our mistakes once again.'

The *middle-aged* (or middle-young) are relatively more influenced by war-and-peace problems (generally and specifically) than the others. They experienced and even participated in the war and its aftermath as adolescents; they are the 'realists' who 'know the realities of the present-day world': power struggles, conflicts, wars.

The *younger* probably have a more diffuse perspective than the other categories and consequently no specific affective preferences or cognitive cues. This may be seen as a function of the relative diffuseness of the 50s and early 60s, where no single issue or problem dominated as in the foregoing period, but several issues competed for attention.[47] Since these problems were brought to the minds of most Norwegians (and for that matter most people in the developed world) *and* became prominent issues in the latest decades only, we assume that the younger are more concerned with and positive toward these matters than are the other groups.

We will also test the hypothesis that the younger are less centrist in their perspective than the other groups; in particular, they should be more change-oriented since they are supposed to be more diffuse (and thus flexible) in their perspective, and since they are not 'settled down in their issues'. This greater flexibility among the younger has been shown in a study by Gergen and Back.[48]

As to questions of consensus and establishmentarianism within the age groups, there is no self-evident theory of variances at hand. One might assume that consensus increases proportionally with age. This seems 'too easy', however. We believe that policy consensus is positively correlated with the degree of political activity of an individual, generally. Voting behavior studies show that activity and involvement decrease after a certain age level.[49] The process of aging could be described as one of progressive social disengagement.

Accordingly, the aged should be thought of as gradually disengaging themselves from the Establishment. This leaves us with the hypothesis that the middle-aged are most establishmentarian; the expected relative diffuseness of the young and the probability that they have not yet been completely socialized to prevailing norms make the younger less establishmentarian. Thus, the aged should be tending in the Right outsider, the younger in the Left outsider direction.

D. *Party affiliation.* Our first problem is on what basis inter-party comparisons should be made. From the low m in both samples in several parties it is clear that not all seven (or six, to exclude the Communists who were the only party not represented in the Parliament at the moment) can be compared. How should we then collapse the groups for the most fruitful analysis?

One method very often used in studies of Western European polities is to compare socialists and non-socialists (or 'bourgeois'). In the field of foreign policy, and in the case of Norway, this a priori distinction should clearly not be adopted uncritically; it may be easily challenged. At the level of public opinion and nation-wide surveys, it may be defended. But even here, and quite evidently higher up in social structure when it comes to foreign policy matters this distinction has proven unvalid. From what has been said above on the development of Norwegian foreign policy thinking, the greatest differences on Establishment and establishment-related items, measured by percentage distance between 'neighbors' on the Socialist-Liberal-Conservative continuum should be found between the Socialist People's Party and the Social Democrats (or Labor Party), exactly the two groups in our sample that would constitute the 'Socialist' category if the party variable is dichotomized.

A trichotomization of the variable offers two alternatives: (Left) Socialists, Social Democrats, and 'Bourgeois'; and (Left) Socialists, Social Democrats and Liberals (Left center), and Right center and Conservatives. According to the parliamentary and government-opposition situation in Norway at the time when our data collection was carried out, the first alternative ought to be preferred, since the four 'bourgeois' or non-socialist parties then constituted the government. Foreign policy issues, however, were not and are not the main basis on which governments are formed in Norway, and they are clearly not the issues which first of all would distinguish Labor leaders (or followers) from Liberal or even Conservative ones. Thus Valen and Katz, when arguing that there is a tendency towards greater differences at the level of leaders than at the level of followers on issues largely involving ideology or strong affect, are not speaking primarily of foreign policy issues (if the strongly dissident minorities are left out).[50] A Labor-Conservative 'Grand coalition' was in fact observed in 1967 when Norway for the second time applied for membership in the European Common Market.[51]

Over the whole range of issues, this coalition would not be very fruitful if considered as one possible category for the comparative purposes of this study. It has been established, for example, that according to the importance they attach to foreign policy as such (relative to other policy fields) *and* to the priority they attach to different foreign policy or international political issues, Laborites and Liberals stand closer to each other than do either the Laborites and the Conservatives, *or* Liberals and Conservatives.[52] Public opinion studies show a similar pattern. These findings will constitute the basis of an hypothesis to be tested here.

There is the possibility of collapsing the party variable into four (treating Laborites separately and collapsing the Center and Christian party categories with either Liberals or Conservatives) or five (treating even Christians and Centerites separately in one group) categories. This would, especially at the elite level, involve problems created by the low m which would then appear for some of the categories. The solution to these problems should clearly not be adopting one single alternative, but using a variety of combinations on the party variables in order to test different hypotheses most fruitfully. The main task is to show the major variations, or 'unexpected' patterns of non-variance, that exist in the samples.

If we relate the party Left-to-Right dimension to the Establishment-outsider dimension, we should expect positive correlation between the two: the Left on the party variable correlates with what we call Leftist outsiders, Right with Rightist outsiders. This argument implies the hypothesis that the Liberals and the Laborites, situated more or less in the middle of the party continuum and relatively close to each other, are Establishment-maintaining, while the other parties in varying degrees are dissenters or outsiders.

This does not necessarily mean that these two parties over a range of dimensions show the highest consensus. Referring once more to the dissensual consensus paradox, 'dissensual (dis-establishmentarian) consensus' may be higher than 'consensual consensus'. In groups where there is a high consistency and monism in the pattern of attitudes (images are less relevant, but may also be included) and where the intensity of attitude-holding, is high, internal consensus will also be high. In this situation, strong disagreement with the prevailing majority consensus (the Establishment), will lead to polarization which in turn strengthens the internal consensus in the dis-establishmentarian group.

The party dimension may also be related to the world perspective, in particular its cognitive parts. While the elite and to a lesser degree the opion-makers are generally rather centrist in their perspectives, the Right should be 'over-centrist' and the Left tend more towards periphery thinking ('periphery' here is 'international periphery', which may well have some similarities with national periphery), as the center perspective is very much based on conservativism, status quo, less change-orientation, etc.

The Right should also be more 'ideological' than other categories in being more inclined to stress what it sees as Western community values in its center perspective and to a large extent *in contrast with* non-center-Western actors or areas. Thus, non-responsiveness towards developing countries and a certain amount of 'anti-Communism' are believed to increase from Left to Right. Also, developing countries responsiveness and 'anti-Americanism' should be highest among the Left.

E. *Establishment-outsider*. Operationalization of the definition has already been indicated. The four indicators, chosen by the respondents themselves, are NATO membership, EEC membership, increase in Norwegian aid to developing countries, and national military units at UN disposal for peace-keeping operations.

The Establishment (E) is made up of positive attitudes on all four indicators; Right outsiders (RO) are negative to increase in aid and UN force (for exact wording, see Appendix F) and positive to NATO and EEC; Left outsiders (LO) take the opposite position. Then the distribution of responses establishes a fourth category – a moderately leftist outsider category positive to aid and UN, but more or less ambivalent on the question of Western cooperation. Once more the problem of the low m arises and we shall have to collapse this fourth category, which may be called the Doubters (D), with Left outsiders where convenient.

The Establishment-outsider dimension gives us a basis for a number of hypotheses. We shall concentrate on three specific ones, one of which will also be tested on several other dimensions.

The first hypothesis concerns *curve shape analysis*. On the public opinion/opinion-makers/elite dimension, and the periphery to center dimension, we had hypothesized that differences between the groups in terms of attitudinal position on dimensions or issues involving affect could be plotted on a linear curve or possibly a flat j-curve (when the parameter is e.g. positive attitude towards some issue). On the Establishment-outsider dimension, our hypothesis is that the curve for the same type of issues will generally approach the steep j-curve with a 'real hook' on the j. This *hook curve* hypothesis is based on the Establishment/Right outsider/Doubters/Left outsider continuum, where the categories are listed in the order mentioned (cf. Fig. 2). The rationale for exactly this ordering of the categories must be given later on (cf. 6.7).

Fig. 2. *The 'hook curve' hypothesis*

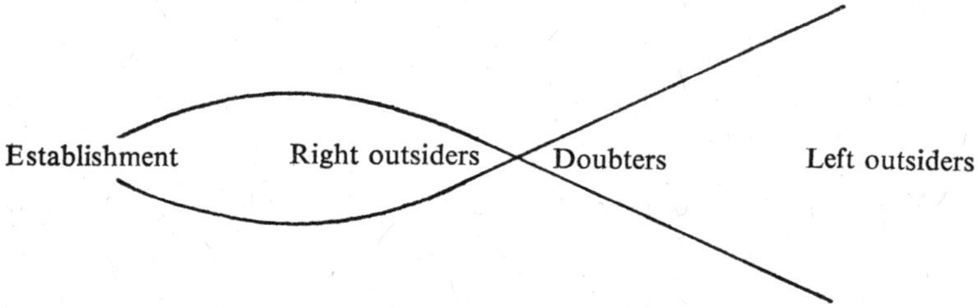

Establishment   Right outsiders   Doubters   Left outsiders

The idea is that the curves represent the position of the four categories as given by percentages (or ratios) where a given value (e.g. positive attitude) on a variable or an index of variables is the parameter i.e. represents the vertical axis. The upper curve would be the case where the RO has the most positive attitude (as towards cooperation with the West), while the lower curve is the case where RO is the most negative (with LO being most negative and most positive, respectively, because according to distances of opinion, these two groups generally represent the end points between which polarization is greatest).

Our second hypothesis is that dissensus between the categories (and consequently polarization between RO and LO) decreases with decreasing Establishment-relatedness of the issues. An issue is related to the Establishment to the extent that it is perceived as such by the milieu, is debated and has been so for some time within the milieu or the whole polity. This convergence of attitudes or steady building-up of consensus as a result of decreasing saliency or 'hotness' of issues is not confined to this dimension only, but it is probably particularly felt here.

The third hypothesis is in fact a mere replication of the hypothesis of the cognitive convergence of affectively diverging units presented above. We mention this general hypothesis in connection with the Establishment-outsider dimension because we suppose it is particularly well confirmed on this dimension.

F. *The influentials or the central policy-makers.* Within the elite there is a nucleus of really influential policy-makers. These are the central communicators: they carry particular prestige or status among the elite members or within the milieu, and they control much of the information the polity is offered and the policy-making process is using.

This nucleus is more structured than the rest of the elite: it communicates more intensely within, is more homogeneous, and recruitment to it is more controlled. Nuclear policy-makers may come into this 'group of eminences' through the different recruitment and socialization channels which exist within the milieu and the elite, and they may to a certain extent represent the pluralism created by this multiple channels structure. But generally they will tend toward more consensus within than the non-influentials.

This tendency will be particularly felt on Establishment and establishment-related items. The hypothesis we are going to test on this variable then is that the policy-making nucleus on Establishment and establishment-related items constitutes an *ultra-elite* (or, with the center-periphery dimension, an ultra-ultra-center) – 'on top of' the consensus pyramidal structure of the polity. This group is extreme in its consensus over those questions and norms on the basis of which they make Norwegian foreign policy.

Who are then these influentials? We chose to decide that by the subjective method: the respondents were asked to state if they considered themselves as personally influential on the Norwegian foreign policy making process. These responses of course will have to be validated with the use of objective data.

PART II

Data

Possibilities and Problems of Comparative Research

As the lack of comparable data makes a cross-national study rather problematic, the real test of our theory of the world perspective as a function of international position will have to wait for another, more comprehensive cross-national study. Also, the possibilities of cross-national comparisons on the other issue-areas and dimensions included in this study are limited. There are, however, *some* possibilities for such comparisons.

One of the first elite studies to focus on foreign policy issues was the study on West German elites carried out by Deutsch and Edinger in the mid-1950s.[1] A more up-to-date and even more comprehensive study of West German and French foreign policy elites was carried out in 1964 by Deutsch, Edinger, Macridis, and Merritt. It dealt mainly with problems of European security and arms control, the Atlantic alliance, and with Western European integration.[2]

Perhaps the most comprehensive, and to us the most interesting study so far is the 1954-1965 series of interviews of British, French, and West German foreign policy elites by Gorden and Lerner. Apart from the great value derived from its being a diachronic and even to a large extent a panel study, it includes several of the issues we have focused on ourselves.[3]

We should also mention some studies of a quantitative approach on American and Canadian elite and opinion-maker samples carried out by Nasatir and Rosenau, and Laulicht et al., respectively.[4] The first two mentioned are based on mailed questionnaires, the latter on an interview survey. In addition, there are several content analysis studies of elites and foreign policy, e.g. one by Singer on American and Russian 'elite papers' which includes some of the items used in our study.[5] In the case of content analysis studies, however, comparisons with data obtained from interview or questionnaire studies clearly pose major methodological problems.

Comparing survey samples cross-nationally, as will be attempted in this report, is by no means unproblematic.[6] Even intra-national comparisons in the case of Norway are problematic since we lack extensive, synchronized multi-item surveys about foreign policy matters on the public opinion level.[7] Moreover, some of the items used are not reliably comparable, even if relatively synchronized with our study, as they differ from ours by content and intention.

In both respects we have the evident problem of synchronization of responses. Even if we allow for some years discrepancy in either direction as compared to the time of our data collection, this does not improve significantly our possibilities of including more comparable data. On the other hand, as shown above, the perspective of elites is fundamentally stable at least within the last ten years.

Perhaps the greatest shortcoming of our reports and data, is that all are from the center class of nations.[8] All these problems and shortcomings taken together the comparative analyses made in this part of our study clearly do not invite rigid conclusions and far-reaching generalizations where the reliability and validity of comparing certain responses is up to question.

Ideally, we should have been able to do comparative research in three directions: between the Norwegian elite and a number of foreign elites, between the Norwegian elite and other strata of the Norwegian public, and between the present and e. g. the pre-war or 1950 Norwegian elite. The ideal design, which would meet demands for cross-national, intra-national, and diachronic research, is shown in Fig. 3. This 'cube' indicates the possibilities for both intra- and international comparisons, taking time (t) and social structure into account.

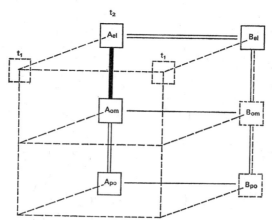

Fig. 3. *The 'ideal design' for cross-national, intra-national, and diachronic comparative research*

Not all relationships between units (A and B represent two different national actors) or levels are equally interesting. Our main interest in this context would be in focussing on the Norwegian elite (A_{el}), relating other units to this one. But in comparing this unit with Norwegian opinion-makers and public opinion, we would like to do the same at the same points of time with respect to the other nations' social structure: this would be the case when we study consensus and agreement in their various aspects. And analyzing the development of e.g. national consensus over time, we would have to focus on all three levels in both units at both time-points i.e. make use of the whole 'cube'.

In the Figure, we have drawn lines to show which relationships we are able to study here. The thick line, between A_{el} and A_{om}, indicates that this relationship may be studied by the use of quite extensive data. We shall further be able to say *something* about the A_{el}–A_{om}–A_{po} and the A_{el}–B_{om} relationships (the two parallel lines). We shall even be saying a few words, and presenting a few data, on the B_{el}–B_{po} relationship as compared with the corresponding one in actor A (broken and the unbroken lines together). Since this is an elite-oriented study, we shall not be interested in A_{om}–B_{om} and the A_{po}–B_{po} relations.

This chapter, as well as chapters 5 and 6, will report on these comparisons, and at the same time testing our hypotheses, to some extent – merely describing our units. In chapter 6 we shall occupy ourselves with intra-elite, to some extent even intra-opinion-maker comparisons.

4. The National Profile: A Center Perspective

4.1. The hypotheses

The hypotheses to be tested and explored in this chapter, were explained and developed in Chapter 2. They are the following:

H 1: *Norway is high on participation in the international system.*
H 2: *Norway is high on opinion-holding concerning international issues.*
H 3: *Norway is relatively low on initiating actions on the international scene, or on initiating interactions with other actors.*
H 4: *Norway has a relatively high acceptance of the existing world order.*
H 5: *Norway in its world image is gradualistic.*
H 6: *Norway is relatively strongly authoritarian with respect to the present international structure and decision-making.*
H 7: *Norway being an 'over-achiever' has moderate mobility aspirations.*
H 8: *Norway has a relatively strong feeling of 'we-ness', i.e. center solidarity.*
H 9: *Norway in its foreign policy thinking is East-West oriented.*
H10: *Norway puts particularly great value in international cooperation as a means to achieve various ends, and as an end in itself.*
H11: *Norway puts its main emphasis in international cooperation on regional policies.*
H12: *Norway's policies and international orientation in particular are directed toward the Euroamerican or Atlantic part of the world.*
H13: *Norway is relatively optimistic concerning the future world.*

Some of these hypotheses, e.g. H1 to H3, will not be subject to much analysis in this context since they are primarily of a behavioral type. As hypotheses are not necessarily taken up in the order they appear above, these hypotheses will be subject to treatment in section 4.7. H13 will be dealt with in 8.1.

4.2. The perspective: frame of reference

When we think of the frame of reference of the Norwegian elite, we are thinking of its *basic* orientations toward the world. More specifically: What

84

are the dimensions, issues, or relationships people structure their world image around? Which cognitive clusters are most present or preeminent when they orient themselves toward the environing world? *Which* and *how many* issue-areas (scope) does the elite perceive as predominant, and in what areas (domain) are they perceived as most important? And: which domain is perceived as the most important?

Boulding points to three major relationships between persons or groups which organize the dynamic processes, the trends of social systems in general: the threat relation, the exchange relation, and the integrative relation. This scheme is not, however, exhaustive; further, it appears to mix two different levels which ought to be kept separate.[1] Galtung and Ruge distinguish between the power relation and the exchange relation, which seems equally unexhaustive.[2]

There is no need here, however, of discussing possible shortcomings in such schemes. It seems that Boulding's threat and exchange relations corresponds to the power and exchange relations, respectively, of Galtung and Ruge. After this we choose to distinguish between the following four types of relationships or issue-areas: (1) the *threat* or power relation – problems of war and peace, etc. (2) the *exchange* relation, which will consist of bargaining, detente, and peaceful competition and thus contain threat reduction and violence modification behavior; (3) the *integrative* relation, which implies questions of peaceful structural change, organized cooperation, etc.; finally, an additional category (4) the status allocation or *socio-economic development* relation, which implies the problems of poverty, under-development, etc.[3]

Various questions about perceptions of threats and trends in the system were used to establish the frame of reference. Some were asked in the beginning of the interview, which should further stress their relevance to the frame of reference problem. The very first question asked for an evaluation of what was the most important problem of today's world, while the second asked what was considered the greatest threat to mankind. In two more questions put later on, respondents were asked to state what trend or trait they found particularly dominant or typical in the present world, and what they hoped that the world in the year 2000 would look like.

The last item will be treated in more detail later on. The other three constitute a continuum, ranging from threat perception as the most to trend perception as the least 'dramatic' cognition of the world. We shall give the detailed distribution of responses on these items in Chapter 5; suffice it here to mention some of the major findings.

Our first observation is that the elite has no clearcut cognition of the trends and problems of the present world; in fact, its image of the world, or its frame of reference, is rather varied. This is particularly true with trend or trait perceptions; and evidentally, our findings here are real and not due to our coding or collapsing of categories. As to problem perception, we may say that war-and-peace problems in general, plus the problems of controlling peace (or war) are seen as most prominent by a majority, but responses here vary from 'The war in Vietnam' to 'Non-proliferation', so this category is rather diffuse.

Following the typology of relationships developed above, we may give the responses of the elite on these two items as shown in Table 4.2.1.

Table 4.2.1. *Present world images of the elite and their distribution on systemic relationships. In percentages.*

	Most prominent trend or trait today	Greatest problem today
Power relationship: war/armaments race/threats to peace	22	39
Exchange relationship: *détente*/disarmament and nonproliferation negotiations	21	34
Integrative relationship: integration or dis-integration/cooperation/UN	38	7
Development relationship: problems of developing countries/hunger/poverty	11	9
Other/DK/NA	8	11
	100	100
	(88)	(88)

When responses are broken down, several interesting observations may be made. Between the two items, there is a radical change of focus from the integrative relation, which captures more attention in the trend perception item, to the power relation. Looking more closely into the responses on the integrative relation, we find that 22% (more than the half of the 38%) in fact have no clear image of world trends: they find the present situation rather confusing, with trends working in different directions, with a marked breaking-up of former trends and traits. On the other hand, this trend or lack of trends is not felt as problematic.

The development relation is not seen as particularly relevant: only about 10% of the elite focus on it on each one of the items. The power relation, which scores on top on the problem item, is divided between one group which sees the Vietnam war as the greatest present problem (20% of the total elite) and another group which thinks in terms of war-and-peace problems in general.

The exchange relation means first of all East-West detente to the respondents: this response accounts for all 21% on the trend or trait item, and for 16% on the problem item, making this response the second overall most cited one.

Presenting these two dimensions together raises the question of the consistency in the elite's perceptions. Now, we should not a priori expect a high degree of consistency in this case: the perceived most important problems of course may be less prominent trends. In fact, this is what the elite seems to think: correlating the two items, we get a Pearsons correlation coefficient of .12, which is rather low. (The corresponding correlation for the opinion-maker sample is .33.)

In its evaluation of the present trends or traits, the elite seems divided in the degree to which it finds them positive or negative. The general tendency seems to be toward a certain ambivalence.

When it comes to domain, it seems that the Norwegian elite goes 'farther out' in the system, i.e. perceives trends and problems from a wider domain, than do elites of the three Western European regional great powers – the French, the British, and the West German. While only 4% of the Norwegian foreign policy elite consider Western intra-regional or intra-bloc problems as the most important today, on the average about 23% of the three above mentioned national elites do the same. On the other hand, China is perceived as far more problematic by the latter than by the Norwegian elite.

This difference in intra-bloc orientation, which seems to make Norway more extrovert than some of its greater alliance partners, may be explained. In the first place, if the Norwegian elite is not very much concerned with intra-bloc matters, it *is* concerned with *inter*-bloc ones: witness its concern about detente. Secondly, intra-bloc affairs are largely connected with decision-making problems or problems of influence which logically interest actors with *some* power, like the three mentioned, but which is of less interest to an actor which has and can have very little influence.

The third item, treated as one of the frame of reference items, is an evaluation of the *threat* or power relationship. Here one may distinguish between value-, actor-, and structure-oriented perceptions; responses typical of these perceptions would be 'Communism', 'China', and 'The East-West power struggle', respectively. Another distinction would be between short- and long-range threats; a third one, between macro- and micro-level threat theories. The three examples mentioned above would represent macro-theories, while 'Man's aggressive nature' or 'Man's lust for power' would indicate micro-theories.

The question we made in our study was rather abstract or general, while a similar one asked by Gorden and Lerner was more concrete and specific, singling out only actor-oriented perceptions for their respondents. Responses in the two studies, then, are not readily comparable.[4]

Our data indicate that the Norwegian elite is relatively structure-oriented in its threat perception, and that it puts main emphasis on macro-level threats. A large part of the elite, however, is rather diffuse on this question: e.g. 28% see war or the danger of war in general as the greatest threat, while 23% more specifically think of nuclear war, the danger of nuclear proliferation, etc., as the greatest threat.

In comparison, the three great powers seem more actor-oriented, and somewhat more short-range oriented.[5] This may perhaps be because the three regional great power elites see themselves as in a position where they (i.e. their countries) may manipulate the international system and as great powers 'hold their umbrella over' mankind. Or, such a position is held by great power elites by the very fact that they *are* great power elites: the idea of the great powers having it in their hands to decide over the life or death of the system has to be held particularly by people who want to see themselves as world leaders, but who perhaps feel that their power is declining.

The distinction between short- and long-range threats is present in the minds of several of our respondents. Some of them state explicitly that to get a non-proliferation treaty, or to achieve real Soviet-US detente are more pressing tasks which may counter the more imminent threat, while e.g. developing the underdeveloped countries and thus countering the threat of hunger, overpopulation, and the 'revolution of rising expectations' are more long-range tasks. Only 18% see this problem as the most threatening aspect of today's world. Another indication that this is a long-range, second priority threat is found when double response is considered: 45% of all double responses on the threat item fall into this response category.

Is the world threatened: perceptions of threat imminence. It has been shown that a nuclear war or a major war in general is perceived as the most threatening prospect of today's world. But *how likely* is such a war, what is the probability attached to it?

It is clearly *not* great: only 3% of the elite expect a World War III before year 2000, and 15% indicated a 50–50 chance. The 3% corresponds very well with expectations of the British, French, and West German elites in 1965: less than 5% in all three found a WWIII rather probable.[6]

The real *concern* with the prospect of a new world war is of course much greater than these figures tell us. But man, and especially elite man, must behave and think rationally, and rational thinking refuses to acknowledge the irrationality of a WWIII. On the other hand, fears of such a war were much more explicitly felt only a decade ago, as the Gorden–Lerner study shows.[7] Their data would probably be valid even in the case of Norway, as public opinion expectations of a WWIII from 1948 seem to indicate.[8]

In accordance with these findings, the danger of a major war emanating from conflicts along the North-South dimension is not perceived as very great by the Norwegian elite. Most elite persons would probably know – although this was not probed – that the present differences in socio-economic development between most rich and most poor countries is very great, both in absolute and in relative terms. How do they perceive these differences as developing? And what consequences do they see from it?

The elite is divided in its predictions of the development of the rich-poor 'gap': 47% believe that it will diminish, 43% that it will increase. A similar division or lack of consensus is found in the evaluation of the probable consequences of a widening of the gap: only about 10% explicitly thought in terms of 'catastrophe', while a much greater percentage, probably about one third of the elite, at the other end did not believe in any serious consequences.

The overall tendency then is to expect a continued gap at the present level, but with not so serious consequences even if it should increase. One reason for this optimism is that the elite expects *both* poor and rich to improve their position in the future, relative to what it is now. The argument of 'relative deprivation', i.e. that the poor countries even if they improve their position over time, will feel increasingly underdeveloped and bad off relative to the rich countries, gets no support among respondents.

The belief that a WWIII may be caused by the poor or rather periphery countries revolting against the center, is held by very few. But *indirectly*, these countries may be the cause of such a war. Escalation, in the sense of involving great powers in a small power conflict, is seen by the elite as the most probable cause of a WWIII: 49% of the elite are of that opinion. 22% believe that the most probable cause will be a great power attack on another great power (and half of these explicitly think of China), while 15% believe primarily in the 'war-by-an-accident' theory. These figures again underline the structure-orientation of the Norwegian elite.

In comparison, super-power elite expectations are far more geared toward *actors* as causing the WWIII, as witnessed by the Singer data. Although this comparison must be made with great caution, and although the variables used were differing in scope, differences are so considerable that we are justified in accepting them.[9]

4.3. *Perceptions of the international system: the structure*

Two of the hypotheses we have put forth on the world perspective of the elite pertain to 'world order' or the international structure, which will here be treated as synonymous concepts. Before we go on to test these hypotheses, we should know *how* the elite perceives the system.

The structure of the international system has both *vertical* and *horizontal* aspects, the vertical having primarily to do with power relations or the stratification of the system; the horizontal aspects implying e. g. the 'breadth' of the stratification pyramid. But horizontal structure also has to do with domain, or more relevant to us: with the relations between the center and the periphery – the 'axes' of the system along the East-West or North-South dimension. On the other hand, this distinction between vertical and horizontal should not be made too strict, as the two would go very much over in each other in the case of e.g. the bipolarity vs. multipolarity dichotomy.

a. *Vertical structure: the stratification of the system.* Only one of the respondents objected to the idea of a stratified international system, while a few did not have any opinion on it. The central tendency (median) was in the direction of four rank categories, which would be referred to as:

> Super-powers, or trans-regional powers.
> Regional great powers, or potential trans-regional powers.
> Middle range powers, or minor states.
> Small states, and 'mini-states'.

This hierarchy of national actors is not perceived as very rigid. As would be expected, ranking is most refined at the top, with a tendency to differentiate more. We have not got responses which may indicate the perceived distance between the rank categories, but we asked respondents to state whether they believed that distance between the top-dogs (the two upper), and the under-dogs (the two lower ranks) is presently increasing or decreasing: whether the system is perceived as developing into a more or a less rigid hierarchical structure.

A majority clearly believes the former: 43 % of the elite believe that the great powers are increasing their power and influence, while 31 % believe that the trend presently is toward more influence for the smaller states. In

90

putting the problem in this way, we have assumed that power in the system is a *zero-sum problem*.[10]

This perceived increasingly rigid hierarchy of power is even more obvious when we add that another 6% of the elite thought that the influence of one particular great or super power, i.e. the United States, was strongly increasing, relative to all other actors. Let us now look at the elite's ranking of the top-dogs.

Practically all of our respondents ranked the United States and the Soviet Union on the same level. Gorden and Lerner in their study asked respondents to rank these two actors relative to each other and got the United States on the very top of the structure. Had we probed specifically into this question, we would most certainly have had similar responses but with the Norwegian elite more inclined to rank them together, i.e. it sees first of all the *dual hegemony*. This will be supported more thoroughly in the following.

The last ranking in the Gorden–Lerner study is from 1965. They asked respondents to rank the top five national actors relative to each other, while we had a more indirect ranking by asking our respondents to give examples of nations falling into the rank categories each respondent individually made up for himself. Their ranking ranged from three to seven ranks, in a few cases even more.

Evidently, these two methods are rather different. To compare the rankings, we made the rankings of all the four national samples into absolute ranks of the given actors.[11] There were no difficulties in obtaining a satisfactory assessment of the ranks of the top-dogs, since they most readily were chosen as examples by our respondents.

Table 4.3.1. *Ranking of the top-dog national actors in Great Britain, France, West Germany, and Norway*

	Britain (1965)	France (1965)	W. Germany (1965)	Norway (1967)
United States	1	1	1	1.5
Soviet Union	2	2	2	1.5
China	4	3	4	3
Great Britain	3	4	3	4.5
France	5	5	5	4.5
West Germany	6	6	6	6
(Japan)	–	–	–	7
(India)	–	–	–	8

The results of these procedures are shown in Table 4.3.1. Overall agreement between the four samples is quite convincing. Apart from the dual hegemony outlook of the Norwegian elite, which gives the two top ranking actors practically the same rank, the interesting thing is the ranking of China. It competes with Great Britain for the status of 'number one pretender'; that is when all four samples are taken into account. Norway sides with France in giving the pretender status to China, an 'alliance' probably based on somewhat different platforms.

Assuming, as many do, that cognitions follow affect, one would have expected that the Norwegian elite because of its 'special relationship' with Britain would have placed her more favorably in comparison with China, whom it largely fears, and with France, to whom it does not look with particularly great affect. As this is not the case, the reason must be found in a rather drastic drop in Britain's prestige during the last few years. There is a time span of nearly two years between the collection of responses in the two studies, and in exactly this period Britain went through some of its most serious troubles in modern times. These must have had some impact on the image of the Norwegian elite.

b. *Bipolarity and the 'dual hegemony'.* Closely connected with the question of how the structure is perceived is the question of what distance is perceived between the top two powers and the rest of the top-dog family. The answer to this question will let us know whether the present international (global) system is perceived as developing into a multipolar structure, i.e. a structure where more than two actors or 'poles' have decisive influence over political relations within it, or is still perceived as basically bipolar.

In the study made by Deutsch et al. in 1964, about $\frac{2}{3}$ of the West German elite believed that the world would remain bipolar. This score parallels extremely well that of our own sample: a little more than $\frac{1}{3}$ (39%) refer China to the category of super-power or trans-regional great power, and although some respondents among the remaining $\frac{2}{3}$ believe that China will reach the top level in the years to come, a majority believes that bipolarity will prevail.

And the minority of multipolarists is only thinking in terms of *tri*polarity: only 6% of the elite think of Britain and France as trans-regional great powers, and practically nobody believes that these two former world powers in the future will rise to their former status again.

In contrast with the West German – Norwegian bipolarity perception, the French elite is – by a strong $\frac{3}{4}$ – convinced that the world will become more and more multipolar, thus creating a rather strong discrepancy between the predictions of three elite groups which one would think were relatively well agreed. The reason for this difference no doubt must be sought in what they *prefer* will happen: the French hope for multipolarity i.e. a higher status, more *gloire*, for themselves, thus probably thinking in terms of a *more* than tripolar world; the two other elites, having no aspirations of the kind, prefer bipolarity. Another reason may be that the French elite perceives multipolarity differently from the two other samples, perceiving the present distance between the upper two and the rest of the top-dogs as smaller than e.g. the Norwegian elite does.

The Norwegian elite then is thinking in terms of bipolarity and 'dual hegemony'. But *what kind of* dual hegemony? Or more accurately: how and how different are the two poles perceived? From the period of alliance formations on, the Soviet Union has been Norway's 'number one enemy'. Its power and its foreign policy have been, at least officially, perceived as a threat, real or potential, to Norway and the West. To what extent are such views held today? Conversely, the United States and her policies have been perceived as positive and friendly. Very recently then, the policies of the two have been perceived more by what distinguishes them than from what they might have in common. In other words: is there one negative and one positive pole in the bipolar structure governing the system?

We believe that this is not so: images have changed. *How* much so is difficult to say. One may conceive of two possible developments in this respect: the respondents *either* maintain their positive evaluation of the United States and gradually come to perceive the other super power more positively under the impression of a certain detente, peaceful coexistence doctrines, and practices of Tashkent diplomacy, etc.; *or*, they converge in their orientations toward modifying their previous positive evaluations of the United States, at the same time modifying their previous negative evaluation of the Soviet Union.

The hypothesized strongly Western-oriented centrism of the Norwegian elite should indicate that the first-mentioned trend is the one to expect. But the Soviet Union is also seen as belonging to the center, and a very strong focus on and interest in the 'dual hegemony' could provide the last-mentioned trend. Still we are inclined to expect the effect of Western-type centrism as stronger, hence our hypothesis would be the first trend. We asked respondents how they perceived the foreign policy of the two super-powers, i.e. their policy *motivations* and policy *aims*. Responses may be compared with similar data from the Singer study of US and Soviet elite papers' perceptions, although as has been mentioned before, methods are different and data are rather non-synchronic. This comparison is shown in Table 4.3.2.

Table 4.3.2. *Perceptions of super power foreign policies*

1. Policy *motivation* is primarily:†	American elite's* perception of Soviet policy (1957–60)	Soviet elite's* perception United States' policy (1957–60)	Norwegian elite's perception of:	
			Soviet policy (1967)	United States' (1967)
'Ideological' or idealistic	69	65	11	30
'Realistic' or power-oriented	31	35	75	53
Other/NA/DK	–	–	14	17
	100	100	100	100
	(347)	(93)	(88)	(88)

2. Policy *aim* is primarily:				
Expansion, world domination	31	24	10	5
Defend own interests and position	69‡	76	32	26
Defend status quo	–	–	25	11
Promote peace and cooperation	–	–	29	23
Help, keep obligations	–	–	0	9
Other/NA/DK	–	–	11	18
	100	100	100	100
	(297)	(59)	(88)	(88)

*) 'Elite' = three leading papers and periodicals in each of the countries.

†) The question in the Singer study was whether the present international strugle was a struggle between two belief systems, two social systems (these two categories were in this context defined as 'ideological'), or between two centers of power ('realistic' or 'power-oriented').

‡) Response categories here were 'Retain and expand own sphere of influence' and 'Self-preservation' (the score on the latter was almost nil in both cases). Thus, this category in the way we use it to some extent is overlapping the first one, which in the Singer study was only 'World domination'.

Looking at the responses of the Norwegian elite separately, we note that US foreign policy is perceived as more dynamic and especially ideologically motivated, while the Soviet Union is seen as more status quo oriented and at least *as* 'peace-loving' as the big Western ally.

Drawing in the time dimension, it is very probable that the mutual perceptions of the two super powers as a result of the détente in the 60s have moved closer to that of the Norwegian elite, i.e. toward stressing 'realism' and status quo orientation (cf. the Nixon administration's stressing of these traits). On the other hand, as has been indicated already, the favorable perception of the Soviet Union in the Norwegian elite has probably dropped somewhat and that of the United States increased due to their respective 1968 performances – the Soviet-led invasion of Czechoslovakia, and the US consent to reduction of hostilities and initiation of peace talks on Vietnam. Despite such possibilities, however, we find our data very convincing in the trend they show, and in fact rather surprising also: our hypothesis cannot be claimed as confirmed; the data rather seem to support the counter-hypothesis, i.e. proposed impact of the dual hegemony image.

At this question, we may have a closer look. We put this item to our respondents in the form of an open-ended question. Thus, we got an evaluation from almost all of them on the super power policies, i.e. their opinions on whether these policies would be evaluated as primarily positive or negative.

Results are shown in Table 4.3.3. The evaluations of the two are strikingly similar, so much so that one may conclude that the hypothesis of the impact of the dual hegemony image or preference is confirmed.

Table 4.3.3. *Norwegian elite evaluations of the foreign policy of the two super powers: positive vs. negative*

	US	Soviet Union
Positive	31	31
Both positive and negative	20	18
Negative	8	6
Neutral: no evaluation in either direction	36	42
DK/NA	5	4
	100	100
	(88)	(88)

Responses on another, separate question show that differences between the two are seen as more prominent than similarities: 51 % see differences as more prominent, while 38 % take the opposite view. This would seem rather contrary to the conclusion just drawn on the basis of the responses presented in Table 4.3.3. However, these percentages refer first of all to *perceptions,* i.e. data given in Table 4.3.2. Moreover, we must distinguish between the image of each respondent individually, and that of the elite as a whole – the latter being in fact what is shown in Table 4.3.2.

But even when we focus on the individual level, as we may do by running evaluations of the two actors against each other, the 'dual hegemony hypothesis' is confirmed, although not so clearly as when the elite level only is considered. This is shown in Table 4.3.4., which is probably *too* much broken down.

Table 4.3.4. *Evaluations of the super powers and the dual hegemony hypothesis*

| | | US | | |
		Positive	Neutral or both/and	Negative
	Positive	22	7	4
Soviet Union	Neutral	8	50	5
	Negative	2	2	0 (n = 84)

A nine-fold table is certainly above the limit we set for our data procession (cf. Chapt. 1). A modifying factor in this respect is probably the unusually high positive correlation we find between the evaluations of the two: it is .89 (Pearsons), which again points to an impressive similarity in evaluations.

The mere 22% clear-cut 'Hegemonists', i.e. those who evaluate both actors positively, is certainly no impressive support for the hegemony hypothesis. On the other hand, there is no doubt a strong tendency toward 'Hegemonism' in the 'Both, and' and 'Neutral' categories. And if these response categories are interpreted as expressing opinions of hegemony *acceptance* if not outright 'love', and thus collapsed with the positive-positive category, making 'Hegemonists' a rather broad category of people who both love and tolerate the dual hegemony, we can present our data in a reduced four-fold table, as in Table 4.3.5.

Table 4.3.5. *Evaluations of the super powers and the dual hegemony hypothesis: the four types of orientation*

| | | US Policy: | |
		Positive or acceptable	Negative
Soviet Union's policy:	Positive or acceptable	'Hegemonists': 87	'Anti-Americans': 9
	Negative	'Anti-Communists': 4	'Anti-Hegemonists': 0

There are only small minorities of 'Anti-Americans' and 'Anti-Communists' in our elite sample. These figures may vary with variations in the international climate, as has already been indicated, although such variations should be less felt or at least less enduring, the higher the structural positions of the persons in question.[12]

As we see, there are no clearcut 'Anti-Hegemonists' in the elite, which further supports the hypothesis of dual hegemony preference; a few respondents, however, seem to lean in that direction. On the other hand, according to our revised definition of the term, a majority of 87% is 'Hegemonists', which is probably a too high figure, compared with 'reality'. The 'Hegemonists' have come to see the structure which has developed out of the post WWII period not only as part of the status quo or the world order, but as a *guarantee* of this order. There is probably a *double* guarantee: on the one hand that given by the NATO pact membership and the alliance with the USA; on the other hand the guarantee derived from the dual hegemony. This may seem contradictory. The rationale behind this inclusion of the 'enemy' as a guarantist is, however complicated, rather easily found in the reasoning of the elite members: the Soviet Union is the 'natural opposite number' of one's own big friend, its policy is now believed to be highly predictable. Moreover, the high value placed in a stable *balance of power* system between East and West makes it necessary that the Soviet Union carry respect and be recognized as one of the two pillars in that balance.

The degree to which this bipolarity positivism is built into the images and attitudes of the elite is further evidenced by its evaluation of the role of alliances or military blocs in the present international system. The respondents were asked to state their appreciation of the alliance system as such, i. e. even including the Warszaw Pact. Only a few of them refused to consider both blocs at the same level: they maintained that one had to distinguish between the two since the Warszaw Pact was something quite different from NATO. 70% of the elite, however, were clearly positive in their evaluation of both blocs, i. e. the bloc system as such, only 6% were negative, while 5% refused to include the Warszaw Pact in their positive evaluation.

The reason for this 'generalized alliance positivism' may of course be found partly in the fact that a positive attitude toward NATO has been extended to include alliances *as such*. But the main reason no doubt is found in the perceived role of the alliances (cf. Table 4.3.6.).

Table 4.3.6. *Alliance 'positivists' perception of the role of alliances in present world. Percent*

Give stability, predictability, security	62	⎫ 76
balance, equal power	14	⎭
Deter the counter-part		15
Promote peace and détente		9
		100
	N = (61)	

Singer is of the opinion that this 'Hegemonism' preference or rather the 'generalized alliance positivism', which exists along with strong affiliations to the Western world, is evidence of a highly 'sophisticated' orientation on the part of the Norwegian elite.[13]

c. *Polycentrism?* Sufficient evidence has now been given of the bipolar image of the Norwegian elite. Still we are left with the question: despite, or rather *under* this perceived continuing bipolarity, are there in the image of the elite trends which point toward more than marginal changes in the structure? Is the trend toward a loosening of the structure – in East and in West, i.e. within the two pillars of bipolarity, or toward its strengthening? This is the question of sub-system integration or disintegration. And it is a question of *symmetry or asymmetry* in the images of the elite: to the extent that the trends within each of the sub-systems are perceived as similar, there is symmetry in its perceptions.

Respondents were asked to state their predictions of future developments within the two blocs or sub-systems. Responses are given in Table 4.3.7. Here responses have also been elicited on three specific relationships: the West vs. China, Soviet vs. China, and Western Europe vs. USA relationships. Developments along these dimensions were not specifically asked for; responses on them therefore are only of the 'spontaneous' type.

Table 4.3.7. *Integration and disintegration in East and West: the question of polycentrism.* (n = 88)

	Intra West	Intra East	West vs. China	Soviet vs. China	Western Europe vs. USA
Disintegration:					
more dissensus, more national independence	22	74	23	18	22*
Status quo: no changes, about as now	8	3	0	2	0
Integration:					
more consensus, less conflict or 'nationalism'	63	21	7	8	0
DK/NA/Other	7	2	70	72	78
	100	100	100	100	100

*) Response categories were: 'More Western European independence of USA' and 'Stronger Western Europe; more WE influence within the Atlantic community'.

We see a significant asymmetry in the predictions of sub-system developments: while the West is seen as becoming more integrated in the years to come, the East is to disintegrate. This Eastern polycentrism is first of all due to predictions of increasing Eastern European independence of the Soviet Union. The number of respondents who believe in a continued and extended split between Soviet and China is greater than the percentage who explicitly state such a belief, but they do not account for much more of the 74% who believe in Eastern disintegration; the Soviet–Chinese split is perceived as fundamental enough already.[14]

In West, 'gaullistic' prescriptions of changed relations across the Atlantic are not given very much credit nor chance. Only a very small minority of the Norwegian elite would support 'Gaullism' – about 6–8% – while a few more would be merely tolerant towards it; the great majority clearly rejects it. Thus one inevitably is confronted with the question: are the predictions of sub-system developments merely a function of hopes?

This is generally not the case, although it may be true with some of the respondents. A majority of the elite perceives the *present* structure as asymmetric or incongruent: the East has been integrated by force into a rigid structure; the West has been integrated by consent, voluntarily and into a looser structure. The development they perceive or predict then is necessary *in order to* create symmetry or congruence between the two sub-systems. As one of the respondents put it: 'The East will have to disintegrate before they once more may join!'

Very few relate the within-bloc development to that which is predicted between the blocs: detente. Thus there seems to be no support for the proposition made by Deutsch et al. that an alliance, set up to counter or deter a threat from outside, will tend to disintegrate as the threat diminishes.[15] If at all, it is only seen as relevant to the East; hence, the idea held by many respondents, that 'liberalization' in the East is a result of increased Western contact with the East (i.e. a one-way relationship).

d. *East-West vs. North-South.* Yet another dimension interests us in this connection – East-West vs. North-South. This dimension – in fact composed of two dimensions of specific importance per se – has been subject to several studies through analysis of the United Nations system. It has been shown that the East-West dimension more or less constantly during the last two decades has accounted for more than half of all the issues taken up in the UN.[16] Does it play an equally important role in structuring the minds and orientations of the Norwegian elite?

From what has been said on 'we-ness' and related aspects of a center perspective, our hypothesis H9 clearly will be that this is so. East-West relations, detente, etc. although they have consequences to the rest of the world, are primarily problems of the *center* world.

This hypothesis is well confirmed by our data. War-and-peace problems are first of all seen in the East-West context; this is true even with the case of the Vietnam conflict, 'located' in the Third World. Measuring rather roughly the ratio of East-West to North-South orientation in elite cognitions, we found the former almost *three times* more important than the latter.

Then the question is whether and to what extent this strong East-West predominance holds when we focus on perceptions of the future world. To this problem we shall return in more detail later on. We would expect that the predominance does *not* hold. The perception of development problems as a long-range threat indicates this. Moreover, the development problems are largely the 'postponed issue-area'. A number of respondents seem to keep a 'package' of issue-areas, i.e. a set of two or more areas which they mention as important or salient to them. The one would be 'East-West detente' or 'East-West-related peace-making'; a second, additional issue-area would be development problems (cf. double response scores, Section 4.2).

Looking at responses on two items on future perception – what they hope and what they predict the world year 2000 to be – we find our expectations confirmed. The international system, in the eyes of the elite, will be dealing more with development problems in the future, but not so much so that East-West relations will be out of the picture. On the contrary, the elite expects the world year 2000 to be occupied equally much with East-West and Norht-South problems.

This indicates both that no great changes are expected in the system, and that being a center nation strongly influences the Norwegian elite. To this aspect, our main concern here, we now turn.

4.4. *Center perspective: the elite evidence*

In Chapter 3 and in the beginning of this chapter, a number of hypotheses on Norway's perspective and its degree of centrism were elaborated and listed. This section will deal with these hypotheses H4 to H8.

H4: *Norway has a relatively high acceptance of the existing world order*

In the preceding section we presented elite cognitions of the existing world order. They constitute the background to what we shall now be focusing on – elite *attitudes* toward this order.

We found that the Norwegian elite perceived the present international structure as increasingly stratified. Does it want to *change* this trend, i.e. reverse it? According to our hypothesis, this should not be the case, and this is quite satisfactorily supported by elite responses.

Only 26% of the elite want to abolish great power veto in the United Nations' Security Council, one of the best expressions of the world hierarchy, while more than twice as many, 59%, definitely want it to stay. On another question – whether they would favor the introduction of a system of weighted voting in the United Nations, a system contrary to the interests of small states – 33% were in favor, 47% against this idea.

The net result then is a 'No change at all' attitude, although one should note that the proposal for *strengthening* the stratification of the system gets more support than the idea of weakening it. This finding is probably a good expression of the 'vested interest' – considering that Norway ranks among the smaller states, one might perhaps call it a 'self-disinterest' – Norway has in the present structure and great power rule of the world.

This is even better reflected when we compare Norwegian elite opinions on the question of abandoning great power veto, with those of a US elite sample studied by Nasatir et al. (cf. Table 4.4.1). A *great* majority of the US sample, as contrasted with the ⅔ Norwegian majority against abolishment, *accepts* this proposed change which should be contrary to the interests of the United States as a great power.

Table 4.4.1. *Comparison of US and Norwegian elite attitudes toward abolishing great power veto*

	US (1959)	Norway (1967)
Veto should be abolished	68	26
Ambivalent, it depends	–	9
Veto should be maintained	15	59
NA/DK	17	6
	100	100
	(575)	(88)

Of course, several explanations may be offered on this point: the United States may feel that they are able to maintain their power without the veto; the US sample may be somewhat (but it should not be much) unrepresentative; or, the Norwegian elite may think as much in terms of what they *believe* the great powers i.e. *also* the Soviet Union, would want, and express their opinion accordingly, not knowing that they may be mistaken.

Another explanation would be the time-lag between the two studies. In exactly this period – between 1959 and 1967 – a vast number of small states have become members of the United Nations, taking over much of the initiative and even some of the decision-making power from the great powers and from the other smaller states, elder members of the organization. Thus, the attitude of the US elite may have changed since then, *and* it is likely that the Norwegian elite has been affected by this new trend, because it has affected the position of Norway within the world organization.[17] Some of the respondents explicitly refer to this with some resentment; indeed one of them talks about the negative influx of the new 'pirate states'.

We should expect a positive correlation between opinions on the two items – veto and weighted voting – in the sense that a positive response on the one should imply a negative reply on the other. However, there is no correlation at all between them (Pearson's correlation .01) 33% of the Norwegian sample wish to maintain the veto right and at the same time wants no weighted voting: they are the *status quo people*. Only 12% are '*egalitarians*' or 'democrats': they wish to abolish the veto right and have no weighted voting. On the opposite side are the '*autocrats*': 15% of the elite want to maintain the veto right *and* at the same time introduce a system of weighted voting. Only 9% want to exchange the veto right with weighted voting.

In 4.3 we showed that the present system, according to the perceptions of the Norwegian elite, is continuously bipolar. Moreover, some indications were given that this trend was approved. This proposed correspondence between cognitive and affective aspects of the perspective is well shown by the West German and French elites; unfortunately, we have no systematic responses from the Norwegian respondents for strict comparison.

More than three out of five West German elite members find continued bipolarity positive, while only one out of ten finds it discomforting. There is a corresponding cognitive – affective relationship in the French elite.[18] This leads us logically to expect that also the Norwegian elite, so close to the West German in its cognitions, positively regard continued bipolarity as a prospect they *want* to see realized. While the French elite here clearly reflects the above-mentioned French aspirations of a higher status, the Norwegian elite has not at its disposal the means and resources for drawing any advantages from a multipolar system, which opens more possibilities for upward mobility.

We stressed in 4.3 the concern with the *stability* of the system, with the *predictability* of trends and acts, with the system changing only under *control* and within the framework of the existing order, which the Norwegian elite shows. We may give further evidence of this concern.

Nearly 100% believe that disarmament, particularly if based on the 'general and complete disarmament' receipe, should be carried out by both sides (East and West) mutually; there is practically no room for unilateralism in the elite. The main reason is surely a feeling that unilateralism may destroy what is seen as the precarious East-West balance. This moreover is well in accordance with what was found by Gorden and Lerner on similar questions.[19]

A good 80% of the elite regard the present balance of power as an important factor in maintaining peace; a similar percentage has the same view of existing alliances.

On the other hand, various proposals which would affect the structure in the direction of changing it, receive little support: only 32% think it would contribute to peace-keeping (in the long run) if there were fewer states in the world, while only 55% think that peace would be strengthened if the smaller states of the world got more influence. The last item is another indicator of an elite 'oligopolistic', great power oriented, perspective.

Stability preferences are perhaps even better reflected by the considerable number of respondents who express their concern that the Warszaw Pact, or the Eastern system, *should not* disintegrate, because this again would threaten the much-wanted stability and predictability of the system.[20] This then would be an indication that predictions and preferences do not go hand in hand; as we saw, a large majority predicted more disintegration in the East.

On the whole, there seems to be no evidence in our data that the hypothesis is disconfirmed. H4 is then seen as fully proved.

H5: *Norway in its world image is gradualistic*

We shall look at this hypothesis by presenting two sets of indicators of the gradualism vs. absolutism dichotomy – one basically cognitive, another affective. 'Cognitive absolutism' would be found when an individual expects or perceives drastic, apocalyptic changes, e.g. a World War III *or* total disarmament within a decade.

Now, we have shown above that only 3% of the Norwegian elite did expect a WWIII before the year 2000. This clear indication of very gradualistic cognitions is backed by further data.

Asked what they believed would be the situation as to armaments and armament levels in the future, only 2% expressed the belief that the world by the year 2000 would be totally and generally disarmed, while 10% expected considerably more armaments within the same period.

Similarly, asked about the most likely development of the 'gap' between the rich and the poor countries up to the year 2000, none of the respondents believed that the gap would be closed or about to be closed within that period, while only about 10% of the elite thought, as indicated above, that a future increase of the gap would result in a major war.

The gradualism hypothesis is, however, more correctly studied from the point of view of attitudes, since this is primarily a question of predispositions, or of the 'mood' of the respondents. We test it by means of three items which ask for opinions on disarmament procedures. On one of these items, we are able to draw comparisons with the three samples in the Gorden–Lerner study.

As Table 4.4.2 shows, the Norwegian elite does not seem *particularly* gradualistic as compared to the three other samples. One should note that questions put in the two studies were slightly different both in content and in form. Thus, it seems that the Gorden–Lerner item includes a larger scope and consequently may lead to comparatively more gradualistic responses: in a way, it seems to include all the three items we have adapted from another public opinion, cross-national study.[21]

Table 4.4.2. *Gradualism vs. absolutism in Norwegian and European elites: the disarmament response*

	Norway* (1967)	Britain† (1961)	France (1961)	West Germany (1961)
gradualistic	74	93	73	95
both/and	1	1	2	–
absolutistic	14	6	9	4
NA/DK/other	11	0	14	1
	100	100	100	100
	(72)	(100)	(100)	(108)

*) This question was put in the form of two response alternatives: 'Disarmament should be done (a) with some weapons to begin with and then stepwise, (b) with all or most weapons as fast as possible'.

†) The question here was: 'Which approach to arms control do you consider more likely to produce useful results – the 'Big Package' agreement such as Khrushchev's proposal for total disarmament with the United Nations, or the 'stage-by-stage' approach to negotiations?' (The first alternative is the absolutist response.)

Another and perhaps more likely explanation of the relative gradualism of the Norwegian elite may be found in the content of the Gorden–Lerner question, referring to the absolutistic alternative as being presented by the then Soviet Russian Prime Minister, Nikita Khrushchev; this may have contributed to reducing the support for this alternative, as it in fact became a matter of support for the Western point of view *as much as* an indicator of absolutism vs. gradualism per se. That this is so is seen by the considerably higher score on the gradualistic (Western) response on the part of the British and West German elites, relative to the less 'alliance-loyal' French elite.

On our two remaining items, asking whether disarmament should be carried out rapidly or step-wise, responses again show a clear preference for the gradualistic, step-wise approach: this is supported by 59% of the sample, while 23% think in terms of the more absolutistic approach. On the third and last item, however, the picture is more confused: asked whether one should aim at disarming throughout the whole world at once (absolutistic) or initially confine oneself, to some chosen areas, respondents were divided almost evenly.

This last finding may be explained by looking at another item on which our units responded: asked whether they would allow some zones to be 'thinned out' to become military *vacua*, 44% responded positively, while a strong 38% responded in the negative. This relative fear or distrust of disarmed pockets or demilitarized zones is probably related to a certain feeling that this might apply to Norway or the Northern European region itself; moreover, the Norwegian elite clearly shares the belief that military 'power *vacua*' are bad constructions which again may threaten the much-wanted balance of power, by inviting non-predictability etc.[22]

Looking at all three disarmament items together, we find a mean acceptance of the gradualistic alternative of 60%, while the mean score for absolutism is 26%. Using a better measure of this gradualism-absolutism relationship, we find a mean ratio of gradualistic to absolutistic response of 3.0, a score which gives sufficient support of our H5. Still, we have to explore further into *how* gradualistic Norway is on an international comparative basis, and perhaps to refine the indicators used for testing the hypothesis.

H6: *Norway is relatively strongly authoritarian with respect to the present international structure and decision-making*

Obviously, this hypothesis is very much related to H4. Thus, some of the data we used to study that hypothesis 'belong' as much to H6.

In the first place, that the elite perceives and approves of the present system as relatively stratified, is support of H6. As shown above, the elite adopted a 'No change at all' attitude and moreover expressed strong positive feelings about the bipolar, dual hegemony world.

While the concept of authoritarianism is in this context primarily adapted to the international system, we have for control purposes included some variables which indicate attitudes toward relevant aspects of the *national* society. Generally, we would expect no important differences on the authoritarian vs. egalitarian dimension in changing the focus from national to international phenomena, or vice versa.

Apart from the variables presented under H4, we may here present two more variables pertaining to the international structure. One asked whether respondents thought that disarmament demanded much inspection: a very strong 86% was convinced of that. Another strong majority – 81% – believed that disarmament depends on the great powers, while only 6% of the elite thought that smaller powers may make an important contribution in that respect, e.g. by acting as an example to others. These two scores – on inspection and great power role – next to the nearly 100% conviction that disarmament must be mutual or multilateral, are the highest ones on the 13 disarmament items included in our study. They seem to be well in accordance with the attitude expressed by the three regional European great power elites.[23]

Three variables with relevance to international problems and at the same time involving the idiosyncratic and the leader-follower aspect of the national context, give further evidence of elite authoritarianism. Two additional variables, both having to do with supra-nationality and the idiosyncratic-international 'continuum', will also be presented.

Authoritarianism means, among other things, that

a. great actors should have decisive influence, small actors not.
b. there should be supra-national decision-making within international cooperation endeavors, but not direct, 'representative democracy' within them (technocracy rather than participation).
c. leaders should have more influence than the followers or the public at large in foreign policy making.
d. followers should be led and taught into international living, while leaders need not.

The first of these 'rules' has been very satisfactorily supported by the evidence given above. Rule b refers to supra-nationalistic attitudes, but at the same time is 'turning the page': respondents are asked if they, in principle, will accept that supra-national governmental organization of which Norway is or may become a member, should select its leadership through democratic elections in the different member countries. The idea behind this 'mirror-image' of international cooperation could be that individuals should basically have not only *duties* – to adapt themselves to supra-national decisions – but also some *rights* in their *contrat internationale* with extra-national actors, the right of participation in selecting those who are to make those decisions.

In Table 4.4.3, Nowegian elite responses on the supra-nationality question are compared with those of the three European elites.[24] As response categories were not identical, we had to make a scaling classification of the responses from both studies which may be somewhat arbitrary, but which is probably reliable enough to make a comparison fruitful.

Table 4.4.3. *Responses on supra-nationality in British, French, West German, and Norwegian elites*

	Britain (1959)	France (1959)	W. Germany (1959)	Norway (1967)
Attitude toward supranationality*				
negative	7	12	1	14
ambivalent	4	8	15	8
moderately positive	45	12	18	26
strongly positive	40	58	65	44
NA/DK	4	10	1	8
	100	100	100	100
	(100)	(100)	(231)	(88)

*) In the Gorden–Lerner study, the question ran: 'Assuming all participating nations would do the same, how far would you be willing to see Germany (France, Britain) limit its sovereignty for the benefit of an international community?' In our study, the question was: 'Do you agree or disagree with the view that those laws and decisions that are valid for an international organization with some degree of supra-nationality should be directly applied on the individual citizens in the member countries – e.g. in Norway?' Response categories were as follows:

	Gorden–Lerner	Present study
(negative)	'Not at all'	'Disagree'
(ambivalent)	'For short term national necessities only'	'It depends'
(moderately positive)	'Also for fundamental political issues'	'Agree to some extent'
(strongly positive)	'As far as establishing a supranational authority'	'Agree strongly'

It seems possible to distinguish between on the one hand France and particularly West Germany as strongly, and on the other hand Britain and Norway as moderately supra-nationalistic. Although we have to take into consideration the time lag between the two studies, this distinction seems to fit well into the picture of actual foreign policy behavior in the late 50s, when Britain *and* Norway, among others, were reluctant to join the European Community. In fact, the British elite in the Gorden–Lerner trend study consistently are the least supra-nationalistic among the three, making the time lag seem less relevant. In the case of Norway, although supra-nationalistic feelings may have increased in recent years, there is still strong opposition within elite as well as public opinion strata to supra-nationalistic designs.[25]

Returning to authoritarianism, we present the two items mentioned together in Table 4.4.4. We see that to the same extent that the Norwegian elite accepts supra-nationality, it *rejects* the idea of an 'international democracy': in fact, the score is 70% in both cases. The argument most often

Table 4.4.4. *Supranationality vs. international democracy: the Norwegian elite responses*

	'Do you agree or disagree with the view that those laws and decisions that are valid for an international organization with some degree of supranationality should be directly applied on the individual citizens of the member countries?'	'Do you agree or disagree with the principle that leaders of an international organization of which Norway is or is to become a member, should be selected by the peoples of the member countries through direct elections?'
agree	70	16
ambivalent	8	7
disagree	14	70
NA/DK	8	7
	100	100
	(88)	(88)

found behind the rejection was that it is better, more safe for democracy, to let the national representatives in such organizations and the top executives of it be selected by nationally elected bodies.[26] Others no doubt found the idea too new to have considered it thoroughly.

One might, from merely looking at the distribution of responses, expect a high positive correlation between responses on the two items. This is indeed what we find: there is a correlation (Pearsons) of .59, which is relatively high, although not particularly impressive. Correlating the two items, we find that 50% of the elite are 'autocrats': they agree in supra-nationality *and* disagree in international democracy; only 2% are 'democrats', accepting the democracy principle and rejecting supra-nationality.

108

This authoritarianism on the part of the Norwegian elite is further confirmed by responses on another question. Asked whether they thought that international integration at the time being would be better promoted by leaders in the respective countries (i.e. Western European ones, as most of the respondents probably had in mind) or whether it in the present situation was more important that people in general contributed toward cross-national cooperation, 63% of the elite said leaders were more important, while only 13% believed more in the people-to-people approach.

Turning now to the last part of the data which is related to our H6, and which covers rules *c* and *d* from the list above, we find again that a majority of the elite, asked whether people in general should have more influence on foreign policy making in Norway, rejects 'democratization': 55% against the idea, 33% in favor. A great deal of those who reject it, do so on the argument that people before having more influence should have more interest and/or information; others think that people *do* have a lot of influence on foreign policy already.

The two items presented in Table 4.4.5 show how the elite relates education into 'international living' to social structure, i.e. the leader-follower dichotomy. Respondents were asked whether they thought it possible to make people more peaceful through education and other stimuli, and whether 'education for peace' should also be applied to politicians or world leaders. Again we find striking evidence of a leader-follower distinction and thus support of our hypothesis. The response here must be viewed in light

Table 4.4.5. *The leader-follower relationship and 'education for peace':*
the elite view

	'Do you agree or disagree that it is possible, through education and other milieu stimuli, to change man and make him more peaceful?'	'Do you agree or disagree with those who argue that such education first of all should be applied on political leaders?'
agree	68	29
ambivalent	2	9
disagree	12	44
NA/DK/Other	8	18
	100	100
	(88)	(88)

of the fact that it is highly unlikely that an elite group, being leaders themselves, should agree to putting themselves on the same footing and prescribing for themselves the same 'peace therapy' as people at large; that would mean admitting that they really needed it. We shall see later on how the public at large looks upon leaders in this respect.

We may conclude that our hypothesis, H6, has received very satisfactory support. As to the problem of a correlation between what we have called international authoritarianism and 'generalized authoritarianism', a correlation we assumed positive, this seems confirmed, although we shall leave the more detailed investigation of this problem to another context. Between the four items used to indicate authoritarianism through opinions on the international structure (the veto, weighted voting, supra-nationality and international democracy variables) we find positive correlations ranging from .36 (between veto and international democracy) to .25.[27]

H7: *Norway, being an 'over-achiever', has modest mobility aspirations*

The concept of 'over-achievement', as indicated above, is related to the question of power or influence. The question is whether or not Norway has more influence in international affairs than her resources or potential for power 'objectively' should give her. Or, in other words, whether or not she has converted her achieved resources into influence on a scale which amounts to over-achievement on the influence dimension, thus making her *satisfied*.

Only one variable is available for testing our hypothesis here. We asked the elite respondents whether or not Norway *had* more influence in the world than might be expected from her resources, etc. Needless to say, it is elite perceptions which should interest us, since the elite here *is* Norway; objective accounts of Norway's influence – if such could be established – do not concern us here, even if they would have been interesting as a check of the elite image. An even more interesting and perhaps much better check would have been foreign elites' evaluation of Norway's influence, because these elites would be the groups to feel the impact, if any, of Norway's influence, since they are interacting with her elite.

Now, the evaluation the Norwegian elite makes of its own strength or 'over-achievement' quite clearly indicates that it *is* feeling over-achieved. 44% of the elite think that Norway has more influence than might be expected, while only 7% feel that she has less than expected, and 42% think she has about as much as can be expected.

A great number of the respondents see Norway as an 'honest broker' in international affairs, as an 'example for others to follow'. Being 'democratic', 'freedom-loving', and 'humanitarianistic' are also assets which make the elite feel their country contributes to making the world more moral, better

110

to live in, and which fit very well in with the picture of Norway's foreign policy as highly '*moralistic*'. The choice of a Norwegian as the first Secretary General of the United Nations is seen as one indicator of Norway's status, and at the same time gives a great deal of the elite members a feeling that they (= their country) are if not *the* ones, so at least among those who have been called upon and see it as their duty to serve the world community.

Although such feelings are widespread, more pragmatic or 'realistic' appreciations are also clearly felt. Some respondents are more inclined, discussing Norway's influence, to turn the coin and look at other actors' influence over Norway i.e. its penetration. To this we shall return (cf. 4.7).

Although some complain about Norway's lack of influence, and have strong aspirations for mobility, most respondents are satisfied with what they perceive as Norway's over-achievement on the status or influence dimension.

H8: *Norway has a relatively strong feeling of we-ness, or center solidarity*

Briefly, 'we-ness' is defined as positive attitude toward center actors, while 'other-ness' is defined as positive attitude toward periphery actors; this is when we look at these matters from the center actor point of view.

We would not argue that we-ness and other-ness are the two opposite ends of one and the same dimension, but we suggest that strong we-ness is often found connected with little other-ness. Further operationalization defines we-ness as consisting of positive attitude to Western cooperation and to the 'Western world', but at the same time also rather positive attitudes toward the Soviet Union and the developed 'Eastern world' Other-ness is defined as positive attitude to the developing countries and to non-aligned countries.

Since we shall be mainly dealing with the concept of we-ness in this context, we should explain it in some more detail. It seem fruitful to talk of a sub-group *within* the we-group: a '*we-we* group'. The we-we group is, in the case of Norway, the developed, Western alliance, the 'North-West'. The '*we-they*' group is then another word for the center or the we group. By increasing loyalty or feeling of solidarity, the Norwegian elite then will see itself attached to the we-we, the we-they, and the they group – in this order of priority.

The we-we priority is proposed in H12 and will be explored in more detail below. Here we shall mainly occupy ourselves with the center-periphery, or the we-ness vs. other-ness distinction. Let us first take a look at elite attitudes toward the Eastern part of the we-they group, i.e. center feelings. We have shown that the Norwegian elite perceives the world as bipolar and that it evaluates the dual hegemony positively. Still we are left with the question what kind of bipolarity, or how strongly bipolar system, the elite perceives and prefers. It should be a loose bipolar system, to use Kaplan's terminology.[28] The question then is how far the Norwegian elite wants to go in the direction of loosening the bipolar structure – in depolarizing it or removing some of the constraints that existed and still exist on interaction between the two poles or the sub-systems led by these poles.

Polarization means, among other things, negative or minimum contact between the two, positive and maximum contact within. Depolarization presupposes positive contact between the poles and allows for negative contact within. Polarization means that interaction (particularly when positive) is between the top-dogs in the two sub-systems, while depolarization implies that even the smaller or middle-range members of the two sub-systems interact positively across the system boundaries, or interact with the top-dog(s) in the other sub-system.

Depolarization further means that interaction as much as possible should be 'contractive', should involve the two parts in an interaction system of some durability and frequency.

It also means that certain military *vacua*, geographically and in terms of military strategy, are accepted.

Several items were included for the testing of attitudes on these questions. On the question of inter-bloc under-dog interaction, we asked respondents whether such interaction ought to go primarily at the bilateral or primarily at the multilateral, bloc level. The former is believed to imply more orientation toward depolarization, as it will be relatively more free from the bloc type, multilateral minimum common denominator and top-dog dominated type of interaction.[29]

The Norwegian elite evidently believes that an East-West detente is going on and will continue, and it is, as witnessed by Table 4.4.6, equally clear that Western European elites agree on this.

Table 4.4.6. *Predictions of continued East-West detente:*
French, West German, and Norwegian elites. Percent

	France (1964)	West Germany (1964)	Norway (1967)
East-West detente will continue	99	83	94
	N = (118)	(162)	(88)

One thing, however, is the near unanimity that detente will continue. Another question is from what state of tension or conflict to what: i.e. how tense do the elites perceive the present period of East-West relations? A considerable number of the Norwegian elite perceived it as continually conflictful, although the majority thought that tendencies to the contrary – peaceful coexistence, cooperation, and a certain political convergence (especially in economic and foreign policy matters) – were more predominant. It seems that the Norwegian elite here stands close to the British, while the two continental elites perceive the situation as more tense.[30]

From this, one would expect that also concerning attitudes toward depolarization, or concrete detente measures, the Norwegian elite will be predominantly positive. Responses on the items chosen to test attitudes towards depolarization indicate that this is only partially so.

A strong 89 % of the elite believe it important to peace that West increase its contacts with East, while only 1 % thinks that such measures are of no relevance to peace. This pro-detente attitude seems to be stronger than similar attitudes reported among Canadian elite samples by Laulicht.[31] An equally strong opinion lies behind the idea that a strengthening of regional cooperation is important to peace. Now the question is what particular region or regions the elite may be thinking of: if it is – in the case of 'their own' region, Europe – the All-European region, that should indicate that the elite *is* thinking in terms of the we-they group, i.e. the center. If it, on the other hand, rather is thinking in terms of Western Europe or Euroamerica, then this is not consistent with a predominantly depolarizing attitude.

This question may be answered by inference from responses on another variable. Respondents were asked to state to which international organization, region, or unit of actors they personally felt greatest loyalty, or with which they felt they had most in common: 30 % chose Euroamerica or Western Europe, only 2 % mentioned the All-European framework. This then would mean that the elite puts a certain restraint on its depolarization willingness.

This is even better seen from responses on the multilateral vs. bilateral negotiations, and the demilitarized zones or military *vacua* items. On the first of these items, opinion is divided: 35 % prefer the multilateral, collective bloc approach to East-West peace and security negotiations, while 31 % prefer the bilateral, and 26 % think that neither one should be preferred, but that both should be adapted.

Gorden and Lerner put a similar question which when responses are compared, seems to indicate that the Norwegian elite is more 'depolarizing' than the three great regional power elites: *they* are far more inclined to take the top-dog approach. Or, more correctly: they are divided between preferring bilateral negotiations between the United States and the Soviet Union – the more extreme form of top-dog approach and not the kind of bilateralism that is implied in our question – and on the other hand, multilateral negotiations where they themselves can play an important role.[32] It seems, judging from these responses, that attitudes toward the problem of negotiations approaches are very much determined by the status and actual or potential influence of the actor. Still we maintain that they are also related to willingness to depolarize, but to make a valid comparison between the Gorden–Lerner samples and ours would certainly require a more thorough, multi-item analysis.

Looking at the other variable which was mentioned, we see the Norwegian elite tending toward accepting the idea of demilitarized zones: 44% in favor of such a measure, 28% against it, with 17% ambivalent and 11% have no opinion. The attitude of the Norwegian elite in this respect seems rather close to that of the British, which in 1961 expressed itself in favor of such a measure, while the French and the West German elites were opposed. Again one might suggest that some other factors are rather determinant, e. g. the fact that such zones have been proposed primarily for Central Europe, thus making France, for strategic reasons, and particularly West Germany, which would probably be included in such a zone,[33] less interested and positive.

On the whole, the main tendency is toward positivism on the depolarization issue, although there is a certain number of dissenters which may be a warning that depolarization should not go too far or fast. This interpretation is backed by responses on another variable. The elite was asked on what fields of activity, or what level, Western countries e. g. Norway first of all should expand their contacts with the East. Responses were classified in three categories: *political* contact (exchange of diplomatic envoys, official state visits and exchange of political information); *economic* contact (trade and production cooperation); and *social* contact (cultural exchanges, sports, and tourism). Political contact appears to involve both parties most and thus is most contributory to depolarization and center community, because this is the top level and the official form. The economic and social forms of contact, in that order, are less involving because they are semi-official and private, respectively, and do not commit the national actor so much.

A double response was obtained on this variable. The result is clearly contrary to the image of strong positivism toward depolarization. The bottom, social level received nearly twice as much support as the most-preferred level, as the political one, which also rated considerably below the economic level: the scores were 62%, 36%, and 53%, respectively.

About this result one might argue that it in fact supports, not rejects depolarization, as it is more important and contributive to depolarization to let the common people in East and West meet and get to know each other, and to knit durable bonds between the two groups through economic ties. Although we would not reject this view as improper, it seems that the elite itself has rejected it by strongly preferring the top level of political leaders as contributive to integration to that of the common people.

Returning to the question of loyalties and feeling of solidarity, we can compare scores for the center and the periphery. Furthermore, a third category is included, comprised of those who pledge their loyalty first of all to the global, center-*and*-periphery system, more concretely the United Nations.

The scores quite convincingly show preference for center before periphery: 48 % mention groups or regions which fall into the center category, while a tiny 2 % put periphery i.e., the less developed countries, first. On the other hand, 41 % of the elite mention the United Nations, giving a strong impression of positive feelings among Norwegians toward that organization or symbol. Attitudes toward the world organization will be taken up in 4.6. Let us now take a look at the evidence of other-ness within the elite.

Judged from responses on several items measuring attitude toward the less developed countries, there seems a rather large amount of other-ness in the elite. 81 % favor an increase in Norway's aid to the less developed countries, which seems to be underscored, in part grossly, by other elites. For instance, of the Canadian elite, according to Laulichts 1963 sample, 66 % were in favor of an increase.[34] And among the three samples in the European panel study, a large proportion in 1965 expressed interest in increasing foreign aid, but they were 'apparently referring to others, not to themselves'. Only one third of the British, one fifth of the French, and less than half of the German samples wanted to increase their own country's aid.[35]

At this point, we should allow for a comparison of how the different countries actually perform, i.e. what their actual amount of aid was at the time of the interviewing. If that is done, the Norwegian relative other-ness, as witnessed by this single variable, becomes less impressive: here, the Norwegian score is the lowest.[36]

This is further modified by looking into responses on a couple of other variables which represent demands for more concrete national sacrifices: 40 % of the Norwegian elite would give help to less developed countries which asked for Norway's assistance in developing a merchant marine and a further 25 % were willing to extend such help on certain premises, while

11 % were against it. Asked whether they were prepared to give the less developed countries customs duty preferences on their products, 44 % answered in the affirmative, 13 % negative.

The Norwegian elite was asked how they thought that the less developed countries should behave toward the rich. From responses obtained on this variable we can say that there is not very much support in the elite of the so-called 'trade union view' of the rich-poor gap, i.e. the view that holds that the less developed countries should put strong emphasis on cooperating *between* themselves and/or do a tougher bargaining with the rich. Only about 10 % take an attitude in line with this view, another 10 % believe that the less developed countries should take a critical attitude toward much of the assistance offered by the rich, while more than $\frac{1}{3}$ of the elite more or less explicitly say that the less developed countries should adopt first of all an attitude of self-criticism, of understanding the rich and *their* problems, even of accepting the conditions which the rich countries set for extending assistance.

Another indicator of other-ness would be elite opinion on the non-aligned countries. Only 16 % think these countries play a great role in today's world, while 46 % believe they play a certain role but not great. 12 % think their role is primarily a negative one, while a little more than $\frac{1}{3}$ believe it is mostly positive. This means that there *is* on the whole a relatively positive attitude toward the non-aligned; however, we should recall that it is not more, but on the contrary rather *less* positive than the elite attitude toward the Soviet Union, the leader of the 'other alliance', to the extent attitudes toward them may be compared.

From these results, we may make several conclusions. In the first place that there *is* a certain other-ness in the elite. Secondly, that this other-ness seems to be inversely proportional to the degree to which it involves Norway as an actor: an unspecified increase in aid in general of course *is* involving the actor, but not so much, or so directly so, as having to allow for the possibility of competition from a new merchant marine – the Norwegian service branch – or new industries. The effects of increasing aid in general and its total amount – what it costs – moreover, may be controlled by yourself, while the other forms mentioned cannot be (at least not to the same extent).

Still, we have not been able to prove sufficiently that the extent of we-ness is particularly greater in the elite than that of other-ness. We have two points to offer. The first has already been mentioned: the strength of we-ness is particularly felt in the *cognitions* of the elite (cf. 4.2 and 4.3) The second case in defense of our hypothesis is the *preferences* of the respondents when asked to select one specific goal or aim as the most important task of Norwegian foreign policy.

We included two items on this problem – one asking for short-range, another for long-range preferences for main goal of Norwegian foreign policy. On the short-range perspective, only 2% of the elite showed a preference for contributions to the solution of development problems as the primary aim of Norwegian policy, while more than $\frac{1}{3}$ of the elite related their preferred aims to center problems (detente, non-proliferation, etc.). On the long-range perspective, however, periphery problems topped center ones: 24% (the highest single score) selected development problems and the rich-poor gap as the main tasks, while about $\frac{1}{5}$ again were centrist.

These responses clearly support our H8: that is when the present or short-range future perspective is considered. As indicated before, development problems and their solution seem to be projected into the rather distant future as a main concern: they *are* the postponed problems.

4.5. *Defending center values: peace thinking*

In this section, we shall be presenting the *peace profile* of the Norwegian elite. This profile is a set of responses expressing elite opinions on a range of stimuli which more concretely are proposals for peace-making. The profile is believed to have both cognitive and affective aspects.

Let us start by showing elite preferences for an immediate or short-range peace policy (cf. Table 4.5.1). Respondents were asked what measures they deemed most important today to secure international peace. Responses may be compared with those obtained from the list of peace proposals to be

Table 4.5.1. *Preferred immediate, short-range peace-making measures: the elite response*

Strengthen international cooperation, the UN	25
Further East-West detente and mutual understanding	17
Maintain the balance of power	10
Achieve agreement on non-proliferation	10
Achieve disarmament and arms control	9
Close the 'gap' between the rich and poor countries, give more development aid	9
Solve the Vietnam conflict peacefully	3
Other	10
NA/DK	8
	100
	(88)

presented below, which implies the more long-range, principal preferences of the respondents. The short-range preferences may also be used to validate the long-range ones.

Responses as shown in Table 4.5.1 are well in accordance with what we have found elsewhere: detente and balance of power rank high, while development questions rank low. The top ranking of international cooperation as a means to peace-making, moreover, is well in accordance with H9.

Singer included a similar variable, classifying 'responses' in three categories, which we may also adapt for comparative purposes as in Table 4.5.2.

Table 4.5.2. *Opinions on peace-keeping in Soviet, US, and Norwegian elites*

Peace can best be obtained by:	Soviet	US	Norwegian
Our own military superiority	18	47	7
Soviet–Western cooperation	67	32	39*
Effective international organization	15	21	31
NA/DK/Other	–	–	23
	100	100	100
	(115)	(287)	(88)

*) On this category, apart from 'Detente', are included 'Achieve agreement on non-proliferation', and 'Achieve disarmament and arms control'.

Perhaps the most remarkable difference in opinion found in Table 4.5.2 is the low Norwegian elite support of the US insistence on military superiority for peace-keeping. This may be due to the considerable time lag: perhaps since then, the Americans have changed their view in the direction of the others. On the other hand, the strong emphasis on international organization in the Norwegian elite is again confirmed, this time on a relative basis. A list of peace proposals was presented to the respondents in a questionnaire. This list of 16 items of course does not contain all the important, relevant proposals which have been put forward, but it does represent a fair sample of such proposals, selected to meet certain purposes.

The proposals are in Table 4.5.3 ranked according to degree of favorable responses they got, i.e. according to *preference*. This ranking gives us the *ideal* peace-making program of the elite – what we shall call its '*optimal peace profile*'.

We see that the results presented in Table 4.5.1 to a large extent resemble and thus validate the optimal peace profile. Co-operation (UN, regional, etc.) ranks high, *détente* also. New is that measures connected with the

Table 4.5.3. *The optimal peace profile of the elite.* %*

Proposal is:	'Especially important to peace'	'Somewhat important to peace'	'Unimportant to peace'	'Against peace'	NA/DK	Total
We must strengthen the UN	79	17	0	0	4	100
Abolish hunger and poverty in the world	69	21	3	0	7	100
Rich countries must give more help to poor	60	31	4	0	5	100
Western countries must increase contact with East	60	29	1	0	10	100
General and complete disarmament must be realized	58	19	4	0	19	100
There must be a military balance between the states so that nobody dares to attack	58	25	3	1	13	100
We must strengthen regional organizations	42	47	3	0	8	100
The military alliances must be preserved	38	42	3	4	13	100
The states must become more democratic	36	46	13	0	5	100
The individual man must be educated to peace	35	55	10	0	0	100
States that naturally belong together must co-operate	28	47	10	1	14	100
Relations between individuals must become more peaceful	28	33	21	0	18	100
The World State must be established as soon as possible	24	15	18	1	42	100
There must be fewer states in the world	10	22	47	1	20	100
The small countries must have greater influence	8	47	23	0	22	100
The nations must become more similar	7	45	31	1	16	100

*) N = 72, as 16 of the total 88 did not fill out the questionnaire.

problems of the developing and poor countries rank high (next to strengthening the UN) in the profile, while they rank low on the list of immediate peace-making measures and on preferences for Norwegian foreign policy. This is again in accordance with the point made above that developing countries and the 'gap' are perceived as more long-range problems. Or: the elite *talks* about these problems because they are part of a general body of items which one *ought to* talk about nowadays; but it does not work them into policy or it postpones their policy inplications.

The varying NA/DK responses may explain some of the variance in the 'especially important to peace' category, which we use as the basis for ranking. Apart from the disarmamemt item, however, most of the items high on NA/DK are at the bottom of the list anyway: they are seen as decisively less important. In general, a high NA/DK score may be taken as a sign of uncertainty as to whether the proposal *is* peace-making or not.

What we have called the optimal peace profile is not necessarily indicative of *policy* preferences. Before becoming policy, the ideal peace program passes through a 'filtering' process, or several processes.

One such 'filter' is the respondents' perceptions of how 'the real world' meets the ideal proposals and makes them 'realistic' – applicable or workable – or not. Another 'filter' is the fundamental attitudes or personality structures of the respondents.

In fact these and other possible filters influence each other *and* jointly influence peace thinking; they are isolated for theoretical purposes. The use of the concept filter may also be somewhat misleading: in the mere evaluation of the different peace proposals (the optimal profile) both affective *and* cognitive factors are at work. The cognitions of the respondent may have a decisive influence on his preferences, making him prefer what he perceives as realistic, and vice versa. Thus it may be incorrect to say that the filter comes in at a second stage in the process of profile building.

However, the exact 'place' of the different factors in the processual sequence is not a main problem here, or an especially relevant one. The process is schematically presented in Figure 4. The end result of the process – the policy outcome – we shall call the *'operational peace profile'*.

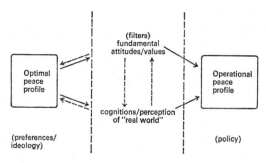

Figure 4. *The cognitive-affective 'filter model'*

Fundamental attitudes which may work as a filter are for instance 'anti-communist' feelings, which 'filter out' East-West *détente*, or regionalism – strong loyalties to specific regional co-operation frameworks – which will to some extent 'filter out' the globalistic proposals represented by 'We must strengthen the UN' (at the cost of 'We must strengthen regional co-operation'). In fact, both examples are supported by our data.

In the following, we shall concentrate on the cognitive filter in the process. It was introduced simply by asking the respondents if they believed that the respective proposals for world peace were 'realistic' or 'unrealistic' – whether or not they might be carried through in the short or in the long run. The results are shown in Table 4.5.4. By calculating the percentage difference between the preference and the perceived 'realism' of the specific items, we get the '*trust status*' of each item. If a highly preferred proposal is seen as highly unrealistic, this proposal represents an extremely *dis*trusted peace proposal. A highly realistic proposal which is less preferred might on the contrary be called a trusted peace proposal, etc. We shall soon return to this problem. Let us first present the operational peace profile of the elite.

We do this by 'sewing' the two dimensions – preference and perception of realism – together in one matrix, where the y axis represents realism, the x axis preference. We plot in the percentage of each single item on each of the two axes and get one point in the matrix for each item. This is shown in Figure 5.

The Figure indicates 7 clusters of items, if arithmetical proximity is taken as a measure of clustering: 13, 10 and 6; 14; 15, 11, 1 and 8; 4 and 9; 3 and 2; 7, 5 and 12; and 16.

We shall use another method of grouping, however: a differentiation on each dimension of the combined preference – realism perception scale between three levels: high, medium, and low. This method gives us *four* groups of proposals:

> *High/High*: proposals 13, 10, 6 and 14
> *High/Medium*: proposals 15, 8, 4, 1, 9 and 11
> *Medium/Medium*: proposals 3 and 2
> *Medium/Low, or*
> *Low/Low*: proposals 7, 5, 16 and 12

The broken lines in the figure indicate the cuts between the three levels mentioned; the range of the levels are somewhat larger on the 'realism' dimension because of the higher average percentage score on that dimension. The cuts roughly are made according to the clustering trends where the

121

distance between two items following next to each other on the dimension in question is the greatest.

Table 4.5.4. *Perceptions of 'realistic' peace proposals: the elite. In percentages*

	'Especially important to peace'	'Realistic'	'Un-realistic'	% difference*
Strengthen the UN	79	61	7	−18
Abolish hunger and poverty	69	42	26	−27
Rich countries help poor	60	64	7	4
West contact with East	60	69	3	9
G & C disarmament	58	36	33	−22
Military terror balance	58	68	6	10
Strengthen regional org's	42	74	1	32
Preserve alliances	38	63	4	25
More democratic states	36	46	24	10
Individual educated to peace	35	61	14	26
Co-operation between 'natural partners'	28	68	1	40
Better inter-indiv. rel.	28	35	35	7
World State realized as soon as possible	24	6	74	−18
Fewer states in the world	10	19	46	9
Small countries more infl.	8	33	32	25
Nations more similar	7	26	39	19

*) Difference 'Realistic' – 'Especially important to peace'. The average score for all 16 items was 8% higher on the response 'Realistic' than on 'Especially important to peace' – 48% and 40% respectively. For a better or more direct comparison between the different proposals, we might take a *weighted* difference score where the average percentage difference is taken into consideration, i.e. – 8% is added to each difference score in the right column.

The order of listing the different proposals also may indicate their relative *rank* within the cluster or group, since it corresponds roughly to their distance from the broken line indicating the level they are closest to.

Table 4.5.4 shows that on several items the difference between degree of preference and degree of realism perception is considerable. This largely answers questions about the relation between affective and cognitive aspects in the respondents' thinking (see 7.1).

A more general test of this difference is the Spearman's rank correlation. Correlating ranks on the preference and the 'realism' perception dimension, we get a rho of 0.33, which gives even better support to the conclusion that the affective-cognitive difference is considerable. *How* considerable it is, however, must be decided on a comparative basis.

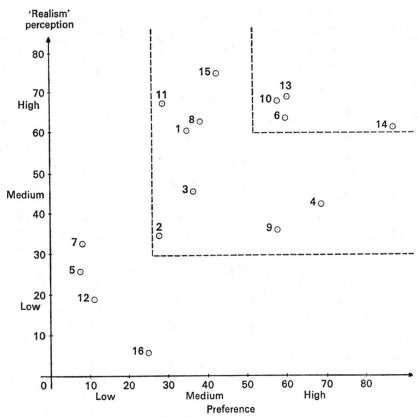

Fig.5. *The graphic combination of peace proposal preference and realism perception*

Table 4.5.5. *Most 'trusted' and 'distrusted' peace proposals**

Most 'trusted'		Most 'distrusted'	
Co-operation between natural partners	40	Abolish hunger and poverty in the	
Strengthen regional organizations	32	world	−27
Educate individuals to pdace	26	General and complete disarmament	−22
Preserve alliances	25	Strengthen the UN	−18
More influence to small states	17	Establish the World State	−18

*) For explanations and comments, see footnote to Table 4.5.4.

Another expression of the cognitive-affective relationship is the *'trust'* or *'distrust'* of the different proposals, already introduced. The measure of trust is the percentage difference between 'realism' perception and preference, as shown in Table 4.5.4. In Table 4.5.5 we give the most 'trusted' and the most 'distrusted' proposals. The last item in each column is not evaluated as having much importance to peace and will be left uncommented here. The others point to a clearer picture of the content of the cognitive-affective dissonance and to some propositions for further research.

That the 'Start with the individual' approach is so much trusted is probably due to a general ideology in the Norwegian society, stressing individualism and possibly Christian conceptions of man's duties and deeds.

A comparison of the two arms policy items listed in Table 4.5.5 – 'Disarmament' and 'Preserve alliances' – indicates that 'tough' proposals are trusted, 'soft' ones distrusted (the two proposals mentioned taken to represent 'soft' and 'tough' policies, respectively). Two other arms policy proposals – 'Keep the balance' (tough) and 'More West contact with East' (soft) – do not support such an hypothesis, however, even if they do not go against it (cf. Table 4.5.5). This point needs more exploration.

That to abolish hunger and poverty all over the world emerges as the most distrusted, is not astonishing. More interesting and perhaps remarkable is that to strengthen the UN – the proposal ranking in the top category of the operational peace profile – ranks number three among the most 'distrusted' proposals. This literally breaks the neat line which the profile is drawing up: to strengthen the UN, although ranking top on both the optimal and the operational profile, will 'in the real life' of politics or policy-making be a less attractive or useful proposal, i.e. more of the High/Medium type of proposals.

Even more convincing is such an argument if we assume – as we feel is quite fair – that policy-makers should stick to 'realistic policies' if they have to choose between the preferred or optimal, and the 'realistic'; or if they see that the much preferred but not so much 'realistic' policy over time is not working or even does not turn out as more 'realistic'.

Thus we shall have to upgrade the 'realist' perception side of the operational profile, which in turn means that the Medium preference/High realism proposals emerge as relatively more operational. Further, it means that the regionalistic, middle-range proposals, which are also the most 'trusted' ones, become *the* policy. This is in fact our H10, to which we shall return immediately.

4.6. 'Internationalism'

As was pointed out in Chapter 2, we must break down this rather unprecise concept into a number of more concrete and unambiguous concepts. A number of such sub-types were offered. We can list an even larger number of 'isms' often connected with an individual's relations with his non-national environment.

As an example, there is no evidence of *'isolationism'*, a much explored attitude in American studies, in the Norwegian elite. There is, according to our data, no objection to Norwegian membership in and support of the United Nations, to giving aid or technical assistance to the developing countries, or on the whole to cooperation on a range of different levels with other peoples and nations.

Probably, no elite will think of itself as *'nationalistic'* – if some kind of 'nationalism' is not explicitly formulated as part of its foreign policy. But it will often think of others as fostering such an attitude. This seems to be the case with the Norwegian elite.

Although this was not probed systematically into, it is quite evident even from other information than ours, that 'nationalism' is rather negatively evaluated in the Norwegian elite. Particular other elites, e.g. the French, are seen as nationalistic.[37] Moreover, Norwegians at large are seen as too nationalistic by their elite: asked what particular national traits or characteristics they thought that Norway should rid itself of, 58% answered Norwegian 'chauvinism', 'selfishness' or 'nationalistic isolationism'. On the other hand, only 4% mentioned what they called 'the national identity' of Norway and Norwegians as a value particularly important to preserve.

Comparing these results with those obtained by Deutsch et al., we see a marked contrast between the elite images. Of the French elite, $\frac{2}{3}$ found that the foreign policy of their country was nationalistic, while of West Germans only 3% had the same image of their country. There are however some important differences in the evaluation of nationalism among the three elites: a great number of the French no doubt evaluate nationalistic policies more positively than do the others; and the West Germans are particularly concerned that nationalistic policies, which recently had such a profound and negative impact on other nations' image of Germany, should not be found.

The Norwegians are in an in-between position: they most probably do not conceive of Norwegian chauvinism as a particularly strong trait and hence do not evaluate it very negatively. To most of the respondents giving the chauvinism response, it is clearly the public opinion, the common Norwegian, who is to blame, not the elite.

The Norwegian elite clearly believes in *'cross-nationalism'*. Asked whether multiple loyalties are possible in the present world, i.e. an individual being loyal both to his national and to some extra- or supra-national authorities without coming into conflict, 58 % believed this was possible, while 13 % believed it was impossible and 27 % were ambivalent.

To some extent such positive attitudes may be explained by the fact that the elite does not fear cooperation with foreign actors. 45 % believed that Norway in a process of increased cooperation and integration in the future would be able to preserve all or most of the traits a specifically hers or most of the values dear to her. A strong 24 %, however, believed that Norway would be losing much in such a process, even such values which were important to her.

Asked what they believe would be the most important consequences to Norway of joining the European Economic Community, $\frac{2}{3}$ of the elite thought these would be found in the economic field, i.e. that is where Norway would have to change most. And, asked what they would gain from increased cooperation and integration in general, $\frac{1}{3}$ answered that the most important gain would be economic. In other words: the kind of activities which they expected would be the most affected, would also give them the greatest gain, another indication of the strong thrust in international cooperation among the Norwegian elites.

We should add that many of the respondents probably are rather selective on this point, thinking of but not explicitly making them clear, certain positive reference groups in particular the European Economic Community. A few of them make it explicit *that* they are selective in answering our question e.g. in the direction of looking negatively on integration with the EEC, but positively on cooperation with the Nordic states.

Above we have seen (cf. 4.2 and 4.4) that international cooperation is high on elite *preference*; further indications of this will be given in 4.7. So far we have presented some evidence of the positive evaluation of international cooperation which may be found in the elite. This evidence has given further support to H9.

What will now be done is to look more closely into some particular aspects of the elite positivism to see what direction it takes. Some of these aspects have already been mentioned.

We found the Norwegian elite relatively *supra-nationalistic* (cf. 4.4.). It is also rather *trans*-nationalistic in approving of international cooperation on the governmental level. We found that this level was preferred to the *cross*-national level as to promoting international cooperation in general, while on the other hand cross-national approaches were preferred in relation with Eastern Europe to the trans-national ones. Further exploration shows, however, that the cross-national, non-governmental approach may have a stronger stand even in general integration or cooperation thinking.

Asked whether international cooperation in the present situation would be best promoted by institutionalized governmental, to some extent supra-national cooperation, or whether it would be better promoted by the non-governmental so-called functional form of cooperation, the elite was strongly divided on the question but did tend slightly in the direction of the latter. 39 % expressed functional preferences, 29 % institutional while 26 % were ambivalent. Whether this relative functionalism is due to long-range preferences or to more ad hoc evaluations, determined e. g. by the probably widespread feeling at the time of interviewing that governmental cooperation in Western Europe did not work, is impossible to say.

One sub-dimension of the broad concept of internationalism would be the *multilateral versus bilateral* cooperation dimension. Both these aspects may be related to the four types of internationalism: i. e. bilateral cooperation may be supra-national, although most often one would conceive of multi-lateral cooperation as taking care of that type of interaction, while bilateral cooperation would be more of the inter-national type.

Comparing Norwegian responses with those of the Gorden–Lerner samples, we get in fact good support of the view that multilateralism or bilateralism is not related to any specific type of cooperation (i. e. according to our typology). The West German elite e. g. which was found to be the most supra-nationalistic, is clearly the most bilateralistic (cf. Table 4.6.1).

Table 4.6.1. *Multilateralism vs. bilateralism in British, French, West German and Norwegian elites*

Aid to the less developed countries should primarily be given	Britain (1965)	France (1965)	W. Germany (1965)	Norway (1967)
multilaterally	42	65		52
both ways/ambivalent	–	–	–	25
bilaterally	31		50	17
NA/DK	25			6
	100			100
	(350)	(200)	(350)	(88)

While French multilateralism stands in sharp contrast with the actual policy of that country, the Norwegian attitude is in good accordance with its policy so far.[38]

a. *Globalism versus regionalism: support of the concentric theory?* We pro-posed in H10 that the Norwegian elite has a preference for regionalistic policies over globalistic ones. Now, the so-called concentric theory of

Norwegian foreign policy claims that there is no conflict between the two, but that both may be pursued at the same time.

There *is* no logical or necessary contradiction between the two hypotheses: a preference for something over something else does not logically, nor necessarily, imply a conflict between the two objects in question. Although we will suggest that there often *is* such a conflict, we shall not be able to substantiate this suggestion by evidence from our own material. The existence of such conflict however, may be shown by e.g. analyzing Norwegian voting behavior in the UN: when global demands meet with regional expectations, as in the case of action over Portugal's colonial policies, or white racialist regimes in Africa, the resulting Norwegian behavior very often has been withdrawal, which may be taken as a strong indication of conflict.[39]

From our data, the concentric theory receives in fact good support, which means it is part of the elite image of its own behavior. Asked whether Norway in international cooperation generally should put priority on global (through the UN or UNCTAD etc.), or regional cooperation (European or NATO) a majority of 56% answered that *both* should be or had to be supported, and that no priority should be given to either of them. On the other hand, 28% were prepared to give priority to the regional type, 16% to the global type of cooperation. Probing on this item (the 56% were asked to state their preference when or if a choice had to be made between the two types) yielded a further 18% support of the regional, 17% of the global, while 21% (all these percentages of the *total* sample) still could not make a choice or rejected it as inappropriate.

The net result thus is a tendency to prefer the regional type of cooperation. This regional preference, however, is based on an image of *harmony* between the various parts and forms of Norwegian external relationships – the concentricism in elite thinking.

Lastly, the globalism versus regionalism dimension may be explored through comparing the Norwegian elite with the West European ones. In the Gorden–Lerner study, respondents were asked to state which external relationship maintained by their own country they thought was the one most important to it; this question is rather similar to our question on personally preferred extra-national loyalties.[40]

For this purpose, we may collapse responses into three categories – the global, inter-regional, and the regional, the first being the UN, the last one, to be explained in more detail later on, meaning Euroamerica (and including rather heterogeneous and partially conflicting entities). The result is given in Table 4.6.2.

Table 4.6.2. *Globalism versus regionalism in the British, French, West German, and the Norwegian elite*

	Britain (1965)	France (1965)	W. Germany (1965)	Norway (1967)
Global	12	1	5	41
Inter-regional*	10	7	0	4
Regional	68	81	74	46
NA/DK/Other	10	12	21	9
	100	100	100	100
	(350)	(200)	(350)	(88)

*) Response values here differed: in the British case they were 'The Commonwealth', in the French '*la Communaute Francaise* or *Francophone*', and in the Norwegian case they were 'All Europe' and 'the developing countries'.

What is clearly shown by Table 4.6.2 is that Norway, although it does follow the trend found in the three other elites of being primarily regional-istic, is far more globalistic *than* the three regional great powers, which are practically equally strongly regionalistic.

This finding may be explained in a number of ways. Certainly it may be due to the framing and the content of the very question, the Norwegian sample responding to a more personal, idealistic stimulus which elicits the optimal choice, i.e. the globalistic response, while the other samples were put more in a position of representing their nation on a 'realistic' policy basis.[41]

But another explanation may be as important as this one: the special Norwegian affection for the United Nations. And this again may be related to a third explanation: the three regional great powers are overwhelmingly regionalistic since 'their' region is where they are able to exert some influence and to gain most, while the small state of Norway although certainly gaining from regionalism, is far less able to exert any influence on it and thus may just as well chose the globalistic line.

b. *Globalism? the UN response.* We shall now show elite attitudes toward the United Nations measured by its willingness to accept concrete proposals on ways in which to strengthen the world organization. There is a nearly 100% consensus that the United Nations *should be* strengthened: only one respondent is against this. This seems to be a rather strong dictum: compared with the Canadian elite samples interviewed by Laulicht, the Norwegian elite is far more favorably inclined. 28% of the Canadian elite was against, while 55% was in favor of the idea.[42]

Nasatir in his 1959 study put a number of questions on plans toward a world federation, built on the United Nations, to a random sample of persons listed in *Who's Who in America*.[43] His results should despite methodological differences lend themselves for comparisons with ours.

Nasatir included eight items in an index. Five of these we found suitable to our purpose, in addition we included two more. Together these seven items were believed to cover central aspects of a possible strengthening of the organization: its legal sphere of influence, its economy, what control functions it should have, and its structure. The two items included were the weighted voting proposal and a proposal, having been put forward, that the United Nation should be given the jurisdiction and the economic rights over the poles, the world sea and the ocean floor – i.e. the 'open areas'.[44]

The two structural items we have presented already, i.e. the veto and the weighted voting variables (cf. 4.4). The remaining five items made up an index of globalistic or United Nations attitudes, to which we will return later. Table 4.6.3 compares the US and the Norwegian responses; at the bottom of the table a percentage ratio of acceptance on rejection is calculated. As the US sample was not asked the question on 'open areas', the ratio of this sample is calculated on the basis of only four items.

We have excluded the 'abolishing the veto power' proposal from the index. This no doubt may be challenged with the argument that the abolishment of the great power veto would strengthen majority rule within the organization and thus the organization itself. While we tend to agree with that argument ourselves, as we have shown, a number of our respondents do not; hence the exclusion of the item from the index. *If* it is included it will greatly contribute to improving the US sample's position vis a vis the Norwegian since the US one as shown in Table 4.4.1 is strongly positive, the Norwegian rather negative to abolishing the veto.

Some of the differences on single items are probably due to the difference in the international position or rank of the two actors. Super-power interests are to some extent reflected in the *relative* US hesitance – majorities in fact support both proposals – toward the UN controling outer space and implementing disarmament plans. On the other hand, it has been shown that the Norwegian elite overwhelmingly believes that disarmament is up to the great powers not to the small, which means that its support of UN implementation in fact is support of the great powers doing the job through the world organization.

One uncertainty is created by the considerable time lag between the two studies. The question is whether positive attitudes toward one or several of these proposals have increased or decreased in one of the countries, or in

Table 4.6.3. *Attitudes toward strengthening the United Nations in American and Norwegian elite samples*

'The UN should have the authority to:		US (1959)	Norway (1967)
Tax the member countries in order to finance its operations	Yes	73	51
	Amb.	–	8
	No	14	25
	NA/DK	12	16
Control that outer space is not used for military and strategic purposes	Yes	70	87
	Ambivalent	–	1
	No	12	3
	NA/DK	17	9
Implement a plan for general or partial disarmament	Yes	53	71
	Ambivalent	–	9
	No	26	10
	NA/DK	21	9
Dispose of the poles, open seas and the ocean floor and of the income of the exploration there of	Yes	–	33
	Amb.	–	3
	No	–	30
	NA/DK	–	33
Dispose of parts of the standing armed forces of member countries'	Yes	68	71
	Amb.	–	2
	No	16	10
	NA/DK	16	17
		(575)	(88)
Mean ratio of positive to negative response:		4.3	7.3
(No. of items:)		(4)	(5)
Mean percentage acceptance, 4 items:		66	70

both, during the period of the time lag. We would think that there has been an increase in the case of the US elite. This however has to be explored.[45]

On the whole, and bearing in mind the differences in data collection time and methods, it seems that the Norwegian elite is more positive toward the UN and hence more globalistic than the US elite. This relative globalism of the Norwegians may be further supported by comparing Norwegian responses on the UN military peace-keeping forces item with those of the British sample from 1965: the latter was 48% in favor of, but a strong 44% against 'the integration of a major part of the British armed forces into a permanent supra-national army under UN command'.[46]

Some of the difference between the British and the Norwegian (and US) elite may be found in the phrasing of the question,[47] but this is not sufficient to cover up the actual difference, which is great.

In the Norwegian elite, there is a strong correspondance between the degree to which proposals are accepted, and the degree to which they are perceived as 'realistic' or realizable. Control of outer space and disposal of military forces are seen as the most realistic proposals, while disarmament, which is highly preferred, drops out as unrealistic.

In another question, respondents were asked what *immediate* measures toward strengthening the UN they would propose themselves: the three most frequent responses were setting up a peace-keeping force, improving the financial situation of the organization, and making its apparatus more effective. These responses to a large extent support the results obtained from the index items, as shown in Table 4.6.3. That UN peace-keeping forces scores high both on the optimal and the realistic is good proof of the strong position of this institution in Norway; furthermore, this is very much compatible with the Norwegian feeling of being called upon to 'clear up the mess' around the world.[48]

c. *Regionalism: 'Westwardness' and the Euroamerican preference.* We have shown above that the Norwegian elite puts more emphasis on regional policies than on global, although its globalism on a comparative basis is strong. This was in accordance with our hypothesis H10.

That there is a strong feeling of 'Westwardness', a strong positive feeling toward cooperation with the Western part of the world, has in fact been shown already in that the two most important foreign policy issues in Norway, according to the elite itself, are both connected with Western cooperation. 'Westwardness', in other words, has been shown to constitute a major part of the Norwegian foreign policy establishment.

Now we need to show the direction this 'Westwardness' takes is primarily toward Euroamerican, Atlantic community. This is what H11 proposes. The hypothesis implies that the Norwegian elite sees no conflict between an Atlantic and a Western European community, but that both are favored – the latter being perceived as part of the former.

This has been shown already, in Table 4.3.7. The Norwegian elite is in agreement with the British in finding little tension in the intra-Atlantic relations, probably a function of the close relationship between the two elites.[49] Or more correctly, a function of the strong Norwegian support of Anglo-American conceptions of the Atlantic community. Gaullism, neither in its cognitive nor in its affective aspects, has any support in the Norwegian elite worth noting, while it has strong support in both respects in the French, and strong support at least in the cognitive sense in the West German elites.[50]

132

In all four samples, however, it seems to be Gaullism *within* the Atlantic framework; possibly we should make an exception for the French elite, as witnessed by the data given in Tables 4.6.6 and 4.6.7. In these Tables, Norwegian responses on the NATO and EEC items are compared with those of the French and the British elite, respectively. Unfortunately, we do not have comparable, synchronized data for all four samples on both

Table 4.6.6. *Attitudes toward NATO in the French and Norwegian elites*

'Are you or are you not in favor of your country being a member of the NATO after 1969?'	France (1965)	Norway (1967)
In favor unconditionally*	34	60
In favor on certain conditions†	50	33
Not in favor	5	5
NA/DK/Other	11	2
	100	100
	(200)	(88)

*) The Norwegian response was as mentioned, while the French was 'Stay (in NATO) with only small changes of the organization'.
†) The conditions mentioned in the French response were a reorganization of NATO, while responses given by the Norwegian sample were 'Should stay if no radical changes in the situation occur' (26 %) and 'Should reconsider Norwegian membership' (7 %).

variables. On the other hand we can, on the basis of the Gorden–Lerner and the Deutsch et al. studies, say that the Norwegian elite is *the* most favorable toward NATO, followed by Britain. Gorden and Lerner report a decline in support of NATO in the British elite, as well as in the other two. In 1956 they found that 82 % of the British, 77 % of the West German and 71 % of the French elites were in favor of NATO.[51]

Concerning attitudes toward the EEC, the Norwegian elite seems almost as pro-EEC as the two members themselves, while Britain is somewhat less enthusiastic (cf. Table 4.6.7). This strong Norwegian positivity may be due to the particularly strong Norwegian tendency toward consensus: it is the small country elite, which no doubt has been much reduced up to recently,[52] standing united as one man behind the desire to join the organization. To some extent it may be due to a certain over-enthusiasm which the small state elite believes it has to show other (and great power) elites in order to be accepted. Or, it may be due to a certain *lag* on the part of the Norwegian elite, maintaining strong Euroamerican or Atlantic feelings, and clinging

Table 4.6.7. *Attitudes toward the EEC in two non-member country elites – the British and the Norwegian*

'Should your country become a member of the European Economic Community?'	Britain (1965)	Norway (1967)
Yes	75	84
Only as associate*	–	6
No	12	5
NA/DK	13	5
	100	100
	(350)	(88)

*) In the British responses, there is no indication of preference for an associate status. It may be that such preference is included in the 'yes' response, as the British respondents were asked to state whether or not they were in favor of joining the EEC; in *what form* was not mentioned.

to the idea of an unbreakable Atlantic unity, at a time when other and allied elites even the British, tend to relax in these respects.

Moreover, although we have no systematic data on this variable, the Norwegian elite is clearly even less willing than the British to see a future united Western Europe as a counter-poise to the two super-powers. When numerous Norwegians in the forced choice of the highest esteemed external unit or organization, choose Western Europe, only a few of them actually harbor such ideas.

To this Atlantica versus Europa dimension we now turn, by means of Table 4.6.8 which shows the responses on the forced choice question, i.e. responses which fall within the Euro-american category only.

From Table 4.6.8 we cannot say that the Norwegian elite is *particularly*

Table 4.6.8. *Atlantica vs. Europa: the intra-regional preferences of the British, French, West German, and Norwegian elites *)*

	Britain (1965)	France (1965)	W. Germany (1965)	Norway (1967)
Atlantica: NATO/relations with the United States	42	9	41	18
Europa: the EEC/relations between France and W. Germany	27	73	33	11
(Nordic countries				15)

*) Percentages on the basis of the *total* sample not only those respondents giving the regional response; percentages in column thus do not add up to 100.

Atlanticist in its orientation, although the Atlantic score is the single highest one. While the French sample clearly is European and the British is predominantly Atlanticist, the Norwegian seems to take the position of the West German sample in dividing itself between the two. However, as we have said, Norwegian 'Europeanism' is with some very few exceptions not contradictory to, but *compatible* with the concept of an Atlantic community.

This may be seen even better if we cross-tabulate the NATO and the EEC responses of the Norwegian sample: 79% of the total sample are in favor of membership in both these organizations, while 4% are against both. These figures, as may be seen from Tables 4.6.6 and 4.6.7, show an almost complete polarization, in the sense that practically all those who are in favor of one of the items are in favor of the other one, and conversely all who are against one are against the other with one exception. Only 9% of the sample take an in-between position, being ambivalent to one and positive to the other item and thus showing moderate Westwardness; bridge-building then is hardly present.

The 'West-Europeans' among the Norwegian elite members are even more regionalistic than the 'Atlanticists' – this is when preferred extra-national units are cross-tabulated against global vs. regional preference. About the 15% 'Nordists' it may be asked whether they constitute a group of potential 'isolationists' since they choose the geographically closest unit. This seems, however, not to be true: a majority of these respondents take the both-and approach to the question of preferred level, while there is a tendency within the minority to make the globalistic choice.

In the French-British conflict – and this relationship *is* perceived as conflictuous by the Norwegian elite – it takes almost completely the side of the British, blaming the French government. The strong Norwegian affinity for Britain, although perhaps subject to some strain in recent years, is further shown in that a sample of Norwegian parliamentarians is clearly less willing to join the EEC without Britain doing so, than the two other Scandinavian countries.[53]

As far as Norwegian feelings toward the United States are concerned, in the within-the-alliance or Atlantic relations there is hardly any tendency similar to the one, as reported by Gorden and Lerner, found in the two continental European great power elites, to question the US leadership and/ or guarantee of the NATO alliance. The lack of enthusiasm for US foreign policy which was found in a considerable part of the Norwegian elite does not apply to Atlantic relations, but first of all to US behavior in the Third World.

To sum up this and the two preceding sections, the Norwegian elite clearly *has* a center or we-they voice, but with a rather strong Western or we-we accent.

4.7. *Norway and system activity: communication and participation*

The hypotheses put forth in relation to Norway's present patterns of inter-action within the international system, propose basically that Norway is high on participation in the system, high on opinion-holding about inter-national issues, and relatively low on initiating actions on the international scene. Norway, in other words, does interact, but very much as a receiver, not an initiator.

As has been stated above, these hypotheses relate to *behavioral* patterns in Norway's foreign policy, patterns which are not the main focus of attention in this context. We shall thus restrict ourselves to a few variables as indi-cators of the hypotheses proposed.

Participation will be measured at two levels, both of relevance in this particular context: the national, and the individual (milieu member) level. Membership in international organizations has been included at the national level in the center-periphery index. Among the seven items included, Norway receives its highest rank on this particular variable, ranking as number 13 as a member of 41 % of all international governmental and non-governmental organizations.[54] If the number of inhabitants in the country is controlled for, however, Norway receives top rank, second only to Israel on number of organization memberships *per capita*.

As these results, however, may be slightly tautological, other variables should be included. One such variable indicating participation is size of the delegation which Norway sends to the UN. Between 1960 and 1965, i.e. from the 15th up to the 20th session of the General Assembly (both inclusive) Norway sent on the average 21.6 persons as her representatives to the UN. This delegation size gives her rank number 28 among all the member countries, which places her in the top quartile.[55]

Another or third indicator would be number of diplomatic exchanges with other countries: on this variable Norway in 1966–67 ranked as number 50 among 127 countries in the world, as measured by the number of diplo-mats it sent to other countries.[56] These indicators (except perhaps for the last one) show that the proposed hypothesis holds at the national level. Turning now to the individual level, we may give some data on the persons on our two samples as to their personal relationship with the international system.

Only 40% of all persons in the two samples were *not* members of any international non-governmental organization, i.e. an organization with national branches but with a wider international organizational set-up. Most of these memberships (⅔ of them) generally went to political organizations (such as the West Europe Movement, the Nordic Association etc.). Only 35% of the elite had not been, or were not at the time of the interviews, member of any official Norwegian delegation to international governmental organizations: 44% of all elite members were or had been a member of two or more such delegations.

Of course participation at the two different levels which have been focused on here, must be positively correlated: when Norway participates, she does so *through* her elite. What our individual level data thus show is basically that our samples *are* Norway's representatives, i.e. yet another validation of the sampling.

A last and fourth variable, which is probably also highly dependent on the national level participation variable, is the frequency of trips abroad undertaken by the milieu members. Our data show that 24% of the elite (9% of the opinion-makers) travel abroad more than 10 times a year, while 52% (29% respectively) go abroad between 3 and 10 times a year. Their participation, however, is limited in domain: they go mostly to the geographically and politically closer regions of Western Europe, the Nordic countries, and North America. Very few go to 'Third World' areas.

On the whole, our participation hypothesis seems to hold. Turning now to the *opinion-holding* hypothesis, we may give information on only one variable at each of the two levels. An indicator at the national level would be the frequency of and tendency to chose abstention in roll-call voting in the United Nations. According to Jacobsen,[57] Norway ranked as number 97 out of 118 states in tendency to take a stand in the period 1965–67 (in all subcommittee votes), that is: she abstained more than most of the others.

There is an opposite tendency at the individual level. The British, French, West German, and Norwegian elite samples explored throughout this chapter were compared according to their tendency to answer with DK-responses or not to answer at all (NA) on a number of different items. The

Table 4.7.1. *NA- and DK-scores among British, French, West German, and Norwegian elite samples as a measure of opinion-holding*

	Britain	France	W. Germany	Norway
Average NA- and DK-score on a number of variables	8.8% (23)	11.6% (23)	7.7% (23)	5.2% (32)

resulting average DK- and NA-score for the four samples is shown in Table 4.7.1.

Relative to other European elites, the Norwegian one seems to be a high overall opinion-holder: it has made up its mind.

When it comes to the third and last hypothesis to be explored briefly in this section, that of Norway as a *non-initiating* actor, relevant information is very scant. We have been able to produce only one indicator of this dimension – participation in sponsorship activities in the UN, i.e. in sponsoring draft proposals for discussion and/or decision.[58]

In fact, what is found when this variable is investigated is that Norway *is* very low on participation in sponsoring proposals submitted to the General Assembly: in 1961 she ranked as number 77 among 107 member countries, in 1965 as number 95 out of 117, which even means that she moved from the next to the bottom quartile *to* the very bottom one over that time period. On the other hand, the pattern of Norwegian sponsorship activity is not very different from that of other center nations: in fact, the sponsorship activists are the Africans, the non-activists the Europeans, which means that sponsorship activity is negatively correlated with international position.[59] This means, moreover, that some doubt as to the validity of this variable as a measure of initiating activity must be admitted, and that the same holds true for abstentions in the UN as a measure of opinionholding at the national level – but not *necessarily* so.

One explanation why the Norwegian elite is probably relatively non-initiating may be found in the relative *penetration* of the Norwegian polity by outside sources, as perceived by the milieu itself. A majority of both the elite and the opinion-maker samples perceives Norwegian foreign policy as being relatively much influenced by foreign milieus – Norway's allies and close 'friends'. And about $\frac{1}{4}$ believe that she is largely dependent on other milieus in making her foreign policy.

As has been pointed out above, however, such perceptions are not coupled with negative evaluations, except for in a few cases.[60] The penetration thus is legitimate. The majority sticks to the rather pragmatic view that the outside influence is a result of an international system of policy-making in which Norway takes her part and has her say.[61]

This view may explain what looks like a contradiction between the perceptions of Norway's influence on the outside, and vice versa: there seems to be little correspondence between these two variables, as the correlation between them is only .13 for the elite, .18 for the opinion-maker sample. Cross-tabulating the two variables, we find moreover no difference between the 'independents' and the 'dependents' in their evaluation of whether or not Norway has more influence in world affairs than she might be expected to have.

In concluding this chapter, the profile of elite thinking which has been drawn and at certain points contrasted with the profiles of other, geographically and politically close elites bears out quite strongly the centrist, truly conservative position of Norway. Another major finding is the strong elite consensus. That consensus will in the next chapter both be contrasted with national consensus and be subject to further analysis of its various components.

5. Consensus Versus Conflict: The National System

In Chapter 3, several types of consensus were discussed and the concepts of 'consensus within' and 'consensus between' were operationalized. In the first sections of this chapter we shall present material for testing the four concrete hypotheses put forward in relation with our discussions of the consensus problem. In later sections, we will deal with problems of centrism, internationalism, and so on.

5.1. *Norwegian consensus: an international comparison*

The types of consensus to be analyzed here are *elite* and *national* consensus. On the latter, which implies a comparison between elite and public opinion in a number of countries, we are not able to do much. Although this to some extent should be possible, we have not been able to compile comparable public opinion data from the other countries used for elite comparisons throughout this report. We have only one set of data from one of these countries. This data set includes five variables responses reported in the Deutsch and Edinger study on Western Germany.

On elite consensus we are able to present a list of twelve variables, most of which have been presented already, and which may be used for a comparison of consensus in the British, French, West German, and the Norwegian elite. In addition we may calculate average scores for each of the elite samples from a much larger number of variables. A total of 32 such variables among a larger number presented to the three samples in the Gorden-Lerner study, has been analyzed by us and averages calculated.

These two data sets will be presented separately in the following. In Table 5.1.1, responses on the 12 items put to the four samples in much the same form and at the same time, are given by means of percentage averages.[1] Under each heading, two figures are presented.

The one gives the *corresponding percentage average* (mean) *of* the group, i.e. its mean percentage score using as parameter the response value which receives the highest score i.e. the modal value, but which at the same time is the modal score for a *majority* of the groups in question.

The other figure represents the *overall percentage mean*, the modal value among the respondents of the group, no matter *what* that value is, as the parameter employed.

The latter parameter gives us the real consensus in a group, i.e. to which degree it is able to agree with itself on a common standpoint. The former – corresponding percentage mean – is of interest when the problem is to what extent two or more groups are able to agree upon one and the same standpoint. This expression then takes care of the 'consensual consensus' case, while there may be 'dissensual consensus' in the case where overall percentage means are taken; if there were no such dissensual consensus, we would only have to calculate *one* figure, as the overall modal score would also be corresponding.

H14: *Norway has a relatively high elite consensus*
H15: *Norway has a relatively high national agreement.*

These are the hypotheses to be tested in this section. Turning to results, we note in the first place that Table 5.1.1 shows a strikingly similar pattern of consensus in all four samples, particularly when overall scores are compared: the difference is within a range of 3%.

Table 5.1.1. *Consensus scores for* 10 *items in British, French, West German, and Norwegian elites. Average percentages*

	Britain (1965)	France (1965)	W. Germany (1965)	Norway (1967)
Mean modal corresponding score	65.3	62.0	69.8	69.0
Mean modal overall score	68.3	71.5	71.3	69.0

When mean corresponding scores are compared, however, the difference rises to nearly 8%, primarily due to the French non-corresponding line, which could be expected. In fact, it is non-corresponding with the other (or the majority of the other) elites only in two of the ten cases, but in these cases the French deviation is so considerable with a percentage drop from 71.5% to 62%.

141

Our H14, however, has *not* been verified by these data: Norway on within-elite consensus takes only a middle position compared to other West European elites. If we turn to the much larger set of variables, mean scores on which are given in Table 5.1.2, our hypothesis is supported. (It should be noted that these 32 variables are the same only between the three Gorden–Lerner samples; those analyzed in the Norwegian samples differ, the overlapping between the two studies being only $\frac{1}{3}$, as is evident our discussion above on the twelve corresponding variables.)

Table 5.1.2. *Consensus scores for 32 partially corresponding items in the British, French, West German, and Norwegian elites.* Average percentages*

	Britain	France	W. Germany	Norway
Mean modal corresponding score	60.7	58.7	62.8	−†
Mean modal overall score	61.3	60.9	64.8	70.4

*) As mentioned in the text, the items were fully corresponding i.e. the same, between the three great power samples; between these three *and* the Norwegian samples there is a little more than 1/3 overlapping.

†) As items are only partially corresponding, it does not make sense to calculate this score for the Norwegian sample.

Taking the two Tables together, we see that the Norwegian sample shows a somewhat higher consensus than the other. On the other hand, it may be argued that the strongest evidence comes from the results on that set of items which is *corresponding* to all four samples, that given in Table 5.1.1. Although the number of variables in the partially corresponding set is relatively high and thus makes spurious scores less felt, we still have a validity problem because sampling of the variables differs.

All we can say is that there *is* a certain tendency over a large range of different variables toward comparatively high consensus in the Norwegian elite, but that this has to be explored into by more data obtained from corresponding sets of stimuli.

Our H14 then is seen as only *partially* confirmed.

Taking up H15, it is clear from what has been said already, that there can be no rigorous testing of it. The five items used for elite – public opinion comparisons in the study by Deutsch and Edinger were all concerned with questions of European cooperation.[2] This should be establishment or close-to-establishment items in the West German context, which means that we

142

may pick out five items of a similar kind from the Norwegian context and use them for comparisons. The results are given in Table 5.1.3. (E = Elite, and PO = Public opinion).

Table 5.1.3. *Comparisons of national agreement in Norway and West Germany*

| | West Germany* | | Norway† | |
	E	PO	E	PO
Mean acceptance of all five items in percentages	74	37	75	54
Mean rejection score in percentages	20	15	12	28
Mean NA or DK scores in percentages	6	48	6‡	15‡
Ratios of acceptance to rejection: mean of all five items	3.7	2.5	6.3	2.0

*) The five items used in the West German studies are 'Western European Union', 'Paris Agreements 1955', 'European Coal and Steel Community', 'NATO membership', and 'European Defence Community'.

†) The five items used are: 'NATO membership', 'EEC membership', 'UN disposal of national force in peacekeeping unit', 'Increase of aid to developing countries', and 'Multilateral aid to be preferred'.

‡) In these scores are *not* included the ambivalent respose, which in the case of the elite accounts for 13 % on the average, in the case of the public opinion 3 %.

The results shown in Table 5.1.3 in fact point in several directions. In the first place, the remarkable similarity between the elite samples is seen once more: the only difference is the relative German tendency to take the negative position – a 20 % mean against the Norwegian mean score of 12 %. This difference makes up for another great difference – in positive to negative ratios.

Our main concern, however, is the difference between the elite and public opinion within each of the two national units. Since the difference between the two levels in acceptance scores is smaller in the case of Norway, one might conclude that Norwegian national agreement is greater. Taking rejection scores into consideration however, and thus looking at the ratios as well, one might draw the opposite conclusion: the Germans are more united, i.e. on how to gain access to the international society again (being rejected after WWII).

One important point of uncertainty is found in the very high NA-score of the West German public opinion: half of it in fact has no opinion on the issues presented. During the years following the mid-50'ies, when the interviews were made, this percentage may well have dropped due to the public being socialized by the elite and being involved in the issues generally. But then the question is what attitudes those 'coming out of the NA box' have adopted. Since the majority of the elite has a positive attitude, and given the strong influence over communication media etc. this majority enjoys, it is very likely that a majority of the former public opinion no-opinion'ers has gone to the positive side, thus making West German national agreement even stronger. On the other hand, the rejecting elite minority may also have shrunk at the same time, a possibility which would work to maintain or even widen elite – public differences, making agreement weaker.

We suggest that much of the explanation why our H15 does not seem to gain support may be found in the collection of items used in the two national context. Those to which the West German public is responding seem to be tapping one single dimension – a kind of 'Euro-internationalism', of attitude toward European cooperation in general. The Norwegian public, on the contrary, responds to a wider range of stimuli, including the foreign aid item which gets relatively strong negative response among public opinion samples in the rich countries.

If only one single variable – opinion on NATO membership – is analyzed, the Norwegians seem to have a higher agreement than the West Germans.[3] Our conclusion then is that even on these questions we need more material in order to make reliable comparison, but that our hypothesis may be maintained as fruitful. Reason for doing so is given in the section to come, where Norwegian elite-public opinion relations are probed by a large number of variables.

5.2. National agreement: social structure and consensus-building

In this section, we shall look at relations between the three levels of social structure we are dealing with in this context – the elite, the opinion-maker, and the public opinion levels. The hypotheses are:

H16: *The higher the social position, the more consensus there will be*

H17: *The opinion of a social group on an issue or a cluster of issues may be projected from that of other social groups in the same universe if we know the exact opinion position of the latter, the position in the social structure of all the groups in question, and their position relative to each other (the projection hypothesis)*

H18: *Systematic elite – public opinion differences will be prominent or particularly great on those dimensions which are part of or closely related to the foreign policy Establishment*

H19: *The Norwegian foreign policy system, as far as Establishment and establishment-related issues are concerned, is moderately oligarchic*

These hypotheses are very much inter-connected, although they do not form a strictly deductive system as presented here.

Altogether 48 items, all of them affective or evaluative variables, were analyzed to measure consensus. On all these variables we had data for both the elite and opinion-makers from our own study. On 32 of them we had data from various national survey or public opinion studies carried out from December 1964 to July 1967.

The choice of parameter, and the calculation of corresponding and of overall percentage means were made as explained above (5.1). In some cases, an alternative *or* extra parameter was employed – a ratio of positive to negative response. Testing inter-group agreement, we used percentage difference on corresponding modal values as parameter, i.e. difference in percentage score on one and the same response value for two or more groups.

In order to obtain a standard percentage value as a parameter, we trichotomized a few variables not already given a three-value form. As most of the variables employed *were* of the trichotomized positive-ambivalent-negative type, this could be made with a fairly reliable end result.

Again we stress that the number of cases where the corresponding percentage mean is not also the overall modal average percentage score, is very low. This in itself could be taken as a sign of high agreement, as it shows an ability to put opinions in the same direction.

Our H16, which proposed that consensus increases with increasing social or structural position, may now be tested. Table 5.2.1 shows it satisfactorily verified in both cases – on modal overall, and on modal corresponding value score – and for both the smaller and the larger sample of variables. The

Table 5.2.1. *Intra-group consensus for elite, opinion-makers and public opinion. Mean (average) percentage scores*

	E	O	P
Mean (average) modal *overall* value for 32 variables	70.4	68.6	62.4
Mean (average) modal *overall* value for 49 variables	68.1	66.4	–
Mean (average) modal *corresponding* value for 32 variables: E's choice*	70.4	67.2	59.4

*) The value on which E scored highest, was chosen as the 'standard' for all three groups; this means that O 'lost' its best score on 3 of the 32 variables: on these 3 it scored higher when the highest overall value was considered. The same was true with P in 4 of the 32 cases.

distance between elite and public opinion, not great in either case, is slightly reduced when we change focus from corresponding to overall score (from 11% to 8%). The distance between elite and public opinion is very small, indeed smaller than one should have expected from our hypothesis of moderate oligarchy. The explanation – or part of it – is found if we break down the total number of variables and look for differences in score on specific issue-clusters included in the total number. This is done in Table 5.2.2.

Table 5.2.2. *Intra-group consensus*: *average percentage scores for* 3 *issue-clusters*

'Cluster':	E	O	P
'Peace proposals' (n = 12)	75.2	71.6	66.7
'Disarmament' (n = 10)	61.2	59.3	59.3
'Globalism' (n = 7): highest overall value	72.2	75.5	58.1
'Globalism' (n = 7): highest corresponding value*	72.2	75.5	45.3

*) P scores lower on modal corresponding value than on modal overall in 3 of the 7 cases.

Only 3 out of the total 32 variables are not included in Table 5.2.2, which should then account for most of the explanation sought here. We see clearly that while the 'Disarmament' variables work toward almost complete inter-group agreement as public opinion on the average scores about as high as the two other groups, the 'Globalism' variables show a contrasting picture. On the one hand, opinion-makers score higher than the elite; this seems in accordance with our hypothesis, H22, to which we shall return. On the other hand, public opinion drops far below the two others on these variables.

The difference between the elite and the public is a measure of what we called the *national* agreement. According to modal corresponding average value (which logically is the only measure of this type of consensus), on the 32 variables the average percentage difference between elite and public was 11%. If we choose as an upper limit for inter-group agreement a percentage difference of 20%, i.e. what falls within a ±20% area is consensual, we find that there is disagreement between the two on 12 of the 32 variables, while there is agreement on the remaining 20. If ±30% is chosen as the upper limit, there is national disagreement on 7 variables or issues, i.e. less than $\frac{1}{5}$ (the extreme case being a 70% disagreement on one variable).

If we look at degree of *milieu consensus*, i.e. agreement between elite and opinion-makers, this is higher, which should be expected. In the case of a ± 20% limit, the number of dissensual cases is 3 for the 32 and 7 for the 48 variables, respectively, while the respective figures in the case of a ± 30% limit are 1 and 2. That is: the milieu consensus is very high.

Even when we lower the upper limit to ± 10% i.e. close to a limit where the probability of a disagreement between the two groups should be rather high, that is random, there is for all 48 variables only about 35% disagreement (on 17 of the 48 variables).

We need of course more data before safe generalizations may be made, but we can venture that *the Norwegian foreign policy milieu is extremely united.* An elite-public opinion difference on the average of 11% seems to indicate relatively strong national agreement on the whole. As Table 5.2.2 shows, this is only valid for a *larger* number of variables or issues. When we focus on a few specific dimensions, there are considerable deviances from the overall trend. This has certain implications for the projection hypothesis, to which we will turn shortly.

Another indication of consensus may be found by looking at how the different groups evaluate the actual Norwegian foreign policy. Elite and opinion-maker respondents were asked if they had anything for which to criticize the present foreign policy. On the whole, apart from the strongest dissenter groups particularly the Leftist outsiders (cf. 5.7) criticisms were not strong, but concerned only minor issues or the very way in which the policy was carried out (cf. 4.7).

In two subsequent national surveys, public opinion was asked to state their opinion on the way the present government handled certain political spheres of activity, among them the foreign policy. Although questions are not the same, response trends may well be compared.

As may be expected, the elite was not particularly critical: only $\frac{1}{5}$ expressed criticism in some form or another. This contrasts with the much more critical opinion-makers, who by more than 50% expressed critical opinions on one or more fields or aspects of Norwegian foreign policy. Most of them, however, were not particularly critical; the result then is not necessarily in contradiction with the strong elite – opinion-maker agreement reported above.

Of the public opinion sample interviewed in the beginning of 1968, only a modest 17% was of the opinion that the government handled foreign policy badly, while 77% on the contrary thought it was handled well. Positive evaluations rose after one year to 82%, putting the sphere of foreign policy well above several other spheres of governmental activity when it comes to public approval.[4]

a. *The opinion-structure*: *'uni-variate'* *consensus*. If the expression of consensus through indices, average modal percentages and mean percentage differences, and mean ratios all are expressions of 'multi-variate' consensus, looking at consensus formations on single items gives what may be called 'uni-variate' consensus. We have done this already, but we shall take a more systematic look at this aspect or way of viewing consensus formation.

What we now will be looking for is ranking of variables according to consensus scores, not so much ranking of social groups or strata. In Table 5.2.3, however, we still focus on that latter aspect. In the that Table, the distribution of modal corresponding scores is given for single variables. Classification is by means of percentage categories with a range of 15%: the upper category represents number of variables which score 85% or more, the next those which score between 70% and 84%, and so on.

Table 5.2.3. *Distribution for the elite, opinion-makers, and the public opinion of 32 variables according to 'uni-variate' consensus*

	E	O	P
> 85% consensus:	25	25	19
70–84% –	28	22	19
55–69% –	19	28	9
< 54% –	28	25	53
	100	100	100
(No. of variables)	(32)	(32)	(32)

The distribution profiles of elite and opinion-makers are rather similar, while that of public opinion differs much from the two others. If 70% consensus is taken as the limit, which actually has been done throughout, we see that 53% of the variables in the case of the elite, 47% in the case of opinion-makers, and 38% in the case of public opinion is within that limit.

While in the elite and the opinion-maker samples the variables are rather evenly distributed among the four categories, in the case of the public opinion they are rather skewed, a slight majority of them falling in the less than 54% agreement category.

If we look at the number of variables which falls into one of the upper two categories in *all three* samples, the number is 8, which means that there is a $\frac{2}{3}$ agreement between the samples on *which* variables to rank highest, the total number of variables being ranked above the 70% limit by the public opinion being 12. Half of these 8 variables again fall into the top category, i.e. $\frac{1}{8}$ of the total sample of variables explored.

148

b. *The projection hypothesis.* The basic idea behind the projection hypothesis is that it should enable us to predict opinions and attitudes in cases where these are not known. In our context this means for instance that knowing the opinion positions of the elite and opinion-maker samples (on a percentage scale) we should be able to give the opinion of the public. There is also the possibility of projecting the opinion of two or more groups, if only the opinion of *one* group were known. What we then need to know is the opinion positions of the groups concerned on a number of other variables – covering a whole set of, or only one specific dimension, depending on the dimension on which opinion is to be projected – and the structural position of the respective groups.

There are several ways of testing the projection hypothesis. One is to select randomly a number of the variables used, take the mean of this sample for all three groups, and then draw the curve which the means make up.

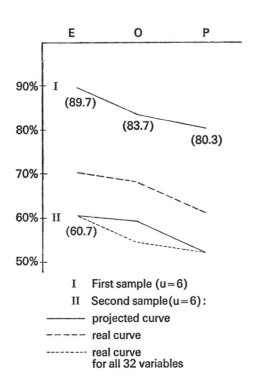

Figure 6. *Projection of opinions for O and P when E's opinion is known*

For another set of randomly selected variables, we take the mean for one group only. By using a matrix where the above mentioned curve is depicted and plotting in the point representing the one-group mean of the second set, we may project the mean opinions of the remaining two groups by drawing a curve parallel to the first one. This is shown in Figure 6, where the twelve peace proposal items are divided randomly in two groups.

The projection test is not quite convincing insofar as the shape of the 'real' curve is somewhat different from the projected one. The difference, however, amounts to less than 5%, and that for opinion-makers only; for public opinion the projected and the real opinion is totally overlapping. As shown in the Figure, the real curve for the 'control' sample (II) tends more towards the curve presented by the totality of 32 variables.

In the long run, and when one is dealing with clusters of variables or indices, a difference between projected and real opinion, a 'deviancy limit' of 5% should probably be allowed for, at least when the number of indicators as low (3–6). When the number increases, the deviancy limit naturally should be lowered.

The probability that one may project with reasonable accuracy the opinion position on one single variable or a set of two variables is generally not high. Out of the total 32 cases, 12 kept the elite-public difference of 11% (for corresponding value) within a $\pm 10\%$ range (i.e. the difference between the elite and the public opinion on these variables varied between 1 and 21%).

The curves shown in Figure 4 all have the 'falling l'-shape, with elite on top and public on bottom. Looking at each single of the 32 variables, 15 of them have this shape, while 8 are A-shaped (with opinion-makers at the top and public opinion at the bottom) and 9 v-shaped (with opinion-makers at the bottom and elite or public at the top: public opinion at the top in 6 of the cases). While the position of the elite and opinion-makers relative to each other may be changing, it is quite evident that they generally will be 'on top of' the public (around 20% deviant cases).

So far we have primarily used absolute percentages as parameters. One might ask whether this will not be somewhat misleading since the number of DK's or NA's should be higher, the lower the structural position: public opinion is generally less inclined than elite people to respond at all to a question. By calculating the NA's and DK's for a random sample of the 32 variables, we find this is true: on 16 variables, the average DK/NA score of the elite is 5.2%, of opinion-makers 4.5% and of public opinion 8.6%. Looking at middle category or ambivalent, 'neutral' scores, the three groups over a greater number of variables seem to be rather similar: all three show scores of about 15 % or so (although on different samples, elite and opinion-makers the same, public opinion another).

On the whole, then, using absolute percentages seems a reliable measure. On some of the variables, however, the public opinion samples have given only two, i.e. negative and positive response, while our two samples included a neutral response category; in these cases, the public opinion will be 'favored' compared to the other two samples. To control for this possibility, we calculated the ratio of positive on negative response on a number of variables (Establishment, establishment-related, and disarmament dimensions) and got partial verification of the projection hypothesis very similar to that obtained using absolute percentages (somewhat more than 50 % of the cases going in the hypothesized 'falling *l*' direction, the rest evenly distributed between the A- and the *v*-shaped curve).[5]

In accordance with the different curve shapes which may be read out of Table 5.2.2 above, we conclude that the projection of foreign policy opinion may reach a sufficient level of accuracy only if *different issue-areas* are considered: projections will vary from one area to another. This is why we now turn to an area which carries particular importance to the foreign policy system: Establishment and establishment-related issues.

c. *The foreign policy system: the hypothesis of moderate oligarchy.* Two related hypotheses, H18, which proposes that systematic elite versus public opinion differences are prominent on Establishment and – related issues; and H19, which proposes that the Norwegian foreign policy system is moderately oligarchic, will occupy us here. In fact they are very much over-lapping, as both concern degree of consensus or dissensus and the opinion curve between the elite and the lower structural positions.

As has been shown already (3.4) we constructed an index of four variables defined as representing the Establishment. Unfortunately, we have not been able to use a similar index for the public opinion, so we shall have to make use of the parameters used so far – mean percentage and ratios.

The general hypothesis, H16, is that consensus increases with structural position. This is well verified by looking into Establishment with the use of both mean modal corresponding value and mean positive/negative ratio (cf. Table 5.2.4).

It is safe to say that the hypothesis would be verified in the case of the index. As we have constructed the index, the number of Establishmentarians in the public opinion would probably be very low, perhaps only 5–7 %, because only 11 % in the national sample asked that question, wanted to increase Norway's development aid (cf. 5.4). But even if this low score, in fact

151

Table 5.2.4. *Establishmentelation and structural position. Mean modal corresponding value and ratio*

	E	O	P
Mean modal corresponding value on 4 Establishment items (positive response)	80.5 %	76.3 %	40.5 %
Mean ratio (positive/negative response) on 4 Establishment items	9.3	5.5	1.8
Index (additive: all 4 Establishment items)			
'Establishment': positive to all items	51	38	
'Right outsiders': positive to two*	31	24	
'Doubters':†	9	23	
'Left outsiders': positive to other two‡	5	14	
NA/DK	4	1	
	100	100	
	(88)	(130)	

*) Positive to NATO and EEC membership, negative or ambivalent to development aid increase and national force under UN command.

†) Ambivalent to NATO and/or EEC, positive to rest.

‡) Positive to increased aid and UN command, negative to NATO and EEC membership.

probably higher today, is corrected for, the number of public opinion establishmentarians by our definition most probably would not exceed 15 %. And: the number of anti-establishmentarians – people who reject *all* four items – would probably be almost as high as that while it is zero in our two top position samples.[6]

It is quite evident that the distance between the elite and the public on Establishment is beyond the upper consensus limit (i.e. 30 % or more if average modal corresponding value is taken). Even if we correct for recent developments which may have narrowed the distance and brought it close to this limit, there is a certain degree of disagreement *between the foreign policy elite and the general population on the central foreign policy issues of Norway.*

It is also evident that our two hypotheses, H18 and H19, have received good support. Taking into account a number of Establishment-related items subsumed under the two dimensions 'globalism' (cf. Table 5.2.2) and 'Westwardness', we get very much the same trend as in Table 5.2.4.[7] H18 may thus be said to be well confirmed.

The same is not yet true with H19: the question may be raised whether the foreign policy system is not oligarchic or even relatively autocratic (cf. Table 3.3.1). All the data we have presented so far seem to go more in that direction than in the direction of moderate oligarchy: the opinion-makers are more close to the elite *than* in a position in-between elite and public. This is even more true in the case of the Establishment and -related issues than in general, but also here it is so. In another context, we explored the relations between the groups by taking the rank correlations on the peace proposals. Even this measure indicates that opinion-makers even if they take an in-between position, are closer to the elite than to the public, i.e. are more in agreement with the former.[8]

Concluding, we may say that the Norwegian foreign policy system *in general* is relatively less oligarchic than we expected, because of the moderate distance between elite and public opinion. When it comes to Establishment issues, however, the distance is great and the position of the opinion-makers is rather close to that of the elite: the system then is rather strongly oligarchic. It may perhaps be added that it is *oligarchic on a 'democratic' basis* since the Norwegian foreign policy Establishment items get the support, individually, of *more than* 50% of the public (except for one case).

5.3 *International versus national agreement*

We have defined 'international consensus' as agreement between different national actor *elites*, while 'national consensus' is elite-public opinion agreement. Now the idea is to compare the two in order to indicate an answer to the question, which was made above, what agreement is the stronger.

To give more than an indication of an answer necessitates our having comparable data for both types of agreement on a *range* of different variables; this we do not have. We are able to present *relatively* comparable responses on 10 variables, 7 of which are affective. They span from attitudes toward NATO and EEC membership via disarmament measures to UN disposal of national armed forces, on the affective side, and from predictions on future disarmament to predictions for a WWIII on the cognitive side.[9]

In section 5.1 we gave some figures on degree of consensus in the British, French, West German, and the Norwegian elite samples, showing ability to agree within the national elites.

What we shall now explore is *between* elite agreement. By means of the material presented in 5.1, we are able to measure international agreement. And we may do this on altogether six *dyads* or pairs of elites, as is done in Table 5.3.1. For control purposes, agreement within the British-French, British-West German, and French-West German dyads is calculated for both the 12 variables which correspond with the variables used in our study, *and* the 32 variables only partially corresponding, presented in Table 5.1.2.

The figures in the Table represent mean percentage differences for modal corresponding values.

Table 5.3.1. *International agreement between the British, French, West German, and Norwegian elites. Percent*

	I*	II†
Dyad		
Norwegian – British	17.0	– ·
Norwegian – French	22.2	–
Norwegian – West German	17.0	–
British – French	11.7	13.8
British – West German	9.1	12.4
French – West German	16.6	14.2

*) For 12 corresponding variables.

†) For 32 variables, corresponding between the British, French and West German samples.

While it is outside the context of this report to comment on the agreement scores found between the three European regional great powers, it is tempting to note that the French – West German relationship, one of the 'special relationships' in modern international politics, does not seem particularly strong as judged from the material which Gorden and Lerner have presented. This may, however, have become comparatively stronger in recent years.

That the three regional great powers seem more in agreement between themselves than with the Norwegian sample, *may* be due to the uncertainty created by the questions used in the two studies and the differences between them. But it may also be accepted as a fact, or rather as a fruitful proposition for further study. Part of the explanation then should be found in the fact that these three elites are higher in international position than Norway, closer to each other in these respects than is any one of them to Norway.

What should occupy us most, however, are the similarities in agreement scores between each of the three regional great power elites and the Norwegian elite, as witnessed by Table 5.3.1. From what has been said above, we would have expected that the Norwegian elite was most in agreement with the British elite, to comply with the idea of a 'special relationship' between Britain and Norway. On the other hand, while the Norwegian agreement with the West German elite is as great as that with the British, the most remarkable finding is the relative Norwegian-French disagreement.

This finding is by no means astonishing, but is well in line with what has been said on the basis of single variables above or on a more qualitative basis. Political disagreement with the Gaullistic France over Euroamerican policies is prominent in the Norwegian elite. The French policy is seen as a deviation from the correct line which must be repudiated.

Our next task is to relate international agreement to national agreement, i.e. agreement in the Norwegian elite-public opinion relationship. This is done by use of the 10 variables which were mentioned in the beginning of this section; this procedure should make comparisons highly reliable.

Table 5.3.2. *International versus national agreement*

	Norway public opinion	elite	British elite	French elite	W. German elite
Mean modal corresponding value, percentages	53.1	73.7	70.0	73.9	69.0
Mean percentage difference with the Norwegian elite, for corresponding values	22.2	–	17.7	20.7	19.8
(No. of items)	(10)	(10)	(10)	(10)	(10)

Results, which are given in Table 5.3.2, show that *inter*national agreement is somewhat if not much greater than the national agreement. That is: the Norwegian elite agrees *more* with some of its closest foreign elite counterparts *than* with its own public opinion. Even the relatively 'alien' French elite is included in that agreement.

Differences however are not very great. If only the 7 affective variables in the list of 10 are analyzed, national agrement or disagrement is approximately 25 %, which is also the score of disagreement between the Norwegian and the French and the West German elites on those variables. The Norwegian-British elite agreement, however, is maintained on 17.5 %.

However much one should warn against too far-reaching conclusions on this international versus national agreement problem, we *may* say that the findings we have presented point toward an important and in some respects very promising perspective on international politics.

In the first place, it shows that the perception of the structure of the international system is not only oligarchic or authoritarian on the level of the nation-states – bipolarity, great power veto etc. being indicators of this – or at the level of individuals i.e. within the nation-states: it even seems to be 'cross-nationally oligarchic', at least within such politico-cultural regions as 'Euroamerica' or Western Europe.

One may of course discuss whether an elite agreement cross-nationally being greater than elite-public opinion agreement intra-nationally by necessity means oligarchy. The term should not be interpreted in a too strictly narrow sense, nor in a strictly negative way. What we have indicated is that the international elite agreement we have found, *being* greater than the national agreement, in a world which still puts strong emphasis on the nation-state as a chief actor in the international system, means elite agreement 'over the heads of', in some issues perhaps even *against* the respective publics. We presuppose then that there is a corresponding elite-public disagreement within the societies of those foreign actors with which we compare the Norwegian society; this of course is an empirical question to which we have not been able to give a sufficient answer (cf. 5.1).[10] Much used concepts such as 'the national interest' seems after this to lose much of their meaning.

Other, perhaps stronger, empirical evidence of the cross-national oligarchy is found if we compare international elite agreement with national agreement on the four Establishment items only (i.e. the Norwegian establishment). As shown in Table 5.2.4, Norwegian national disagreement is a big 40% on these items, while the Norwegian elite is in 21% disagreement only with the British elite on those same items. Since the Establishment takes such an important place in the foreign policy system, this *is* a strong indication of the cross-national oligarchy.

One explanation of the structure of opinions which we have termed international oligarchy, is of course that the elite tends to interact more with other elites than with their own public. Furthermore, our findings may be seen as evidence in support of the *penetration* thesis. One may argue that high elite consensus in a number of countries is an international, but not inter-related phenomenon: elites by virtue of their very position in their society, no matter what the issues, will *have to* agree within themselves. The argument then would continue: the mere fact that elites strive to get as close to complete consensus as possible, and more often than other social groups do succeed in that respect, explain why agreement scores *between* elites become so comparatively high.

To a certain extent this 'elite position effect' explanation must be accepted. We feel, however, that it cannot satisfactorily explain why and how images and attitudes on a variety of different issues become so parallel, take the same direction, the same value. While elite position in itself contributes to consensus and agreement on anything, *what* the elites will agree on is very largely determined by communication cross-nationally, and often – as would probably be true in the case of British-Norwegian elite relations – through penetration.

5.4. *Centrism and social structure*

Our hypothesis proposes that H20: *centrism increases with increasing structural position*. We shall test this hypothesis by breaking it down into five sub-hypotheses, covering each one of the five aspects of centrism which were outlined and studied in 4.4.

In some instances, as will be well understood by now, rigorous testing is impossible due to lack of information on public opinion attitudes. In such instances comparisons will have to be reduced to elite – opinion-maker relations.

Let us first look at the '*frame of reference*' dimensions – the traits and trends most salient to the groups, and the hopes the various groups have for the future. Doing this we shall also be able to have a look at the logical prolongation of H9, which concerns the degree to which world images are East-West-centered: that the elite is most East-West-centered among the social groups we study.

a. *World images and social structure.* We have information on the public opinion only on two of the socalled 'frame of reference' items – threat perceptions and hopes for the year 2000. Threat perceptions are compared in Table 5.4.1.

Table 5.4.1. *Threat perceptions and structural position: what is the greatest threat to mankind today?*

	E 1967	O 1967	P 1964
Nuclear war/nuclear weapons/the proliferation danger	23	36	59
War/war danger in general (nuclear war not mentioned)	28	10	13
Hunger/overpopulation/the rich-poor gap	18	39	5
East-West tension/the balance of terror/the armaments race	12	3	0
China/Chinese aggressiveness	3	8	4
Communism	1	0	3
DK/NA/Other	9	4	16
	100	100	100
	(88)	(130)	(1000)

We see at least two striking dissimilarities between the groups. The fear of or concern with nuclear weapons or the 'nuclear reality' seems conversely proportional with structural position: the lower strata are far more concerned with it than the higher. Does this indicate that public opinion is more 'soft on' nuclearity, while elite is 'tough' in relation to it? Or is the explanation rather that the elite has a more 'realistic' appreciation of present threats and problems, those 'underlying' and more structurally determined as contrasted with the more visible or surface-like phenomena as 'The Bomb' is?

Both explanations may in fact be given some credit. We may mention one single item as an indicator of 'toughness'. This one indicator supports the argument just followed concerning differences in 'toughness' (cf. Table 5.4.2).

Table 5.4.2. *'Toughness' and structural position: tolerance level for nuclear war*

		E 1967	O 1967	P 1967
Can you conceive of any value so high or important that it would justify taking the risk of a nuclear war?:	Yes	27	15	7
	No	58	80	89
	DK/ NA	15	5	4
		100	100	100
		(88)	(130)	(539)

The 'toughness' variable furthermore may be seen as an indicator of *degree of identification,* i.e. identification with the nation or the social group to which respondents belong, as shown by Berelson and Steiner.[11] As the elite has most to defend, personally, and sees its interest in the survival of the nation most at stake as a group (from the simple fact that it is leading and representing the nation) – it will also identify itself most with the nation, *or* possibly some greater unit (e.g. the 'Euroamerican' or Western politico-cultural entity).

Another dissimilarity between the groups is, as seen in Table 5.4.1, the relative occupation of the opinion-makers with the 'social misery threat' – hunger, overpopulation, under-development. This finding is well in accordance with what was found in 5.2 (cf. Table 5.2.2). We shall return to this aspect of 'internationalism' later in this chapter.

Turning to hopes for the future world, responses on this item give the preference of people for long-run developments, but also their more immediate concerns – what their present activities would be directed at; this latter aspect is seen when responses on this variable (cf. Table 5.4.3) is compared with those given on threat perception.

Table 5.4.3. *Hopes for the world year* 2000 *and structural position*

	E 1967	O 1967	P 1967
Problems of the less developed are more central/being solved	28	25	14
More international cooperation/stronger UN	26	10	4
Peace/security	14	22	53
Detente/more trust between nations	13	22	0
Disarmament/non-proliferation secured	9	2	15
Other (more advanced technology/more peaceful indiv.)	10	7	8
NA/DK	0	12	5
	100	100	100
	(88)	(130)	(539)

The projection of present concerns into future hopes seems to be most prominent in the public opinion: their orientation is toward war-and-peace issues in general. While the elite and opinion-makers expose a more diffuse set of preferences, the public opinion has one very salient preference. This will be true even if one in order to control for a possible coding effect, collapses 'detente' and 'disarmament' – the exchange relationship items – with the 'peace' category.

Elite is relatively more concerned with cooperation – the integrative relation – which was mentioned as an indicator of centrism (the 'compensation through intermingling hypothesis'). On the other hand, the opinion-makers do not put more emphasis than the elite on the development problems, as might be expected.

But these conclusions may be based on more information, i.e. from the two items giving perceptions of the present world's most prominent trends and problems. This is done in Table 5.4.4. The Table points to some modifications of the conclusions mentioned.

159

Table 5.4.4. *Present world images and their distribution on systematic relations: for elite and opinion-makers*

	Most prominent trend		Most important problem	
	E	O	E	O
I Power relation: war/armaments	22	32	39	53
II Exchange relation: detente/disarmament/ non-proliferation	21	5	34	9
III Integrative relation: integration stability-lability/cooperation*	38	16	7	0
IV Status relation: problems of developing countries/rich-poor gap	11	25	9	32
DK/NA/Other	8	22	11	6
	100	100	100	100
	(88)	(130)	(88)	(130)

*) The answer 'instability' was given by 22 % of E and 11 % of O, on the question of the most prominent trend today.

The strong elite concern with the integrative relationship – problems of cooperation and stability in the structure – is very well confirmed. On the other hand, the opinion-makers' relative preoccupation with development questions and the elite's striking disinterest for or 'non-perception' of these questions point to what was indicated above: the opinion-makers are ahead of the elite on such 'new' issues. The opinion-makers have to a large extent (note that it is true only with between $\frac{1}{3}$ and $\frac{1}{4}$ of the sample) internalized the international development issue already, while the elite is 'catching up with' opinion-makers over time on that issue. (Cf. what was said above, in 4.4 and 4.6.)

This means also that opinion-makers are less East-West-oriented than the elite – another indication that the elite is more centrist. In the image of elite members then, the 'switching hypothesis' – that the system will move from being East-West to becoming North-South centered – as a consequence of this receives more backing than among opinion-makers, who have already 'switched' the system in their world image.

One logical implication of this should be that opinion-makers show a higher consistency or constancy in cognitive orientation than does the elite, if consistency is defined as (high) positive correlation between the perceptions on two cognitive items. That should be true over time, i.e. between the 'hopes for year 2000' item and the present trend', 'problem' and 'threat perception' items. This is confirmed, although the correlations in neither case are high.[12]

But what does this result really mean? That opinion-makers are relating future hopes more to present 'realities' and concerns, while the elite is 'thinking of something else'? Or rather that the elite simply had a less consistent or consonant cognitive structure than the opinion-makers? Correlating the three present world cognitive items we find the same pattern: opinion-makers show a higher (positive) correlation than elite in all three cases, a correlation of .49 between problem and threat perception being the highest one (and the corresponding one for the elite .16). We leave the problem for further discussion in sections 7.1 and 7.2.

For all three groups, we have found that war (or nuclear war in particular), seconded by the threat emanating from the rich-poor gap and the social misery aspects of world developments, are perceived as the most problematic or threatening factors in the system. How strong are these problems felt to be, how likely is it that the threat will be manifest – in a war or another destructive 'event'?

Such questions point to the relationship between 'catastrophe perception' and structural position. To a certain extent they may also be seen as related to the optimism-pessimism dimension, but will not be treated primarily as such here.

In a more general sense, catastrophe perceptions will be related to centrism or strong concern for center values and the very status or position *as* a center nation. One would expect that those who were most centrist and most center-status conscious would be most inclined to feel these values threatened. Catastrophe perceptions should thus increase with structural position.

Against this proposition speaks the argument that catastrophe perceptions naturally and logically are strongest in the lower social strata. For one thing, they have less to lose in a catastrophe. More important relative deprivation or a feeling that things are going pretty bad anyway, that there is a steady, on-going catastrophe process so that the Big Catastrophe does not make *that* much difference, is more prominent in these strata. Catastrophe thinking accordingly should be most prominent also.

We believe that the last proposition carries most weight, and we shall subject it to testing. This was do by relating structural position to the two most salient threat dimensions – the war or 'nuclearity' (East-West-related primarily), and the 'social misery' or gap (North-South) dimension. Table 5.4.5 shows the predicted *development* of the system along these dimensions, while Table 5.4.6 indicates the *consequences* expected from the more serious development alternative.

Table 5.4.5. *Catastrophe thinking: predicted development along 'threat dimensions'*

	In East-West relations, detente will continue:				Is a World War III likely before year 2000?			Will the gap between the rich and the poor countries be greater than today within year 2000?‡		
	E	O	P	P*	E	O	P	E	O	P
Yes	94	79	56	38	3	7	12†	43	40	
Perhaps	2	7	–	47	15	42	–	3	12	
No	2	4	26	12	68	43	–	47	32	
DK/NA	2	10	18	4	14	8	–	7	16	
	100	100	100	100	100	100		100	100	
	(88)	(130)	(1000)	(539)	(88)	(130)	(539)	(88)	(130)	

*) From the 1967 youth study.

†) This response was obtained on a question asking for predicted development of East (socialist)-West (Capitalist) relations.

‡) The question was somewhat differently phrased (cf. Appendix F) and the response values actually were 'Yes' = The gap will be greater; 'Perhaps' = The gap will remain about as now; 'No' = The gap will become smaller.

Table 5.4.6. *Catastrophe thinking. Expected consequences if worst development alternative for 'threat dimensions' should materialize*

What will be the most likely consequences of a World War III to Norway?

	E	O	P 1967	P 1964
Total destruction	35	9	37	39
Irreparable losses	15	33	24	20
Heavy but not irrep. losses	17	35	35	32
Not so heavy losses	5	2	3	3
DK/NA/Other	28	21	1	6
	100	100	100	100
	(88)	(130)	(539)	(1000)

What will be the most likely consequences if the gap between the rich and the poor countries becomes greater?*

	E	O	P
War between them	8	9	12
Serious conflicts/war danger	42	42	41
Other (not so serious) consequences	39	36	44
DK/NA/Other	11	13	3
	100	100	100
	(88)	(130)	(539)

*) This question was asked E and O; the question posed to the public opinion sample was 'Between now and the year 2000, what do you think is most likely to happen in the relation between the rich and the poor countries?'

The difference between the groups are marginal only. In three of the five cases the hypothesized trend is confirmed, one case is deviant (WWIII consequences to Norway) and the last one (development of the gap) is 'open': here we lack data on the public; opinion-makers on the other hand seem to be less optimistic than the elite and this is in accordance with the proposition, which, *on the whole*, seems to have received good support. (For further evidence of 'optimism', cf. 5.6).

The higher the structural position, the less concern there seems to be about possible threats to the system and the center values. Does this mean that *affections* about the stability of the system also are less prominent at higher structural positions, so that our hypothesis does not hold? We shall present two sets of variables which may shed some light on the problem.

H 20.1: *Acceptance of existing world order increases with increasing structural position*

Table 5.4.7. *Acceptance of world order and structural position: balance preferences*

	E	O	P
To keep the present balance of power is important to peace	83	67	76
To preserve present military alliances is important to keep peace	80	60	40*
General and complete disarmament should be carried out mutually (by both sides disarming at the same time)	95†	64	89

*) The question in the 1967 youth study (P on the other two items being from the 1964 study) was 'To obtain peace countries should be members of military alliances so that no country or group of countries dare attack others.'
†) This question was not directly asked the respondents in E; the score is more or less arbitrary, but based on other information.

From the three indicators in Table 5.4.7, balance thinking seems especially prominent in elite, while opinion-makers at least as much as the public take a more detached, 'unilateralistic' attitude. This difference between elite and opinion-makers may be further explored by responses on questions about possible changes in the present international structure (vertically), given in Table 5.4.8.

There is more change-orientation on the part of opinion-makers in both cases, which is in accordance with the trend found in balance thinking.

Table 5.4.8. *Acceptance of world order and structural position:*
status quo preferences

| | The veto right in the UN should be abolished | | A system of weighted voting should be introduced in the UN | |
	E	O	E	O
Yes	26	44	33	32
Perhaps	9	15	11	18
No	59	34	47	38
DK/NA	6	7	9	12
Ratio: pos. neg.	0.4	1.3	0.7	0.8

With the usual restriction imposed by the insufficiency of public opinion data, we may thus conclude that our initial hypothesis has been established as a fruitful proposition for further exploration and testing.

H20.2: *Gradualism increases with structural position*

There are one cognitive and one affective dimension to this problem also, and consequently we present two sets of data to shed some light on it. The first set, presented in Table 5.4.9, gives indications of absolutism; the second one (cf. Table 5.4.10) is a compilation of opinions on disarmament procedures which indicate attitudes toward the absolutism-gradualism dimension.[13]

Table 5.4.9. *Absolutism vs. gradualism: indications of 'cognitive*
absolutism' as related to structural position (1967 responses
in all groups

	E	O	P
Disarmament within year 2000:			
total disarmament	2	2	13
more armaments	10	12	25
War within year 2000 (WWIII):	3	7	12
The rich-poor gap within year 2000:			
closed	0	2	26
has resulted in a war	8	9	12

What Table 5.4.9 really shows is the tendency, which increases with structural position, toward more dispersion in the direction of absolitistic perceptions; this tendency is seen in all the five rows presented. The public is more inclined than higher strata to perceive *either* the Big catastrophe *or* the 'Heaven on earth'.

Turning to the affective component of absolutism-gradualism – and this component is naturally the most interesting and perhaps inportant – the picture is more diffuse. What is included in the set of variables presented in Table 5.4.10, is the time, the domain and the scope dimensions. It was shown above that the elite very clearly was gradualistic on all the three variables. From what has been found above on the general difference between the groups, we expect that the two other groups also will be gradualistic *more than* absolutistic, which is also confirmed.

Table 5.4.10. *Absolutism vs. gradualism: indications of 'affective' gradualism*

Disarmament should be done:	E 1967	O 1967	P 1964
1. as rapidly as possible	23	32	29
carefully and step-wise	59	58	67
2. over the whole or most of the world at once	42	30	63
in some chosen areas to begin with	46	55	33
3. with all weapons as fast as possible	14	5	20
with some weapons to begin with and then stepwise	75	85	75
(n)	(72)	(130)	(1000)
average % gradualistic response:	60.0	66.0	58.3*
average ratio of gradualistic/absolutistic responses:	3.0	6.9	2.2

*) That this score is so relatively high almost equalling E's, is due to the fact that an ambivalent value was used in our study for E and O, while so such middle category was used for P.

In only one case – public on the second question – is there a preference for the absolutistic alternative, while the elite on that same item is almost equally divided between the two alternatives. The opinion-makers on this set of variables are the most gradualistic, although the difference for instance between elite and opinion-makers is not very great, as the average ratios may indicate. This was not expected. We offer one explanation. In the two last variables there is an aspect of balance thinking: you should take the whole world and all weapons, if not there may be some danger of 'cheating' or insecurity from the fact that *some* areas and weapon categories are 'thinned out', while others are left 'un-touched'. This argument is supported by responses on a question about the advisability of thinning out or disarming certain zones militarily (cf. 4.4): 54% of the opinion-makers, against 44% of the elite, were positive to this idea.

H20.3: *Authoritarianism increases with increasing structural position*

As shown in 4.4., by authoritarianism we are primarily thinking of attitudes toward the international system, but as it may be expected that there is a kind of 'generalized authoritarianism', we included even some variables on the national system for control purposes. The hypothesis is tested by means of a number of variables, on some of which are given both acceptance and rejection response percentages (cf. Table 5.4.11).

There is very satisfactory support for the hypothesis. While the relationship between the opinion-makers and the public is disputed by the public opinion being more authoritarian than the opinion-makers on two of the four variables on which there are public opinion responses, the position of the elite relative to the other two is quite clear. The general trend that the elite is more authoritarian, which is our hypothesis, is reversed in only one of the ten cases (on the variable 'Increased influence for the smaller countries is important to peace'). And even this one exception may be interpreted as not unfavorable to the hypothesis, since the higher strata may well nurse aspirations of upward mobility on behalf of their country – a small country – *and thus themselves*. To this problem of influence and mobility aspirations we now turn.

H20.4: *Feelings of 'over-achievement' and thus moderate mobility aspirations are more prominent the higher is the structural position*

Table 5.4.11. *Authoritarianism and structural position*

A.	E	O	P
Disarmament depends on the great powers	81	65	48
Disarmament agreements demand much inspection in their implementation	86	68	77
More influence for the smaller countries is important to peace	55	52	48
The great power veto in the UN should be maintained	59	34	–
Weighted voting systems should be introduced in the UN	33	32	–
International governmental organization leaders should be pointed out by democratic elections*			
should	16	27	–
should not	70	48	–
International governmental organizations should be given supranational power over the inhabitants of member states	70	63	–

166

Table 5.4.11. (*cont.*)

	E	O	P
B.			
People i.e. the public at large should in general have more influence over foreign policy†			
should	33	41	36
should not	55	32	40
To raise and educate individuals to peace is important to peace in world	90	81	70
Political leaders should be taught to behave more peacefully			
should	29	49	
should not	44	20	

*) The question was: 'Do you agree or disagree with the principle or idea that the leaders of an international governmental organization of which we are or are going to be members, should be elected by the peoples in the member countries through direct.elections?'

†) The questions in the public opinion study (1964) was about politics in general, or national public affairs, not particularly foreign policy.

Again only one single variable is available for a clearcut testing of the hypothesis (cf. 4.4). We feel, however, that this one variable gives a reliable picture of the feelings of 'over-achievement' in the various social strata under study. Although mobility aspirations cannot be immediately read out of the responses on this variable, they do give a good indication of such attitudes. As is done above, responses on the question of personal mobility aspirations are included in the Table 5.4.12, which shows the responses.

Table 5.4.12. '*Over-achievement*' *and mobility aspirations* (1967 *data*) *in the elite, opinion-maker, and public opinion samples*

Norway's influence in today's international system is:	E	O	P	Do you personally want more influence on Norway's foreign policy?:	E	O	P
less than it should be	7	5	52	yes	48	58	47
about as may be expected	42	56	44	somewhat more	3	13	–
more than may be expected	44	25	0	no, I am satisfied	39	20	50
DK/NA	7	14	4	DK/NA	10	9	3
	100	100	100		100	100	100
	(88)	(130)	(539)		(88)	(130)	(539)

Looking at the macro-level variable only, our hypothesis gets good support. We note that the perception of over-achievement is totally absent in public, which shows a slight majority for the 'under-achievement' notion. The difference between the elite and the public here is almost dramatically large: in fact, their images of Norway's position in the international system seem to be quite opposing. Who is the closer to 'reality' is an interesting question and could possibly be answered by having other, third party or foreign, evaluations on the issue.

What public opinion seems to say is that the high up strata, representing the country abroad, should work to get Norwegian policies more heard, more influential, while especially the elite is saying that there is nothing more to be done: their voice *is* heard and their role *is* that of a relatively influential actor. Some respondents even express surprise that Norway's influence *is* that high. Other seem to explain moderate influence by referring to Norway (= its elite) being already agreed with those (= Euroamerican elites) whom she want to influence.

What is important to us however is not whether the public opinion is misinformed about Norway's actual performances, or whether the elite is exaggerating them. The important thing is that differences in opinion exist and that they seem to be related to social structure in the way which was hypothesized.

H20 5: *A feeling of we-ness or center solidarity is most prominent in the elite and least in the public*

The hypothesis by implication seems to present another hypothesis, namely, that what we have called other-ness – the logical opposite end of the we-ness – other-ness continuum – is most prominent in the public. This is however, probably not so; at least we do not think such a hypothesis very fruitful. The problem has to do with relations to the outside, foreign world – the international environment. It certainly has to do with 'internationalism' in the very unprecise sense of the term. Thus it is believed that the elite will be both more we-ness *and* more other-ness oriented than the public, from the simple fact that elite has far more interaction with, knowledge about and internalized favorable attitudes toward the outside world than the public, and both the n-1 (Norway being the one) countries in the 'we' group and the 'other' are outside.

Operationally, we-ness was defined above as positive attitude toward center actors, while other-ness is expressed by positive attitude to periphery actors. In both cases, actors of course are international actors.

We shall look at these two aspects separately, since it is suggested that they do not constitute opposite ends on one and the same dimension. It was shown above that elite attitudes to the Soviet Union were said to be 'sophisticatingly' positive (cf.4.3). Unfortunately, we have not obtained the same kind of data for the other two groups. It is therefore impossible to give a good measure of feelings toward the 'we-they' reference group, of the effect of centrism on relations to the 'big opposite number' at lower social strata. We do have some indications, however, which seem to point to a not inconsiderable amount of positivism toward the Soviet Union in the Norwegian public.

In a nation-wide 1964 survey, Russians ranked above Italians and far above Negroes as acceptable marriage partners for Norwegian girls.[14] In the same year, a question was asked whether Norway should have relations in sports competitions with several politically criticized countries; relations with the Soviet Union were clearly more acceptable than relations with both Spain and South Africa.[15]

This relative Soviet positivism in Norwegian public opinion is more due to admiration than love. In 1960, Soviet ranked number one in the Norwegian public as the most successful country in the 50s, and in 1946 the Russians were believed to have contributed most to the allied victory over Germany. Norwegian polls after the WWII also show a relatively high degree of symmetry in the evaluation of the super powers.[16]

On the other hand, the USSR is still a strongly negative reference group to many Norwegians. In 1963, people were asked who or what they considered the greatest threat of war; 20% answered they believed the Soviet Union was the greatest danger – and this was also the number one response.[17] This score is clearly greater than it would be in the elite, although elite responses were taken four years after and the public opinion might have changed toward more positivism in the meantime.

From all this we may conclude that there *is* at the public opinion level a tendency to include the Soviet Union – although in the 'we-they' framework – in the 'we' group, and that this tendency probably is due to what we have called the 'centrism effect'. A certain 'anti-Communism' or fear in some parts of the public and especially in periods of great international stress may push the Soviet into the 'they' group, and the *negative* 'they' group. But insofar as such attitudes still are salient – and they *are* – they seem to be removed from Communist Soviet to Communist China, which now to most Norwegians with an opinion on this probably is the most prominent member of the negative 'they' group.

In Table 5.4.13, various items on which we have comparable responses

Table 5.4.13. *We-ness and structural position*

		E	O	P
More Western contact with the East is important to peace		89	87	87
East-West negotiations in security matters should be conducted	multilaterally	35	18	
	both/ambival.	26	53	
	bilaterally	31	25	
Certain geographical areas or zones should be demilitarized or neutralized for disarmament or arms control purposes:	agree	44	51	
	ambivalent	17	15	
	disagree	28	30	
Preferred level of contact with East is	T	36(3)	28(3)	(3)*
	M	53(2)	65(1)	(2)
	B	62(1)	54(2)	(1)
Greatest personal feeling of loyalty to:	Euroamerica	30	24	17
	Europe	2	5	0
	Rich/Northern† (We) countries	47	47	51
Average percentage of positive response to NATO and EEC		85	72	53
Rich countries should cooperate more between themselves vis a vis the less developed countries/should extend help to them in their own interest‡		22	6	

*) These figures, in brackets, represent the ranking of the preference of the levels in each group. The rankings of the public opinion sample are done from responses obtained in a national survey made by the Norwegian Gallup agency in September 1968. Asked if they thought that relations between Norway and the Soviet Union should be cut off in three specifically mentioned fields, responses were:

	State visits (T)	Cultural cooperation (M)	Sports (B)
Should be cut off	57	47	42
Should not be cut off	39	48	53
NA/DK	4	5	5
	(n = 1624)		

To let 'Cultural cooperation' represent the middle level here is not in accordance with the procedure of classification used in the case of the elite and the opinion-maker samples, where cultural cooperation was classified as 'Bottom level' activity. However, it is felt that it is more 'elevated' and thus may be separated from sports.

†) This category includes 'Euroamerica', 'Europe', and 'The Nordic countries'.

‡) These responses were obtained as two among several others on an open question which ran: 'How do you think that the developed countries should act or what attitude should they take in relation to the less developed countries concerning the gap between them and the problems of development?'

for the elite and the opinion-maker samples, are presented. They focus on the degree of we-ness in the different strata, but also give some indications on the 'we-we' and the 'we-they' aspects of the concept.

Our hypothesis is here clearly supported, although the data given in the Table do not discriminate as do those which were presented in the next above, between the elite and the public.

As to the position of opinion-makers, this seems not very different from that of the elite, although we see from the second to the fourth (from the top) items in the Table that the opinion-makers are somewhat more 'we-they'-oriented than the elite, as they respond more positively to these three items. The elite clearly is the most 'we-we'-oriented. From the final item in Table 5.4.13 the opinion-makers may seem more other-ness oriented than the elite, a suggestion to which we now turn.

Table 5.4.14. *Other-ness and structural position*

		E	O	P
Norway's official development assistance to the less developed countries should				
	be increased	81	85	11
	remain as now	15	13	42
	be reduced	1	0	12
	be ended	0	1	21
'If a less developed country asked Norway for our help in building up a merchant marine, do you think we should give such help?'	yes	65	72	36
	rather not	18	12	–
	no	10	6	53
'The less developed countries have asked for customs duty preferences for some of their products. Are you prepared to grant them that?'	yes	44	63	24
	perhaps	27	22	–
	no	13	4	66
The less developed countries should cooperate more in relation to the rich countries to their own interest*		18	33	
Index of the three development assistance items:				
	all three accepted	34	49	[8]†
	two accepted- two negative	55	45	[30]
	all three rejected	5	1	[45]

*) The question was: 'How do you think the less developed countries should act or what attitude should they take in relation to the developed countries concerning the gap between them?'

†) These scores are arbitrary, but close to findings reported in another study on the same sample. See text.

Our only comparable information on the public opinion on the other-ness dimension, is the set of development assistance items.[18] On the whole, however, they should give a good and a valid measure of attitudes on this dimension. On the relationship between the elite and the opinion-makers, which interests us most in this context, we have a few more variables appropriate for testing the hypothesis that the opinion-makers show greater other-ness than the elite. (Cf. Table 5.4.14).

We see that our suggestion or hypothesis about the relative 'other-ness' of the opinion-makers is confirmed. The role of the opinion-makers as an avant garde in the relationship with the less developed countries is again established. Generally, one may say that their role is to broaden the 'we-we' attitude, which seems to be predominant in the elite, and to a certain extent even in the public opinion.

5.5. 'Internationalism' and structural position

There is hardly any need to present much evidence for the hypothesis, H21 that *higher social strata are more 'internationalistic'* in the broad and un-precise meaning of the concept, *than lower ones.* Our own material, some of which is presented in Table 5.5.1, clearly shows that this is true.

Table 5.5.1. *Internationalism' and structural position*

	E	O	P
Norway should cooperate less with other countries*	0	0	9
Norway should not give aid to the less developed countries	0	1	21

*) From the question of which IGO or unit respondents felt greatest loyalty toward or had most in common with (Cf. Table 5.5.3).

'Isolationism', which seems to be a problem in some other countries, is relatively unproblematic, both in its affective and in its cognitive aspects, in Norwegian society. This may be further shown by a number of variables: Norwegians have relatively good knowledge of other peoples and of extra-national phenomena; one third of them can speak a non-Scandinavian language; and less than one third has never been abroad.[19]

a. *Supranationalism*. What we shall be concentrating attention on in this section, are the two (or three) sub-dimensions of 'internationalism': supra-nationalism, and regionalism vs. globalism. The hypothesis on structural differences on the dimension of supra-nationalism is

H22: *Supra-nationalism increases with structural position.*

National surveys made during the last years, although scant and with few indicators of this dimension, indicate that the Norwegian public is relatively supra-nationalistic. At least supra-national institutions are not perceived as *the* great danger in cooperation with other countries, as witnessed for instance by attitudes toward the EEC from the beginning of the 60-ies.[20]

The reason for this however, may very well be that this 'danger' has not been felt – is not very salient. Further, we must distinguish between the generalized supra-nationalistic or anti-supra-nationalistic attitude of people, and the more differentiated attitude. Thus, attitudes toward some regional supra-national institution may be negative, while the same person holds a positive attitude toward some other regional, or some global, institution. This differentiation was in fact made by some of our elite and opinion-maker respondents.

Public opinion surveys which have been carried out recently seem to indicate that supra-nationalism increasingly is being perceived as a threat, as witnessed by an increased opposition against Norwegian membership in the EEC. In particular, an impact by the perspectives raised by the socalled Werner plan and Davignon report seem to explain this development.[21]

Table 5.5.2. *'Supra-nationalism' and structural position*

	E	O	P
To establish the World State is important to peace	39	47	27
IGO's should have supra-national powers over the inhabitants of member states:			
yes	70	63	
no	14	13	
What do you think will promote international cooperation the most: supranational institutional cooperation, or functional cooperation?			
supra-national	29	34	
both	26	19	
functional	39	36	

As seen from Table 5.5.2, there is no difference between the elite and the opinion-makers on supra-nationalism. This conclusion may perhaps be qualified if we look at responses on the other dimension we shall focus on – regionalism vs. globalism. In fact this is our hypothesis

H23: *The elite is the more regionalistic, the opinionmakers the more globalistic among the social groups*

that their supra-nationalism takes different directions.

As in 4.6, the regionalistic vs. globalistic responses will be derived from two sets of information. The first set, which shows preferences when a forced choice is offered, is presented in Table 5.5.3.

Table 5.5.3. *Regionalism vs. globalism : the evidence of the forced choice variables*

	E	O	P
When it comes to the question what attitude we should primarily or principally adopt toward international cooperation endeavors – do you think that Norway should concentrate on the global or the regional fields?			
global	16*	30	
both/ambiv.	56	55	
regional	28	15	
NA/DK	0	0	
If you should state which international organization or unit you personally identify yourselves most closely linked with, would you then mention†			
The United Nations	41	36	28
NATO/Atlantica	20	16	17
Western Europe	11	8	–
The Nordic countries	15	18	34
Europe	2	5	0
Developing/non-align.	2	12	7
NA/DK/Other	9	5	14

*) In a follow-up question, the elite respondents who answered 'Both' in the first question were asked to indicate their preference if and when a choice between the two became necessary: 33% of these respondents (56% of the total 88) answered 'global', 36% regional, while 20% still thought a choice was unnecessary or unrealistic, and 11% did not answer. (Cf. Section 4.6).

†) The question in the public opinion sample from 1964 was: 'What do you think Norway should do today, should we establish closer ties with the Nordic countries, the NATO countries, the nonaligned and the developing countries, the socialist countries, the United Nations, or do you feel that Norway should participate less in international cooperation?'

Several observations should be made from Table 5.5.3. From the first question, our hypothesis seems to have received some backing. We note however, that the ambivalent or both-and score in both samples receives a majority: this is in fact proof that the so-called 'concentric theory of Norwegian foreign policy' has strong backing in the milieu.

If we extract responses on this global-regional dimension even from the second answer, making the 'UN' and 'Less developed countries' responses indications of globalism, we get although less pronounced, the same tendency: 48% of the opinion-makers against 43% of elite gives a 'globalistic' response, while 48% of elite and 47% of the opinion-makers are 'regionalistic'. The corresponding scores for public opinion would be 35% and 51%, making it the least 'globalistic'. But *is* the public at the same time the most 'regionalistic' of the groups?

We cannot answer this question without looking into the *content* of 'regionalism'. From Table 5.5.3 it is clear that the region the public opinion primarily has in mind, is the Nordic countries: Norway's neighbors. Combining responses for NATO and Western Europe and comparing the scores for this 'Euro-american' region with those of the Nordic, we get the following ratios (of Euro-american on Nordic response):

$$E: 2.0 \quad O: 1.3 \quad P: 0.5$$

This pattern is consistent with the one we found on Establishment.

If the public's choice from 1964 is compared with its choice between Nordic and European economic cooperation in 1957, there seems to have been a certain movement toward more Nordic positivism in the last years: then there was an even choice.[21] The two items of course may not be directly comparable and this may explain the difference over time. On the other hand, there might have been a drop in (Western) European preference due to the set-backs of EEC-EFTA relations from 1963 on with an effect lasting for some years, reaching a new setback after the second French veto against EEC entry *and* subsequent plans for extended Nordic cooperation. On the other hand, developments after 1969 and the renewed EEC offer of membership to among others Norway, may have changed the situation. As a direct result of this offer, the plans for Nordic economic cooperation were dropped and elite attention once more turned to Western European cooperation.

In 4.6, level preference was further explored by use of the peace proposal responses presented in 4.5. As we have complete information only on the elite and the opinion-makers, we cannot carry out the same kind of analysis here, for all three structural levels. We have to confine ourselves to twelve of the sixteeen peace proposals included in our study, because only these twelve were used in the 1967 public opinion study (the youth study). This means that there is no item to represent the 'intra-regional' level, which really was the one most preferred by the elite. Moreover, as parameter we shall have to use overall acceptance of the proposals, not the graded acceptance scores employed above.

The result (given in Table 5.5.4) still shows enough support for what we have found so far. The most prominent difference found in Table 5.5.4 is

Table 5.5.4. *Systemic level orientation and structural position. Average percentage of acceptance*

Level	No. of items	E	O	P
Global	(4)	75	76	69
(Inter-)regional	(3)	85	75	61
National	(3)	63	59	61
Individual	(2)	76	73	75
Average % acceptance of all items:	(12)	75.2	71.6	66.6

that between the groups on 'regionalism' – on preference for the regional or inter-regional level. Inter-group differences on the other three levels are not very great. But at this point we should take into account that the elite on the whole shows a higher acceptance than opinion-makers, and that the same is true with opinion-makers vis a vis the public. If this overall difference in acceptance, or in consensus (cf. 5.2) is corrected for, the picture of inter-group relations becomes clearer: the opinion-makers *are* the most 'globalistic', while the elite still is the most 'regionalistic'.

In assessing public opinion preferences, we should look at the columns, not the rows in the Table. By this operation we see that the public has a preference for the individual approach – to improve man himself or man-man relations. Reading the Table column-wise still leaves us with an elite preference for the inter-regional, and an opinion-maker preference for the global level (although the latter shows a very narrow predominance over the inter-regional and individual).

The conclusions to be drawn from the material presented in Tables 5.5.3 and 5.5.4 should thus be clear. First, there *are* differences in what 'circle' – if the socalled 'concentric theory' is applied – is to be preferred; although we may say nothing on how *strongly* these preferences are held, we may say that they *do* exist. Secondly, the public opinion seems to prefer the 'innermost' circle, while the opinion-makers go farthest out, leaving the elite in the in-between position. The elite circle is the Establishment circle, i.e. Euroamerica. Or, we may say that the opinion-makers are trying to pull the elite and actual Norwegian policies toward a more globalistic, a wider framework, while the public opinion is acting as a brake on the elite, trying to confine policies and preferences to the closer relationships. On the other hand, this public close-relationships preference is not necessarily 'isolationistic' or less worthy than the preferences of the other groups.

It should also be noted, and we make it a proposition for further study, that the tendency toward neutralism or non-aligment preferences – expressed by preference for Nordic cooperation and by loyalties to the less developed and the non-aligned countries – is inversely proportional with structural position.

As to level orientation, our conclusion – also tentative – is that *there is a tendency toward greater belief in the lower levels of the system, the lower is the structural position.* In other words: the 'individual man' approach to peace – and we may say to international relations in general – is most accepted relatively by the 'common man'.

c. *Regionalism and 'Westwardness'.* The two most important items on this dimension – opinions on membership in NATO and the EEC, the two Western cooperation set-ups which attract most attention – have been referred to already. The detailed responses are now given in Table 5.5.5.

Table 5.5.5. *'Westwardness' and structural position: opinions toward Norwegian membership in the NATO and the EEC*

		E	O	P*
Do you at the present time think that Norway after 1969 should stay in the NATO – or do you think that we should withdraw?	Should stay	86	60	52
	Should reconsider the membership/ both-and	7	22	22
	Should withdraw	5	17	20
	DK/NA	2	1	6
		100	100	100
		(88)	(130)	(1000)

*) On NATO membership, P responses are from 1964, while on EEC membership they are from July 1967, shortly after we completed our own data collection. The NATO response given here probably is a little too unfavorable, other polls show more positivism.

(cont. overleaf)

Table 5.5.5. (*cont.*)

		E	O	P*
On what conditions do you think that Norway should relate itself to the EEC?	As full member	84	83	54
	As associate member	6	1	–
	Should not relate itself to the EEC	5	14	21
	DK/NA	5	2	25
		100	100	100
		(88)	(130)	(1600)

From polls taken in the preceeding years, it seems clear that positive public opinion attitudes toward both NATO and the EEC have not increased, but this is most felt in the case of EEC memberships, where recent polls show a certain decrease of support.[23] On the other hand opposition for instance against NATO membership has remained very stable since the 50s, accounting for about $\frac{1}{3}$ of the total population (being against the membership in this organization). This percentage was found even after Czechoslovakia August 1968, which had a rather strong effect on the Norwegian public. Again, these events raised the percentage in favor of membership to a peak 72%, but this increase then was 'taken' from the prior Don't Know's or the ambivalent. We would expect that this increase over some time will have dropped to the 'natural' level of support which could be around $\frac{2}{3}$ of the population.[24]

It has been shown that the two items are moderately related, as we found a .30 correlation between them in the case of the elite. While the opinion-makers in a number of cases, reported above, have shown higher correlation in the 'expected' cases, than the elite, the opposite is true in this case: the correlation for the opinion-maker sample between NATO and EEC responses, is. 21. This should indicate that the elite is more polarized into a 'multi-issue conflict' than the opinion-makers, in the sense that one specific opinion value (positivism) on one item tends to imply the same opinion value on the other item. There is no buffer, no strong group of respondents taking an intermediate or overlapping position. And we do in fact find a somewhat higher number of intermediates among the opinion-makers when the NATO and the EEC responses are cross tabulated (cf. 4.6). On the other hand, it is of course correct to say that the elite is not so much polarized *as* it is *integrated*: the 'pole of opposition' on NATO and EEC is not numerically strong; acceptance of these organizations on the contrary is high, which is a sign of strong integration

C. *Globalism*. Information on public opinion again is scarce or not comparable to that obtained in our study. However, in national surveys from 1947 to 1967, positive public opinion attitudes toward the UN show an increasing trend: in 1967 a total of 79% thought that the world organization had lived up to, fully or partially, expectations to it, while only 15% said that it had not.[25] This score is exceptionally high and indicates the general UN positivism in Norway. And in this very general form there is probably not very much less positivism in the public than in the elite or the opinion-maker groups.

In Table 5.5.6, only three of the variables included give responses for the public. It seems, however, safe to conclude that the public on these more *specific* items is less positive than the elite and the opinion-makers toward the UN and thus less 'globalistic'. On the other hand, it seems equally safe to say that public opinion is *more* positive than negative toward the world organization, and that the ratio here is at least as large as in the case of 'Euro-american' organizations, probably larger. The peace-keeping forces and the idea of Norwegian participation in them was thus accepted by as much as 70% of the population as early as in 1957 – a score quite unusual for such a new item.[26] Clearly the general UN positivism made this possible but also the feeling of Norwegian 'responsibility' for 'cleaning up the mess', reported above.

Table 5.5.6. *'Globalism' and structural position. Attitudes toward the UN*

	E	O	P
To strengthen the UN is important to peace	96	89	87
Greatest loyalty to or preference for the UN	41	36	28
There have been made several proposals as to which functions the UN should be given the authority to perform – in the short or in the long run. Would you personally approve of disapprove of the UN having the right to:* tax the member countries to be able to finance its activities	2.0	12.3	–
control that the outer space is not being used for military purposes	29.0	47.0	–
carry out a plan for general disarmament	7.1	14.5	–
dispose of the polar areas, the open seas and the ocean floor	1.1	1.5	–
dispose of parts of the national armies of the standing military forces of member countries	7.1	7.0	3.4

Table 5.5.6. (*cont*).

	E	O	P
Index of last five items as a measure of UN positivism (percentages):			
1: positive to all five items	19	38	–
2–3: positive to four items/positive to three and negative to one	36	46	
4–5: negative to two or three items	21	11	
6: positive to none/negative to four or to all items	3	1	
NA/DK	21	4	
Average (mean) percentage approval of the 5 items	62.6	77.8	

*) Ratios for approval/disapproval of the proposed items are taken.

The conclusions which may be drawn from Table 5.5.6 are essentially two. First, that the opinion-makers on the whole are more 'globalistic' than the elite, which we hypothesized. Secondly, and this is a modification of the conclusion just drawn, the support of the elite for the UN is more general, more 'rhetoric' and less committed, while that of the opinion-makers on the other hand is more specific and more committed. This becomes particularly evident when we separate the first two items listed in Table 5.5.6 from the five concrete proposals: the elite ranks higher on the former, the opinion-makers very clearly so on the latter, with one exception where scores are even.

We have taken ratio of approval to disapproval of the five concrete proposals in order to control for the differences in NA responses. For all five items, there is a percentage average of NA or DK responses of 14.6 for the elite, 4.8 for the opinion-makers. The NA score for the elite is particularly great in the case of the index, largely due to one item only (polar areas, etc.) The difference in NA scores, however, cannot make up for all the difference in positivism which the index and the ratios show very clearly.

5.6. *Future expectations: the evidence of optimism*

The hypothesis has been tentatively proposed that

H24: *Optimism increases with structural position.*

Some evidence of future thinking has already been given in 5.4, notably in Tables 5.4.5 and 5.4.6. On what was called catastrophe thinking, the conclusion was made that the higher the structural position, the less concern there seems to be about possible threats to the system.

We have some more items to present on this problem, and we do have information on the public opinion in these items. In Tables 5.6.1 and 5.6.2, two sets of cognitive variables presenting expectations of future developments along several dimensions, are compiled. The first set contains a variety of such variables. The second one shows expectations about the consequences of disarmament.

From Table 5.6.1, we see very clearly that the elite is the most optimistic among the groups: this is confirmed by each single one of the five variables presented, except in the case where ratio is taken on the 'war avoidance in general' item. The opinion-makers, while showing a more optimistic profile than the public opinion on the first three variables listed in the Table, look with less optimism on the prospects of disarmament. This is well in accor-

Table 5.6.1. *Optimism vs. pessimism: expectations of future development*

	E 1967	O 1967	P 1967
Norway's position will be better in general in the future than it is	79	47	36*
Ratio: Better/worse	11.2	4.7	3.3
War may generally be avoided	60	56	55†
Ratio: Yes/no	6.0	11.2	1.3
Man is the master of developments	76	66	55‡
Ratio: Yes/no	25.3	16.5	1.3
Within the nearest future,§ there will be:			
disarmament	39	21	35
stable armament level	34	51	21
more armaments	18	30	34‖
Within the year 2000, there will be:			
disarmament	59	24	48
armament level about as now	13	35	15
more armaments	8	12	25‖

*) From the 1964 study: the question was 'Do you think that in the years to come your living standard will increase, decrease or stay the same?' (% increase).

†) The question here was 'Do you think that man can learn how to avoid war, or is it not in man's power to prevent war?'

‡) The question ran: 'Do you expect your own future to be determined largely by what you yourself make of it or by external circumstances over which you have little control?' (First alternative used as parameter.)

§) 'Nearest future' = 'Within 10–15 years' in the E/O study, 'Within 20 years' in the P study.

‖) If the response category 'War', which somewhat illogically was used at the armament end of the disarmament-armament continuum in the public opinion study, is included, responses of P become even more pessimistic (cf. Table 5.4.5).

dance with opinion-maker evaluations of disarmament possibilities: 49 % of them, against 33 % of the elite, believes that general disarmament in the nearest future is unrealistic. On the other hand, the public is declaredly more pessimistic in this respect. In other words: it shows the diffuse, absolutistic image exposed above, while opinion-makers stick to the middle-of-the-road line, is *moderately* optimistic *and* – pessimistic. The second set of items (cf. Table 5.6.2) not only gives an indication of optimism, but also of what may be called the 'belief in panaceas' of the different groups. Disarmament here is seen as a *means* to obtain certain aims.

Table 5.6.2. *Optimism vs. pessimism: the 'belief in panaceas'*

	E	O	P
1. One should start disarming in order to create trust	22	45	46
One should first create trust and then start disarming	50	37	48
2. The economic differences in the world could be evened out if all disarmed	12	24	29
The economic differences will continue to exist even after disarmament	74	66	65
3. Disarmament will create greater stability and peace-keeping possibilities	42	40	42
Serious conflicts may arise even if there were complete disarmament*	36	35	47

*) The response alternatives used in the 1964 study for P were, respectively: 'Do you think that the relationship between the nations would be changed by a general and total disarmament?', and 'Do you think serious conflicts could arise in a disarmed world?'

The conclusions to be drawn from Table 5.6.2 are clearly different from those drawn on the basis of Table 5.6.1. The trend seems to be quite reversed, as the elite is the more pessimistic, the opinion-makers the most optimistic in two of the three cases. This must be explained by the difference in the very nature of the two sets of variables we have employed to measure optimism-pessimism: one thing is expectations for the future, another thing evaluations of the effect of concrete measures which are expected. What the elite seems to say is that the world will change for the better and there will even be disarmament, but one should not expect very much *more* than that.

Is the relative optimism on the part of the elite due to the fact that this group, which counts so many policy-makers or *responsables, has* to show belief in the future of the system which it itself (at least to some extent, and together with other elites) will be creating? This seems rather plausible. But then elite disbelief in the panaceas is all the more natural: on the one hand they *have* to show belief that the system (which is to be managed by themselves) will improve; on the other hand they have to be the 'realists' who can see the complexity of things and can warn against over-optimism and too great demands or expectations from those not in charge.

The opinion-makers, on the other hand, believe that much could be achieved through disarmament *if* it only was carried out; that is, however, not what they believe or expect will happen.

This really amounts to an indirect *dialog* between the elite and the opinion-makers, which may also be found in other connections. The opinion-makers may have strong preferences, may put forth concrete proposals which may deviate rather strongly form those of the elite; as has been said *passim*, the role of an avant garde, of initiator, of proposal-carrier, is that of the opinion-makers particularly in their relationship with the elite. But since the elite is going to decide which means will be adopted, what proposals attempted, *and* is going to implement them, and since this role of the elite is well known to the opinion-makers, they are not very optimistic about what will actually be done.

The elite message to their opinion-making *critici,* on the other hand, is that they should not press too much, go too far, expect too much or be too far-fetched in what they propose.

6. Elite Consensus:
The Extent of Inter-Group Conflicts

The purpose of this chapter will not be to present all the relevant material which could be said to 'deserve' presentation in this context. We will be analyzing inter-group similarities and differences by limiting ourselves to the various hypotheses developed in Chapter 3.

The reader will find, however, that certain topics or issue-areas will be taken up in all or most of the sections which follow, e.g. degree of centrism, consensus and agreement problems, and various aspects of internationalism. What will be attempted is to restrict as much as possible both the quantitative evidence presented and the comments which accompany it.

Before proceeding, we present an answer to two, related questions. First, what is the relative strength i.e. *discriminatory power* of the independent variables employed? Secondly, what are the *relations* between these independent variables – how do they interact?

Both these questions have important theoretical relevance. The reason why they are taken up here is that we will answer them by use of empirical evidence; thus, they naturally should be related to the data part of our report. On the other hand, answers to the questions will have to be considered and if necessary incorporated, in passing from theory to the empirical testing of hypotheses, which follows.

6.1. *Variable effect*: *the discriminatory power of independent variables*

The independent variables to be analyzed are those presented, i.e. sample category or institutional affiliation, age, party preference, Establishment-outsider preferences, and social position. Personal assessment of foreign policy making influence, taken up as an independent variable at the end of this chapter, was left out of this part of the analysis.

The method employed is a trivariate analysis where all possible combinations of two independent variables (among the total five) are run against a third, dependent variable. The total number of such dependent variables used in our analysis is 10; the four Establishment variables are included.[1] The total number of combinations of independent variables is $\binom{5}{2}$, i.e. 10.

Analysis was according to the *multivariate percentage analysis method*.[2] As parameter we used the percentage of a given group or category responding with one specific answer, i.e. the group modal value. The distribution on the dependent variable, as expressed by this percentage, is seen as *a function of the combination of the two independent variables* in all possible cases of combination between them, when each independent variable is treated separately. Each trivariate run produced a table where the total number of entries represented these cases of combination.

The variance in each of the possible combinations is given by the greatest difference in percentage found between any two entries in the column and the row, which give the variance of each independent variable when the other independent variable is kept constant.

An mean percentage differences is then taken for each of the independent variables by calculating the mean difference on all the dependent variables. This procedure is exemplified in Table 6.1.1, which gives the results in

Table 6.1.1. *Social position and sample category against attitude toward economic sanctions. Elite sample only: the total matrix*

| Social position | Sample category | Economic sanctions | | | | | | | |
		1 Pos.	2 Amb.	3 Neg.	4 Other	5	9 NA	Sum	(n)
1 P	1 PO	61.1	11.1	27.8	0	0	0	100.0	(18)
1 P	2 AD	33.3	33.3	0	33.3	0	0	99.9	(3)
1 P	3 MM	42.9	28.6	28.6	0	0	0	100.1	(7)
1 P	4 IO	85.7	0	14.3	0	0	0	100.0	(7)
2 M	1 PO	20.0	60.0	20.0	0	0	0	100.0	(5)
2 M	2 AD	50.0	20.0	10.0	20.0	0	0	100.0	(10)
2 M	3 MM	57.1	0	42.9	0	0	0	100.0	(7)
2 M	4 IO	44.4	44.4	0	0	11.1	0	99.9	(9)
3 C	2 AD	11.1	33.3	44.4	0	0	11.1	99.9	(9)
3 C	3 MM	57.1	28.6	14.3	0	0	0	100.0	(7)
3 C	4 IO	33.3	16.7	33.3	0	0	16.7	100.0	(6)
Total		47.7	22.7	22.7	3.4	1.1	2.3	99.9	(88)
		(42)	(20)	(20)	(3)	(1)	(2)	(88)	

185

percentage of the trivariate analysis i.e. *all* entries; and in Table 6.1.2, which presents the percentage differences and the mean percentage differences *when* the greatest possible percentage difference only is calculated, as explained above. The example is a trivariate analysis where social position and sample category are run against attitude toward economic sanctions, in the case of the elite sample.

The analysis now is done by means of the percentages in the left-hand column of the Table, *in casu* the percentages of positive attitude toward economic sanctions. We find the variance, or the percentage difference, for the sample categories by keeping social position constant, and vice versa. In Table 6.1.2, we have indicated between what entries the greatest percentage difference is found, in parentheses.

Table 6.1.2. *Variance (mean percentage difference) for social position and sample categories in trivariate runs against attitude toward economic sanctions. (See also Table 6.1.1).*

	Variance for social position: sample category is kept constant	Variance for sample category: social position is kept constant
	41.1 % (P − M)*	52.4 % (AD − IO)
	38.9 % (M − C)	37.1 % (PO − MM)
	14.2 % (M/C − P)	46.0 % (AD − MM)*
	52.4 % (P − C)	
Mean percentage difference:	38.9 %	45.2 %

*) The combination C/PO, or center politicians, was lacking, i.e. no respondents fell into this category.

As indicated by this single run only, sample category shows greater variance on the average than social position: it seems to have greater discriminatory power on attitudes toward economic sanctions. As we shall see later, the 'power' which sample category 'holds over' social position in this respect holds true for the total number of ten dependent variables explored.

The mean difference for each of the independent variables in combination with another independent variable, is then compared by calculating the *ratio* between them. According to these ratios, a *ranking* of the independent variables may be made which indicates their *partial effect,* i.e. the effect of each independent variable on the number of (or all) dependent variables when the independent variables are combined, but treated separately. This ranking may also be graphically presented as in Figure 7. The arrows indicate the relationship between the variables (in combination); the ratios are attached: the first (left) one is the ratio for the elite, the second one for the opinion-maker sample.

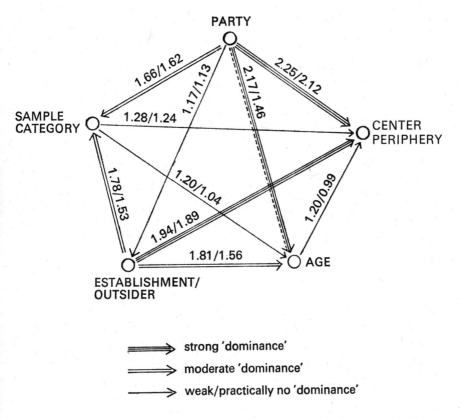

Fig. 7. *Relationship*
between independen variables according to their discriminatory effect

The *ranking* one may derive from this graph, the ratios in both samples taken into consideration, would be the following:

I   Party affiliation
     Establishment-outsider
II   Sample category
(III) Age
     Center-periphery (social position)

The most convincing pattern is the *dominance* over the remaining three variables of the party and the Establishment-outsider variables. Another result which comes out clearly is the bottom ranking of the center-periphery and the age variables. This seems to confirm very well our assumptions that these variables do not account for much of the variance in the kind of samples we are studying.

The ratios for the opinion-maker sample are lower than that of the elite in all ten cases but are at the same time very similar. This means that the variables in the former (one case of the elite) interact less than in the latter. Or: polarization tendencies are less prominent in the elite. Another pattern which emerges is the much stronger effect of the age variables in the opinion-maker sample; it is especially seen in the party-age combination, where age does very well against this generally influential variable in the case of the opinion-makers. Age then accounts for more in this sample; this is even shown by the fact that it 'matches' the sample category, but on the other hand contradicted by the fact that it fares less well against the center-periphery variable, which is contrary to the general pattern.

Against the type of analysis we have made here, one may on the basis of 'Norwegian realities' object that if the leftist and deviationist groupings (the Communists and the Socialist People's Party) were kept out, the party effect would be much less prominent. To check such a possibility, we made an analysis which omitted these groups from the party variable. The analysis then was not made on the principle of the greatest possible difference in the row and the column. Instead, two values (i.e. party groups) were chosen on the variable on which variance was analysed and the differences between these two when combined with all possible values on the other independent variable (kept constant) were taken.

This analysis, which on the party variable used the difference between the Labor and the Conservatives (and on the other variables used a pair of values which we believed would show the greatest difference possible on that variable) in fact gave the same result: *the party variable outranked all the other four independent variables* (in about the same ranking order as from the initial analysis) *in effect*.

6.2. *Relations between the independent variables*

The next problem to be taken up before we proceed to the presentation of data and the testing of hypotheses, is the question: *how* and *to what extent* do the independent variables interact and *influence each other* when no third (dependent) variable is considered?

This is a question of correlations or of how the five independent variables are distributed on each of the other four. Distributions may create a certain bias, particularly in the case where a variable with strong effect (party) is very unevenly distributed on a variable with weak effect (center-periphery) to the extent that the variance of the latter on a dependent variable in fact is determined by the former.

Another relevant question is whether it is fruitful to use both the party and the Establishment-outsider variable, since the two may be expected to correlate rather positively with each other. This is in fact the case, but the correlations as expressed by Pearson correlation coefficients, are only moderately positive: .18 for the elite, .14 for the opinion-maker sample. This indicates that the two variables *should* be treated separately.

We shall leave the Establishment-outsider variable out of this discussion, since it will be dealt with rather extensively in the following sections. We shall mainly occupy ourselves with relationships between the party and the sample category variables on the one hand, and their respective relationship with the remaining variables, on the other hand. From 6.1, it is evident that special attention should be paid to how the party variable interacts with the other independent variables, which for the purpose of this analysis are seen as dependent ones.

Variable A may be said to have potential influence on variable B if the values of A 1. has a highly scattered or skewed distribution on B, and 2. has more discriminatory power than B.

The *party* variable seems to have some influence on the *sample category* variable, in both samples. In the elite sample, half of the parliamentarian or Politician group belongs to the Labor party, which in fact is quite purposive, as sampling in this case was made according to party distribution in the Parliament. In the opinion-maker case, half of the Mass Media and nearly half of the Education samples are Liberals, which, assuming that the Liberals occupy more or less a middle position among the party groups, should not create too much bias. It is worth noting in that respect that the Interest organization category is by 42% both samples made up of Conservatives.

The *party-age* relationship shows no particularly uneven distributions, except that 44% of the oldest category is Labor, in the elite case. On the other hand, half of the Labor and the Socialist People's party group in the opinion-maker sample is of the youngest category, which *may* be of some significance as age in the case of the opinion-maker sample has relatively strong discriminatory power.

As to *party-social position* relations, there should be more influence as

189

half of the periphery group is Labor, half of the middle group is Conservative as far as the elite sample is concerned; and nearly half of the center category is Conservative in the case of the opinion-makers. Considering the relatively weak discriminatory power of social position, party *should* have some effect on this variable.

Looking at relations between *sample category* and *age*, half of the oldest in the elite, but half of the youngest in the opinion-maker sample comes from the Politician category, which in fact shows a striking difference in the age composition of this category between the two samples. Among the opinion-makers, nearly half of the oldest age category is of the Interest organizations category. Sample category and *social position* relations are marked by the complete absence of elite Politicians in the center (cf. 6.1), and a corresponding very strong influx of Politicians in the periphery category. We should also note that the Civil servants (elite only) are relatively 'center-oriented', while the Interest organization category occupies that position in the case of the opinion-makers. In this sample, the Politicians strongly resemble their elite counterparts in that they account for 47 % of the periphery category.

Most the uneven distributions reported above have been on the level of a 50 % of the group concerned falling into one single value or category on another variable. There certainly are higher scores, or higher modal values, to be found and thus more uneven distribution, but they do not have the importance of those reported so far. That e.g. a 100 % of the Christian/ Center party category in the elite, and 72 % in the opinion-maker sample come from the Politician category does not have any serious consequences to our analysis, because these parties in both samples do count only a small number of respondents and thus will not be subject to rigorous study, and because the unevenness is found on a variable with less discriminatory power than the party variable. Most of the other very uneven distributions found also are due to the Christian/Center party, or the Socialist People's/Communist party categories.[3]

6.3. *Sample category comparisons*

In the first place, we want to test the assumption that

H25: *The civil servants category is a communication nucleus within the elite, both in terms of within- and in terms of between-group communication.*

We shall test the hypothesis by looking at the structure of communication within the milieu.

a. *Communication structure.* The structure is primarily drawn by the flows of information and the trends in the personal contacts taken in foreign policy matters. Again we may show the flows and trends only as they are seen in the preferred information sources and preferred contacts as stated by the respondents themselves. Opinion-maker responses are included for validation and for comparative purposes.

In Table 6.3.1, preferred sources of information on international politics and foreign policy questions are shown by single and multiple response. Questions included both domestic (Norwegian) and foreign sources. Responses are collapsed according to certain criteria; this is shown in footnotes to the Table.

Several conclusions may be drawn from Table 6.3.1. First the elite is more oriented toward public sources of information than are the opinion-makers, a finding well in accordance with their recruitment and the roles they play.

On the other hand, there is a striking difference between on the one hand

Table 6.3.1. *Preferred source of information in the elite, opinion-makers and (elite) sample categories. Single and multiple responses.**

Norwegian source:	Elite		Op. makers		PO		AD		MM		IO	
	sr	mr	sr	mr	sr	mr	sr	mr	sr	mr	sr	mr
Public†	38	52	16	32	52	83	77	82	0	10	18	28
Semi-public	13	40	16	79	4	39	14	41	15	25	23	66
Non-public	43	102	66	152	26	91	9	87	57	97	46	133
NA/Other	6	6	12	12	18	18	0	0	28	28	13	13
	100	214	100	275	100	231	100	210	100	150	100	240
Foreign:												
Public‡	17	25	11	18	22	35	41	50	0	10	5	5
Non-public	54	95	64	112	31	57	46	87	90	148	55	96
NA/Other	29	29	25	25	47	47	13	13	10	10	40	40
	100	149	100	155	100	139	100	150	100	168	100	141
(n)	(88)		(130)		(23)		(22)		(21)		(22)	

*) Multiple response are calculated in the case of domestic (Norwegian) sources, on 3 responses, in the case of foreign sources on 2 responses only.

†) The response categories were collapsed as follows:
'Public' = Foreign service/Foreign minister/Foreign relations committee in the Storting.
'Semi-public' = Radio and/or TV; in Norway, these institutions are state-owned and monopolistic, but retain a certain independence from the state.
'Non-public' = Press/Special publications/Private organizations.

‡) The response categories in this case (foreign sources) were made up of:
'Public' = Diplomats/Politicians and civil servants 'Non-public' = Press/special publications/colleagues and/or friends.

the Politicians (PO) and the Civil servants (AD), and on the other hand the Mass media (MM) and the Interest organizations (IO): the former strongly prefer public sources of information, the latter the non-public ones.

But this means that the within-group communication seems to be very strong, particularly in the case of the Civil servants and the Mass Media people: a majority in both these groups seeks information primarily from own group. This tendency is particularly strong in the case of the Civil servants, and their preference must be interpreted as proof that they base themselves very much on the diplomatic channels of information plus their own ministry evaluations.

There is a certain sender-receiver relationship between on the one hand Civil servants and Politicians, the former being the source of public information to the latter; and on the other hand between the Mass media and the

Table 6.3.2. *Preferred group contact for foreign policy-making influence purposes: elite, opinion-makers and (elite) sample categories. Single and multiple response* *)

	Elite		Op. makers		PO		AD		MM		IO	
	sr	mr	sr	mr	sr	mr	sr	mr	sr	mr	sr	mr
Foreign minister/ the government members	31	36	23	31	26	34	41	46	19	29	32	32
The Storting/the foreign relations comm.	20	33	25	48	52	70	0	19	19	24	14	24
Party leaders†	13	29	14	22	9	52	9	9	10	20	23	32
Civil service	15	23	2	5	0	4	41	55	5	5	14	28
Mass media‡	13	17	18	33	9	13	5	5	39	49	5	10
Interest organizations	1	3	5	11	0	0	0	0	0	5	5	10
NA/DK/Other	7	7	8	8	4	4	4	4	8	8	7	7
	100	148	100	166	100	177	100	138	100	140	100	143
	(88)		(130)		(23)		(22)		(21)		(22)	

*) Multiple response is made on 2 responses.
†) This category might of course have been collapsed with one of the first two groups in the column, as it is to a large extent composed of, or recruiting, them; as it is difficult to assess, however, to which one of the groups it would be appropriate to add this one, it is listed separately.
‡) The most often found response in this category was one which stated that respondents would contribute an article, interview to the press making their case to the public.

192

Interest organization people, the former sending information to the latter. As the Politicians are considered one of the most policy-influential groups, at least on legitimizing policies, the role of the Civil servants as witnessed by the preferences of the Politicians helps support our hypothesis.

It is, however, not well supported if we take multiple response as an expression of between-group communication: the mass media and the interest organizations do not seem to be taking much information from the civil service, when multiple response is considered. Whether this is due to lack of esteem, *or* is rather due to lack of access, is difficult to say from the material we have, but it *may* be the latter.

Another indicator of the structure of communication is, as mentioned above, preferred channels of contact when the purpose is to exert maximum influence on the making of Norwegian foreign policy. Responses, both single and multiple, are shown in Table 6.3.2.

Preferences of elite and opinion-makers are rather similar on this variable. The opinion-makers are somewhat more in preference for the 'democratic' way of influence, i.e. through the parliament and through mass media.

Again, within-group communication comes out strongly: not only does each one of the four groups show a stronger preference for itself than other groups show – this is rather natural – but three of them (Interest organization people being the exception) rank themselves top among all groups. As indicated already (3.4 A), this may be due to evaluation of access, not ranking according to influence: the within-group contact is the easiest one. But the total elite ranking in Table 6.3.2 of preferred contacts corresponds exactly to the ranking obtained on another variable giving the evaluations of the respondents of the actual influence on policy-making of the various groups. Thus it is not only a question of access.

We note, from Table 6.3.2, that the Civil servants and the Politicians rank each other very low; even on double response the other group does not get much support. May this be taken as an indication of a certain competition between the two, a desire for maintaining a certain distance although (or because of) on information exchange they are close.[2] A number of people in both groups seem to think in terms of the 'non-political' civil service, whose task it is to collect, process and send information, but not to take decisions. Others, however, come closer to our own view of the handling of information as a key to policy-making influence.

From the material presented here, we are not able to say that our H 25 has been satisfactorily supported. More thorough investigations will have to be carried out on this problem.

b. *Consensus and Establishmentarianism.* We have put forth the following hypotheses on these issues for the sample category variable:

H26: *The civil servants and to a lesser extent the Politicians are Establishmentarian.*

H27: *The civil servants and the Politicians are the groups showing the highest consensus.*

In her study of the West German elite, reported above, Keller found that the politicians and the civil servants showed the highest average modal value scores among West German foreign policy sub-elites.[4] This finding was obtained by calculating mean acceptance of five specific items (cf. Table 5.1.3). We may compare the scores on the four Establishment items in our own elite sample with these results, although items are only partially corresponding and the position of the five items in the West German case as Establishment items is not at all certain as has already been indicated. Comparisons are made in Table 6.3.3.

Table 6.3.3. *Comparison of West German and Norwegian elite sample groups: European cooperation, and Establishment items respectively*

| | West Germany* | | | | | Norway | | | |
	PO	AD	MM	IO		PO	AD	MM	IO
Mean modal value in %	80	79	70	76		79	88	74	80

*) Figures taken from a table quoting Suzanne Keller's study, in Deutsch and Edinger, *Germany Rejoins the Powers.*

The Norwegian Civil servants clearly are strongly Establishmentarian, while the Politicians in contrast with their West German counterparts seem to be somewhat relaxing in their support, although not remarkably so.

Another interesting result – and there is a striking similarity between the two national elites in that respect – is the Mass Media score which shows a *relative* dis-Establishmentarian attitude in this group. Considering the role of the mass media in mobilizing public support for elite and Eastablishment policies, this attitude may have some consequence to public attitudes as well.

There is however, the question whether the Norwegian Mass Media dis-Establishmentarian score is somewhat spurious: the Mass Media group in the opinion-maker sample is the *most* Establishmentarian, showing a mean score of 86% on the four items, while the three other opinion-maker groups have means of about 73%. The opinion-maker Mass Media score, however, is probably more biased than the elite Mass Media score, because in the former group there is practically no leftist or Socialist respondent.

Another and probably better test of the hypothesis is obtained through the Establishment-outsider index; the results on this kind of analysis are shown in Table 6.3.4. The Civil servant strongly pro-Establishmentarian

Table 6.3.4. *Establishment and sample category: index scores*

	Elite				Opinion-makers			
	PO	AD	MM	IO	PO	ED	MM	IO
Establishment	48	64	38	55	48	32	50	31
Right outsiders	35	32	33	23	12	25	31	31
Doubters	13	0	14	9	22	29	13	22
Left outsiders	4	0	10	5	18	11	6	16
NA/DK	0	4	5	8	0	3	0	0
	100	100	100	100	100	100	100	100
	(23)	(22)	(21)	(22)	(40)	(28)	(16)	(45)

attitude is again confirmed, while the opinion-maker Mass Media Establishmentarianism is considerably modified. On the whole, it seems that the index confirms the picture drawn up by mean modal value scores. Except that the elite Politicians, i.e. the foreign relations committee, are somewhat less Establishmentarian than expected, our hypothesis has been satisfactorily confirmed.

Turning to H27, on consensus, our assumptions are well confirmed. In Table 6.3.5, average scores for corresponding modal values on the 48 items employed in previous sections (cf. 5.1–3) are shown for the elite group. The differences between the sample categories are not great, which stresses the strong tendency toward consensus in the Norwegian elite. On the other hand, there is inter-group disagreement of $> 20\%$ (between any two groups) on 22 of the 48 items, – 46% of the items. Considering the low group subtotals, however, this disagreement score is not very high. If the $> 30\%$ disagreement limit is applied, there is inter-group disagreement in only 21%

Table 6.3.5. *Consensus and sample category: elite average scores for corresponding modal values on 48 items*

	PO	AD	MM	IO
Average percentage scores for corresponding modal value on 48 items	67.4	69.4	63.7	65.0

of the cases. As disagreement scores of $> 20\%$ with such low sub-totals may occur randomly, thus making the $> 30\%$ limit more realistic, there *is* strong agreement between the sample categories.

Between the two Establishment-holders, the Civil servants and the Politicians, agreement is almost strikingly high: only 5 out of the total 48 items show a $\gtrsim 20\%$ disagreement between these two groups, that is only 10% of the cases. On only one single item there is more than 30% disagreement between them, while in *less* than 40% of the cases there is a $\gtrsim 10\%$ disagreement! This certainly is a very strong indication of the close connections which exist between these two communicators and policy-makers. These connections probably are one of the chief instruments in creating the Norwegian foreign policy consensus.

c. *Centrism.* The rather tentative hypothesis has been put forth that

H 28: *The Civil servants are the most centrist sample category.*

By use of most of the variables employed for the testing of centrism in 4.4 and 5.4, we shall briefly look into how the institutional groups or sample categories relate themselves to the centrism dimension.

On preference for the existing world order, the hypothesis seems to hold: the Civil servants are matched by the Mass Media people on the five variables testing attitude toward world order, but they are well above Politicians and Interest group people.

On both the gradualism vs. absolutism, and the authoritarianism dimensions, the Civil servants *and* the Mass Media people are the gradualists and authoritarian, while the other two groups although safely on the gradualistic and authoritarian side as well, are *relatively* absolutistic and egalitarian. There is on the six variables measuring authoritarianism a difference in mean acceptance percentages of nearly 10% between the Mass Media as the most authoritarian and the Politicians and the Interest group people as equally egalitarian.

The over-achievement and the we-ness versus other-ness aspects of centrism present a somewhat different picture. As is shown in Table 6.3.6, feelings of over-achievement seem much related to the status or position of the group concerned in the Norwegian foreign policy system: those who think that they themselves are influential, also believe that Norway on the international scene has maximized its influence. This will be even better seen in section 6.8.

The we-ness of the Civil servants, as hypothesized, comes out very

196

strongly from Table 6.3.7. And judging from the responses we are able to present, it seems that the Civil servants are *both* most we-they *and* we-we oriented among the categories: it is really *the* we-ness group in our sample, according to the definition of we-ness we have adopted.

In particular, the relatively strong preference the Civil servants show for top level contact with the Eastern countries is both remarkable, if only the first response is considered (cf. footnote to Table 6.3.7) and interesting. In

Table 6.3.6. *Perceptions of Norway's influence in the international system: over-achievement and the sample categories*

Norway's influence in the international system is	PO	AD	MM	IO
greater than may be expected	70	50	33	23
about as expected	26	41	38	64
less than it should have been	0	0	19	9
NA/DK/Other	4	9	10	4
	100	100	100	100
	(23)	(22)	(21)	(22)

Table 6.3.7. *We-ness and sample category*

		PO	AD	MM	IO
To increase contact with East is important to peace		90	87	89	89
Contact with Eastern	Top level	26	51†	39	28
Europe should pri-	Medium level	52	64	48	50
marily be sought at the:*	Bottom level	82	54	43	69
Soviet foreign policy	Positive	35	27	33	27
is primarily:	Negative	5	0	0	9
Personal loyalty first	Euroamerica	26	54	24	19
of all to:	All Europe	0	0	5	5
	Rich world/Northern	48	63	49	33
Average NATO/EEC acceptance		80	100	71	86
US foreign policy is	Positive	43	27	29	23
primarily:	Negative	9	0	10	14

*) Double response is included.

†) On the first response, which would give the 'first-on-the-mind' or top preference form of contact, this group chose by a strong 46% the top level form.

fact the Civil servants are the only group *defending* this form of contact: among the other groups, there are rather outspoken rejections of this form. Moreover, with the exception of the Mass Media people (when double response is considered) they show a low preference for it.

The explanation of the Civil servants' preference may be sought in the fact that top level contact is very much *their* contact, since they maintain it on a day-to-day basis through diplomatic relations and since they most often both plan and participate in top level visits. The reluctance of the Politicians, another potential participator in this form of contact, may perhaps be explained by this group not being familiar with the top contact, and perhaps a little bit 'suspicious' toward it. It should be noted that in the period just before this interview study was carried out, Norwegian top officials paid several visits to Eastern European countries. A number of elite members, including parliamentarians, seem to have been rather critical toward, or at least dubious of the value of these visits.

The other-ness responses are presented in Table 6.3.8. As pointed out above, we do not suggest any direct or necessary relationship between we-ness and other-ness in the sense that strong we-ness implies weak other-ness and vice versa. We expected that the fact that the Civil servants are relatively more exposed to the world at large, as is the Mass Media group, should make them relatively more other-ness oriented than other less exposed groups.

The results as presented in Table 6.3.8 do not give completely satisfactory support of this rather tentative hypothesis although the trend generally seems to be in favor of it. On the foreign aid attitude index, the Civil servants are *not* showing the most positive attitude, while the Mass Media is. On the

Table 6.3.8. *Other-ness and sample category*

		PO	AD	MM	IO
Foreign aid attitude index:*	1	22	32	52	32
	2–3	69	55	38	45
	4–5	9	5	5	9
	NA	0	8	5	14
Evaluation of nonaligned	Positive	39	50	43	23
countries' role is:	Negative	13	0	10	18
Opinion on the 'bargaining					
of less developed countries	Positive	21	32	10	14
is:	Negative	43	23	24	41

*) The categories are those used in Table 5.4.14, i.e. 1 = All three items accepted; 2–3 = Two accepted – two negative; and 4–5 = all three rejected.

two other items, however, the Civil servants come out as clearly the most positive.

This leads us to believe that even on the different aspects of 'internationalism', which we shall now scrutinize, the Civil servants and the Mass Media groups are more generally favorable than the other groups. That is: we may expect the former to be both more regionalistic and more globalistic than the others, *on* those variables where there is no forced choice, between these two directions. This would then – to the extent it is true – lend support to the contention that it is *degree of day-to-day exposure* to the outside world at large which is the main factor.

d. *'Internationalism'*. From what we have said above, we make the following

H 29: *The Civil servants and the Mass media people are both more globalistic and more regionalistic, leaving out forced choice variables, than the remaining groups.*

The forced choice variables are left out of the testing of this hypothesis, but we shall nevertheless have a look at them at the end of the section. Regionalism and globalism responses are presented in Table 6.3.9.

Table 6.3.9. *Regionalism and globalism: the sample category responses*

	PO	AD	MM	IO
Average percentage of NATO and EEC membership acceptance	80	100	71	86
To strengthen regional organization is important to peace	95	87	89	84
To strengthen the UN is important to peace	100	93	94	95
Globalism (UN attitude) index: 1:*	26	9	24	18
2–3:	48	45	14	36
4–5:	17	23	29	14
6:	0	5	5	0
NA	9	18	29	32

*) Response categories explained in Table 5.5.6.

Our H 29 is evidently *not* confirmed. While the number of variables on the regionalism sub-dimension probably is too low to show any clear pattern (in fact, the items show different trends), the globalism sub-dimension is satisfactorily covered (by six items altogether). The data show that while the Mass Media group more or less is matching the Interest organizations group, if not the Politicians, the Civil servants clearly are *least* globalistic

199

among the sample categories. The great differences in NA scores make comparison somewhat difficult, but the relative non-globalistic attitude of the Civil servants is fairly well established.

The reason for this somewhat unexpected finding may be sought variously. We may point to three different explanations. First, it may well be that the UN as an institution and as an indicator of globalism is already so well established within the Norwegian milieu that any exposure effect is negligible: the low-exposure groups, as the Politicians and the Interest organization group are, have been sufficiently exposed to it or even over-exposed to it.

Attitudes toward the less developed countries and the nonaligned then is something different, because these issues have not been so much exposed; thus, high exposure makes a difference. There is, however, a correlation (Spearman's) of .48 between the UN and the TA attitude indices, which points toward a relatively strong connection between the two issue areas.[5]

On the other hand, and this explanation is much related to the one just mentioned, the strong UN positivism in the elite, particularly as it is found among the Politicians and the Interest organization people, is a kind of 'idealism' which the 'realists' (represented by the Civil servants and the Mass media people) to some extent reject. This may be seen by the fact that the two latter groups show a relative distrust in the 'Strengthen the UN' and 'Disarmament' peace proposals (cf. 4.5). This civil servant 'realism' seems to be shared by the West German counterparts, who also show least support of disarmament.[6]

Table 6.3.10: *Regionalism vs. globalism: the sample category responses*

		PO	AD	MM	IO
Preference to: (first response)	Global policy	17	5	19	23
	Neither: both to be pursued	57	64	62	41
	Regional policy	26	32	19	36
Preference to: (probing: second response)*	Global	13	14	14	27
	Regional	22	18	29	5
	Neither: no choice necessary/wrong problem	22	32	19	9
Personal loyalty to:†	United Nations	48	23	43	50
	Euroamerica	26	54	24	19
	Nordic area	22	9	19	9

*) Percentages made on the basis of the total sample i.e. n = 88.
†) Percentages not adding up to 100.

The third possible explanation would be that there *is* a connection between globalism and regionalism in the sense, mentioned above, that being high on the one means being low on the other. This may be explored by the forced choice variables, shown in Table 6.3.10.

There *is* a strong tendency in the direction of this third explanation. Both variables, the probing question included, show that the Civil servants are the most regionalistic group, while globalistic attitudes seem to be most prominent among the interest organization, the remaining two groups being more or less equally divided between the two options.

The Civil servants' score on the 'neither' or ambivalent value in both the first and the probing response is interesting in the sense that it shows a relatively strong reluctance on the part of this group to make a choice between the two directions or levels of cooperation. This of course is well in accordance with the Establishmentarian role of the Civil servants, which is in cooperation with politicians and government to reconcile, to harmonize different and potentially conflicting policies. When in a more indirect manner, the group is asked to state its preference, however, it comes out very strongly in favor of regionalistic policies.

6.4 *Age*

The most important problem to be explored in this section is what we have called the 'period of basic socialization effect'. Our hypothesis is that

H 30: *The world perspective of a person is to a large extent a result of the socialization he went through in his years of maturing (15–25); the prominent issues and beliefs of that period influence his perspective.*

The operationalization of this hypothesis was made above (cf. 3.5) and we shall not repeat it in detail here.

The testing of it will be made in three parts, as we have hypothezised a set of specific attributes to be found in the perspective of each one of the three age groups into which our respondents have been divided.

H 30.1: *Cooperation and integration concern is more prominent in the category of old than in other age categories.*

Several variables related to various aspects and levels of cooperation are presented in Table 6.4.1.

The results leave hardly any doubt: the hypothesis is verified in six of the seven cases, and it is very convincingly verified when mean percentage acceptance scores are calculated.[7]

Table 6.4.1. *Cooperation concern and the age groups* *

	MY	M	O
Supranationality accepted	69	65	80
To maintain alliances is important to peace	67	83	89
In order to achieve peace in the present situation, cooperation should be strengthened†	15	24	32
To strengthen cooperation between states which naturally belongs together is important to peace	71	73	83
To strengthen UN	96	94	100
To strengthen regional organization	83	90	94
To establish the World State	42	37	39
Average percentage score, 7 items:	63.3	66.6	73.9
(n)	(26)	(37)	(25)

*) The age groups are: MY = 'the middle-young', those ≥ 44 years old; M = 'the middle aged', those from 45–54; and O = 'Old', those ≥ 55 years old.

†) This question is a multiple choice question, asking for preferred immediate peace-making measure. Cf. Appendix F.

The 100% acceptance among the 'old' of the proposal of strengthening the UN as important to peace, leads us to take a look at the UN attitude index. Although for various reasons, most of them mentioned already, we would not suggest that high cooperation or integration concern necessarily means strong UN positivism, we expect at least *some* tendency in that direction. For control purposes, we include the data for the opinion-maker sample (cf. Table 6.4.2.).

The expected tendency is *not* found in the trends Table 6.4.2 presents. On the contrary, the younger age groups are the ones showing the strongest

Table 6.4.2. *Age and attitudes toward the UN: elite and opinion-makers*

	Elite			Opinion-makers			
	MY	M	O	Y	MY	M	O
UN attitude index:							
1:	39	11	12	42	33	39	32
2–3:	38	27	48	44	51	39	53
4–5:	12	27	20	10	12	11	11
6:	8	0	0	2	3	0	0
NA	3	35	20	2	1	11	4
	100	100	100	100	100	100	100
	(26)	(37)	(25)	(41)	(33)	(36)	(19)

*) For an explanation of the categories, see Table 5.5.6.

UN positivism; this is true in both samples; and this is true if we control for the very great difference in NA score among the elite groups.

This may be interpreted as a certain, if not great distrust among the elder, more 'experienced' toward *concrete* measures of strengthening the world organization, whereas they still maintain the strong consensus on the very general dictum that the UN should be strengthened. Age, in other words, has fostered a certain scepticism: UN positivism, because it is part of the Norwegian foreign policy Establishment (and because it is relatively strongly supported by the public) is still highly *expressive* among the elder, while it has lost some of its instrumentality. The younger, on the other hand, are high on both aspects of this parsonian variable, but particularly on the latter.

H 30.2: *War and peace problems, fear of war etc. are more salient among the middle-aged than among the elder and younger.*

Before going into the testing of this hypothesis, let us substantiate the argument that the middle-aged are the ones who have been most exposed to the war, i.e. WWII. This is done in Table 6.4.3, which shows the war situation of the respondents and their own evaluation of the impact their war experiences have had on themselves. We see that the middle-aged have been most involved in the war (as participants) and that they also report greatest impact (although the 'old' opinion-makers report a similarly strong impact.

Table 6.4.3. *War exposure and war impact : the age groups*

	Elite			Opinion-makers			
	MY	M	O	Y*	MY	M	O
War situation:							
Participated in military ac-							
tivities†	23	41	20	0	9	50	42
Imprisoned‡	12	22	20	0	3	17	26
Exiled§	0	8	24	0	0	0	6
Impact of WWII experi-							
ences have been:							
great	31	62	44	7	48	53	53
moderate	42	24	36	24	39	39	47
none	12	8	4	32	6	6	0

*) This age group of course was too young (12 or younger) to be directly involved, or participating in war activities of the kinds listed.
†) Abroad in the allied forces, or in the 'home force'.
‡) In Germany or in Norway, for a shorter period or till the end of the war.
§) In London, United States, or in Sweden.

Table 6.4.4. *'Peace and war concern' and the age groups*

	Elite			Opinion-makers			
	MY	M	O	Y	MY	M	O
The greatest threat to mankind in the present world: war*	46	70	44	36	61	39	56
Value justifying the risk of a major war?:							
yes	35	19	32	10	15	19	21
no	54	68	48	68	61	79	68
War may perhaps not be avoided	23	46	36	24	42	52	47
A WWIII is unlikely within year 2000†	61	76	64	42	42	44	42
The consequences of a major war to Norway would be disastrous‡	62	43	48	59	46	28	26

*) Responses from the multiple choice threat question, cf. App. F.

†) Unlikely = less than 50–50 % likely.

‡) Disastrous = 'Total destruction' or 'Irreparable losses'.

Turning now to the testing of the hypothesis, it clearly *is* middle-age war fear, as seen from the first two items in the Table: the middle-aged see war as a more salient threat (except for the opinion-maker case) and are least willing to risk it. These findings easily fit in with the hypothesis, supporting it.

The results on the three remaining items, however, need some elaboration. From these items, what may be said of the middle-aged and their point of view, is more or less the following: in *general*, war is difficult to avoid, but the *big* war, a World War III, may be avoided. And *if* the big war *should* come, it will not carry such tremendous destruction as is often believed. In other words: World War II, which they more than any other age group experienced and participated in, was *the* great war (which will not happen again). In fact, it was *their* war. *Minor* wars, however, will have to be experienced in the future.

But at this point, it is necessary to put the question: *is* it really age, or is it *war experience* (or non-experience in the case of the young) which counts when it comes to attitude formation?

This may be explored by using personal war situation (cf. Table 6.4.3) as an independent variable and the Establishment variables as dependent ones. This operation yields a few interesting results: those among the elite sample who were actively fighting the war (mostly abroad) are very strongly

Establishmentarian (89 percent) and strongly pro NATO; those who were prisoners of war show the same tendency, but moderately so. None of these groups, however, are particularly EEC positive although they abstain from opposing it.

On the other hand, those who took part in the resistance movement at home clearly are less Establishmentarian (only by 41 percent) and less pro NATO. In fact, their position judging from the data is rather similar to that of the group of elite members who were too young to participate in any way in the war activities and who were consequently little exposed to the war.

This difference between the out and the home fighters seems to reflect the historical (but may be ever latent) split between the two factions in the foreign policy elite before and during the war which was described above. On the other hand, the group of elites who were exiled during the war and for the most part took up positions in the exile administration, casts some doubt on this home-abroad controversy as this group although it is more Establishmentarian (both according to the index and to the NATO variable) than the home resistance people, nevertheless seems to be closer in its attitudes to them than to the out fighters.

With this interpretation of the results, an interpretation we believe well in accordance with the notions of war exposure and war impact, the hypothesis is satisfactorily verified.

Table 6.4.5. *Age groups and attitudes toward the less developed countries*

	Elite			Opinion-makers			
	MY	M	O	Y	MY	M	O
Greatest threat to mankind: development problems	23	19	12	49	30	39	32
Most important peace-making measure: solve devel. problems	16	13	8	29	12	14	26
To abolish hunger is important to peace	91	90	83	88	93	88	84
Rich countries help poor is important to peace	88	93	88	85	88	90	87
TA attitude index:							
1:	58	30	16	59	52	47	21
2–3:	31	59	64	34	39	39	74
4–5:	8	3	12	0	3	8	0
NA	3	8	8	7	6	6	5

H 30.3: *The younger age groups are more concerned with and more positive toward the less developed countries than the elder*

Table 6.4.5 shows relatively good support of this sub-hypothesis in our data, although the trend is not consistently in the same direction on all counts. The conclusion then may be is that it is the combined experience of both fighting the war (also in a foreign prison) *and* doing it abroad (together with allied forces) which has an effect upon peoples' minds. Although there are indications of some such effect – indications which tell us that war experience should be further explored – our investigations so far do not give us any strong reason to dismiss the importance of age and the hypothesis on the effect of the socialization period.

Two multiple choice questions at the top of Table 6.4.5. deviate from the rest in that the 'middle-young' opinion-makers on these items show least concern with development problems. On the other hand, this group is not less concerned than the middle-young (or the youngest) elite group. And the index, which is the best measure of attitudes and which at the same time

Table 6.4.6. *Age groups and systemic relationship 'cues': another test of the 'period of socialization effect*

| | | Elite | | | Opinion-makers | | | |
		MY	M	O	Y	MY	M	O
'Most important prob-	I*	23	51	40	51	52	58	47
lem of today's world'	II	46	27	32	5	9	14	11
	III	4	5	16	2	3	0	0
	IV	15	11	0	37	33	22	37
'Hoped main difference	I	8	19	8	20	22	24	16
between now and year	II	31	22	16	22	21	17	48†
2000'	III	19	22	40	12	15	8	5
	IV	32	32	20	29	18	31	16
'Preferences, Norwe-	I	27	19	28	12	15	16	14
gian foreign policy now'	II	27	40	24	20	27	20	16
	III	16	30	28	22	30	33	47
	IV	8	0	0	32	6	0	5
'Preferences, Norwe-	I	15	16	20	10	12	8	11
gian foreign policy in	II	16	11	20	7	12	20	11
the future'	III	19	28	29	24	24	22	26
	IV	31	30	8	37	21	3	5

*) Categories: I = Power (war-peace) relationship II = Exchange (detente, disarmament) relationship; III = Integrative relationship; and IV = Development relationship (cf. 4.2).

†) All of them responding 'detente'.

206

reflects 'instrumentality' in the thinking of the respondents, shows the expected trend.

H30 may be given another close look by using the typology of relationships (cf. 4.2 and Table 4.2.1) which in fact reflects the different aspects of the perspectives of the age groups. Table 6.4.6 shows responses of the age groups on four different items – 'Most important international problem today', 'Hopes for year 2000', and preferred Norwegian foreign policy task now and in the future.

From the scores presented for the different types of relationship, we see each one of our sub-hypotheses receives support in 3 out of 4 cases in both samples. The only exceptions are the elite middle-aged, who score highest in only two out of four cases on the power (I) relationship, and the opinion-maker old, who are on top on two out of four items in the integrative (III) relationship. In a few other cases, however, the expected top score is a very narrow one, as for instance with the middle-young elite group being equalled by the middle-aged on the development relationship in two out of four cases.

Although the results in Table 6.4.6 are less convincing than those shown above, we may conclude that our H30 on the whole has received satisfactory support.

We made the tentative hypothesis that the younger age groups were less *centrist* than the elder. Particularly, we thought that they, due to expected greater flexibility, would be less inclined to accept the existing world order, and less structurally authoritarian, and thus more change-oriented and 'democratic' than the elder groups.

Results do *not* seem to support this assumption. Concerning preference for the existing world order, we do find that the middle-aged show greatest preference in both samples, but the younger show less preference for the world order than the old age group only in the opinion-maker case. Similarly, only the very young opinion-makers show less authoritarianism than all elder groups. This *may* mean that age differences on centrism disappear when people reach a certain age (i.e. 35 years or more) and that only in the very young age groups is centrism low – because it has not been affictively socialized, and/or accepted yet. or: it may be that the present young, those of 30–35 or less, will maintain their relative lack of centrism – which means that the periphery perspective only recently has started being adopted, and only by those who are still young and still relatively 'unsocialized'.

It is in accordance with this that other-ness increases when age decreases. On the other hand, the younger groups are practically as we-ness oriented as the elder, the younger putting somewhat more stress on the we-they relations, but not much more.

Lastly, we shall test the hypothesis that

H31: *The middle-aged are the most consensual and most Establishmentarian age group.*

These are in fact two hypotheses, as they relate to issue-areas which have been treated separately so far. We have lumped them together because the same trend is proposed on both issues. They are tested against the results shown in Table 6.4.7.

Table 6.4.7. *Consensus and Establishment among the age groups*

| | Elite | | | Opinion-makers | | | |
	MY	M	O	Y	MY	M	O
Mean corresponding modal value: 32 items	63.6	60.1	55.0	62.5	63.9	60.0	57.9
Mean NA score for 12 disarmament items:	7.7	18.9	28.0		–		
Mean ratio of acceptance to rejection on 32 items:	4.0	5.9	2.9		–		
Establishment index:							
Establishment	54	55	44	29	36	52	37
Right-outsiders	27	30	36	17	28	22	37
Doubters	4	11	12	34	18	14	21
Left-outsiders	15	0	0	20	18	8	5
NA	0	4	8	0	0	4	0
	100	100	100	100	100	100	100
	(26)	(37)	(25)	(41)	(33)	(36)	(19)

The mean corresponding modal value, indicating consensus, is not a reliable measure in this case, as is indicated by the inclusion of mean NA scores. The latter show rather great variance between the elite age groups; a similar, but much less pronounced variance is found between the opinion-maker age groups.

This NA score variance is controlled for in the average ratios shown in the Table: in fact, these ratios seem to confirm our hypothesis about the middle-aged as the most consensual group. Such conclusions, however, are hasty, since the high average ratio of the middle-aged (5.9) is very much due to only a small number of items on which this group scored very positive ratios: taking each single item separately, the middle-young group scores highest ratio on more items than the middle-aged.

208

What we *may* conclude, however, is that *our suggestion of a gradual disengagement on the part of the elder – the old – seems fruitful.* As far as our data go, this suggestion has been confirmed. And it is even better confirmed if we only take into account the distribution of the age groups on the Establishment index, which – moreover – confirms our hypothesis although very narrowly so in the case of the elite, where the middle-young are practically as Establishmentarian as the middle-aged.

This is first of all due to the fact that the middle-young score particularly high on the UN and the TA variables which account for half the indicators of the index. If only the two 'Western' indicators – attitudes toward NATO and EEC membership – are observed, there is a mean percentage of acceptance of memberships for the middle-aged of 89 %, while the middle-young and the old score 82 %, both of them.

These scores, as well as e.g. the opinion-maker age group scores on the Establishment index, seem to correspond with findings in the study made by Deutsch et al. They conclude that the middle-aged of the French elite 'is somewhat different from the elder and the younger, who resemble each other'.[8] They also conclude that the middle-aged are more Gaullistic than the others,[9] which again corresponds fairly well with the relative Establishmentarianism of the middle-aged Norwegian respondents, as foreign policy Gaullism at the time of data collection was the foreign policy Establishment of France.

In concluding then, we may say that our hypothesis that the middle-aged were the most consensual has not been satisfactorily confirmed. On the other hand, it has been shown that they are the most Establishmentarian group. Furthermore, the hypothesized 'disengagement of the aged' and, by implication, the importance of being involved in, being active in foreign policy activities for making the middle-aged the most Establishmentarian, has been confirmed.

6.5. *Social position*

It has been shown above, both theoretically and empirically, that social position within the context of high status group like the elite and the opinion-makers does not have a strong discriminatory effect, or importance to speak in more general terms, compared to other independent variables, and compared to the effect it has on the general public opinion levels.

This is rather obvious. It is a variable that refers to the total system – Norway – not merely to a small part of it like the elite.

This may be substantiated by looking at consensus scores for the center, middle and periphery categories: they are practically equal; in fact, the difference on corresponding modal value averages for 32 variables is *less* than 1% between the elite periphery and the elite center. On only 13% of the 32 variables is there a ≳30% disagreement between these two categories. Center-periphery differences within the opinion-maker sample are practically the same, but even smaller when disagreement scores are compared: this sample in fact shows *no* ≳30% disagreement on any of the 32 variables selected for study.

The second proposition, which is rather a hypothesis as it has not yet been tested empirically, implies that

H 32: *The importance (discriminatory effect) of social position is inversely related to structural position.*

We are able to test it against a number of items on which we have social position scores for all three structural levels. The representativity of these items, as they cover disarmament and technical assistance problems mainly, may be questioned. On the other hand, the number of items is 13 and the variety of aspects of disarmament problems covered rather great. The results presented in Table 6.5.1 thus should be given some weight.

Public opinion responses are taken from studies made by Galtung and Eide.[10] Two sets of responses are included for two different definitions of the periphery and center categories, but the one set which corresponds best to the definition we ourselves employ, is PO I.[11]

Employing this definition, we see that our H 32 does *not* receive support, but on the contrary seems to be rather disconfirmed by results when average percentage differences are compared. Contrary to expectations, social position seems to have a stronger effect on the top, foreign policy elite level of society *than* on lower levels, even though its effect on the top level, compared to that of other variables, is moderate.

We have two explanations to offer in relation to this finding. In the first place, the low n of the elite sample compared to that of the public opinion sample (88 against 1000) make intra-elite differences *comparatively* more likely; they are to a larger extent random. If we take a look at the single variable differences, 4 out of 13 are of the ≥30% category, while 6 out of 13 i.e. little less than half of the variables, are of the ≳20% category, both of which according to our definition above are nonrandom differences.

Table 6.5.1. *Relationship between social and structural position: percentage differences between periphery and center *)*

Item:	EL	OM	PO(I)	PO(II)
Disarmament should be carried out stepwise	− 33	9	− 14	− 30
Disarmament should be carried out in some selected areas first	− 6	6	− 4	− 21
Disarmament should start with a few selected weapons	34	6	− 19	− 35
Disarmament depends on great powers	− 31	− 21	− 10	− 17
One should increase confidence before disarming	28	21	− 12	− 24
Much inspection is needed for disarmament	6	3	− 16	− 19
All states want disarmament, but dare not before others do	− 3	8	− 11	− 10
Some states will try to hide weapons under disarmament	21	− 15	− 9	− 18
UN police forces should be established	7	− 13	− 8	− 17
World state should be established	12	− 3	− 4	− 27
Norway should assist less developed countries in establishing merchant marine	− 13	− 8	− 15	− 15†
Customs duty preferences should be extended to less developed countries	30	26	− 33	− 33
Norway should give more technical assistance to less developed countries	8	13	− 1	− 1
Mean percentage difference, between P and C (+ or −):	± 17.8	± 11.0	− 12.2	− 20.5

*) The parameter used is percentage differences between the periphery and the center on acceptance of the items. The items were most often not presented to respondents in the way they are seen here.

†) The P and C categories under PO I and PO II are the same on this and the following two items.

Thus, there *are* differences between elite center and periphery which cannot be explained by randomness alone.

It is noted – and this *may* to some extent be an indication that differences are random – that the trend in periphery-center difference is very unsystematic in the case of the elite and the opinion-makers, while it is monotonous in all 13 cases for both definitions of public opinion periphery and center. That is: while in the case of the elite and the opinion-makers, the center is sometimes 'above' the periphery, a pattern expressed by a negative difference score, sometimes 'below' it, the center is monotonously and systematically 'above' the periphery in the case of the public opinion.

Some of the reason for this must lie in that the public opinion at large is very much *structured* along the periphery – center dimension, while the top strata are not. But this does not explain the fact of greater elite periphery – center differences.

A second explanation is found in party differences. It was shown above (6.2) that the distribution of the party variable on the social position variable was somewhat biased. This may account for much of the difference on *single* variables, although it cannot answer for the whole set of variables employed here, as party differences on these variables do not show any systematic trend either.

As an example, let us see how party and social position interact on the three absolutism-gradualism variables listed on top of Table 6.5.1. We saw that the Conservatives made up one half of the elite center, while Labor accounted for half the elite periphery. On the first item – rapid versus step-wise disarmament – the trend is as expected: the Conservatives *and* the center take the gradualistic (stepwise) attitude; moreover, percentage differences between center-periphery and Conservatives–Labor are practically the same.

On the second item – the whole world versus selected areas approach – periphery-center differences are practically none, while the Conservative–Labor difference is of the order of 30 %, *but* with Labor as the more gradua-listic this time. This may mean that the role of Labor is that of neutralizing the effect of the center Conservatives on this variable. This is further indicated by the third item – all versus some selected weapons – where the Conservatives once more are the gradualists, and where there is a periphery center difference in the expected direction of the center as the most gradua-listic.

The gradualism-absolutism dimension brings us over into the problem of *centrism*. As we have no complete theory for world perspective according to social position at the level of the foreign policy milieu, we shall restrict our analysis of centrism to only a few of its aspects, on which there *is* some theory (cf. Chapt. 3) to lead us.

As shown by results in Table 6.5.1, there is no clear trend in the direc-tion of center gradualism and periphery absolutism within the elite and the opinion-maker samples, like the trend reported on the part of public opinion. The elite center is more gradualistic in two out of three cases, while periphery – center differences in the opinion-maker sample are too small to make conclusions meaningful. There is a slight tendency toward gradualism in the periphery, not in the center, if all three items are seen to-gether.

Another aspect of centrism is the we-ness versus other-ness problem. Our hypothesis is

H 33: *The social center is we-ness, the periphery otherness oriented*

The evidence is given in Table 6.5.2.

Table 6.5.2. *We-ness, other-ness and social position*

	Elite			Opinion-makers		
	P	M	C	P	M	C
(We-ness)						
Primary loyalty to Euro-America	17	39	41	24	29	15
Accept NATO membership	69	80	96	44	64	65
Favor EEC membership	71	87	95	77	84	82
More contact with Eastern Europe important to peace	91	96	76	82	87	88
The rich should cooperate more vis a vis the less developed countries	31	19	14	12	3	6
Favor demilitarized zone (Other-ness)	38	44	53	62	48	48
TA attitude index:						
1:	37	35	27	53	50	41
2–3:	54	55	46	41	39	50
4–5:	3	7	14	0	2	9
NA	6	3	13	6	9	0
	100	100	100	100	100	100
	(35)	(31)	(22)	(34)	(62)	(34)

As to other-ness, the hypothesis is satisfactorily confirmed, although differences between the categories are not great. We-ness scores present a more confusing picture, however, and the hypothesis at this point does not seem to get sufficient support:

Among the elite, it is confirmed in 4 out of 6 cases, a clear trend. On the other hand, the trend is in the hypothesized direction in only 2 out of the 6 cases for the opinion-makers. The only safe conclusion on we-ness and social position seems to be that elite 'we-we' feelings, i.e. favorable attitudes toward Euro-American relations, increase with increasing social position. A corresponding pattern is not found among the opinion-makers, which should lead us to believe that the opinion-maker center contains a moderate, but recognizable amount of *'isolationism'* or *protest* against *any* kind of cooperation or affiliations with external actors.

Concretely, this should imply that the opinion-maker center is less globalistic (as well as less regionalistic, as Table 6.5.2 in fact shows it *is*) than at
least one of the other two social position categories, *and* that it even is less
Establishmentarian. What is now proposed then is that our

H34: *The center is the most Establishmentarian social position category*

does not hold for the opinion-maker sample. This is exactly what is found
(cf. Table 6.5.3).

Table 6.5.3. *Globalism, Establishmentarianism, and social position*

		Elite			Opinion-makers		
		P	M	C	P	M	C
UN attitude index:							
	1:	26	19	9	35	44	29
	2–3:	46	29	32	49	43	47
	4–5:	17	26	18	15	8	12
	6:	0	3	5	0	2	3
Establishment index:							
	Establishment	49	48	59	29	45	35
	Right outsiders	23	42	27	21	21	32
	Doubters	14	7	5	29	19	24
	Left outsiders	11	0	0	21	15	6

While the hypothesis holds for the *elite* center, which shows a safe majority
of Establishmentarians, the opinion-maker center is relatively right outsider
oriented. The implications of this relative 'isolationism' on the part of the
opinion-maker center are difficult to assess, but its effect may be that of
reducing socialization of the public into 'internationalism' in general, and
of putting pressure on the elite not to go too far on the various 'internationalistic' inroads. These suggestions are made on the assumptions that the
opinion-maker center is better placed than the middle and the periphery
categories in performing the functions of socialization and elite or policy-
making influencing – assumptions which do seem to be justified by our data
on the communication structure.

The question was raised above whether the social center of the society
at large might represent a challenge to the foreign policy elite or the milieu
of policy-makers, if relations between them were characterized by relatively
strong differences in attitudes and images (cf. 3.3). We have shown that elite
– public opinion relations in the Norwegian foreign policy context approach
a rather hierarchical or oligarchic structure (cf. 5.2). Our final problem in

this section is to see to what extent the *general* (i.e. national) social center tends to bridge the gap found between the elite and the public opinion at large.

We may analyse this problem by breaking down public opinion responses on a number of different variables on social position. In Table 6.5.4 these variables are divided into two sets, the one including Establishment or E–related items, the other consisting of gradualism versus absolutism indicators

Table 6.5.4. *Relations between the elite and the general public social center*

| | Public social positions:* | | | | |
	1	3	6	8	Elite
Establishment or E–related items:† ratios of acceptance to rejection, in *average* (n = 5)	0.7	0.7	1.3	1.8	6.4
Gradualism versus absolutism items:‡ ratios of gradualistic to absolutistic response, in *average* (n = 6)	2.0	2.0	2.7	5.8	4.6

*) Positions are categories according to the Galtung index of social position, an additive index ranging from 0 (as the extreme periphery) to 8 (as the extreme center).

†) Items are attitude to NATO and EEC membership, attitudes toward merchant marine assistance and customs duty preferences for the developing countries, and preferences for NATO versus Nordic area on international loyalty question.

‡) Items are all taken from among the disarmament questions: the three indicators of gradualism versus absolutism (cf. Table 5.4.10), whether disarmament should precede increasing confidence or vice versa, whether economic differences will persist after disarmament or not, and whether much inspection is needed under a disarmament agreement.

and three more disarmament questions. Average ratios were calculated for each set of variables, as shown in the Table.

The results in short are: while the social center on non-Establishment items seems to be playing the role of bridgebuilder between the foreign policy elite and the rest of the public, on Establishment matters it is not. That the social center scores higher than the elite on the six disarmament attitude items is due to an extremely high score on one single item; if this item is deleted, the mean score of the social center (category 8) becomes approximately 3.5, which would have 'fit the curve' much better, putting this category in-between the elite and the others.

The distance between the foreign policy elite and the general social center on Establishment is rather great, supporting the notion of the Norwegian foreign policy system as relatively hierarchic or oligarchic. On the other hand, the center lends considerable support to the regionalistic, Euro-american part of the Establishment. The average ratio on the two items representing this part is 3.1, which is still well beyond the elite score, but a strong majority according to our standards. It is particularly on the technical assistance questions that the center 'holds back' its support, although it is more positive toward these questions than the middle and periphery public opinion.

6.6. *Party preference and the foreign policy milieu*

We will start this section by substantiating the claim made in 3.4 that the Socialist – Non-Socialist dichotomy is not the most fruitful classification in dealing with the party variable within the Norwegian foreign policy context.

As has been said above, on the other hand, it is a formally logical classification as it represents the present government structure of Norway. From this structure one should expect that the Non-socialists, being in government at the time of the interview, would be the most Establishmentarian category, while the Socialists (Labor took over as a minority government in March 1971) would be leaning toward the left. As is shown in Table 6.6.1, this is not true, particularly if the analysis is confined to the elite only – as one very well may argue it should be as far as Establishment is concerned.

Table 6.6.1. *Socialists versus Non-socialists and Establishment*

| | Socialists | | Non-socialists | |
	EL	OM	EL	OM
Establishment	58	15	45	51
Right outsiders	12	8	47	33
Doubters	15	35	4	16
Left outsiders	9	42	2	0
NA	6	0	2	0
	100	100	100	100
	(34)	(39)	(45)	(83)

Clearly, it is the very strong impact of Right outsiders which 'deprives' the Non-socialist elite of its expected Establishmentarianism. The Non-socialist opinion-makers show a pattern more in accordance with the suggestion of relative Non-socialist Establishmentarianism. The 'Rightism' of the elite should be attributed mainly to the fact that the Conservatives make up

216

more than half this group, but the distribution is probably not totally unrepresentative of the universe.

Another striking fact is the considerable difference between the Socialist elite and opinion-makers. To a large extent it is due to a relatively much larger number of Left Socialists in the opinion-maker than in the elite sample. But it should certainly also be attributed to what may be called the 'elite effect' on the Labor party: the involvement, not the least through two continuous decades of post-war government, of the Labor party leaders in Norway's foreign policy making have created a relatively strong Establishmentarianism among them, which stands in sharp contrast with attitudes held by Labor rank and file. This observation has already been made on the basis of foreign policy and military policy questions by Valen and Katz,[12] and we shall give it more proof later on in this section.

Let us now show the distributions on the Establishment dimension for other classifications of the party variables. We may relate results to the hypothesis that the Labor and the Liberals, as 'middle parties', would both show the strongest inter-party agreement and be more Establishmentarian than other parties, which is our

H 35: *Labor and Liberals are the most Establishmentarian party groups.*

We see from Table 6.6.2 that the hypothesis holds for the elite, but not for the opinion-maker sample. Elite – opinion-maker difference is particularly great within Labor as already indicated: the Labor elite is strongly Establishmentarian, its opinion-makers are as 'Doubters' challenging the wisdom of their leaders' Establishmentarianism.

Table 6.6.2. *Establishmentarianism and the party groups*

	Elite*			Opinion-makers				
	Lab.	Lib.	Con.	SPP†	Lab.	Lib.	C/OP‡	Con.
Establishment	67	76	35	5	26	46	72	50
Right outsiders	14	8	65	0	16	21	21	44
Doubters	14	8	0	20	53	33	7	6
Left outsiders	0	8	0	75	5	0	0	0
NA	5	0	0	0	0	0	0	0
	100	100	100	100	100	100	100	100
	(30)	(13)	(27)	(20)	(19)	(33)	(16)	(34)

*) Only three of the five party groups employed in the case of the opinion-makers, are presented; the remaining two had too low m's to make analysis meaningful.
†) This group includes 2 Communist party supporters.
‡) This group includes 9 Christian People's Party supporters, 7 Center Party supporters.

This challenge, however, is limited: it does not include the dramatic rejection of the Euro-american component of the Establishment as the Socialist People's Party and Communist group shows. Thus, even if the Labor opinion-makers are swinging toward the left, they do not make the last great 'leap' into Leftism: only 5%, against 75% of the Socialist People's Party, are Left outsiders. Even the Liberal opinion-makers show a certain swing to the left; the one Left outsider among the Liberal elite group (note the low *m*) is rather spurious.

The Rightism of the Conservatives, has already indicated, comes out very strongly in Table 6.6.2. It was shown in 6.3 that among the institutional groups the Civil servants were the most Establishmentarian, although with a large number of Conservatives in the ranks. A comparison of administrative and Conservative Establishmentarianism then should tell us that – particularly when also the strong effect of the party variable is taken into consideration – the adminstation effect is large: being a member of the foreign service *counteracts* the party effect of being a Conservative.

If we combine the Labor and the Liberals, as proposed above, into a 'middle party' group, we find that 69% of this group among the elite (against only 31% among the combined Conservative-Christian-Center group) is Establishmentarian. The respective figures for the opinion-maker sample are 40% and 58%.

A better measure of party relations, however, are scores of agreement or disagreement between the different party groups. The hypothesis was made that

H 36: *Labor and the Liberals in foreign policy matters stand closer to each other than do any other party groups.*

Table 6.6.3 gives agreement scores between the five party groupings as classified in Table 6.6.2; the scores are mean percentage difference for 32

Table 6.6.3. *Mean percentage differences between party groups for corresponding modal values on 32 variables as a measure of agreement between them*

| | Elite | | | Opinion-makers | | | |
	Lab.	Lib.	Con.	Lab.	Lib.	C/CP	Con.
SPP/C	–	–	–	21.0	24.8	26.2	30.0
Labor		7.5	13.7		14.6	25.6	21.6
Liberals			14.9			16.2	11.3
Chr/Center	–	–	–				16.3

variables. In the case of the elite, the small *m* of the Left Socialist and the Christian-Center groups excludes them from analysis.

When single differences are analyzed, by means of the number of cases of $\geq 30\%$ and $\geq 20\%$ differences (cf. *passim* above) the patterns are practically the same.

Considering the relatively strong discriminatory effect of the party variable and comparing these results with those obtained on other variables, the Lib-Lab agreement is striking. It is a very strong indication that the present government-opposition structure is *not* representative of foreign policy attitudes and international images among leading strata of the political parties. This is however not tantamount to saying that the non-representativity of this structure is 'dangerous' or tends to create 'instability': although the party variable as such has considerable effect, this is not necessarily proof that the *party system* has a decisive influence over policy-making. Most probably it has not. This may be shown very simply by presenting the figures for party distribution on the policy-maker variable: elite party groups, according to themselves, have a share of the policy-maker group practically *equal* to their respective share of the total elite sample. That is: The opposition participates in policy-making to the same extent as the Government party or parties.

Our next problem is related to the one we have just been discussing, but presents another aspect of party relations *and* a more general problem as well. This is the question seen from the following:

> In groups where there is a high consistency and monism in the pattern of attitudes, and where the intensity with which these attitudes are held is high, consensus within the groups will also be high.

As has been explained above (cf. 3.4) this is largely due to what we shall call the 'polarization effect'. The reasoning behind this, given above, leaves us in fact with two hypotheses: one proposes that intensity and monism creates consensus, the other that polarization makes for consensus.

What we shall do here, however, is to re-allocate the pattern of causal relationship. In fact we shall propose that intensity leads to polarization which in turn leads to monism and consistency which at least create consensus.

Let us show consensus scores for the party groups over the whole range of items employed for measuring consensus so far. Results are shown in Table 6.6.4.

Table 6.6.4. *Consensus and the party groups*

| | Elite | | | | Opinion-makers | | | |
	Lab.	Lib.	Con.	SPP	Lab.	Lib.	C/C	Con.
Mean percentage modal value, *corresponding* value (n = 32)	70.4	70.4	58.7	54.3	66.8	64.1	58.8	65.6
Mean percentage modal score, *overall* value (n = 32)	70.4	70.4	62.0	66.3	71.8	66.3	67.5	68.3

Labor is the most consensual group in both samples and for both corresponding and overall values. That the Liberals, who among the elite sample put up the same strong consensus as the Laborites, do show some defection among the opinion-makers may be attributed to various causes, e.g. the relative heterogeneity or 'built-in' dissensus of that party.

But the best explanation *may* be exactly the position of the Libereal party as a middle party, where attitudes are more dispersed and where people are attached to the two 'wings' of the party system. Now, the label of 'middle party' has also been attached to the Labor party; and the reason why this party *is not* dissensual, but on the contrary the most consensual, is probably its built-in ability to create consensus among its rank-and-file.[13]

Turning now to the proposed causal relationship and the related hypotheses, we shall deal first with intensity and then test the hypotheses about consensus.

Intensity of course must be related to what we throughout this report have called Establishment and –related issues. These are the issues about which there is political struggle, and it lies implicit in the concept of struggle that attitudes on such issues are particularly intensely and consistently held.

Thus, we selected ten items – all the four Establishment items plus six which we found were related to them – and calculated party distributions.[14] These items, with the exception of three, were dichotomized into the values 'positive' and 'negative', i.e. acceptance or rejection of the item. The three non-dichotomized items were trichotomized with a middle, 'neutral' value. This had some, but not decisive effect on the end result (cf. Table 6.6.5).

The way of analysis now was to calculate the average percentages scores of positive and negative responses (the two types of responses taken separately) for all the party groups. In this part of the study even elite Left Socialists and Christian-Center people were included, despite the very low *m*'s for these groups, in order to arrive at a complete picture.

The results very clearly substantiate that attitudes on these ten items are subject to rather strong polarization: average percentage differences between e.g. the Conservatives and the Socialist People's Party groups are 66.4% in the elite, 51.2% in the opinion-maker case. The corresponding opinion-maker figure for the totality of 32 variables was found to be 30% (cf. Table 6.6.3). And this polarization does not only take place between the extremes: there is an 'inside-the-extremes' difference e.g. between the opinion-maker Labor and Socialist People's Party of 26% (against 21% for all 32 variables) and between the elite Liberals and Conservatives of 20% (against 15%, respectively). Elite Labor – Socialist People's disagreement on the ten Establishment-related items is another case in point when contemplating 'Socialist unity': on the average there is 59% disagreement between them.

Turning now to the effect of intensity and polarization on consensus, our hypothesis which follows from the above analysis, is that

H 37: *On issues where there is strong intensity in the attitudes held, and where polarization is high, consensus will be strongest at the extremes.*

In other words, the Consevatives and the Socialist People's Party should be the most consensual groups on the average over the ten Establishment-related items analyzed in this context. The results are shown in Table 6.6.5.

Table 6.6.5. *Consensus as a function of intensity and polarization: the evidence of ten Establishment-related items*

		SPP	Lab.	Lib.	C/CP	Con.
Percentage mean, *positive* re-						
sponses on ten items:	EL	0	53.8	35.1	58.0	62.4
	OM	11.8	31.0	45.8	50.0	59.2
Percentage mean *negative* re-						
sponses on ten items:	EL	70.8	29.5	39.4	24.0	18.7
	OM	74.0	47.4	33.7	30.0	23.9
No. of cases where pos. *or* neg.						
response is not modal value.	EL	1	1	1	1	1
	OM	0	2	1	2	1

Our H 37 is firmly backed in all four cases: the Conservatives show the highest mean score on positive, the Socialists People's Party the highest score on negative responses. The party group which shows the strongest tendency toward an *even score* i.e. toward equally high (or low) average scores on both positive and negative response is the Liberals, with Labor following suit: this is exactly what should be expected according to the 'middle party' conception.

The polarization effect, or the combined polarization – consistency effect, may be read out of the results obtained in another way as well: by looking at *intra-party distances* between mean positive and mean negative scores. This indicates to what extent the party groups tend to take one specific position i.e. chose one particular response value consistently over a number of items. In fact this procedure is not very different from the one already shown, but it employs the results given in Table 6.6.5 in another way.

In terms of these intra-party distances, we arrive at the following ranking of the party groups (the top ranking is the one with the greatest distance):

	Elite	Opinion-makers
1. Socialist People's Party	− 70.8	− 62.2
2. Conservatives	43.7	35.3
3. Christian-Center parties	34.0	20.0
4. Labor	24.3	− 16.4
5. Liberals	− 4.3	12.1

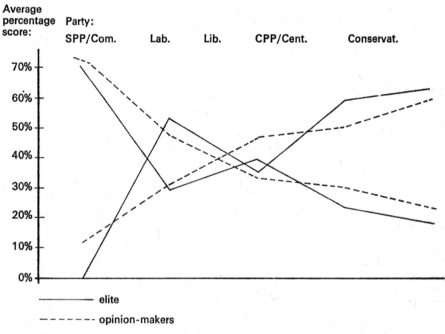

Figure 8. *Intra-party distances in the elite and opinion-maker samples between acceptance and rejection attitudes on* 10 *items*

What this ranking actually gives is a refined picture of the effects of polarization shown in Table 6.6.5.

The effect of polarization on parties may be visualized by means of a diagram where the parties are placed on a left-to-right dimension (on the horizontal axis) and the intra-party distance are plotted in (on the vertical axis). This is shown in Figure 8.

This curve shape is found for 7 out of the 10 single items in the case of the Socialist People's Party being close to 0 and the Conservatives on top approaching 100, and in 8 out of the 10 items when the curve is in the opposite direction (Conservatives at the bottom, Socialists at the top).

Attitude formation in questions related to Establishment then is very consistent and thus relatively predictable. Another conclusion from our data is that the polarization effect seems strongest at the elite level, which is well in accordance with the proposition presented by Valen and Katz.

6.7. *Establishment-outsider variations*

The first hypothesis to be tested in this section represents another case of curve shape analysis, and it is also related to issues involving affect – where attitudes are held relatively intensely and consistently and where there is polarization.

The hypothesis is that,

H 38: *On issues involving high affect, attitudes will tend to distribute themselves on the Establishment-outsider dimension, in the order of Establishment-Right-Doubters-Left, according to a j-shaped curve.*

There is no mystique about this hypothesis: if the order of the categories on the Establishment-outsider dimension were changed, the curve shape would also change, e.g. to the linear curve shape found for party groups from Left to Right, *if* Right outsiders and Establishment simply changed position on the proposed continuum.

The idea of looking for the 'hook' curve is that the ordering of categories proposed is believed to represent the relative order in which the four categories are represented in the group of policy-makers. *This is exactly what our data show,* as may be seen from Table 6.7.1.

The main importance of this lies in the position of the Right outsiders as really *competing* with the Establishmentarians for policy-making influence (according to own perceptions, that is). This position means they are able to 'pull' policies in the direction of their own stand, an act which may be visualized by the 'hook' curve conception. Choosing the Establishment

Table 6.7.1. *Policy-makers and Establishment-outsider*

| | Percentage of policy-makers in Establishment-outsider categories for: | |
	Elite sample	Opinion-maker sample
Establishment	40	11
Right outsiders	36	19
Doubters ⎱		7
Left outsiders ⎰	25	10

position as a starting-point, the Right outsiders represent *one* direction of thought, the Doubters and Left outsiders another and opposite one.

As to testing H38, we shall jump over the figures and present the visualized confirmation of the hypothesis (cf. Figure 9).

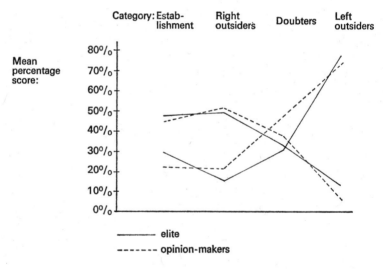

Figure 9. *The test of the 'hook curve' hypothesis*

We see from Figure 9 that the *j*-shape of the curve is seen for both sets of responses (positive and negative) on the eight items scrutinized. Looking at each single item separately, we also find the same *j*-curve distribution in a majority of the cases.

As has already been shown by measuring its effect as related to that of the party variable, the mean (as well as single-item) difference between the extreme categories – the Right and the Left outsiders – is not so great as that

224

between the extreme party groups. It is seen from the Figure that Establishmentarians and Right outsiders are closer to each other than is any other dyad of categories on this dimension: this is another indication of the strong influence on policy-making of 'Euro-americanism'.

The role of the Establishmentarians of course is very much that of making compromises between the positions of the extreme groups. This compromise-making role is revealed by the distribution of responses on the three items presented in Table 6.7.2.

Table 6.7.2. *The compromise-making role of the Establishmentarians*

	Elite				Opinion-makers			
	E	RO	D	LO	E	RO	D	LO
Foreign policy should primarily be:								
global	12	15	13	100	12	16	40	83
both	67	41	87	0	76	42	60	11
regional	12	44	0	0	12	42	0	0
Technical assistance should primarily be:								
bilateral	11	33	13	0	24	42	13	0
both	18	37	25	0	48	29	20	0
multilateral	71	22	50	100	26	19	57	78
Security policy contacts with East mainly:								
bilateral	31	26	38	75	16	29	27	39
both	22	30	50	0	64	39	60	39
multilateral	44	33	0	0	18	29	10	6

The compromise-role is seen in the tendency of the Establishmentarians to pick out the 'both' response on these single choice questions: in four of the six cases, this response is the majority choice.

But another piece of evidence may also be extracted from the distribution in the Table: the reality in the position of *doubt* of the category which has been given that name. This category also in four of six cases picks the 'both' response.

The second hypothesis presented under the Establishment-outsider heading is in reality a logical deduction from H 38 and proposes that by decreasing affective involvement in the issues, the difference between the outsider categories (or any two categories on this dimension) will also decrease.

We scrutinized the 32 variables employed for various explorations throughout this study, *minus* the four Establishment items. We found in short that this deduced hypothesis is well supported by the data. This means that H 38 is firmly backed as concerns the criterion that the issues should involve high affect or saliency to respondents; if not the expected j-surved distribution does not come out.

6.8. Differences according to self-perception: the policy-maker variable

The problem to be investigated here is much related to the one just discussed, in that a distinction is made between Establishment-related and other issues. We propose

H 39: *On Establishment and – related issues, the policy-maker group constitutes an ultra-elite 'on top' of the consensus pyramid of the polity.*

Thus, we expect that the policy-makers on such issues, but *only* on them and not on a whole range of different issues (non-salient, not involving affect) tend to be particularly consensual on taking the Establishment line.

The hypothesis is supported as far as the Establishment index is concerned, although the difference is not as great as expected (cf. Table 6.8.1). While

Table 6.8.1. *Establishment-outsider distributions and the policy-makers*

	Elite		Opinion-makers	
	Policy-makers	Rest*	Policy-makers	Rest*
Establishmentarians	59	46	33	37
Right outsiders	32	28	40	23
Doubters	6	11	13	25
Left outsiders	3	7	14	14
NA	0	8	0	1
	100	100	100	100
	(31)	(53)	(15)	(109)

*) Those who score NA on the policy maker variable, i.e. those who do not specify their policy-making influence in terms of the two categories, have been excluded.

the hypothesis is not confirmed in the case of the opinion-makers, this should not be attached much importance to as the policy-makers in that sample really do not take part in policy-making activities to the same extent as the elite policy-makers. One should, however, note the great influence of Right outsiders on the opinion-maker policy-makers: this is in line with what was found above about the 'rightwing' protest role of some of the opinion-makers (cf. 6.5).

If we confine ourselves to the elite policy-makers in the following, we may make another test of the hypothesis by looking at two sets of data: one being the mean modal value scores for each of the two categories on the totality of 48 variables, the other being a selection of Establishment-related variables. (Cf. Table 6.8.2).

Table 6.8.2. *Establishment and consensus scores for policy-makers and non-policy-makers*

	Policy-makers	Non-policy-makers
Mean corresponding modal value on 13 Establishment and – related items	67.1	60.4
Mean corresponding modal value on totality of 48 variables	66.7	65.6

The difference between the two categories is very small when a large number of different items is explored. This means that *in general* policy-makers *and* non-policy-makers are practically equally consensual. On Establishment-related items, however, the policy-makers get over-consensual, which is very logical as Establishment is the basis on which they make policy.

Another and even better indication of the very strong agreement between policy-makers and those outside the policy-making 'nucleus', are the single item agreement scores, measured by percentage differences on corresponding response values: in *none* of the 48 cases is there disagreement of the $\geq 20\%$ type, while there is $\geq 10\%$ disagreement in only 13 or 27% of the total number of cases explored. Compared with disagreement scores found on other variables above, this is certainly strong agreement. It means that *whether or not an elite member is also member of the policy-making group has seldom any influence on his foreign policy attitudes.*

It may also be inferred from this that there must be a lot of inter-communication and mutual influencing of images and attitudes between the policy-makers and the rest of the elite. In fact, the results obtained here are another strong proof of the homogeneity of the Norwegian foreign policy elite.

That some people do consider themselves policy-makers while others do not, of course should have *some* effect on some issues. Apart from the not very strong effect this has in relation to the foreign policy Establishment (making the policy-makers not only more positive toward Euro-america, but toward the UN and the developing countries as well – although only

227

slightly more positive in the latter two cases – than is the rest of the elite) it has some effect on e.g. perceptions of Norway's influence in the international community, where 61% of the policy-makers think that Norway has more influence than might be expected, while only 34% of the rest has the same image. On the other hand, a majority of the policy-makers also believes that Norway makes up its foreign policy within the context of international cooperation: only 16% of them, as against 40% of the rest, believe that Norway on the whole makes up its policy rather independently of what other states do.

Concluding this chapter, one is again struck by the degree of consensus and agreement which exists within and among the various sub-groups. At the same time, certain invariances point to interesting conclusions. One is that the party variable indicates the prominent role of political parties as socializing agencies in the Norwegian polity. Another important finding which should be followed up by more detailed research is the importance of the formative years to image-building. It has implications for what is discussed in the final chapter (8): future Norwegian elite attitudes and images.

PART III

Conclusions

III. Conclusions

This part is divided into two only partially related chapters. In the first, we shall face the problems of consonance, cognitive-affective consistency, and affective-to-cognitive convergence. In the second and final chapter, we shall focus on the world year 2000 as it can be derived from the expectations and images of the Norwegian elite; we shall make some 'projections' on what Norwegian foreign policy could be like in the future: and lastly we shall discuss possibilities of further research on the problems this study has dealt with.

7. Problems of Consistency, Consonance and Convergence

Our use of these three concepts differs somewhat from the way in which they are normally used. Thus, while Festinger's classical study of consonance and dissonance mostly deals with them in terms of the relationship between two (or more) cognitive elements (but in a wider conception of the word 'image') we use them in connection with cognitive – affective relationships.[1] The term 'consistency' in this context is reserved for the relationship between two cognitive *or* between two affective (or evaluative) elements. 'Convergence', lastly, is the process by which one element approaches another to which it is related.

7.1. *Consistency*

Two distinct types of consistency are explored in this context. The one may be called 'logical consistency', the other should be termed 'statistical consistency'. The concept has been discussed to some extent already (cf. 5.4). We shall in the following concentrate our discussion of consistency on the statistical type.

According to Galtung,

> consistency is the property a set of variables has if all inter-correlations are high, or all correlations with a measure of the dimension they are supposed to tap are high ...[2]

We shall deal with the first case, i.e. that of inter-correlations between a number of variables, adapting our method of measuring consonance to the peace proposal items (cf. 4.5). Our hypothesis will be that

H40: *Consistency increases with structural position.*

In order to test the hypothesis, a matrix of inter-correlations between all the 16 items (only 12 in the case of the public opinion sample) was made out. H 40 clearly holds, as is seen from Table 7.1.1.

Table 7.1.1. *Highest and lowest inter-correlation coefficients between peace proposals for the elite, the opinion-makers, and the public opinion*

	Elite	Opinion-makers	Public opinion
Highest	.986 (Rich help poor/Small states more influence)	.789 (Strengthen the UN/ Disarmament)	.468 (Raise individuals to peace/Better interindividual relations)
Lowest	.653 (Maintain alliances/ Realize the World State)	.286 (Small states more influence/Realize the World State)	−0.059 (Maintain alliances/ Disarmament)

The relative diffuseness on the part of the elite, tentatively pointed out in 5.4, is clearly not borne out by the information we present in this section. Diffuseness at least statistically should be defined as the tendency of a unit to divide itself between two or more different values on a given parameter.

Consistency may be further explored by means of cluster and factor analysis. We made the peace proposals subject to both these types of analysis, and the results are as follows:

Cluster analysis was made according to the rather simple method developed by McQuitty.[3] The resulting clustering is shown in Appendix I, where the Pearson's correlation coefficients 'linking' the variables are also given.

The statistical consistency reported above is again confirmed: in the elite case there are two (three), in the opinion-maker three (four), and the public opinion (youth) case five clusters. In the latter case, the clusters are clearly separated from each other, while in the two former there are linkages of high inter-correlations between the clusters which make them less separated and which further stress the (statistical) non-diffuseness of the profiles of the elite and the opinion-makers.

The extremely high inter-correlations coefficients found in the case of the elite – nearly all of them in the range of .90 or more – make it less relevant to single out specific clusters or sub-clusters. One may, however, in the four item cluster singled out in the Figure in Appendix I, find a specific category of 'global egalitarianism'.

In the case of the opinion-makers, specificity is less prominent than in the case of the elite. An 'impure' variable, 'Rich help poor states in development', distorts an otherwise logical internal consistency which would have singled out three specific clusters in the profile: one 'tough integrationist' ('Maintain alliances', etc.), one 'soft integrationist' (Strengthen the UN', etc.) and one 'World federalist' cluster.

The other way of exploring coherent 'bodies of belief' in the three samples is by way of *factor analysis. Using rotated* factor loadings, we arrived at the following list of factors for the three samples (cf. Figure 2 in Appendix I) for the loadings of the various items on the factor):[4]

The elite showed only *one single factor,* another strong proof of the specificity in the thinking of the elite. The opinion-makers showed three factors: one 'internationalist', one 'anti development assistance' and one 'anti-internationalist'. The public opinion sample (the youth sample) showed five factors: 'soft internationalist', 'anti tough integrationist', 'individualist', 'world federalist', and 'anti development assistance'.

Between the opinion-maker and the public opinion samples there is a certain but limited similarity: while in both cases an 'anti development assistance' factor emerges, the 'internationalist' opinion-maker factor is split in two factors with different value in the case of the public opinion.

We have shown that in terms of what we have called statistical consistency our H40 holds true. Differences between the structural positions represented by our three samples are so considerable that we may claim our findings valid for the social strata the samples represent.

But what does this mean? Where does the importance of such findings lie?

One problem with the use of such methods as cluster and factor analysis is found in the very methods. The results they yield often seem to be used with too much confidence and for too far-reaching conclusions. In other cases they present results which are either inexplicable or rather trivial.

In this context, we find it particularly relevant to combine correlation analysis with the study of consensus. The ways in which consensus and consistency in social groups may interact present some interesting and potentially far-reaching problems. An attempt at combining the two dimensions is made in Table 7.1.2.

The Norwegian elite clearly approaches the upper left corner of the Table: it shows high consensus and high consistency. Its action potential, i.e. its capacity to act *in common* as a prerequisite for being able to act at all, is thus – when no other factors are considered – high.

The case of high consensus and low consistency would indicate that action potential is high, but only when issues are taken separately. Persons

Table 7.1.2. *The interaction between consensus and consistency and its possible consequences*

| | | Consensus | |
		High	Low
	High	Very homogeneous, closely knit together group. Action potential is high	Polarized group, disagreement between internally consistent sub-groupings Action potential is low
Consistency			
	Low	Pluralistic opinion structure Action potential is high on single issues	Very heterogeneous disintegrated group No action potential

who agree on one issue will not necessarily agree on another. High action potential thus must be based on a capability of forming new alliances from issue to issue. Such a situation of much criss-cross is conceivable. Many foreign policy elites would probably approximate a position somewhere between the high consensus/high consistency and high consensus/low consistency categories.

The combination of both low consensus and low consistency is, however, not conceivable. Where such a combination were found, it would not be possible to talk about the social group concerned being an elite: in such a situation that group would not be able to perform prominent elite functions, such as acting and forming opinions.

But even in the fourth and final case – the situation when there is low consensus but high consistency – the question whether the group concerned may perform elite functions would have to be asked. Internal disagreement combined with high consistency does not *necessarily* mean manifest internal conflict. But the probability that conflict will be found is indeed very high. And where there is internal conflict, there is most often little external action. Thus, the action potential in this case is most likely low.

The ideal position, from an elite point of view, is that close to which the Norwegian elite seems to find itself. Whether and under what conditions that position may be changed depends on developments both within and outside the elite group or the foreign policy milieu itself.

The changes that took place before, during and just after WWII (cf. 2.5) in Norway's foreign policy were a result of external stimuli working on the images of elite members combined with an internal power struggle. The impact of external stimuli was probably most felt on the consensus side, breaking the old consensus down, gradually to replace it with a new one.

In this process, and at some stage when disagreement was at its highest, there was not one but two Norwegian foreign policy elites. Whether and to what extent elite members maintained high consistency in the process, is not possible to assess, but in the period of disagreement between roughly equally numerous subgroups within the elite, it probably approached the low consensus/high consistency category.

Elite members, naturally and as a function of position, will strive to achieve both high consensus and high consistency. Both may be difficult to achieve, but the former probably more so than the latter, because the individual elite member has more control over consistency. We would not say complete control, as a person e.g. through the pressure of conflicting external factors forcing him to take specific stands, is also forced to take mutually inconsistent positions.

It is, however, part of the life of elite persons to reduce inconsistencies in his profile. This is not always easy because he has to live up to expectations from his group, saying that reducing or wiping out inconsistencies should not be done at the expense of group consensus.

7.2. Consonance

In this section we shall deal primarily with the problem of *affective-cognitive consonance,* and in a more systematic way than has been done above (cf. 4.5) and on an individual not group, basis. In the first place, we shall test the hypothesis that

H41: *Affective-cognitive consonance increases with increasing structural position.*

Again, data are available only for the elite and the opinion-maker samples and the most reliable and valid data available are responses on the peace proposals. Both these conditions put restrictions on the generalizations we can draw.

Generally, a person will seek consonance and avoid dissonance. This tendency should be particularly felt among elite persons, because they in their role can less easily 'live with' strong affective-cognitive dissonance. In the feed-back system of creating attitudes and images, deciding policy and implementing it, and in receiving reactions to it, there will be a process of adjusting the affective and cognitive aspects of the perspectives of the persons involved.

Another reasoning speaks against this hypothesis, however. In a foreign policy milieu, particularly its elite part, there may be an influx of 'quasi-preferences' – peace policies are preferred as a tribute to e.g. the lower strata, to public opinion, but not *really* felt. The elite thus pays 'lip service' to influential parts of the public. They compensate for this 'restriction' on their true ideology by excluding the 'quasi-preferred' items from their cognitive image of which policies are 'realistic'. This point may explain some of the lack of 'trust' which certain policies experience (cf. 4.5).

One way to test the hypothesis would be by means of rank correlation. We found above that the elite sample shows a (Spearman's) *rho* of .33 between the preference and the 'realism' it attaches to the peace proposals. The corresponding *rho* for the opinion-maker sample is -0.10. It is probably even more negative in the case of public opinion.[5] Rank correlations, however, are no proof of the matter, and we have to turn to the data for further exploration.

Affective-cognitive dissonance may, as Festinger points out, be made more consonant in a number of ways. This can be done through one of the elements being stripped of its dissonant content and *adapted* to the other, brought close to it. This would probably happen to the element which is most deviant, according to some criteria, possibly the preferences of the individual (so that the cognitive element is adapted to the affective one). Further, one of the elements may be *reduced* or deliberately played down, so as to more or less disappear. Lastly, the two elements may *converge,* both of them being stripped of some of their dissonant content. Or, the same can be done with the relationship between the elements.

In the case of the Norwegian foreign policy milieu, the latter approach has been most commonly practiced. On the one hand, continued detente is perceived; on the other hand, the perception of military alliance as necessary is upheld and sometimes reinforced. To some extent, therefore, one has to maintain an image of the 'they' part of the 'we-they' group as an 'enemy' (at least potential). At the same time, however, one's own partners – the 'friends', or particularly the *big* friend – is perceived in a somewhat changed frame of reference with somewhat reduced affection.

Another case of cognitive dissonance turned into consonance, at least in the image held by most of the milieu, is probably represented by the 'concentric theory' of Norwegian foreign policy. Whether the consonance obtained in these and other cases is satisfactory to the persons concerned, is another matter. What we shall discuss very briefly, however, is the general problem: what are the possible or probable *implications* of dissonance, particularly for persons who hold a highly dissonant set of images and attitudes?[6]

Table 7.2.1. *Affective-cognitive dissonance and personality types*

| | | Preference: | |
		High	*Low*
'Realism' perception:	*High*	The consonant or well balanced	'The cynic' or 'The sheer realist'
	Low	'The sheer idealist'/ 'The disillusioned'	'The withdrawer: the out of-this-world man'

Among other things, this depends on the *intensity* with which the ideas concerned are held, *how* unrealistic they are thought to be, and for *how long* such feelings and thoughts exist.

A person with a peace profile high on preference, low on realism may be a 'sheer idealist' able to live well with his dissonant peace thinking. Or he may *not* be able to do that and end in frustration or disillusion, which may further result in forms of desperate action, or in inaction. He will perhaps blame the world ('it is rotten, nothing will work') or his leaders ('they don't want peace, really'; 'they are the true causes of war'). A study of the British Peace Pledge Union – an organization of 'radical peace activists' – has given some evidence on this.[7]

Another position may be that of a 'cynic' or 'realist': peace proposals are not highly preferred or evaluated, but the measures or methods they indicate are seen as quite realistic. The various personality types we may draw from such reasoning on affective-cognitive dissonance can be listed schematically as in Table 7.2.1.

Consonant personalities are found on the Low/Low to High/High diagonal axis. The elite person will generally be found at the High/High end of the axis, while lower social strata will spread to the other categories. But there are, as has been shown, important exceptions to this picture: a considerable part of the elite is placed in one of the two dissonant High/Low categories.

The opinion-makers, who were said to have a slightly more dissonant profile than the elite, are more free to be dissonant *and* (at least from some parts of society) probably are *expected* to be more so. This group, standing between the elite and the general opinion, in some respect must represent both 'sheer realism' and 'sheer idealism': it shall compensate for the lack of such positions or personalities in the elite and at the same time give vent to such more or less manifest attitudes among the general opinion.

In Table 7.2.2 below, correlation coefficients between preference and realism perception of the 16 peace proposals are given for both samples.

The items are ranked according to the correlation found in the case of the elite.

Table 7.2.2. *Spearman's correlation coefficients between preference for and realism perception of peace proposals in the elite and the opinion-maker samples*

(Elite rank)		Elite	Opinion-makers	(Rank)
(1)	'Maintain alliances'	.796	.397	(4)
(2)	'Strengthen regional organization'	.785	.515	(1)
(3)	'Maintain balance of power'	.784	.346	(7)
(4)	'West increase contact with East'	.773	.377	(6)
(5.5)	'Strengthen the United Nations'	.764	.337	(8)
(5.5)	'Rich help poor states'	.764	.392	(5)
(7)	'Raise individual to peace'	.754	.285	(12)
(8)	'Natural partners should cooperate'	.743	.440	(3)
(9)	'More democratic states'	.735	.300	(11)
(10)	'Abolish hunger and poverty'	.730	.234	(15)
(11)	'Small states more influence'	.728	.180	(16)
(12)	'Better inter-individual relations'	.711	.330	(9)
(13)	'States should become more similar'	.708	.443	(2)
(14)	'Disarmament'	.678	.244	(14)
(15)	'Fewer states in the world'	.677	.270	(13)
(16)	'Realize the World State'	.665	.306	(10)

In the first place, we note very strong support for the hypothesis, H41, that consonance increases with structural position: in fact, *none* of the correlations in the case of the opinion-makers are higher than the *lowest* correlation for the elite sample.

Secondly, the ranking of the items seems to coincide somewhat with our findings, established above (4.5), on the 'trust' and 'distrust' of the proposals, although important differences are found and although it should be stressed, of course, that the two *types of analysis* are not at all corresponding.

Thirdly, there is a Spearman's rank correlation coefficient between the ranking of the two samples of .54, not very high, but which still seems to show a certain similarity in the perceptions of the two.

7.3. *Convergence*

We have showed above that there will tend to be a convergence of opinions among individuals or groups, as one moves from items involving high affect to items involving little or no affect (cf. 6.6).

A similar convergence may take place *from* affective *to* cognitive components of the same issues or issue-areas: the affective components are adjusted to the cognitive, attitudes to perceived reality. This hypothesis:
There is a convergence of affectively dissident opinions on a cognitive basis is our H42.

It is obvious that a relatively great affective – cognitive dissonance, and a non-convergence on the two between some units, may be completely consistent and rational: one may *perceive* an armaments race as taking place and yet *wish* for disarmament. The relationship between affective and cognitive elements of a person's perspective becomes interesting only when in certain situations *one would expect* consonance between them.

To take only two examples: we have shown above that persons who expected the gap between the rich and the poor countries to increase in the future were *not* more inclined than others to have a positive attitude toward an increase of Norwegian technical assistance vis à vis the less developed countries. We did also show that a large number of respondents did not adopt a positive attitude towards depolarization or the promotion of *detente,* which was perceived as a future prospect by almost everybody.

The important thing in this connection may be whether the respondent in question views a decreasing rich-poor gap or an increasing detente as positive values. In other words, there is an intervening factor, another affective element working in between the affective and cognitive element, or on the relationship between these elements. It has been substantiated already that in the concrete examples mentioned, the intervening variables may be or in fact *are* what in our terms should be referred to as strong 'we-they' feelings, in others' terms 'self-interest', and 'we-we' feelings or 'ideology'.

On the other hand: how much and for how long can an individual perceive one thing and prefer quite another? Can one witness a gallopping armaments race and at the same time ardently support disarmament, *without* being subjected to internal conflicts, frustrations, possibly withdrawal? Will one not, confronted with the real world, tend to adjust one's own hopes and preferences according to that reality, in order that the gap between the preferred and the experiences shall not be too great?

Moreover: *if* values, evaluations and preferences largely determine or influence perception, would not one's cognitive image of the world become too remote from the real world, because one's ability to perceive is blurred one's images distorted by one's preferences? The result may be called *cognitive discrepancy.*

If it is true, as we think it largely is, that the strong 'Westwardness' in the Norwegian elite tends to arrange the cognitive elements of the perspective held by the elite members, this may explain the relatively limited perspective they actually hold. A certain bias is clearly introduced in the images of the respondents.

We now return to the testing of H42. As the peace proposals still represent the best, i.e. most valid and reliable, arsenal for testing such a hypothesis in a systematic and valid manner, we shall once again have a look at these variables. We shall first compare agreement between the elite and the opinion-makers on the two peace proposals elements; secondly, we shall look at agreement rates between the party groups in the opinion-maker sample.

As Table 7.3.1 shows, there *is* an affective to cognitive convergence in the case of the elite and opinion-maker samples: the mean difference, as

Table 7.3.1. *The affective to cognitive convergence hypothesis and elite and opinion-maker samples*

	Preferences: 'especially important to peace'	Preferences: 'Important to peace'*	Realism perception
Mean elite – opinion-maker differences	6.8%	7.6%	4.9%
No. of cases of ≥ 10% difference	5	5	0

*) Comprises both 'Especially important to peace' and 'Somewhat important to peace'.

well as the single-item difference measured by the number of cases of ≥ 10% difference, is smaller in the realism perception side than on the preference side.

This convergence is even better reflected by looking into some of the single variables (cf. Table 7.3.2). We see that on those proposals which have a – 10% difference on the preference side, the convergence is particularly, perhaps surprisingly great, almost amounting to total agreement between the two samples on the realism perception side.

Testing the hypothesis, H42, on opinion-maker party groups (cf. Table 7.3.3) we are obviously looking into the independent variable accounting for most of the variance in the samples, and thus one of the variables which should offer the most valid testing of H42. As seen from the Table, only half of the 10 cases shows a confirmation of the hypothesis, while 3 out of 10

Table 7.3.2. *Elite versus opinion-makers on some selected proposals:*
the convergence hypothesis in percentages

| | 'Especially important to peace' | | 'Realistic' | |
	E	OM	E	OM
Keep the balance	58	34	68	64
Preserve alliances	38	22	63	63
Educate individuals to peace	35	46	61	59
Establish the World State	24	36	6	10
Strengthen the UN	79	68	61	64

Table 7.3.3. *The convergence hypothesis and party groups: the case*
of the opinion-makers

	Preferences: 'Important to peace', mean percentage difference	Cases of ≥ 30% diff.:	Realism perc.: 'Realistic': mean percentage difference	Cases of ≥ 30% diff.:	Hypothesis confirmed:*
Socialist-Conservatives	20.1	3	15.1	3	+
Socialist†-Christians‡	20.1	5	16.3	3	+
Socialist-Liberals	14.1	3	15.6	3	−
Socialist-Labor	13.8	5	21.0	4	−
Labor-Conservatives	14.2	1	12.1	1	+
Labor-Christians	12.8	3	13.0	3	/
Labor-Liberals	9.9	1	10.4	1	−
Liberals-Conservatives	8.2	0	5.9	0	+
Liberals-Christians	12.3	1	12.3	2	/
Christians-Conservatives	14.6	1	11.0	2	+

*) Confirmed = + ; disconfirmed = − ; neither confirmed nor disconfirmed = /.
Only differences of ± 0.5 % (mean difference) or more are taken as confirmation or
disconfirmation.
†) Comprises the Socialist People's Party and the Communists.
‡) Comprises the Christian People's Party and the Center Party.

disconfirm it, the remaining 2 cases neither confirming nor disconfirming it.

This is not an impressive support of the hypothesis, although the evidence
is *in the direction of* it. Looking more closely into the data presented in
Table 7.3.3, we might suggest that the convergence is found particularly
between groups which are by definition politically at some distance from
each others. Following the Socialist-Labor-Liberals-Christians-Conserva-

tives continuum, we see that e.g. the Socialists on the one side, the Christians and the Conservatives on the other converge most; they are also at the greatest 'political distance' from each other, *and* most in disagreement affectively. On the other hand, close 'neighbors' as e.g. the Socialists and Labor in particular, are seen as more in disagreement cognitively.

If we distinguish between 'neighbors' and 'non-neighbors' according to the continuum indicated, we see that in 4 out of 6 cases the 'non-neighbors' are converging (one case being ambivalent), while the opposite pattern is found in 2 out of 4 cases between 'neighbors' (one case being ambivalent).

On the whole, we feel that the hypothesis of an affective to cognitive convergence has been established as a fruitful proposition for further exploration and confirmation.

8. Perceptions
of Future Norwegian Foreign Policy

8.1. *Perception of the World Year* 2000

Predictions about the future are useful, difficult to make, and meaningless –
at the same time. They are useful because man ought to look ahead and see
what comes after today, or what *may* come. They are difficult to make
because societies are so complex and their development may take so many
directions that prediction, except in a very gross and superficial way, may be
beyond man's capability. And they are at the same time meaningless because
a prediction that includes certain possibilities while ruling out others (as
any prediction will have to) may give rise to counteracting and transcending
forces – self-denying as well as self-fulfilling.[1]

The 'magic year' 2000 was not always explicitly referred to in the questions
about future developments that we asked the respondents: in some cases,
a shorter time-span was referred to. The type of analysis adopted in this
section is about some preferences and expectations concerning the future
of the international system, found among members of the Norwegian
foreign policy milieu. It is a rather superficial analysis because conclusions
drawn (by the author) on the predictions made (by respondents) are necessarily based on certain preconditions (many of which are not known today)
and on wide margins for intervening variables.

Attitudes and images of elite people are one set of conditions among a
large number that shapes the future. But as the 'objective' social world is
subject to changes, so are attitudes and images, and the two of course
interact. Such changes, on the other hand, should not be over-estimated.
Stability, slow transformation etc. seem to be equally prominent features of
social development.

It was our hypothesis that

H13: *Norway is optimistic about the future.*

The hypothesis actually has been supported by data presented above (cf.

244

Chapter 4 and sections 5.4 and 5.6). In Table 5.4.3, elite, opinion-maker, and public opinion hopes for the future world were shown. In addition to expressing hopes for the future, the elite sample was invited to state what they *expected* the world to look like in the future, 'the year 2000'.

There *is* a tendency to expect a better world in the future, and this seems consistent with the expressions of hopes. The *rank order* of preferences and expectations are the same: those items which are most prefered are also most expected. *But* there is no real consonance in the data when these two variables are compared: by correlating the two, we find practically no correlation between them (finding a Pearson's correlation coefficient of -0.13).

An interpretation of this in fact would be that optimism is not as strong as expected. We would not say it is non-existent; other findings show the opposite. One possible explanation of the low correlation is that thinking about the distant year 2000 future is not well developed and that the low salience of the issue itself contributes to low consonance; responses are given to some extent at random.

What the elite *hopes* but does not expect about the world in 30 years seems to be: that the actors at that time will cooperate and understand each others more, that this cooperation will take place within or under the guidance of a supra-nationalized world body, possibly the UN, *and* that they in particular will cooperate to solve the problems of the less developed countries, and to bridge present inequality gaps in the system.

Peace-and-war thinking is not, in its direct expression, so prominent in the future as it is in the present, which seems to indicate that the elite largely expects these problems to be partially solved or at least played down in importance by then. We note, on the other hand, a certain pessimism towards these problems: there is a tendency to hope that they are solved by that time, but at the same time to disbelieve it. This may be interpreted quite contrary to the above mentioned interpretation, to mean that the elite neither really hopes nor expects the ever-lasting problem of peace to be settled by the year 2000, when peace is defined as absence of war.

Deutsch et al. contend, with particular reference to the French elite, that

> we think it quite valid to argue that feasible political developments, for both the present and the near future, can to some extent be gauged by the degree of elite consensus upon desirable developments.[2]

While we find this contention valid to a certain point, certainly a number of factors may intervene to make desired developments non-feasible. This seems to be more true the less power, i.e. capability of imposing its desires upon the world, the elite in question possesses. Thus, what the Norwegian elite desires certainly will not have much chance of being realized, unless those desires happen to coincide with what is desired by some or a number of other actors' elites, possessing far more power. But this is what seems to be the case: Norway's preferences for the future world coincide to a large extent with those of other Western states, which *do* possess power. And this, due to penetration, historical developments and resulting Atlantism in the elites preferences, is more by *intention* than by chance[3]. This Western-Norwegian coincidence has been more than indicated by the comparative analysis engaged in above.

On future prospects, there seems strong agreement between the four elite samples that there will some change in the system, but that it will remain basically bipolar. China is seen as on her move upwards, West Germany is also expected to move upwards but to a lesser degree, while the two traditional great powers Great Britain and France are expected to move downwards. Other contenders are not given much chance; only Japan is mentioned as an upward mover by some of the Norwegians. This seems well to reflect the centrism, if not the *ego*-centrism of European elites.

To summarize what may be seen as the image of the future of the Norwegian elite, concentrating on the structure, trends of integration or disintegration, and the threat or power relationship, the following profile could be drawn:

There will be more international cooperation, as a function of increasing integration of the system throughout the last decades of the century. Some sub-systems, however, will have been particularly much integrated: this is true with Western ones; the East will have been less integrated, while the South will remain as little integrated as it has been since decolonization.

The conflict between the East – or the North-East - and the West will have been partially removed, substituted by a narrower and more positive network of cooperation. The traditional East-West conflict will to some extent have lost ground to another conflict dimension – the North-South. In the year 2000 the gap between the rich North and the poor South has not decreased; at the same time, the world at large is becoming more occupied with the gap and North-South relations in general. That the gap is not decreasing does not, however, have serious consequences to international relations. On the other hand, the lack of major progress in large parts of the 'developing world' will create a state of distrust and discontent which results in polarization, middle-range wars, and so on. The rich countries will be somewhat more concerned with helping the poor countries, much to their own interest.

Western Europe has become a well integrated unit, with an extensive network of cooperation with Eastern Europe. Western Europe is, however, not on its way to any big or super power status. And the socalled 'gaullism', which to some extent made itself felt during the 1960s, has vanished.

Much because China is moving upwards, she and the Soviet Union have had some serious conflicts amounting to military clashes. This trend, plus the increasing understanding between the North-East and the West, have laid the ground for extensive Soviet-US cooperation. This cooperation is increasingly the essential content of the bipolar structure, making it a bipolar hegemony. This hegemony is to the benefit of the system as a whole, because it secures stability, predictability, change under control.

While the world has witnessed a number of minor and middle range wars, the great nuclear war has been avoided by the year 2000. The level of armaments reached its peak in the 1970s and 1980s, and after that it started to decline due to disarmament treaties and their successful implementation.

The partial disarmament achieved has, however, not had the effect on the world structure and the possibilities of avoiding conflicts as some optimists in the 1960s believed it was possible to obtain.

Contacts between nations and peoples have been steadily improved. Great technological achievements have revolutionized among other things the network of communication and made this possible. At the same time, nations have become more similar to each others: they have moved closer to the Western model of society and culture.

And finally, Norway has bettered its position throughout the end of the century, compared to the one it had in the 1960s.

Among the sub-groups of the sample, differences on the whole are not great or substantial concerning the image of the world year 2000. Given that in the future there *will* be a stable, predictable and controlled change in the world society, there is no reason to expect great differences in image as elite membership is renewed. There are, on the other hand, certain differences between the age groups which should be brought out here.

The younger elite members in Norway, as well as in France, are more 'internationalistic' or 'anti-nationalistic' than their elder colleagues, at the same time as they are more pessimistic about the prospects of international integration in the future. The younger are more inclined to expect tripolarity in the structure; they are more optimistic when it comes to bridging the rich-poor gap in the world; and they are more moderate in their optimism concerning further integration of the West. In other words, the younger have a more balanced image of the world year 2000 than do the elder groups: their image of world structure contains a greater amount of symmetry in the relationship between sub-systems.

8.2. *Future Norwegian foreign policy*

How will the Norwegian elite think and act in the future? That question is a logical follow-up of the last part of the last section: what the younger age groups think and how they react today should be a good indicator of how the Norwegian elite in the future will think and act. That is, to the extent we may assume that they will basically maintain their images and attitudes. This we *may* on the basis of the proposition about the importance of the formative years on the image building.

But for a number of reasons we should rather free ourselves from hard data at this point. We should be free to speculate on the future.

It has been stressed before that Norway is an actor much dependent on the environment. Penetration from outside, and the more or less willing internalization of the message which the penetrating agents carry (we are still thinking of Euro-Atlanticism) is related to the dependency.

But in objective terms, Norway is not *that* dependent on external forces. To some extent, she seems to have chosen the position of a responding, not an initiating actor. She has the feeling of the achieved – and this feeling must be at the core of why she is not more initiating.

The high consensus of the elite reflects a pattern of general relevance to Western polities at the manifest elite level: the passing away of ideologies and the introduction of more pragmatism – the shift from empathy to expathy. In the case of Norway, the lack of major ideological controversy at the elite level seems to have been carried to the point of profound self-satisfaction among elite members.[4]

But will or can this situation last? That depends on developments both inside and outside the foreign policy milieu itself. Also, it may be dependent on the degree to which elite images reflect the real world.

What that real world looks like is in itself a controversial question, but we must assume that one can establish that objectively, an 'objective' world as a set of phenomena existing independently of the minds of men.

We may think in terms of two opposite types of relationship between the real world and the images of man. According to one, images reflect the real world: the objective and subjective world is one and the same. The opposite type would be the no relationship one: images are formed on their own, from within the social group of which a given person is a member, or within that person himself, and without reference to the outside world.

These are ideal types. But one may find examples of social groups or single individuals who come close to them: on the one hand the *clairvoyant* or the insightful social scientist, foreign policy practitioner or international man: on the other hand the sectarian, who need not be a Hippie or a religious sectarian, but might be e.g. a scientist or practitioner.

The Norwegian elite and foreign policy milieu falls somewhere in between these two models. Exactly *where*, depends upon an assessment of what the objective world is like. Elite images of course must largely reflect that world; if not, will put itself and the actor it represents in a potentially dangerous situation. On the other hand, the centrism of the Norwegian elite (and to a somewhat lesser extent the milieu) probably points to the possibility that people may stick to images which are relatively consistent with the realities of 'their part of the world', but which do not necessarily reflect very well the objective global system.

Moreover, the Atlanticism of the Norwegian elite seems so entrenched that it could scarcely be changed in the foreseeable future. The only thing that could change it is a serious threat to its very basis, in terms of a series of discontinuous changes like the one the Norwegian elite experienced from 1940 to 1949.

The Norwegian elite, or the whole milieu, sees no such threat in the present world. Again we must ask: does it reflect the real world?

What is that real world like? Let us think of *one* possible real world: the confusing one, a world of contending trends, actors, ideologies. The strong emphasis on integrationist trends in the image of the milieu does not reflect well the actual trends in a real world: disintegration, at the national as well as the inter-national or global level, would seem as prominent.

And although the conception of a basically and continuously bipolar world structure would seem relatively 'correct', there seems to be too little reflection of both certain moral issues (whether the structure is a 'good' one e.g. for those actors or groups which find themselves at the bottom of it and do make grievances about their position) and of tensions within the structure. The low salience of the development and the North-South issues shows this.

It is thus an evaluation of this author that the Norwegian foreign policy milieu does not reflect particularly well the real world in the way the milieu conceives of the world particularly in the case of the elite sample, taken as a whole. But then we have made the observation that the younger parts of the elite and gradually the whole milieu are coming closer to a realistic world image, and that this is the important thing for the future.

This observation must be qualified by certain others. First, the differences between the perceptions of the younger and those of the older are relatively marginal *except* when the very young in the opinion-maker sample are included. These differences, however, may point to changed images and there-fore changed policies in the future. Unless no drastic discontinuous changes occur in the meantime to prepare the ground for revolutionary global developments, the probability of evolutionary gradualistic development is high.

But again one has to face certain facts. The younger parts of the milieu are going to take over image building and policy-making only in ten or fifteen years, when the present power-holders – the middle-aged – have become old and are in their turn disengaging themselves. Will these new power-holders – the present young – at *that* time reflect the real world better than the present power-holders reflect today's world? Or will the real world have changed so much that the images of the younger elite will have become more or less out-dated, irrelevant, when they become established, dominant elite images?

We predict, on the basis of variations between the age groups, that the Norwegian foreign policy milieu will be more positive toward developing countries, including China. But what would that attitude mean – how far would it go? Would it e.g. include a situation of 'class conflict' between the rich and poor countries, where the two sides are opposed due to conflicting interests, and the developing countries form a militant trade union vis a vis the rich – the latter presumably including Norway?

There are many reasons to believe that it would not and most of them are found in the pages above. 'Partners in development' would seem a much more acceptable (and realistic) 'scenario' to the present Norwegian elite than the 'class conflict' one, although this is probably less true for the younger parts of the milieu than for the older.

But there are other scenarios, some of which are already being prepared for the stage: e.g. that of smaller countries opposing big ones, most recently and most prominently in the case of Indochina. Although the Indochina war has not had any major effect on the Norwegian foreign policy milieu so far, it may have a long-range effect. There is no doubt – as has already been indicated in our report – that US policy in Indochina is disapproved of by great parts of the milieu. The question is on the one hand, whether the effect of that conflict in the long term may be that the case of small versus big powers, i.e. the highly unequal distribution of power in the world as something basically negative, is put to the Norwegian elite. The question then is whether the elite will take sides, or take a new side, by stressing Norway's position as a medium-range or smaller state, thus making a new point of identification, and at the same time playing down the fact that it is rich and developed. Lastly, the question is whether this may lead to a weakened identification with Euro-Atlanticism.

It is more probable that Norway will take sides with small nations against big, powerful ones than that Norway will side with the under-developed against the developed; this follows from the mere fact that she is relatively small *but* developed, i.e. the international position of Norway.

But this is not a very high probability. It *may* become so if e.g. the Indochina situation is globalized – extended to more parts of the world. Then the situation will be very close to the type of discontinuous changes in the real world which we see as a prerequisite for drastic changes in the images of the Norwegian elite.

A fourth scenario is that of changed images due to influences from within the milieu itself, or within the Norwegian polity. The Student Revolution, the emergence of the New Left (these phenomena occurred in Norway after the time of the interviewing, but largely only after they were seen on the continental European scene) may be forerunners of such influences to come. And they may already be represented by the young part of the opinion-maker sample which with its Leftist tendencies may not be the most probable recruits to the future elite, given that present recruitment patterns are continued, *but* which may be so if these patterns are changed.

But such domestically originating effects may just as well go in the other direction, toward reaction through reemergence of past, or towards re-inforcing present positions. A combination of environmental real-world dis-continuous changes and a reinforcement of present images and attitudes to enable them to resist those environmental influences, is not unlikely. But then of course the milieu would move closer to the type of relationship between the objective and subjective world described above as a non-relationship: images and attitudes are formed and held *irrespective of* what happens in the objective world.

In that perspective, the more the bipolar world and the super-power domination of it is felt and resented throughout the world, the more the Indochina effect is felt, the more the gap between the rich and the poor is widening, and the more entities are disintegrated throughout the world – the more Norway's foreign policy elite will stick to or even reinforce its belief in bipolar dominance, US protection through Euroatlanticism, Nor-way's status as developed and her place in the Center-Western world. 'You know what you have, you do not know what you may get' is a rather precise description of the thinking of the major part of the Norwegian milieu.

And after all: can the foreign policy milieu escape from the international position of the country it represents? Does it not follow from the theory we have developed that it cannot: that as long as that position is not changed, dominant images and attitudes held by the elite and milieu concerned can-not change either?

It should be clear from the very basis of our theory that the international position of an actor may and will often change over time. To a large extent due to environmental changes, to some extent (depending on the range of manouvering it has) on the acts of the (elite of that) actor itself. As was indicated above, the possibility (as in the case of Norway) of redefining one's position through manipulating the various components of the international position profile would seem to present a range of self-determination leaving much room for action.

Norway may be joining the European Communities in the beginning of the 70s. This would be a step with more far-reaching consequences than is commonly expected, at least in the long run. To most members of the Norwegian milieu, EEC membership is just another way of practicing Euroatlanticism. If the EEC turns out to be something else, something more European (even if still Western) than Atlantic and not necessarily reconciling the two very well, this may become a major problem for the future Norwegian elite, whose perceptions have the two as one and the same and whose policies thus are founded on such perceptions.

EEC membership would create no problem with respect to centrism and the continued status of a developed, an achieved country. It would, however, create problems in relation to the USA and with respect to the bipolarism presently found in the elite. It would not, on the other hand, make redefinition of her status in terms of more emphasis on size and lack of power more probable, and the probability that Norway may take sides with the small and/or poor countries (the two characteristica, as we know, are positively correlated) would become not stronger but most certainly lesser. Neither would her globalism increase, but on the contrary decrease.

And then comes the question: considering what this report has proved, that there exists a wide difference in the images and attitudes on dominant political issues between the elite and the general population – should the elite not redefine its positions to become more in line with the thinking of the people at large? This would not automatically mean a more precise, realistic, or objectively based relationship to the real world; in some cases it might mean the contrary. But it would mean a better reflection of groups and interests which are not well represented at the level or elites: the national *and* international periphery. No doubt there is a danger that elite – public opinion differences may become even wider in the future, than they are today.

What are then likely predominant images and attitude sets of the Norwegian elite and foreign policy milieu in the future?

It is our prediction that the real world is going into a period of more conflict, less stable structures, and conflicting trends of integration and disintegration. Viewing the world 'superstructure', we feel bipolarity will see competing if not (in the nearer future) equally strong alternative structures; center nations will develop more cooperation among themselves but at the same time – as alternative structures will to a large extent be established within and among this group – see more conflicts of interest crossing lines of cooperation; periphery nations will to a lesser extent develop cooperation between themselves but at the same time achieve some reductions in internal conflicts of interest, thus preparing the ground for a development towards a trade union of poor (and small) nations. Such a development may be accelerated by new Indochinas, by an increasing rich-poor gap, and by racial polarization (e.g. over the 'postponement' of a just solution to racial discrimination over the world).

If there are going to be no far-reaching changes in these directions; if there is no basic change in Euroatlantica forcing a choice on Norway of the type which has been mentioned; if there is no 'militant' challenge from the underdeveloped countries which really calls to the forefront of political thinking the moral issues involved in underdevelopment, the lack of power among poor and small and the crucial role rich and big countries play in depriving the poor and small development and power; and if there is no change in the detente trend (in either direction) – *then* there is strong reason to believe that Norwegian elite and milieu images and attitudes will remain much the same as today for a foreseeable future, except for the gradual change of emphasis predicted by the age variations.

But if several of the conditions just mentioned are met – then Norway's international position is bound to be affected, and by consequence the images and attitudes of her elite and leading foreign policy-debating strata. The latter *may* of course overlook changes in the 'objective' position of the country and stick to the established ways of perceiving it, but we must assume that this subjectivism is not possible in the long run. It need not be (will most probably not be) a change *from* center to periphery, but from one type of centrist position to another, including some changes in the elements defining the position, and including a changed structure in the center which affects the position, a Euroatlantic split being one such type of change.

The Norwegian outlook is rigid in the sense that it is well established and based on a rather deep self-satisfaction. At the same time it is flexible because to a large extent (the extent decreasing proportionally with decreasing structural position) the Norwegian foreign policy milieu is accustomed to being led by other elites. New leadership with new images thus would mean a new Norwegian outlook. One may wonder what Norwegian images and attitudes would have looked like if great parts of the elite (the potential as much as actual) had not been forced to take refuge in London and Washington at a crucial moment, but had gone instead to – Moscow.

For the future, going to Brussels means in the longer run at least that a partially alternative leadership is established. It will most probably affect the bipolarism, globalism, and the Atlanticism of the milieu, creating a new type of centrism in reducing the role of these elements.

Changes in the environment are a necessary condition for changes in the images and attitudes of Norwegians. Such changes make *people* change their outlook, or *some* people change so that consensus is replaced by disagreement. In such a situation, where new channels of recruitment to the elite positions also will be opened, the conditions may be created for 'internal factors' to work themselves out. Then today's young with really alternative images, represented in the opinion-maker sample, may make their way to the leading opinion-making and policy-making positions 'before their time' and with far greater effect than otherwise would have been possible. But the probability that this 'third force' would be able to pose as an alternative to two regionalisms fighting each other, is not great.

This is under present circumstances: it is a task for everybody who cares about it – and the author of this report does – to make a 'third force' both possible *and* probable.

Appendices

APPENDIX A:

Sampling procedure

As mentioned elsewhere, a total of 100 persons were selected for interviewing in the *elite* study, 25 from each of the four categories mentioned (cf. Appendix B).

Galtung, in discussing the question of the minimum average m per cell in a table which present the data, mentions two lines of argumentation on the question how large the m ought to be: first, that the m should be able to get out the variation in the universe; secondly, that the percentages one makes out of the information presented in a table, are not 'too subject to fluctuations with some small changes in the absolute figures'.[1]

He sets, as a 'rule of thumb', the average m per cell to be not lower than 10 and preferably 20 or more. If on the average (deviances from the rule must of course be allowed) there are three variables per table and two values per variable, the m has to be 80 (when the requirement is 10 cases per cell, 160 when the requirement is 20 cases per cell). And in the case of two variables per table and three values per variable, the m has to be at least 90.[2]

As we generally will make use of trichotomies on the value side, and bivariate analysis on the variable side, it seems satisfactory to have a total m of about 100, although the requirements set up initially of course are *minimum* requirements and to some extent based on 'scientific guess-work'.

On the other hand, an m of 100 in fact is strongly supported by Gorden and Lerner, who on the basis of experiences with changing m's in their panel studies, find that

> Except for the m requirements of cross-tabulation, soundings of elite opinions may require many fewer respondents than imagined to achieve a reliable measure of opinion. Our middle years rule of thumb of 100 panelists is close to insensitivity (of changing m's) and the addition of a very few more respondent would achieve a high degree of reliability. [3]

Although this is not made explicit in their report, we take it that they would think of a higher per-cell m than the minimum we have adopted; their excluding cross-tabulation from the conclusions they make then is not to be taken as a proof against the proposals we have made: a total m of 100 in the case of the elite.

In the case of the opinion-makers, the m, both the total and thus logically the sub-group m's, were made much higher, nearly three times as high, because we expected a lower response rate in this case. Moreover, the un-

256

certainty as to what constituted the universe and what was the correct sampling in the first stage, made this necessary.

Among the Parliamentarians, we included all the 24 members of the extended Foreign Relations Committee in the Storting plus one MP from the Socialist People's Party; the selection of people from the administration was made by three judges independently, and 15 from the Foreign, 5 from each of the two other ministries were included; from the mass media – the press and radio – we selected the foreign editors of the dailies and weeklies appearing in Oslo or, in those cases where there was no foreign editor, the chief editor, and from the radio/TV we included the heads of the news and foreign departments and their 'second hands' (redaksjonssekretærer) plus the news commentators (journalists, editors, or researchers); and among the interest organizations we included the administrative heads from the main organizations in four different fields: Norwegian branches of international organizations (WAWF, Red Cross), general political organizations ('Atlanterhavs-komiteen', the Nordic Association, etc.), economic interest organizations (Norwegian Shipowners' Association, etc.) and the peace or defense organizations (War Resisters and 'Folk og Forsvar').

Totally, we got interviews with 88 persons on a practically even distribution between the four groups. No reverse sampling was made to replace those with whom we did not get an interview.

The opinion-maker sample was also selected partly by formal criteria, partly by the use of judges, but in two cases – in the case of mass media and the teachers – randomly. Four groups were included: members of *the political parties' committees on foreign policy matters* (standing or the last *ad hoc* commitee), journalists on the foreign 'desk' in the Oslo *press* and editors of 'province' newspapers (appearing outside Oslo) plus all employed in the radio/TV's two relevant departments (those who were not included in the elite sample), administrative heads (or in the cases where there were no such permanent heads: the chosen chairman) of relevant *interest organizations* which were not included in the elite sample, and *teachers* in history and social science ('samfunnskunnskap') in the secondary school and the universities.

The party committee members were all included, except in two cases: half of the committee of the Socialist People's Party was selected randomly, as the committee was relatively much more numerous than the committees of the other parties; and the Communist Party 'excluded' themselves by not responding when we asked for a list of members of the party's foreign relations committee. In the case of the Center Party, we had to include the party's executive committee, since it had no special committee on foreign relations.

The people in the press were – as mentioned – selected randomly. We used a catalogue of all papers appearing weekly or more often. The number of respondents to be contacted was determined by the official data on the paper's circulation. Papers with a circulation below 12,000 were excluded. In most cases only one respondent – the editor – was included from each paper, but in the case of the biggest papers, a larger number (from 2 to 5, depending on circulation) was included.

The interest organizations were selected by the use of a catalogue of Norwegian associations and interests organizations.[4] All organizations with a membership total above 500 and which were relevant to foreign policy or international political matters were included, and one respondent was chosen from each organization.

The secondary school and university teachers were chosen randomly from a list of members in the History Section of the Norwegian Secondary School Teachers' Association.

NOTES

1 Galtung, *Theory and Methods*, p. 61
2 ibid., p. 60
3 Gorden and Lerner, op. cit. p. IX-4
4 Jorolv Moren, *Oppslagsboken norske organisasjoner* (Oslo: Johan Grundt Tanum, 1967)

APPENDIX B:

Response rates of the samples

A total of 100 persons in the case of the elite, 278 in the case of the opinion-maker sample were selected and contacted through an introduction letter, and through the mailed questionnaire accompanied by an introduction letter, respectively The total number of persons contacted, and the total number of respondents actually obtained, are shown with a breakdown on the various sub-groupings of the samples, in Table B. 1.

Table B. 1. *Response rates for the sub-groupings of the elite and the opinion-maker samples*

	Selected number of persons		Number of persons actually responding		Response rate in percentages	
	EL	OM	EL	OM	EL	OM
Politicians	25	77	23	40	92	52
Civil servants	25	67	22	28	88	42
Mass media	25	55	21	16	84	29
Interest organizations	25	79	22	45	88	57
Total	100	278	88	130	88	47

The response rates among the sub-groupings of the opinion-maker sample is of course too unequal to be satisfactory. In particular, the low return of the mass media group despite two follow-up letters to the selected persons, is deplorable *and* rather inexplicable. As has been mentioned, the opinion-maker selection was told that another study of 'top' people in various fields had been carried out recently; this was believed to help increase the return from the opinion-makers.

APPENDIX C.

Validation of the differentiation between the elite and the opinion-maker samples

The validation will be done according to the three dimensions for differentiation shown in Figure 1: social position, exposure, and participation.

According to *social position,* the difference between the two samples is as expected: the elite is more recruited from center positions than the opinion-maker sample (cf. Table C. 1), according to two different definitions of 'center' and 'periphery'.

Table C. 1. *Social position of the elite and opinion-maker samples*

	Elite		Opinion-makers	
	I*	II†	I	II
Center	25	59		26
Middle	35	29		48
Periphery	40	13		26

*) Definition I: Center = 8; Middle = 6, 7; Periphery = 0–5.
†) Definition II: Center = 7, 8; Middle = 5, 6; Periphery = 0–4.

As to degree of *exposure,* and to place in the communication structure, we shall view the two together, as they certainly may be. A number of variables some of which have already been mentioned (cf. 4.7) may be used as indicators. A selection of them is found in Table C. 2.; the rationale for the selection made should be relatively self-evident.

Table C. 2. *Exposure and place in the communication structure of the elite and opinion-maker samples*

	Elite	Opinion-makers
'Would you say that you have any personal influence on the making of Norwegian foreign policy?'		
Yes	36	12
Little or no	60	84
'Have you been or are you at the moment member of any official Norwegian delegation to international organizations?'		
Yes, 3 or more	26	1
Yes, 1–2	36	9
No	35	79

Table C. 2. (*cont.*)

	Elite	Opinion-makers
'When you discuss foreign policy matters, would you say that you yourself most often take contact with others, or are you more often contacted by others?'		
I most often take the contact myself	16	12
Both/it depends	46	53
I am most often contacted by others	24	7
How often do you have contact with the foreign minister or a member of the government in foreign policy matters:		
More or less daily	26	3
More or less weekly	25	14
Once a month or so	32	22
Once a year or so	9	2
Never	0	25
How often do you go abroad?		
More than 20 times a year	6	0
Between 10–20 times a year	18	9
Between 3–10 times a year	52	29
One or two times a year	23	45
Very seldom	1	15
Never been abroad	0	2

We see from the Table that the elite is more exposed (more contacted, more often going abroad, etc.) than the opinion-makers, and that they also are more centrally placed in the foreign policy communication and/or policy-making structure. The possibility of a 'tie' between the 'Going abroad' and 'Being member of an international organization delegation' does not weaken this conclusion.

APPENDIX D.

Distribution of some key properties among the samples. The problems of heterogeneity, representativity, and bias

We shall survey the distribution among the samples of a total of eight variables, only two of which have been treated in the text above (age and party affiliation). On some of these variables, we may make comparisons with the nation, i.e. the distribution in the Norwegian population as a whole, *or* in a representative sample of the population. On a few of the variables, we shall also be able to draw comparisons with distributions found in one of the samples of foreign elites with which comparisons have been made throughout this report.

To start with *sex*, there is in both samples an overwhelming majority of men: only 3% of the elite and 5% of the opinion-maker sample are women. These figures seem to correspond fairly well with the actual situation in most Western societies: elite positions are held by men. In comparison, there were only 5% women among the respondents in the survey made by Nasatir (op. cit.), on a more representative sample of the US elite universe. And as to the composition of the Norwegian Storting at the time of our interviewing, only 7% of the members were women. The present distribution according to sex in the Norwegian population is close to the 'normal distribution', i.e. a slight majority of women.

According to *educational background*, our two samples are similarly equal: ¾ of each has higher (post-secondary school) education, from the universities, colleges of higher education etc. (cf. Table D. 1).

Table D. 1. *Educational background of the samples*

Level of education	EL	OM	Type of higher education*	EL	OM
Primary school	5	0	Humanities	24	29
Junior secondary	7	5	Law	33	10
Senior secondary	9	15	Economics	12	5
Technical/lower officer ed.	1	5	Social sciences	8	20
Teacher school/higher			Business	1	4
military ed.	11	5	Technical fields	4	5
University/higher college			Agriculture	4	3
education	67	70	Military	8	4
			Other	6	20

*) Includes only the 'Teacher school/higher military education' and the 'University/higher college education' categories. Percentages on the basis of sub-totals.

Moving now to *occupation,* Table D. 2 shows both type and sector of occupation. Most of the difference between the samples on these variables obviously is due to the very sampling itself, where e.g. civil servants were selected from the foreign service in the elite, from the education and research categories in the opinion-maker case. When however, occupational sector is considered, the similarities again are striking.

Table D. 2. *Occupational background of the samples*

Type of occupation: position.			Type of occupation: by sector.	Population (1960)*	EL	OM
	EL	OM				
Civil service: central administration	28	12	Primary	19.5	8	3
			Secondary	36.5	8	10
Civil service: education and research	11	39	Tertiary	44	84	87
Mass media	24	13	Public sector (civil service/ education/radio/military forces)		54	55
Administration: nonpublic	19	15				
Agriculture/fishery	8	3	Private sector		46	45
Business/service	3	6				
Industry	2	3				
Military forces	2	0				
Other	3	9†				

*) Source: Ståle Seierstad, 'Norsk Økonomi', in Ramsøy (ed.) *Det norske samfunn.* p.93.
†) Including several student leaders.

So far we have reported strong similarities between the samples, according to sex, education, and occupational sector. These similarities lead us to conclude that the sampling has been meeting the standards set up. There is, however, one more variable to look into, *income* distribution.

From Table D. 3 we see that the elite generally has a higher income than the opinion-makers, which certainly should be expected, given the higher status and generally more important role functions of the elite.

Table D. 3. *Income distribution in the samples*

	Elite	Opinion-makers
Less than 28,000 N. kr.	3	18
28,000–48,000 N. kr.	23	40
48,000–62,000 N. kr.	33	25
More than 62,000 N. kr.	41	17

Thus, we are inclined to say that the income distribution data do not oppose the conclusion just drawn: the samples, according to several background variables generally considered of some importance in characterizing survey samples, show reasonable degrees of heterogeneity, representativity, and do not seem particularly biased (one possible source of bias being the high number of public servants in the sample).

It is evident that the samples are far more educated, have more 'white collar' jobs, and have a much higher income than the overall Norwegian. But it is hard to say whether they have more of these assets compared to the public, than should have been expected *given* the fact that these groups have a higher socio-economic status in the society.

It has already been found that according to *age,* both samples probably are somewhat younger than might have been expected, or compared to certain other elites. On the other hand, an explanation was offered for the fact that the elite in particular is very much 'middle-aged'; we certainly should not expect an age composition more or less in line with the one found among the adult population at large.

Even when it comes to *party affiliation,* another of our independent variables, there is no reason to expect a composition according to that found among the general population: there is probably a certain bias in the opinion-maker sample, but as far as the elite sample is concerned, it probably represents the universe – *the* elite. Not only did we mention that those parties which are under-represented in the elite, if one compares with the distribution of party affiliation in the general population (cf. Table D. 4) are relatively much recruited from periphery social strata; we also showed that most of them were the least active when it comes to foreign policy activity.

Table D. 4. *Party affiliation in the samples and the population*

	Elite	Opinion-makers	Population*
Labor	34	15	43.1
Conservatives	31	28	21.0
Liberals	15	25	10.4
Center party	3	5	9.9
Christian People's Party	2	6	8.2
Socialist People's Party	3	15	6.0
Communists	1	1	1.4
Would not vote	2	4	–
NA/neutral	9	1	–

*) Parlimentary elections, 1965. Voters only.

APPENDIX E.

Methodology

The explorative part of the research design may be said to favor an informal setting where the stimuli are presented in an un-systematic way to elicit as much information as possible. When we chose a wholly formal setting, the reason was two-fold: first, that an informal setting was found to involve more research facilities and resources than were available; secondly, and most important, that an informal setting would exclude the other part of the design – its testing of hypotheses.

The purpose of exploration, however, made its case in the choice between an unstructured and structured setting: the both-and attitude again was applied, but with a relatively strong emphasis on an unstructured setting (although it may be found, cf. Appendix F), that structured items are in a majority).

At this point we should make clear that the instrument or instruments available were the interview schedule and the questionnaire. Content analysis clearly was inappropriate as the requirement that the setting be the use of systematic stimuli, was definite. The use of systematic observation or non-verbal acts, as opposed to verbal, was further excluded, for two principal reasons: first, that resources would not allow, secondly, that it would be very difficult to administer, given the problems of designing the universe and given the composition of the sampling categories. (Parliamentarians would be fairly easily administered, but not Mass Media people).

Several authors speak strongly in favor of structuring the interview schedule and/or questionnaire, and most of them speak on the basis of experience from empirical research.[1] Our pretest, on the other hand, made it clear that quite a number of the respondents might object to a too rigidly structured schedule; hence our compromise on this point. At this point, it should be made clear that the choice of instrument – whether oral (verbal) or written – also was a compromise, due to lack of resources, technical and other reasons. Interviewing was found to be a 'must' vis a vis elite respondents, while the opinion-maker sample could 'make do with' a mailed questionnaire.

As mentioned already, the interview schedule was made subject to a pretest on about ten persons not very different, in terms of status and expected opinions, from the elite universe; some of them in fact may probably be seen as members of that universe. On the basis of this pretest, the final schedule was prepared, taking due notice of the responses from the pretest respondents in making the structured questions. The interview schedule was prepared during the period September 1966 to February 1967, and was subject to extensive discussions and several drafts, mainly at the International Peace Research Institute, Oslo. At the very beginning, explorative interviews with the use of an almost totally unstructured schedule were carried out among a number of persons estimated as good informants.

In preparing the questionnaire to be sent to the opinion-maker sample, preparations of which took place at the end of the period mentioned *and* during and directly after the interviews were made, we benefited greatly from the experiences made from the use of the interview schedule, particularly in the pre-coding of responses. A preliminary draft of the questionnaire was mailed to a number of persons, approximately 40 – half of whom responded – believed to cover most of the characteristica of the opinion-maker sample.

The interviewing was carried out by three student colleagues, all senior students, from the Institute of Political Science, University of Oslo, and the author. These three assistants carried out about $\frac{2}{3}$ of the total number of interviews obtained, the author did the rest. All had some training in interview techniques, although not on foreign policy questions. The age and the background of the interviewers in most respects of relevance were about the same; thus, the probability that there is an interviewer effect is not considered as great.

The respondents, after receiving the introduction letter (cf. Appendix H) were contacted either directly in their offices, or by telephone, and appointments for an interview were made. The interviews took from $1\frac{1}{4}$ to 2 hours and were conducted mostly in the office, or at the working place of the respondents. A number of interviews were abrupted, but only a very few had to be broken off and resumed on another day.

The interviewer assistants were instructed to make extensive notes where extra information could be obtained, and they were told to probe on those questions where they felt that probing might be useful or necessary. The interviewees were asked to state their personal opinions and were assured that the interviews were strictly confidential. By and large, we believe that the interviews were taken under fairly satisfactorily conditions.

The questionnaire to the opinion-maker sample was mailed, the first one being sent out in April 1967, enclosed with introductory letters. Two reminders were sent out after periods of 15–25 days. The respondents were asked to give extra comments, criticisms etc. on an open space beside each item.

A few of the respondents made criticisms against the form or even the purpose of study being undertaken; other had less substantial criticism to voice. The great majority, however (more in the case of the elite) did not voice any specific *or* any general form of critique against the study.

The elite responses were coded by the author himself, while the opinion-maker responses were coded by an assistant, after receiving detailed instructions, both through a codebook and verbally from the author. The author also controlled the coding of the assistant. The data were punched on IBM cards.

NOTES
1 Hyman, op.cit.; Gorden and Lerner, op.cit.

APPENDIX F

The interview schedule and the questionnaire. With marginals

Most questions were put to respondents in both samples, i.e. both in the schedule and the questionnaire. Where this is not true, a note – (IS) in the case where the question was only included in the interview schedule, (Q) where it only appeared in the questionnaire – is made.

Most questions were put in practically the same form (order and phrasing) in both cases; exceptions of importance are mentioned (see notes at the end of the Appendix).

Questions which were *not* given precoded responses in the questionnaire, are attached the note *pc* (postcoded). Other information is given in notes at the end.

Questions 75 to 103 were all put in a similar form and phrasing to both samples, i.e.: they were presented to the elite sample in a question near which they themselves filled out, *but* at the *end* of the interview.

Marginals are, unless otherwise mentioned, given for the elite to the *left,* for the opinion-makers to the *right.*

(Some of the questions actually put to respondents have been left out of the following list. Some of them may be found in other appendices, i.e. Appendices C and D; others will be found in the text).

1. *What do you personally consider the most important problem in contemporary international politics?*

	(EL)	(OM)	*pc*
1 War-peace problems in general	20	32	
2 The Vietnam war / US policy in Vietnam	20	21	
3 Nuclear weapons, proliferation danger	9	7	
4 Armaments race / terror balance / disarmament problems	9	–	
5 East-West relations / detente	16	2	
6 Integration, cooperation problems	7	–	
7 European market problems / trade	1	2	
8 Developing countries' problems / the rich-poor gap .	9	32	
9 NA/DK/Other	9	4	

2. *What do you consider the greatest threat to mankind in the contemporary world?*

1 War / major war / war danger in general	28	36
2 Nuclear weapons / nuclear war / proliferation	23	10
3 Armaments race / terror balance.................	5	1
4 East-West relations conflict	7	2
5 China, China's foreign policy....................	3	8
6 Under-development / hunger and poverty / the rich-poor gap in the world	18	39
7 Man himself / the world's leaders................	7	
8 Other (nationalism)	5	
9 NA/DK..	3	

3. *What do you personally consider the most important aim of Norwegian foreign policy today and in the near future?*

1 Contribute to peace and security.................	24	14	*pc*
2 Secure a nuclear non-proliferation treaty..........	3	1	
3 Contribute to disarmament and arms control agreements	5	7	
4 Promote international understanding / East-West detente.......................................	25	13	
5 Participate in international cooperation / promote integration support UN	17	20	
6 Solve West European market problems	8	12	
7 Assist in the solution of developing countries' problems / give more aid	2	12	
8 Other	10	9	
9 NA/DK..	6	12	

4. *Looking further ahead, let us say 15–20 years into the future, do you think that some other aim by then should be more important to Norway's foreign policy?*

1 Yes..	48	26	*pc*
2 No, same as today's..........................	43	52	
9 NA/DK.......................................	9	22	

(Both 'Yes' and 'No' answers):

1 (response categories)	17	10
2 (as in above question)	11	–
3	1	2
4	13	10
5	23	19
6	3	5
7	24	19
8	7	6
9	9	29

5. *Would you say that you think much about what the world will look like in 15 to 20 years' time, or say in year 2000?*

1 Yes, much	61	55
2 A great deal, but not very much	17	36
3 No, little or nothing	14	6
9 NA/DK	8	3

6. *What do you hope will be the main difference between the world today and the world year 2000?*

1 Peace and security prevails.......................	13	22	pc
2–3 Disarmament is achieved / non-military conflict resolution.........................	9	2	
4 More international understanding, openness / detente	14	22	
5 More cooperation / supra-national institutions established	25	10	
6 Market and trade problems solved	1	1	
7 Hunger and poverty overcome / developing countries' problems being solved...........................	28	25	
8 Other (man better, more peaceful)	10	7	
9 NA/DK	0	11	

7. *If you should describe contemporary international politics by one single trait or trend which you think is predominant – which one would you mention?*

1 Insecurity / war / danger of major war	11	13	pc
2 Armaments race / nuclear proliferation	11	19	
3 The stability / balance of power	8	0	
4 East-West detente / Soviet–US cooperation	21	5	
5 Increased cooperation, integration	8	5	
6 The instability / dissolution of old traits...........	22	11	
7 Development problems / rich-poor gap	11	25	
8 Other	3	2	
9 NA/DK	3	20	

8. *Which trait or trend do you expect will be predominant in the world year 2000?*

1 Insecurity / war / danger of major war	1	–
2–3 Armaments race / nuclear proliferation	1	(IS)
4 East-West detente / Soviet–US cooperation	10	

5 Increased cooperation, integration	18	
6 The instability / dissolution of old traits...........	1	
7 Development problems / rich-poor gap	21	
8 Other	13	
9 NA/DK.......................................	36	

9. *Do you believe that Norway will be better or worse off in the future?*

1 Better...	56	45
2 Better if outside, world conditions allow...........	23	2
3 About as today................................	7	29
4 Norway will have difficulties which may make her worse off	6	0
5 Worse...	1	10
6 Other	6	0
9 NA/DK.......................................	1	14

10. *When it comes to the question what attitude we in general and principally should take toward international cooperation – particularly in the political field – do you think that Norway should concentrate on the global or the regional (West European) level?*

1 Global primarily..............................	16	30
2 Both at the same time..........................	56	55
3 Regional primarily.............................	28	15
9 NA/DK.......................................	0	0

(If respondent answers 'Both at the same time'):
If there in a particular situation, in an important matter, comes to a conflict between the two and Norway had to make a choice between them – which one should she choose?
(Percentages of those who answered 'Both' only).

1 Global	30
2 Regional	32
3 Hypothetical question: conflict not conceivable.....	10
9 NA/DK.......................................	28

11. *In the present situation, do you think that Norway should continue as a member of NATO after 1969, or do you think that she should leave the organization?*

1 Should continue (without reservations)	60	18
2 Should continue if the situation by then is not radically changed	26	42
3 We should reconsider our membership and make a decision in 1969	7	22
4 We should leave................................	5	17
5 Other	2	1
9 NA/DK.......................................	0	0

12. *What role do you think military alliances play in today's world?*

1 Stabilizing role................................	32	(IS)
2 Act as deterrents	13	
3 Give security, predictability	17	

4 Balancing, equilibrating role	11	
5 Give detente	8	
6 Create insecurity / terror balance	2	
7 Obstacle to detente and peace	2	
8 Other	6	
9 NA/DK	9	

13. *If you consider present trends in international politics – would you then say that the influence of the great powers is increasing, or would you rather say that the influence of minor and small states is increasing to the disadvantage of the great powers?*

1 The influence of one big power, the United States, is increasing..................................	6	5
2 Great power influence is increasing................	43	35
3 Power relations are stable, constant	14	24
4 Influence of minor and small states is increasing....	31	22
5 Other	6	0
9 NA/DK	0	14

14. *If you should rank nation-states according to their power or influence – how many different rank categories do you then conceive of?*

1 Two	3	1
2 Three	33	11
3 Four..	28	17
4 Five	23	22
5 Six..	3	16
6 Seven or more................................	1	12
9 NA/DK	9	21

15. *Which states do you consider real big powers?*

1 United States and Soviet Union	56	42
2 United States, Soviet Union and China............	29	41
3 The five nuclear powers	6	14
4 Other	5	0
9 NA/DK	4	3

16. *If you characterize, briefly and with reference to one specific trait which you find predominant, the foreign policy of the two super powers* (or the powers mentioned as big powers) – *which trait would you then mention?*

	(IS) United States	Soviet Union
1 Secure own national interests......................	19	18
2 Maintain status quo in world......................	11	25
3 'Internationalistic', cooperative	1	2
4 Peace-seeking / works for detente.................	22	27
5 Generous / comes to others' assistance	9	0
6 Fears the other big / containment policy...........	15	7
7 Expansive / policy of dominance..................	5	10

272

8 Other (wrong policy)............................	15	6
9 NA/DK.......................................	3	5

1 'Ideological'....................................	30	11
2 'Realistic' / national interest policy................	43	69
3 'Power policy'..................................	10	6
4 Other...	11	9
9 NA/DK.......................................	6	5

17. *Do you think that Norway on the whole has the amount of influence in world affairs she ought to have, or do you think she has more or less influence than she deserves?*

1 Less than she ought to have.....................	7	5
2 About as she ought to have.....................	42	56
3 More than she deserves, should normally have had..	44	25
4 Other...	3	2
9 NA/DK.......................................	4	12

18. *Do you think that Norway on the whole determines her foreign policy herself, or do you believe that certain other countries or international organizations she is member of, have much influence on her policy?*

1 Determines more or less herself..................	11	18
2 She is more independent than other states in a similar position.................................	19	7
3 In some cases she determines herself, in others not..	30	36
4 Others have a relatively great influence on her policy	24	25
5 Norway is more or less *not* making her own foreign policy...	11	11
6 Other...	3	0
9 NA/DK.......................................	2	3

19. *It has been proposed that a system of weighted voting ought to be introduced in the United Nations. Do you agree or disagree with such a proposal?*

1 Agree completely...............................	14	10
2 Agree to a certain extent........................	19	22
3 Both agree and disagree.........................	11	18
4 Disagree to a certain extent......................	13	9
5 Disagree completely............................	35	29
6 Other...	2	2
9 NA/DK.......................................	6	10

20. *Several proposals have been made as to which powers the United Nations should be given, in the short or in the long run. Do you personally agree or disagree with the idea that the United Nations should be given the power or authority to:*

A. Tax all member countries in order to finance its operations

1 Agree completely...............................	32	59
2 Agree to some extent............................	19	27
3 Both agree and disagree.........................	5	5
4 Disagree to some extent.........................	7	3
5 Disagree completely............................	18	4

6 Other	3	0
9 NA/DK	16	2

21. B. Control that outer space is not used for military and strategic purposes

1 Agree completely	81	89
2 Agree to some extent	6	5
3 Both agree and disagree	1	1
4 Disagree to some extent	1	2
5 Disagree completely	2	1
6 Other	0	0
9 NA/DK	9	2

22. C. Implement a plan for total or partial disarmament

1 Agree completely	60	72
2 Agree to some extent	11	16
3 Both agree and disagree	7	3
4 Disagree to some extent	0	2
5 Disagree completely	10	5
6 Other	2	0
9 NA/DK	10	2

23. D. Abolish the big power veto in the Security Council

1 Agree completely	11	24
2 Agree to some extent	15	20
3 Both agree and disagree	9	15
4 Disagree to some extent	13	10
5 Disagree completely	46	24
6 Other	0	0
9 NA/DK	6	7

24. E. Dispose of the pole areas, ocean floor and the open seas and of the income of the exploration thereof

1 Agree completely	22	29
2 Agree to some extent	11	17
3 Both agree and disagree	3	11
4 Disagree to some extent	2	4
5 Disagree completely	28	26
6 Other	0	0
9 NA/DK	34	13

25. F. Dispose of parts of the standing armed forces of member countries

1 Agree completely	48	59
2 Agree to some extent	23	19
3 Both agree and disagree	2	7
4 Disagree to some extent	2	2
5 Disagree completely	8	9
6 Other	2	0
9 NA/DK	15	4

274

26. *Which of all these proposals do you believe is the one most realizable?*

1 Proposal on weighted voting		2	12
2 – – taxing............................		14	19
3 – – outer space		39	36
4 – – disarmament......................		6	5
5 – – abolishing veto power..............		1	1
6 – – poles, ocean floor etc................		2	5
7 – – disposal of armed forces.............		17	12
8 None of them are realizable.....................		0	1
9 NA/DK..		19	10

27. *Do you think that one in the present situation should take concrete steps to strengthen the United Nations as a peace-keeping institution? If yes: which concrete step would you personally propose?*

1 No: the United Nations should not be strengthened.		1	2
2 Yes...		99	98
(Which one:)			
1 Strengthen the economy		17	19
2 Establish permanent peace-keeping force..........		19	26
3 Strengthen the organization and its ability to act....		16	17
4 Pool more development assistance aid through UN .		2	18
5 Strengthen and widen the political unity		10	16
6 Make China Rep. a member		3	1
7 Other: several of these steps should be taken		21	2
9 NA/DK..		12	1

28. *In order to promote and develop international cooperation in general – do you think it is most important:*
   A. *That the governments and leaders in the various countries have the proper political will to cooperate*
      or
   B. *That the people at large in the various countries want cooperation?*

1 Agree completely with A		35	34
2 Agree more with A than with B		28	36
3 Ambivalent: both are right.......................		22	15
4 Agree more with B than with A		8	8
5 Agree completely with B.........................		5	3
6 Other		1	0
9 NA/DK..			

29. *For the same purpose – do you think it is most important:*
   A. *That formal, supra-national institutions are set up*
      or
   B. *That non-governmental organizations, or the socalled functional cooperation, are strengthened?*

1 Agree completely with A		18	18
2 Agree more with A than with B		11	16
3 Ambivalent: both are right.......................		26	19

4 Agree more with B than with A	18	21
5 Agree completely with B.	21	15
6 Other	1	2
9 NA/DK	5	9

30. *Do you agree or disagree with the principle that the leaders of international organizations of which Norway is a member or is going to be a member, should be elected by the citizens of the member countries through democratic elections?*

1 Agree completely	8	9
2 Agree to some extent	8	18
3 Both agree and disagree	7	14
4 Disagree to some extent	14	13
5 Disagree completely	56	35
6 Other	1	0
9 NA/DK	6	11

31. *Do you agree or disagree with the view that those laws that are valid for an international organization with some degree of supra-nationality should be directly applied on the individual citiens in the member countries – e.g. in Norway?*

1 Agree completely	44	42
2 Agree to some extent	26	21
3 Both agree and disagree	8	11
4 Disagree to some extent	8	4
5 Disagree completely	6	8
6 Other	1	1
9 NA/DK	7	13

32. *Would you say that the persons behind the foreign policy play any role in making the policy which is conducted, or is the policy more or less independent of persons or personalities?*

1 Persons play a role	68	52
2 It depends on the persons / on situation	22	40
3 Policy is more or less independent of persons	6	6
6 Other	1	0
9 NA/DK	3	2

33. *If you imagine the world year 2000 – how far do you think the world has come by then when it comes to international cooperation?*

1 There has been a setback	1	1
2 About as today	5	1
3 Somewhat longer than today	25	36
4 Much longer than today	42	46
5 Very far	8	5
6 Other	3	1
9 NA/DK	16	10

34. *What do you consider the most important measure to help achieve peace today?*

1 Maintain balance of power / NATO	10	5

2 Non-proliferation treaty	10	15
3 Disarmament / arms control	9	12
4 More understanding / detente East–West	17	37
5 Strengthen international cooperation	24	2
6 Close the rich-poor gap / more aid...............	9	2
7 Solve the Vietnam conflict	3	19
8 Other	10	2
9 NA/DK	8	6

35. *Do you think it likely that the world within the next ten–fifteen years has moved towards partial or complete disarmament, do you think the situation will be like today, or do you rather think there will be more armaments at that time?*

1 More armaments	18	30
2 Armament level about as today...................	34	51
3 Partial disarmament............................	38	9
4 Total disarmament.............................	1	0
5 Other	2	0
9 NA/DK	7	10

36. *What do you think the situation will look like about the year 2000?*

1 More armaments	8	12
2 Armament level about as today...................	13	35
3 Partial disarmament............................	56	22
4 Total disarmament.............................	3	2
5 Other	3	0
9 NA/DK	17	29

37. *Do you think it is possible to avoid war, or do you you think it is mostly impossible?*

1 War may be avoided	60	55
2 War may sometimes be avoided, sometimes not.....	26	34
3 War may mostly not be avoided	10	5
4 Other	1	1
9 NA/DK	3	5

38. *On the whole – what do you think of man's possibilities of directing developments in the world?*

1 They are great.................................	76	66
2 It depends: sometimes great.....................	11	23
3 Not so great: developments direct man	3	4
4 Other	1	2
9 NA/DK	3	5

39. *How likely do you think it is that a world war or a major war involving the use of nuclear weapons will occur within the year 2000?*

1 Very unlikely..................................	58	43
2 Rather unlikely................................	10	0
3 More or less 50–50 chance	15	42

        4 Rather likely.................................... 1   2
        5 Very likely...................................... 2   5
        6 Other 5   0
        9 NA/DK... 9   8

40. *If a world should break out, how do you think it most likely would happen?*
        1 By technical accident / human failure.............. 15   10
        2 Escalation of a limited conflict 49   69
        3 A great power attacks another great power......... 11   9
        4 China starts it.................................. 11   1
        5 By miscalculation................................ 3   0
        6 Other 7   1
        9 NA/DK... 4   10

41. *What do you think will be the consequences for Norway of a major war in the future?*
        1 Total destruction 35   9
        2 Irreparable losses............................... 15   33
        3 Big, but not irreparable losses 17   35
        4 Not so great losses.............................. 5   2
        5 Other / it depends 16   2
        9 NA/DK... 12   19

42. *Can you imagine any value or aim which should justify taking the risk of a major war, where nuclear weapons are used?*
        1 No 58   79
        2 Yes.. 27   15
        3 Other 6   2
        9 NA/DK... 9   4

43. *Do you agree or disagree that it is possible, through education and other milieu stimuli, to change man and make him more peaceful?*
        1 Agree completely 60   52
        2 Agree to some extent............................. 18   29
        3 Ambivalent...................................... 2   8
        4 Disagree to some extent 7   10
        5 Disagree completely.............................. 5   1
        6 Other 1   0
        9 NA/DK... 7   0

44. *Do you agree or disagree with those who say that such education first of all should be applied to political leaders?*
        1 Agree completely 13   27
        2 Agree to some extent............................. 16   22
        3 Ambivalent...................................... 9   15
        4 Disagree to some extent 11   5
        5 Disagree completely.............................. 33   15
        6 Other 3   0
        9 NA/DK... 15   16

278

45. *Some people argue that peace first of all must be based on good relations between individuals, in the family, within organizations, and at work. Do you agree or disagree with such a view?*

1 Agree completely	34	30
2 Agree to some extent	22	21
3 Ambivalent	11	18
4 Disagree to some extent	8	16
5 Disagree completely	14	9
6 Other	0	0
9 NA/DK	11	6

46. *Concerning relations within a nation-state and the importance they may have to peace, different views are held:*

A. *Some believe it is most contributive to peace if the nation-state is as homogeneous as possible, so that it consists of only one ethnic group or socio-cultural group, because it may then be possible to avoid e.g. race conflict.*

B. *Others believe it may often be more contributive to peace if the nation-state is to a large extent heterogeneous, because this may create e.g. more tolerance among people.*

Which one of these views is closer to your own?

1 Agree completely with A	17	9
2 Agree more with A than with B	27	22
3 Ambivalent: agree some with both	9	13
4 Agree more with B than with A	14	24
5 Agree completely with B	22	9
6 Other	1	1
9 NA/DK	10	22

47. *Concerning relations between states –*

A. *Some believe that it is most contributive to peace if the nation-states are similar to each other – in political system, culturally and in their economic systems, while*

B. *Others believe it is more contributive to peace when the states to a large extent are dissimilar in such respects.*

Which one of these views is closer to your own?

1 Agree completely with A	11
2 Agree more with A than with B	18
3 Ambivalent: agree some with both	31
4 Agree more with B than with A	7
5 Agree completely with B	10
6 Other	0
9 NA/DK	23

48. *Do you believe that the nation-states in the world will be more or less similar to each other – in political, economic, social and cultural respects – e.g. in year 2000 than they are today?*

1 Will be more similar to each other	80	75

279

2 Will be more similar to each other in *some* of these respects	14	2
3 Will be about as now	1	6
4 Will be less similar to each other	0	1
5 Other	1	1
9 NA/DK	4	17

49. *If you look at what you think is the most likely development in the next 10–15 years, do you believe that the split between the Communist countries will be deeper or be less during those years?*

1 Will be deeper................................	39	69
2 There will be more national independence among them, more differences	35	1
3 Will be about as now	3	14
4 Will be less	21	5
9 NA/DK	2	11

50. *Looking at the relations between the Western countries in the same period – do you believe that the differences and strains which can be seen today in these relations will become greater or lesser?*

1 Will become greater............................	14	27
2 Will be more national independence..............	8	0
3 Will be about as now	8	29
4 Will become lesser	63	32
5 Other	3	0
9 NA/DK	4	12

51. *Considering relations between the Communist and the Western countries – do you believe that detente and the tendencies toward cooperation will be strengthened or weakened in the same period?*

1 Will be strengthened	94	79
2 Will be about as now	2	7
3 Will be weakened.............................	2	4
4 Other	1	2
9 NA/DK	1	8

52. *On what conditions do you think that Norway should become a member of the European economic community?*

1 Norway should *not* become a member.............	5	14
2 Should only become a member on certain economic and/or political conditions	35	52
3 Should try to get certain conditions fulfilled before we join as member.................................	27	4
4 Norway should join without making any conditions.	19	27
5 Norway cannot make any conditions..............	8	0

6 Other	3	0
9 NA/DK	3	3

53. *Do you believe that an eventual membership in the Community will have great internal consequences in Norway – or do you think that consequences will be of less importance?*

1 Consequences will be of little importance	27	2
2 Consequences will be of some importance..........	34	72
3 Consequences will be great.......................	23	24
4 Consequences will be very great	2	1
5 Other	7	1
9 NA/DK	7	0
(Consequences mainly on:)		
1 Economic policies, structures....................	38	18
2 Greater industries.............................	7	13
3 Small industries	0	3
4 Agriculture and fisheries.......................	5	15
5 Cultural life..................................	3	0
6 Social life, labour market......................	2	12
7 Political life, party relations...................	7	8
8 Other	5	8
9 NA/DK	33	23

54. *Do you believe that Norway in the years ahead, because of a growing cooperation and contact with other countries and peoples, will lose much of her national characteristica in some or all spheres of society – or do you think she will be able to maintain most or all of her national characteristica?*

1 She will maintain most of them..................	38	17
2 She will maintain what is of particular value	7	20
3 She will lose something, preserve something.......	24	32
4 She will lose much, even what is of particular value	24	23
5 She will lose practically all her characteristica	0	4
6 Other	5	0
9 NA/DK	2	4

55. *What do you think Norway will gain, first of all, on an extended cooperation and contact with other countries and peoples?*

1 Economic benefits: export incomes...............	31	24
2 Culturally: greater richness, impulses.............	10	11
3 More understanding of others, tolerance..........	24	28
4 More understanding for our own problems *in* other countries and peoples	2	1
5 Greater possibilities for influence	5	15
6 More security	7	2
7 Other	6	2
9 NA/DK	15	17

56. *What kind of national characteristica do you think that Norway should try, as much as possible, to rid herself of?* (double response)

1 Cultural: 'pettiness', religion, language quarrel	13	11
2 Political: sovereignty, self-determination	7	0
3 Social: high social security and wages	1	0
4 Economical: investment and concessions policies, tariff protections.............................	8	3
5 Individualism	1	0
6 Nationalism, chauvinism, isolationism.............	58	49
7 Our 'untouched' nature, recreation areas..........	2	2
8 Other (should not rid herself of anything).........	14	4
9 NA/DK	7	39

57. *– and what characteristica or values do you think she should try to preserve as much as possible?*

1 Cultural: religion, language	28	19
2 Political: political system, self-determination	23	7
3 Social: security system, wages etc.	9	6
4 Economical:	0	1
5 Individual liberties, rights.......................	20	17
6 National values, symbols	4	6
7 Our 'untouched' nature, recreation areas..........	14	11
8 Other	9	5
9 NA/DK	14	38

58. *Do you believe that increased cooperation and contact between nations lead to less conflict between them, or do you rather believe they will make increased conflict possible?*

1 Will make increased conflict possible	1	5
2 It depends, ambivalent	15	29
3 Will lead to less conflict	82	65
4 Other	2	0
9 NA/DK	0	1

59. *What form of contact do you think Norway, e.g. in relation to the Eastern European countries, should put particular emphasis on in the future?* (Double response)

1 Tourism, sports cooperation	17	14
2 Cultural cooperation, student exchange............	46	41
3 Trade...	45	55
4 Exchange of political information.................	7	23
5 Production cooperation..........................	8	10
6 Exchange of diplomatic representations............	8	2
7 State visits, top-level contacts	21	3
8 Other (most or all these forms)	15	2
9 NA/DK	0	3

60. *How do you think contact between East and West in political or particularly 'security policy' questions should be taken: at the organizational level (through NATO and the Warszaw Pact) or bilaterally, between the different countries?*

1 At the organizational level primarily	35	18
2 Both	26	53
3 Bilaterally	31	25
4 Other	6	0
9 NA/DK.......................................	2	4

61. *Within nations, we know that the individual may maintain bonds of loyalty both to the local community and to the national government. Do you think that a similar multiple loyalty position can be applied even toward some international organization or unit of which we are a member as well as to the national government, without such a position leading to conflicts?*

1 Yes, it is possible............................	58	49
2 It depends, ambivalent: sometimes conflict, sometimes not	27	40
3 It is not possible.............................	13	6
4 Other	1	0
9 NA/DK.......................................	1	5

62. *If you should say which international organization or unit you yourself feel the greatest loyalty toward or think that Norway should be most closely related to – would you then mention*

1 United Nations...............................	41	36
2 The Atlantic community or NATO	19	16
3 Western Europe	11	8
4 All Europe...................................	2	5
5 The less developed countries	2	12
6 The Nordic countries..........................	15	18
7 Other	6	2
9 NA/DK.......................................	4	3

63. *There are different opinions about the role of the nonaligned countries in the world. What is your own opinion about that role?*

1 They do not play an important role..............	31	12	pc
2 They play a certain role	46	62	
3 They play an important role	16	22	
4 They play a sometimes decisive role..............	0	3	
5 Other	4	0	
9 NA/DK.......................................	3	1	

1 Positive role	39	45
2 Both positive and negative role..................	10	1
3 Negative role.................................	10	17
4 No evaluation made	11	25
5 Other	2	2
9 NA/DK.......................................	23	10

283

1 Nationalistic, opportunistic	3	15
2 Bridge-builders, mediating role	24	39
3 Avoid taking sides	8	4
4 Have some influence on big powers	7	23
5 Prestige seekers only	8	2
6 They are not heterogeneous, not *one* role	8	1
7 Other	9	8
9 NA/DK	33	8

64. *Do you believe that the socalled 'gap' – the primarily economic differences – between the poor and the rich countries will increase or decrease within e.g. year 2000?*

1 It will increase	34	39
2 It will increase for some time, but then start decreasing	9	1
3 It will remain about as now	3	12
4 It will decrease	47	32
5 Other	3	0
9 NA/DK	4	16

65. *What consequences on world politics do you think that an increasing or remaining gap may have in the long run?*

1 May lead to a catastrophe, to explosion	8	9
2 Will increase the danger of war	13	3
3 Will increase possibilities of conflict, increase differences	21	2
4 Will lead to race conflict	1	1
5 Will create more unrest, instability	26	2
6 Will disrupt international cooperation	6	25
7 Will create more hatred, discontent, increase the moral burden on the rich	7	36
8 Will lead to stagnation, starvation, etc. in the poor countries	7	9
9 NA/DK	11	13

66. *How do you think that the developed countries should act or what attitude should they take in relation the less developed countries concerning the gap between them and the problem of development?*

1 Give it more attention in general	10	8	pc
2 Help, increase their aid	31	27	
3 Help in their own interest	11	5	
4 Strengthen cooperation between themselves	11	1	
5 Strengthen cooperation with the less developed countries	8	17	
6 Try with various means to bridge the gap between them	18	25	
7 Other	7	4	
9 NA/DK	4	13	

67. *Do you think that Norway should give more aid to the less developed countries, about as now, or should she give less aid?*

1 Norway should not give such aid	....	0	1
2 Norway should give less aid	....	1	0
3 Should give about as today	....	15	13
4 Should give more aid	....	66	31
5 Should give much more aid	....	15	53
6 Other	....	1	0
9 NA/DK	....	2	2

68. *Do you think that Norway's aid to the less developed countries should be given primarily on a multilateral or a bilateral basis?*

1 Multilateral only	....	3	12
2 Primarily multilateral	....	49	27
3 Both about equally much	....	25	30
4 Primarily bilateral	....	17	20
5 Bilateral only	....	0	2
6 Other	....	4	0
9 NA/DK	....	2	9

69. *How do you think the less developed countries should act or what attitude should they take in relation to the developed countries concerning the gap between them?*

1 Should demand more, put pressure on them	....	9	13	pc
2 Should be critical, decide conditions for aid and assistance	....	10	6
3 Should be self-critical, try to understand the problems of the other part	....	24	11
4 Should not demand, should more or less accept the conditions the developed countries make for giving aid and assistance	....	9	17
5 This is their own business	....	11	3
6 No evaluation made, neutral on the matter	....	14	5
9 NA/DK	....	23	45

1 Cooperate more between themselves	....	8	2
2 Cooperate more with the developed countries	......	9	15
3 Become more realistic	....	18	12
4 Establish more stable, effective regimes	....	6	7
5 Become less nationalistic	....	5	2
6 Become more independent, self-relying	....	15	11
7 Other	....	10	6
9 NA/DK	....	29	45

70. *Do you think it is possible to decrease and eventually bridge the gap between the rich and the poor countries unless the former cut down on their living standard, or in other ways sacrifice something?*

1 No, not possible	....	35	22
2 No, they will have to sacrifice the increase in their living standard	....	5	9

285

3 They will have to sacrifice some of the increase in their
   living standard 24   35
4 Yes, it is possible 26   27
5 Other 4   2
9 NA/DK 6   4

71. *If a less developed country asked Norway to assist in building a merchant marine, of its own, do you think that Norway ought to give such assistance; or do you think that she should not?*

1 Yes, definitely 40   13
2 Yes, if the scheme is realistic 25   59
3 We should discuss it and try to convince that country
   to drop the scheme 18   12
4 No 10   6
5 Other 3   0
9 NA/DK 4   12

72. *The less developed countries have asked for customs duty preferences for a number of their export products. Do you think that Norway should agree to give them such preferences, or do you think that she should not?*

1 She should 44   63
2 It depends, if others do 27   22
3 No, she should not 13   4
4 Other 5   0
9 NA/DK 11   11

73. *Do you approve or disapprove of the use of sanctions, particularly economic sanctions, in international politics?*

1 Yes, in general 48   41
2 Both approve and disapprove 23   35
3 No, disapprove 23   19
4 Other 4   2
9 NA/DK 2   3

74. *Do you think it has any importance to the possibilities of maintaining peace if the number of states in the world was greater than it is today?*

1 No 53   15
2 Yes: peace possibilities become greater 1   14
3 It depends, both yes and no 15   32
4 Yes: peace possibilities become smaller 13   20
5 Other 7   0
9 NA/DK 11   19

Below is a number of views on DISARMAMENT on which we would like to have your own opinion. The views concern a number of important questions as to how disarmament *should* be carried out, how it is believed that it *will* take place, and *what consequences* it is believed that it will carry. The views are expressed as alternatives: for each combination of alternatives we ask you to state your own view – or choose the stated opinion which comes closest to your own. (Please mark the appropriate place)

75. A. Disarmament should be carried out as rapidly as possible.   B. Disarmament should be carried out carefully and stepwise.

1 Agree completely with A	12	15
2 Agree more with A than with B	11	16
3 Ambivalent	18	8
4 Agree more with B than with A	38	35
5 Agree completely with B	21	24
6 Other	0	0
9 NA/DK	0	2

76. A. Disarmament should be carried out only after sufficient confidence has been established.   B. One should start disarming in order to create confidence.

1 Agree completely with A	24	19
2 Agree more with A than with B	26	19
3 Ambivalent	25	16
4 Agree more with B than with A	15	28
5 Agree completely with B	7	17
6 Other	0	0
9 NA/DK	3	1

77. A. One should disarm over the whole or most of the world at the same time   B. One should start disarm in a few selected areas and then proceed to others.

1 Agree completely with A	21	14
2 Agree more with A than with B	21	16
3 Ambivalent	7	12
4 Agree more with B than with A	32	35
5 Agree completely with B	14	19
6 Other	2	0
9 NA/DK	3	4

78. A. A disarmament agreement demands much inspection to be implemented.   B. A disarmament agreement demands little inspection to be implemented.

1 Agree completely with A	49	37
2 Agree more with A than with B	37	31
3 Ambivalent	4	12
4 Agree more with B than with A	5	9
5 Agree completely with B	0	6
6 Other	1	0
9 NA/DK	4	5

79. A. *All governments want to disarm, but*   B. *Some states do not really want dis-*
      do not want to start in fear that the   *armament, but keep military forces*
      others will not.   *not only for defence, but also for*
            aggressive purposes.

1 Agree completely with A	21	10
2 Agree more with A than with B	25	25
3 Ambivalent	31	15
4 Agree more with B than with A	15	25
5 Agree completely with B.	4	21
6 Other	0	0
9 NA/DK	4	4

80. A. *It is likely that some states will try to*   B. *It is not likely that some states will*
      hide away some military equipment in   *try to hide away military equipment*
      a disarmament scheme.   *in a disarmament scheme.*

1 Agree completely with A	20	23
2 Agree more with A than with B	26	39
3 Ambivalent	19	13
4 Agree more with B than with A	17	15
5 Agree completely with B.	7	4
6 Other	1	0
9 NA/DK	10	6

81. A. *In implementing disarmament, one*   B. *In implementing disarmament, one*
      should abolish all weapons as rapidly   *should start with some selected*
      as possible.   *weapons e.g. nuclear ones, and then*
            proceed to others stepwise.

1 Agree completely with A	7	4
2 Agree more with A than with B	7	2
3 Ambivalent	1	5
4 Agree more with B than with A	47	45
5 Agree completely with B.	28	39
6 Other	3	0
9 NA/DK	7	5

82. A. *Disarmament is first of all dependent*   B. *The smaller states can contribute*
      on the great powers.   *much in showing an example for*
            others.

1 Agree completely with A	31	30
2 Agree more with A than with B	50	35
3 Ambivalent	11	12
4 Agree more with B than with A	3	9
5 Agree completely with B.	3	12
6 Other	1	0
9 NA/DK	1	2

83. A. *The economic differences in the world would more or less disappear if all states disarmed.* B. *The economic differences in the world would remain even after worldwide disarmament.*

1 Agree completely with A	1	10
2 Agree more with A than with B	11	14
3 Ambivalent	14	6
4 Agree more with B than with A	50	39
5 Agree completely with B	24	26
6 Other	0	0
9 NA/DK	0	5

84. A. *The power relations in the world would be radically changed if all states disarmed.* B. *The power relations in the world would remain more or less unchanged even after world-wide disarmament.*

1 Agree completely with A	10	9
2 Agree more with A than with B	18	15
3 Ambivalent	11	12
4 Agree more with B than with A	42	41
5 Agree completely with B	15	13
6 Other	0	0
9 NA/DK	4	9

85. A. *Disarmament would create more stability and greater possibilities of maintaining peace in the world.* B. *Serious conflicts may arise even in a completely disarmed world.*

1 Agree completely with A	13	17
2 Agree more with A than with B	29	23
3 Ambivalent	21	23
4 Agree more with B than with A	19	18
5 Agree completely with B	17	18
6 Other	0	0
9 NA/DK	1	1

86. A. *In order to control armaments and maintain peace in the near future, certain areas or zones should be demilitarized.* B. *In order to control armaments and maintain peace in the near future, forces and arms ought to be as much dispersed as possible so that military vacua are avoided.*

1 Agree completely with A	20	22
2 Agree more with A than with B	24	29
3 Ambivalent	17	15
4 Agree more with B than with A	21	19
5 Agree completely with B	7	11
6 Other	4	1
9 NA/DK	7	3

87. *A. Disarmament should be carried out*   *B. In order to get the disarmament*
     mutually with all sides disarming at   *process started, one side e.g. the*
     the same time and equally much.   *West should disarm somewhat and*
                                                                                   then wait for the other side to follow
                                                                                          suit.

1 Agree completely with A	52	35
2 Agree more with A than with B	40	29
3 Ambivalent	4	9
4 Agree more with B than with A	2	16
5 Agree completely with B.	0	8
6 Other	0	0
9 NA/DK	2	13

The second and last part of the questionnaire touches upon some of the questions we have covered already, but in a new form, besides presenting a number of new questions.

Again we present a number of views on how best to MAINTAIN or SECURE PEACE in the world.

What we are asking you to do, is to

1. state *what importance* you personally would attach each of the views mentioned, when it comes to their ability to maintain or secure peace, and
2. state whether or not you believe that each of the views mentioned is *realistic* or *unrealistic*, i.e. whether or not it may be implemented – in the long or in the short run.

If you in some case do not want to state any opinion, you are free to do so, but of course we do hope that you will answer to all our questions.

At the bottom of the list, you will be able to express any other personal opinion, if you want to, concerning the topic we are covering.

After each single item, a number of possible responses, both on the *importance* and the *realism* of the item, are listed. Please check the appropriate response, i.e. the answer which comes closest to your own opinion.

88. '*The individual man must be educated to peace*'

1 Especially important	35	46	1 Realistic	61	59
2 Somewhat important	55	35	2 Ambivalent	0	1
3 Without importance	10	7	3 Unrealistic	14	19
4 Is against peace	0	0			
9 NA/DK	0	12	9 NA/DK	25	21

89. '*Relations between individuals must become more peaceful*'

1 Especially important	28	29	1 Realistic	35	41
2 Somewhat important	33	35	2 Ambivalent	1	2
3 Without importance	21	24	3 Unrealistic	35	34
4 Is against peace	0	0	9 NA/DK	29	23
9 NA/DK	18	12			

90. '*The states must become more democratic*'

1 Especially important	36	32	1 Realistic	46	49

2 Somewhat important....	46	43
3 Without importance	13	12
4 Is against peace	0	0
9 NA/DK..............	5	13

2 Ambivalent....	3	2
3 Unrealistic	24	26
9 NA/DK.......	27	23

91. *'Hunger and poverty must be abolished throughout the world'*

1 Especially important	69	67
2 Somewhat important....	21	18
3 Without importance	3	4
4 Is against peace	0	0
9 NA/DK..............	7	11

1 Realistic	42	51
2 Ambivalent....	0	0
3 Unrealistic	26	28
9 NA/DK.......	32	21

92. *'The nations must become more similar'*

1 Especially important	7	12
2 Somewhat important....	45	39
3 Without importance	31	32
4 Is against peace	1	0
9 NA/DK..............	16	17

1 Realistic	26	35
2 Ambivalent....	2	2
3 Unrealistic	39	39
9 NA/DK.......	33	24

93. *'The rich countries must give more help to the poor'*

1 Especially important	60	60
2 Somewhat important....	31	25
3 Without importance	4	5
4 Is against peace	0	0
9 NA/DK..............	5	10

1 Realistic	64	70
2 Ambivalent....	3	1
3 Unrealistic	7	5
9 NA/DK.......	26	24

94. *'The small countries must have greater influence'*

1 Especially important	8	13
2 Somewhat important....	47	39
3 Without importance	23	33
4 Is against peace	0	1
9 NA/DK..............	22	12

1 Realistic	33	29
2 Ambivalent....	1	0
3 Unrealistic	32	52
9 NA/DK.......	34	19

95. *'The military alliances must be preserved'*

1 Especially important	38	22
2 Somewhat important....	42	38
3 Without importance	3	5
4 Against peace	4	20
9 NA/DK..............	13	15

1 Realistic	63	63
2 Ambivalent....	0	1
2 Unrealistic	4	10
9 NA/DK.......	33	26

96. *'General and complete disarmament must be realized'*

1 Especially important	58	59
2 Somewhat important....	19	24
3 Without importance	4	2
4 Against peace	0	2
9 NA/DK..............	19	13

1 Realistic	36	28
2 Ambivalent....	4	3
3 Unrealistic	33	49
9 NA/DK.......	27	20

97. *'There must be a military balance between the states so that nobody dares to attack'*

1 Especially important	58	34
2 Somewhat important....	25	33
3 Without importance	3	5
4 Against peace..........	1	13
9 NA/DK..............	13	15

1 Realistic	68	64
2 Ambivalent....	3	1
3 Unrealistic	6	10
9 NA/DK.......	23	25

98. *'States that naturally belong together must cooperate'*

1 Especially important	28	27
2 Somewhat important....	47	42
3 Without importance	10	15
4 Against peace..........	1	2
9 NA/DK..............	14	14

1 Realistic	68	75
2 Ambivalent....	4	2
3 Unrealistic	1	1
9 NA/DK.......	27	22

99. *'There must be fewer states in the world'*

1 Especially important	10	3
2 Somewhat important....	22	18
3 Without importance	47	58
4 Against peace..........	1	4
9 NA/DK..............	20	17

1 Realistic	19	24
2 Ambivalent....	3	1
3 Unrealistic	46	48
9 NA/DK.......	32	27

100. *'The Western countries must increase contact with East'*

1 Especially important	60	59
2 Somewhat important....	29	28
3 Without importance	1	3
4 Against peace..........	0	0
9 NA/DK..............	10	10

1 Realistic	69	72
2 Ambivalent....	0	0
3 Unrealistic	3	4
9 NA/DK.......	28	24

101. *'We must strengthen the United Nations'*

1 Especially important	79	68
2 Somewhat important....	17	21
3 Without importance	3	8
4 Against peace..........	0	0
9 NA/DK..............	1	3

1 Realistic	61	64
2 Ambivalent....	2	1
3 Unrealistic	7	14
9 NA/DK.......	30	21

102. *'We must strengthen regional organizations'*

1 Especially important	42	35
2 Somewhat important....	47	41
3 Without importance	3	8
4 Against peace..........	0	2
9 NA/DK..............	8	14

1 Realistic	74	79
2 Ambivalent....	2	2
3 Unrealistic	1	1
9 NA/DK.......	23	18

103. *'The world state must be established as soon as possible'*

1 Especially important	24	36
2 Somewhat important....	15	11
3 Without importance	18	14
4 Against peace..........	1	7
9 NA/DK..............	42	32

1 Realistic	6	10
2 Ambivalent....	6	2
3 Unrealistic	74	77
9 NA/DK.......	14	11

104. *What would you say is particularly wrong or criticizable in the foreign policy line your political antagonists (in Norway) advocate?*

1	Their one-sidedness / anti-ism	19	19
2	Lack of realism / their 'moralism'	23	12
3	Their irresponsibility, opportunism	14	9
4	Lack of initiative, action, determination	8	13
5	Outdate policies, cold war-ism	7	12
6	Falseness, dishonesty	1	0
7	Isolationistic	3	2
8	Other	0	2
9	NA/DK	25	31

1	The NATO policy, attitude towards Western policy of Norway	32	27
2	The EEC policy	10	7
3	Development assistance policy, attitude toward the less developed countries	3	5
4	*Detente* policy, attitude toward the East	1	3
5	Disarmament policy	2	3
6	Vietnam policy	1	3
7	UN policy, attitude toward the UN	2	4
8	Other	1	6
9	NA/DK	48	42

105. *Would you say that you have personal influence on the making of Norwegian foreign policy?*

1	Yes	13	2
2	To some extent, in some fields: yes	23	10
3	Little influence	9	35
4	No	51	49
5	I am neutral, civil servant	1	0
6	Other	3	0
9	NA/DK	0	4

106. *Have you ever taken an initiative to promote a view or try to influence the policy on a particular question?*

1	No, never	(Q)	49
2	Once		13
3	Two times		2
4	Three times or more		5
5	Other		5
9	NA/DK		26

107. *Do you wish you personally had more influence on the making of Norwegian foreign policy?*

1	Yes	33	29
2	To some extent, in some fields: yes	15	29
3	A little more influence	3	13
4	No	39	20

5 I am neutral, does not apply to my job............	7	0
6 Other...	1	0
9 NA/DK.......................................	2	9

108. *Do you agree or disagree that people in general should have more influence on Norwegian foreign policy?*

1 Agree completely..............................	11	22
2 Agree to some extent...........................	22	19
3 Ambivalent....................................	9	18
4 Disagree to some extent	18	11
5 Disagree completely............................	21	23
6 No: they should have more information...........	5	0
7 No: they should have more interest...............	9	0
8 Other...	0	0
9 NA/DK.......................................	5	7

109. *How many people would you say have real personal influence on the making of Norwegian foreign policy (approximately)?*

1 More than 500	6	6
2 Between 200 and 500...........................	9	10
3 Between 100 and 200...........................	7	11
4 Between 50 and 100............................	17	13
5 Between 20 and 50.............................	25	18
6 Between 5 and 20..............................	19	15
7 Less than 5	2	3
8 Other...	0	0
9 NA/DK.......................................	15	24

115. *Are you a member of an international non-governmental organization (e.g. World Federalists, The Nordic Association, etc.)?*

1 No, none.....................................	43	40
2 Yes, member of one............................	38	29
3 Yes, member of two	13	11
4 Yes, member of three	3	3
5 Yes, member of three or more...................	3	5
6 Other...	0	0
9 NA/DK.......................................	0	12

117. *Would you say that any particular moral or religious conviction or belief has played and plays a role as far as your views on international politics or foreign policy matters are concerned?*

1 No	36	32
2 Religious conviction	10	13
3 Humanistic, humanitarian beliefs	11	13
4 Ethics in general...............................	14	8
5 Political beliefs................................	14	10
6 Other (world solidarity, unity)..................	14	7
9 NA/DK.......................................	1	17

1 An almost determinant role	1	22
2 A great role..................................	14	22
3 A certain role	32	8
4 Other	0	1
9 NA/DK......................................	53	47

120. *Would you say that your personal situation or position or on the whole what you experienced, during the Second World War has had any importance for your views on international politics and foreign policies?*

1 No, no importance............................	8	13
2 Some importance.............................	33	36
3 Great importance.............................	47	25
4 An almost determinant importance...............	1	12
5 Other	1	1
9 NA/DK......................................	10	13

1 Came to understand peace / war problem, danger of war..	8	9
2 Saw the necessity of military defence	11	4
3 Became a pacifist	3	2
4 Became more positive toward West	13	3
5 Saw the dangers of totalitarianism	1	6
6 Other (experience what unity means)	1	17
9 NA/DK......................................	63	61

125. *If there was a general national election tomorrow – for which political party would you vote?*

1 Labor Party	34	15
2 Conservative Party............................	31	28
3 Christian People's Party	2	6
4 Communist Party..............................	1	1
5 Center Party	3	5
6 Socialist People's Party.........................	3	15
7 Liberal Party.................................	15	25
8 Would not vote	2	4
9 NA/DK......................................	8	1

APPENDIX G

International position of nation-states

According to the international social position index.*

Rank position	Nation-state	Index score
3	France	16
3	German Federal Republic	
3	Italy	
3	Soviet Union	
3	United Kingdom	
9.5	Czechoslovakia	15
9.5	Netherlands	
9.5	Poland	
9.5	Spain	
9.5	Sweden	
9.5	Switzerland	
9.5	United States	
9.5	Yugoslavia	
17.5	Austria	14
17.5	Belgium	
17.5	Canada	
17.5	Denmark	
17.5	German Democratic Republic	
17.5	Hungary	
17.5	Japan	
17.5	Rumania	
23.5	Argentina	13
23.5	Bulgaria	
23.5	Finland	
23.5	Norway	
28.5	Australia	12
28.5	Chile	
28.5	Greece	
28.5	Luxembourg	
28.5	Portugal	
28.5	Turkey	
35.5	Brazil	11
35.5	Colombia	
35.5	Ireland	
35.5	Israel	
35.5	Mexico	
35.5	South Africa	
35.5	United Arabic Republic	
35.5	Venezuela	
42	India	10
42	Iran	

Rank position	Nation-state	Index score
42	New Zealand	
42	Philippines	
42	Uruguay	
46.5	Andorra	9
46.5	Monaco	
46.5	Pakistan	
46.5	San Marino	
56.5	Algeria	8
56.5	China	
56.5	Cyprus	
56.5	Ecuador	
56.5	Guatemala	
56.5	Iceland	
56.5	Indonesia	
56.5	Iraq	
56.5	Lebanon	
56.5	Libya	
56.5	Lichtenstein	
56.5	Morocco	
56.5	Peru	
56.5	Syria	
56.5	Thailand	
56.5	Tunisia	
72.5	Burma	7
72.5	Ceylon	
72.5	Costa Rica	
72.5	Cuba	
72.5	Ethiopia	
72.5	Ghana	
72.5	Honduras	
72.5	Jordan	
72.5	Korea, North	
72.5	Korea, South	
72.5	Kuwait	
72.5	Panama	
72.5	Rhodesia	
72.5	Saudi Arabia	
72.5	Taiwan	
72.5	Zambia	
85.5	Albania	6
85.5	Congo-Kinshasa	
85.5	Dominican Republic	
85.5	El Salvador	
85.5	Jamaica	
85.5	Nicaragua	
85.5	Nigeria	

Rank position	Nation-state	Index score
85.5	Sudan	
85.5	Vietnam, North	
85.5	Vietnam, South	
97	Afghanistan	5
97	Bolivia	
97	Haiti	
97	Ivory Coast	
97	Kenya	
97	Madagascar	
97	Malaysia	
97	Malta	
97	Muscat and Oman	
97	Senegal	
97	Singapore	
97	Tanzania	
97	Uganda	
108.5	Cambodia	4
108.5	Cameroon	
108.5	Guinea	
108.5	Mongolia	
108.5	Paraguay	
108.5	Quatar	
108.5	Trinidad and Tobago	
108.5	Trucial Oman	
108.5	Western Samoa	
108.5	Yemen	
116.5	Bahrain	3
116.5	Bhutan	
116.5	Laos	
116.5	Liberia	
116.5	Mauritius	
116.5	Nepal	
123.5	Congo-Brazzaville	2
123.5	Gabon	
123.5	Gambia	
123.5	Malawi	
123.5	Maldive Islands	
123.5	Mali	
123.5	Niger	
123.5	Upper Volta	
134.5	Aden	1
134.5	Botswana	
134.5	Burundi	
134.5	Central African Republic	
134.5	Chad	
134.5	Dahomey	

Rank position	Nation-state	Index score
134.5	Guinea, Equatorial	
134.5	Lesotho	
134.5	Mauretania	
134.5	Ngwane	
134.5	Rwanda	
134.5	Sierra Leone	
134.5	Somalia	
134.5	Togo	

N = 141.

* Index: 1. Age of nation. 2. Population (total) 3. Memberships (total number of) in IGO's and INGO's. 4. Geographical centrality. 5. Literacy level. 6. GDP at factor cost. 7. GDP per capita. 8. Industry's output as % of total GDP.
Classification: Each of the eight indicators has been trichotomized.

APPENDIX H

Introduction letter

Translation of letter sent to the elite sample, prior to contacting
UNIVERSITY OF OSLO
INSTITUTE OF POLITICAL SCIENCE
Professor dr. philos.
Knut Dahl Jacobsen,
Head of institute.

OSLO, January 1967
Fritznersgt. 12
T. 44 24 87

Research Assistant Helge *Hveem* will this spring carry out a study about international politics and Norwegian foreign policy. The study, which is carried out as a field work for his thesis for the *magister* of political science degree, will be based on interviews with a number of persons who occupy central positions in the field of foreign policy.

Hveem's primary aim is to analyze how one in these central positions – in the Storting and within the political parties, in the foreign service, in the press and the Norwegian Broadcasting, and within various interest organizations – generally and in specific fields conceive of international politics and the factors which influence it. He will also study which factors are expected to play a prominent role in the future developments. Lastly, he will explore how and to what extent international politics can be said to influence Norwegian foreign policy, and vice versa.

This institute considers the study as very important, as it may yield new insights in a field where little research has as yet been done in our country. We therefore do hope that you will respond positively to the study and take time to, during one and a half to two hours, answer to some questions. In the near future, you will be contacted by Research Assistants J. E. Kolberg or Bjørn Johannesen, who will assist Mr. Hveem in the interviewing, or by Mr. Hveem himself.

We should like to stress that the material which is obtained will be used for research purposes only, and that all information, including your own identity, will be treated confidentially in the analysis of the material.

Cordially,
Institute of Political Science

Knut Dahl Jacobsen,
Professor

APPENDIX I

Cluster (McQuitty)
analysis of peace proposals

a. *Elite:*

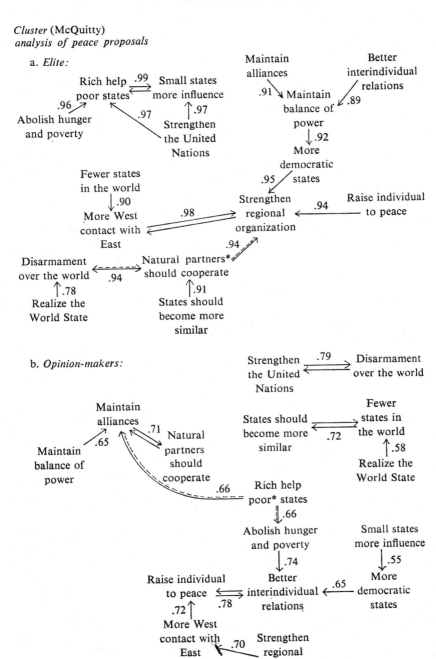

b. *Opinion-makers:*

c. *Public opinion*
   (youth):

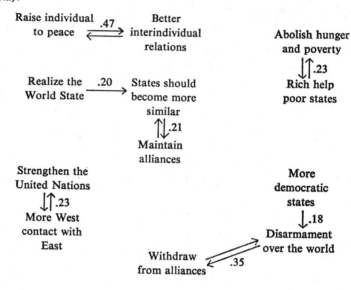

Fig. 2. *Factor analysis of peace proposals.*

Elite: *One single factor*
               On which 'Strengthen regional organization' and 'Rich help poor
               countries' loaded most heavily (with correlation coefficients of .91
               and .90 ,respectively).

Opinion-makers   I 'Cooperative' or '*Internationalist*'
               'Disarmament' .51 / 'Natural partners cooperate' .46 / 'Streng-
               then the United Nations' .43 / 'Maintain alliances' .40 / 'Maintain
               balance of power .38.
               II '*Anti development assistance*'
               'Small states more influence' −.47 / 'Abolish hunger and poverty'
               −.38 / 'Rich help poor states' −.36.

III '*Anti-internationalist*'
'Realize World State' −.47 / 'Strengthen regional organization −.40 / 'Fewer states' −.39 / 'More similar states' −.33 / 'More West contact with East' −.31.
'Impure' variables:*
'Raise individuals to peace' / 'Better interindividual relations' 'More democratic states'.

Public opinion: I '*Soft internationalist*'
'Strengthen the United Nations' .48 / 'More West contact with East' .48 / 'More democratic states' .36 / 'Disarmament' .31.

II *Anti*-'*Tough internationalist*'
'Withdraw from alliances' .56 / 'Maintain alliances' −.52.

III '*Individual level approach*'
'Raise individuals to peace' .59 / 'Better inter-individual relations' .59.

IV '*World federalist*'
'Realize the World State' .57 / 'States should become more similar' .48.

V '*Anti-development assistance*'
'Abolish hunger and poverty' −.53 / 'Rich help poor states' −.53.

*) Variables which do not load on any particular factor, but on two of them practically equally much.

Bibliography

Allardt, Erik, 'Värdeorientering inom amerikansk politisk forskning', *Tidsskrift for samfunnsforskning,* 2/3-1967, pp. 232–246.

Alker, Hayward Jr, and Bruce M. Russett, *World Politics in the General Assembly* (New Haven: Yale University Press, 1965).

Almond, Gabriel, *The American People and Foreign Policy* (New York: Praeger, 1965).

Alstad, Bjørn (ed.), *Norske meninger I–III* (Oslo: Pax, 1969).

Andrén, Nils, 'Nordic Integration', *Cooperation and Conflict,* 1967, pp. 1–25

Bendix, Reinhard and Seymour M. Lipset (eds.), *Class, Status, and Power: A Reader in Social Stratification* (New York: Free Press, 2nd ed. 1966).

Berelson, Bernard and Gary A. Steiner, *Human Behavior: An Inventory of Scientific Findings* (New York: Harcourt, Brace & World, 1964).

Blumer, H., 'Attitudes and the Social Act', *Social Problems,* 3, 1955, pp. 59–64.

Bonham, Matthew, 'Scandinavian Parliamentarians: Attitudes toward Political Integration', *Cooperation and Conflict,* 3, 1969, pp. 149–161.

Boulding, Kenneth, *The Image* (Ann Arbor: University of Michigan Press, 4th ed., 1966).

Brecher, Michael, Blema Steinburg, and Janice Stein, 'A Framework for Research on Foreign Policy Behavior', *Journal of Conflict Resolution,* XII, 1, 1969, pp. 75–101.

Brundtland, Arne Olav, *Sikkerhetspolitisk omprøvning?* (Oslo: Tidens Ekko, 1968).

Brundtland, Arne Olav, 'Hvorfor ikke skandinavisk forsvarsforbung?' *International Politikk* nr. 2, 1964.

Burgess, Philip M., *Elite Images and Foreign Policy Outcomes: A Study of Norway* (Ohio State University Press, 1968).

Coser, Lewis, *The Functions of Social Conflict* (Glencoe: Free Press, 1956).

Dahl, Robert A., *Who Governs? Democracy and Power in an American City* (New Haven and London: Yale University Press, 1961).

Deutsch, Karl W., *Arms Control and the Atlantic Alliance* (New York: Wiley, 1967).

Deutsch, Karl W., *The Nerves of Government* (New York: Free Press, 1966).

Deutsch, Karl W., Lewis J. Edinger, Roy C. Macridis, and Richard L. Merritt, *France, Germany, and the Western Alliance. A Study of Elite Attitudes on European Integration and World Politics* (New York: Scribners, 1967).

Deutsch, Karl W. and Lewis J. Edinger, *Germany Rejoins the Powers: Mass Opinion, Interest Groups, and Elites in Contemporary German Foreign Policy* (Stanford: Stanford University Press, 1959).

Deutsch, Karl W. et al., *Political Community and the North Atlantic Area* (Princeton: Princeton University Press, 1957).

Eckhardt, William and Theo F. Lentz, 'Factors of War/Peace Attitudes', *Peace Research Review*, I, 5, October 1967, p. 20.

Eckstein, Harry, *Division and Cohesion in Democracy. A Study of Norway* (Princeton: Princeton University Press, 1966).

Edinger, Lewis J. and Donald D. Searing, 'Social Background and Elite Analysis: A Methodological Inquiry', *American Political Science Review*, LXI, June 1967, pp. 428–445.

Etzioni, Amitai, *Political Unification* (New York. Holt, Rinehart & Winston, 1965).

Fanon, Frantz, *Les damnés de la terre* (Paris: Maspero, 1961).

Farrell, R. Barry (ed.), *Approaches to International and Comparative Politics* (Evanston: Northwestern University Press, 1966).

Festinger, Leon: *A Theory of Cognitive Dissonance* (New York: Harper & Row, 1957).

Field, G. Lowell and John Higley, 'Elite-konsensus i et utviklet politisk samfunn', *Tidsskrift for samfunnsforskning*, 1, 1971, pp. 1–28.

Frydenlund, Knut, *Norsk utenrikspolitikk* (Oslo: Tidens Ekko, 2, 1966).

Frankel, Joseph, *The Making of Foreign Policy* (London: Oxford University Press, 1963).

Galtung, Johan (ed.), *Cooperation in Europe* (Oslo: Universitetsforlaget, 1970).

Galtung, Johan, 'Foreign Policy Opinion as a Function of Social Position', *Journal of Peace Research*, 3–4, 1964, pp. 206–231.

Galtung, Johan, 'Images of the World in the Year 2000', European Coordination Centre for Research and Documentation in Social Sciences, Vienna, 1970, mimeo.

Galtung, Johan, 'A Structural Theory of Aggression', *Journal of Peace Research*, 2, 1962, pp. 95–119.

Galtung, Johan, *Theories of Peace* (Oslo: Universitetsforlaget, forthcoming).

Galtung, Johan, *Theory and Methods of Social Research* (Oslo: Universitetsforlaget, 1967).

Galtung, Johan and Mari Holmboe Ruge, 'Patterns of Diplomacy', *Journal of Peace Research*, 2, 1965, pp. 101–135.

Gergen, Kenneth W. and Kurt W. Back, 'Aging, Time Perspective, and Preferred Solutions to International Conflicts', *Journal of Conflict Resolution*, IX, 2, June 1965, pp. 177–186.

Gleditsch, Nils Petter, *Norge i verdenssamfunnet* (Oslo: Pax, 1970).

Gleditsch, Nils Petter, 'The Structure of the International Airline Network' (Oslo: unpublished magister's thesis, 1968).

Gleditsch, Nils Petter and Helge Hveem, 'On an International Center-Periphery Index' (forthcoming).

Gorden, Morton and Daniel Lerner, *Euroatlantica* (Cambridge, Mass.: M.I.T. Press, 1969).

Halle, Nils H., 'Social Position and Foreign Policy Attitudes', *Journal of Peace Research*, 1, 1966, pp. 46–74.

Hambro, Edvard, 'Demokrati og nøitralitet', *Fritt Ord*, 1939, pp. 107–116.

Hambro, Edvard, 'Small States and a New League: From the Point of View of Norway', *American Political Science Review*, October 1943, pp. 903–909.

Haskel, Barbara, 'Is there an Unseen Spider?', *Cooperation and Conflict*, 1967, Vol. 2 pp. 229–234.

Haskel, Barbara, 'A Mirror for Princes? Elite Images', *Cooperation and Conflict*, 4, 1968, pp. 240–246.

Hellevik, Ottar, *Stortinget – en sosial elite?* (Oslo: Pax, 1969).

Herz, John, *International Politics in the Atomic Age* (New York: Columbia Paperback, 1959).

Holst, Johan Jørgen, *Norsk sikkerhetspolitikk* (Oslo: Norsk Utenrikspolitisk Institutt, 1968).

Homans, George C., *The Human Group* (New York: Harcourt, Brace, 1950).

Hunter, Floyd, *Community Power Structure* (Chapel Hill: University of North Carolina Press, 1953).

Hveem, Helge, 'Foreign Policy Thinking in the Elite and the General Population', *Journal of Peace Research,* 2, 1968, pp. 146–170.

Hveem, Helge, 'Images of International Stratification: The Ranking of African States', paper presented to the University Social Science Conference, Nairobi, 8–13 December, 1969.

Hyman, H., et al. *Interviewing in Social Research* (Chicago: University of Chicago Press, 1954).

Høivik, Susan (ed.), *10 innlegg om EEC* (Oslo: Universitetsforlaget, 1971).

Haavelsrud, Magnus, 'Views on War and Peace Among Students in West Berlin Public Schools', *Journal of Peace Research,* 2, 1970, pp. 99–120.

International Encyclopedia of the Social Sciences (New York: Macmillan and Free Press, 1968).

Jacobsen, Kurt, 'Sponsorships in the United Nations: A System Analysis', *Journal of Peace Research,* 3, 1969, pp. 235–266.

Jacobsen, Kurt, 'Voting Behavior of the Nordic Countries in the General Assembly', *Cooperation and Conflict,* 1967, pp. 139–157.

Kaplan, Morton, *System and Process in International Politics* (New York: Wiley, 1957).

Kaplan, Morton A. (ed.), *New Approaches in International Relations* (New York: St Martin's Press, 1968).

Katz, Elihu, 'The Two-Step Flow of Communication. An Up-To-Date Report on a Hypothesis', *Public Opinion Quarterly,* 1957, pp. 61–78.

Kelman, Herbert (ed.), *International Political Behavior* (New York: Holt, Rinehart & Winston, 1966).

Koht, Halvdan, 'Neutrality and Peace. The View of a Small Power', *Foreign Affairs,* January 1937.

Koht, Halvdan, *Norsk utanrikspolitikk fram til 9. april 1940* (Oslo: Tiden, 1947).

Koritzinsky, Theo, *Partiene og utenrikspolitikken* (Oslo: Pax, 1970).

Krech, David and Richard Crutchfield, *Theory and Problems of Social Psychology* (New York: McGraw-Hill, 1948).

Kreitler, Hans and Shulamith, 'Crucial Dimensions of the Attitude towards National and Supra-National Ideals', *Journal of Peace Research,* 2, 1967, pp. 107–124.

Laulicht, Jerome, 'Public Opinion and Foreign Policy Decisions', *Journal of Peace Research,* 2, 1965, pp. 147–160.

Lerner, Daniel, 'French Business Leaders Look at EDC: A Preliminary Report', *Public Opinion Quarterly,* XX, 1, Spring 1956, p. 220.

Lie, Trygve, *Hjemover* (Oslo 1958).

Lindgren, Raymond, 'International Cooperation in Scandinavia', *Yearbook of World Affairs,* 1959.

Løchen, Einar, *Norway in European and Atlantic Cooperation* (Oslo: Universitetsforlaget, 1964).

Macridis, Roy C. (ed.), *Foreign Policy in World Politics* (Englewood Cliffs: Prentice-Hall, 2nd ed., 1962).

Martinussen, Willy, 'Velgerne og de politiske stridsspørsmål', *Tidsskrift for samfunnsforskning*, 2/3, 1967, pp. 163–186.

McClosky, Herbert, 'Consensus and Ideology in American Politics', *American Political Science Review*, 58, 1964, pp. 361–382.

McQuitty, L. L., 'Elementary Linkage Analysis for Isolating Orthogonal and Oblique Types and Typal Relevancies', *Educational and Psychological Measurement*, 1965, pp. 207–229.

Merton, Robert K., *Social Theory and Social Structure* (Glencoe: Free Press, 2nd ed., 1957).

Michels, Robert *Political Parties: A Sociological Study of the Oligarchical Tendencies of Modern Democracy* (Glencoe: Free Press, 1958).

Milgram, Stanley, 'Nationality and Conformity', *Scientific American*, Dec. 1961, 205 (6), pp. 45–51.

Miller, Warren E. and Donald E. Stokes, 'Constituency Influence in Congress', *American Political Science Review*, LVII, 1, March 1963, pp. 45–56.

Mills, C. Wright, *The Power Elite* (New York: Oxford University Press, 1956).

Modelski, George, *A Theory of Foreign Policy* (New York: Praeger, 1962).

Moren, Jorolv, *Oppslagsboken norske organisasjoner* (Oslo: Johan Grundt Tanum, 1967).

Nadel, S. F., 'The Concept of Social Elites', *International Social Science Bulletin*, 8 1956.

Nanda, Krishan, 'Elite Nuclear Policy Thinking in India', *Bulletin of Peace Proposals*, Autumn 1969, International Peace Research Institute, Oslo, pp. 125–135. Mimeo.

Nasatir, David et al., *Attitudes of Prominent Americans toward 'World Peace Through World Law'* (New York: Columbia University Bureau of Applied Social Research, September 1959). Mimeo.

North, Robert C., Ole R. Holsti, M. George Zaninovich, and Dina Zinnes, *Content Analysis: A Handbook with Applications for the Study of International Crisis* (Evanston: Northwestern University Press, 1963).

Parsons, Talcott, 'On the Concept of Political Power', *Proceedings of the American Philosophical Society*, 107, 3, June 1963, p. 261.

Parsons, Talcott and Edward Shils, *Toward a General Theory of Action* (Cambridge: Harvard University Press, 1951).

Proceedings of the International Peace Research Association, Inaugural Conference (Assen: Van Gorcum, 1966).

Proceedings of the International Peace Research Association, Second Conference (Assen: Van Gorcum, 1968).

Proceedings of the International Peace Research Association, Third Conference (Assen: Van Gorcum, 1970).

Protho, James W. and C. W. Grigg, 'Fundamental Principles of Democracy: Bases of Agreement and Disagreement', *Journal of Politics*, 22, 1960, pp. 276–294.

Raestad, Arnold, 'Nøitralitet og nøitralitetspolitikk', *Tidsskrift for rettsvidenskap*, 1940, pp. 43–58.

Ramberg, Trygve, 'Stortingsdebatten om paragraf 93 i Grundloven', (Oslo: 1967 mimeo)

Ramsøy, Natalie Rogoff (ed.), *Det norske samfunn* (Oslo: Gyldendal, 1969). English version *Norwegian Society* (Oslo: Universitetsforlaget, forthcoming).

Reinton, Per Olav, 'International Structure and International Integration: The Case of Latin America', *Journal of Peace Research*, 4, 1967, pp. 234–265.

Riesman, David, *The Lonely Crowd* (New York: Doubleday Anchor, 1953).

Riggs, Fred W., 'International Relations as a Prismatic System', *World Politics*, XIV, 1, October 1961, pp. 144–181.

Robinson, J. A., 'Survey Interviewing Among Members of Congress', *Public Opinion Quarterly*, 1960, pp. 127–138.

Rokkan, Stein (ed.), *Comparative Research Across Cultures and Nations*, Publications of the International Social Science Council, 8 (Paris: Mouton, 1968).

Rose, Arnold M., *The Power Structure: Political Process in American Society* (New York: Oxford University Press, 1967).

Rosenau, James, *The Attentive Public and Foreign Policy: A Theory of Growth and Some New Evidence* (Princeton: Center for International Studies, Princeton University, 1968).

Rosenau, James, *National Leadership and Foreign Policy* (Princeton: Princeton University Press, 1963).

Rosenau, James N., *Public Opinion and Foreign Policy* (New York: Random House, 2nd ed., 1964).

Russett, Bruce M., *Community and Contention: Britain and America in the Twentieth Century* (Cambridge, Mass.: M.I.T. Press, 1963).

Russett, Bruce M., *International Regions and the International System: A Study in Political Ecology* (Chicago: Rand McNally, 1967).

Russett, Bruce M., '*Methodological and Theoretical Schools in International Relations*', Monograph no. 2 of the American Academy of Political and Social Science, Philadelphia (Oct. 1970), pp. 87–105.

Russett, Bruce M., *Trends in World Politics* (New York: Macmillan, 1965).

Russett, Bruce M. et al., *World Handbook of Political and Social Indicators* (New Haven: Yale University Press, 1964).

Schwartzmann, Simon and Manual Mora y Araujo, 'The Images of International Stratification in Latin America', *Journal of Peace Research*, 3, 1966, pp. 225–243.

Simon, Herbert A., *Administrative Behavior* (New York: Free Press, 2nd ed., 1965).

Singer, J. David (ed.), *Human Behavior and International Politics* (Chicago: Rand McNally, 1966).

Singer, J. David, 'The Levels-of-Analysis Problem in International Relations', *World Politics*, XIV, 1, October 1961, pp. 77–92.

Singer, J. David, 'Man and World Politics: The Psycho-Cultural Interface', *Journal of Social Issues*, XXIV, 3, 1968, pp. 127–156.

Singer, J. David, *Quantitative International Politics: Insights and Evidence* (New York: Free Press, 1968).

Singer, J. David, 'Soviet and American Foreign Policy Attitudes', *Journal of Conflict Resolution*, VIII, 4, pp. 424–485.

Singer, J. David and Melvin Small, 'The Composition and the Status Ordering of the International System, 1815–1940', *World Politics*, 1966, pp. 236–282.

Snyder, Richard C., H. W. Bruck, and Burton Sapin, *Decision-Making as an Approach to the Study of International Politics* (Princeton: Princeton University Press, 1954).

Snyder, Richard A. and James A. Robinson, *National and International Decision-Making: Towards a General Research Strategy Related to the Problem of War and Peace* (New York: Institute for International Order, 1961).

Terhune, Kenneth W., 'Nationalistic Aspiration, Loyalty, and Internationalism', *Journal of Peace Research,* 3, 1965, pp. 277–287.

Torgersen, Ulf, 'Borgerkrigen som ble vekk', *Tidsskrift for samfunnsforskning,* 2/3 1967, pp. 247–256.

Valen, Henry and Daniel Katz, *Political Parties in Norway: A Community Study* (Oslo: Universitetsforlaget, 2nd printing 1967).

Waltz, Kenneth, *Man, the State, and War* (New York: Columbia University Press, 1959).

Wiberg, Håkon, 'Social Position and Peace Philosophy', *Journal of Peace Research,* 3, 1968, pp. 277–292.

Willetts, Peter, 'The Behavior of the African Group in the General Assembly', University of Strathclyde, M. Sc. dissertation, 1968/69. Mimeo.

Yearbook of National Accounts Statistics, 1967 (New York: United Nations).

Ørvik, Nils, *Hovedlinjer i norsk utenrikspolitikk* (Oslo: Tidens Ekko, 5, 1962).

Ørvik, Nils (ed.), *Norwegian Foreign Policy: A Bibliography 1905–65* (Oslo: Universitetsforlaget, 1967).

Ørvik, Nils, *Sikkerhetspolitikken 1920–39,* Vols. I og II (Oslo: Forsvarets krigshistoriske avdeling, 1960–61).

Ålvik, Trond, 'The Development of Views on Conflict, War, and Peace among School Children. A Norwegian Case Study', *Journal of Peace Research,* 2, 1968, pp. 171–195.

Åmlid, Johanne, *Ut av kurs* (Oslo: Pax, 1966).

Notes

CHAPTER 1.

1 Milton Rokeach, 'The Nature of Attitudes', in *International Encyclopedia of the Social Sciences I* (Macmillan Co & Free Press, 1968), pp. 449–57.

2 Talcott Parsons and Edward Shils, (eds) *Toward a General Theory of Action* (Cambridge: Harvard University Press, 1951) pp. 58 ff.

3 Leon Festinger, *A Theory of Cognitive Dissonance* (New York: Harper & Son, 1957).

4 Cf. H. Blumer, 'Attitudes and the Social Act', *Social Problems*, 3, 1955, pp. 59–64.

5 Cf. J. David Singer, 'Man and World Politics: The Psycho-Cultural Interface', *Journal of Social Issues XXIV*, 3, 1968, pp. 127–56.

6 Kenneth Boulding, *The Image* (Ann Arbor: University of Michigan Press, 1966) p. 12.

7 David Krech and Richard Crutchfield, *Theory and Problems of Social Psychology* (New York: McGraw Hill, 1948) p. 153.

8 Herbert Kelman, 'Social-Psychological Approaches: Definition and Scope', in H. Kelman (ed.) *International Political Behavior*, (New York: Holt, Rinehart & Winston, 1966) p. 26.

9 William A. Scott, 'Psychological and Social Correlates of International Images', in Kelman (ed.), op. cit, p. 72.

10 Suzanne Keller, 'Elites', in *International Encyclopedia of the Social Sciences 5*, pp. 26–29.

11 Karl W. Deutsch, et al., *France, Germany, and the Western Alliance* (New York: Scribner's, 1967) pp. 4–5.

12 Cf. C. Wright Mills, *The Power Elite* (New York: Oxford University Press, 1956) p. 19.

13 Society is, according to Riesman, ruled by a multiplicity of such veto groups which have the power, each one of them, to stop or constrain the exercise of power or will by any other group. Cf. David Riesman, *The Lonely Crowd* (New York: Doubleday Anchor, 1953).

14 Robert A. Dahl, *Who Governs? Democracy and Power in an American City* (New Haven and London: Yale University Press, 1961).

15 Cf. Floyd Hunter, *Community Power Structure* (Chapel Hill: University of North Carolina Press, 1953).

16 William Spinrad, 'Power in Local Communities', in Reinhard Bendix and Seymour M. Lipset (ed.) *Class, Status, and Power* (New York: Free Press, 1966) p. 222. Spinrad contends that these extrapolations have been made in order to give support

to Wright Mills, but that they should be rejected as invalid. While I think that this criticism, which refers to the so called 'fallacy of the wrong level', to a large extent should be accepted, it does not invalidate the reputational approach as a useful tool of analysis.

[17] Arnold M. Rose, *The Power Structure: Political Process in American Society* (New York: Oxford University Press, 1967).

[18] For a brief and very clarifying review of the literature, and an original treatment of the concept 'elite', see S. F. Nadel, 'The Concept of Social Elites', *International Social Science Bulletin* 8, 1956.

[19] Ulf Torgersen, 'De politiske institusjonene', in Natalie Rogoff Ramsøy (ed.) *Det norske samfunn*, (Oslo: Gyldendal 1969) p. 256. English version *Norwegian Society* (Oslo: Universitetsforlaget, forthcoming).

[20] See for instance Deutsch et al., op. cit.; Morton Gordon and Daniel Lerner, *Euratlantica*, (Cambridge, Mass.: M.I.T. Press, 1969); and the theoretical work by Gabriel Almond, *The American People and Foreign Policy* (New York: Praeger, 1965).

[21] We prefer the concept 'policy-maker' to that, which is more often used, of 'decision-maker'. The latter tends to dramaticize policy-making by focusing on the specific event, delimited in time (When was the decision taken?) and in space (By whom?) The former points, more fruitfully, to the *process*.

[22] Karl W. Deutsch, *The Nerves of Government*, (New York: Free Press, 1966).

[23] Raymond Aron, 'Social Class, Political Class, Ruling Class' in Bendix and Lipset (ed.), *Class, Status and Power*, p. 204. According to Aron, the empirical study of a leading stratum includes essentially four aspects: the social background and manner of recruitment; the career patterns; the manner of thinking or cognition in this category; and the coherence and feeling of solidarity of its members. He argues against the use of the word 'elite', which he finds misleading.

[24] Elihu Katz, 'The Two-Step Flow of Communication', *Public Opinion Quarterly*, 1957 pp. 61–78; Deutsch et al., op. cit.; Almond, op. cit.

[25] Cf. James N. Rosenau, *Public Opinion and Foreign Policy*, (New York: Random House, 1964) and *National Leadership and Foreign Policy* (Princeton: Princeton University Press, 1963). In the latter, Rosenau employs the concept 'national leader' to mean a kind of sub-elite of prominent opinion-makers. A similar meaning has the concept 'sub-leader' in Dahl, op. cit., although it is employed at the local, community level.

[26] Johan Galtung, 'Foreign Policy Opinion as a Function of Social Position', *Journal of Peace Research* 3–4, 1964, pp. 206–231.

[27] The concept of influence in relation to foreign policy making is given a definition in Karl W. Deutsch and Lewis J. Edinger, *Germany Rejoins the Powers*, (Stanford: Stanford University Press, 1959) p. 195. Partially, we are in agreement with these authors when they see 'the continuing enjoyment of substantial status and prestige' as important aspects of their definition. We do not agree, however, when they also define influence on foreign policy making as 'repeated association with prevailing policies': a person who is only complying with any prevailing policy is simply a follower, not an influential. Of course the influential cannot repeatedly or over a longer period of time be dissociated from prevailing policies: that would probably be proof that he is a non-influential. On the other hand it must be shown that he is an activist, an initiator in the foreign policy making process, or at least that his

opinion on some issues at some time, if he is sought out for advice, has some importance to the policy resulting from the policy-making process.

28 Keller, op. cit. p. 28.
29 Cf. Johan Galtung, *Theory and Methods of Social Research*. (Oslo: Universitetsforlaget, 1967). Probability samples usually are the basis sampling methodology set up for drawing generalizations, the main reason being that they makes it possible to evaluate *how* indicative findings from testing a sample are of the universe; p. 55.
30 A similar approach was employed in the study of Deutsch et al., op. cit.
31 The influence of the military leadership, although it is probably relatively modest compared with a number of other states, should not be underestimated. In times of international crisis or perceived foreign threats, it may be decisive. On the other hand, in 'normal' times it is not felt as particularly great, or rather: the military leaders by other elite groups are not given particular competence in and thus access to foreign policy-making. For an evaluation of the influence and role of the military during the inter-world war period, see Nils Ørvik, *Sikkerhetspolitikken 1920–39*, (Oslo: FKA, 1960–61) Vols. I and II.
32 The response rate we obtained for the elite sample was almost the same as that obtained by Robinson in his study of American congressmen, cf. J. A. Robinson, 'Survey Interviewing Among Members of Congress', *Public Opinion Quarterly* 1960, pp. 127–38.
33 Galtung defines these concepts as follows: *heterogeneity* is found when the units of analysis show high dispersion on the variables of interest; *representativity* means that all combinations of variables/units shall be represented in the sample in the same proportion as in the universe; and *bias* means a higher degree of verification in the sample than is found within the total universe. Cf. Galtung, *Theory and Methods*, pp. 51–52.
34 Much of the reasoning and the argumentation behind the choice made here is found in Galtung, ibid. pp. 109–160.
35 Cf. Helge Hveem, 'Foreign Policy Thinking in the Elite and the General Population', *JPR*, 2, 1968 pp. 146–170. Unfortunately, we can present only two items which were used in both the interview guide and the elite questionnaire: the socalled 'intra-individual' and 'interindividual' approaches to peace-making. The results as mentioned show no bias, as can be seen from the following table:

Test of the data collecting method. %

	E*		OM		E†	OM
	Pos	Neg	Pos	Neg		
Individuals should be educated to peace	78	12	81	12	35‡	46
Better relations between the individuals	56	22	51	25	28	27

* The data for the elite sample here are based on responses on the interview guide.
† Elite data here are from the questionnaire.
‡ The percentages here represent those who think that the item is 'Especially important to peace'.

E = Elite; OM = opinion-makers.

On the intra-individual item, the opinion-makers are more positive than the elite in both cases, while on the interindividual item the elite is the more positive in both cases. If the table is read vertically, looking at the relationship between the two items, the trend is also consistent in all four cases: the intra-individual approach is the most preferred.

36 See for instance Nils Ørvik, *Hovedlinjer i norsk utenrikspolitikk* (Tidens Ekko 5, Oslo 1962); Knut Frydenlund, *Norsk utenrikspolitikk* (Tidens Ekko 2, Oslo 1966); Einar Løchen, *Norway in European and Atlantic Cooperation* (Oslo: Universitets-forlaget, 1964). For a detailed bibliography of books, articles etc. on Norwegian foreign policy, see Nils Ørvik (ed.), *Norwegian Foreign Policy: A Bibliography 1905–65* (Oslo: Universitetsforlaget, 1967).

37 According to Laulicht, one should not be afraid of too long interviews, even with elite people; cf. Jerome Laulicht, 'Comparative Studies of Foreign Policy Opinions', in *Proceedings of the International Peace Research Association*, Second Conference, (Assen: Van Gorcum, 1968) Vol. 1, pp. 401–416. Robinson, on the other hand, warns against too long interviews, cf. Robinson, op. cit.

38 In fact, all studies referred to through out this report *and* from which data for comparisons have been taken were either not publicized or were not known to us when we selected our variables and the data collection took place. The only exceptions were studies by Deutsch and Edinger, op. cit., and David Nasatir et al., *Attitudes of Prominent Americans toward 'World Peace Through World Law'*, Bureau of Applied Social Research, Columbia University, September 1959.

39 Laulicht, op. cit. puts forward 10 issue-areas which he proposes should be included in any comparative study of this kind. We have in fact 7 of the 10 included, and the remaining 3 are briefly referred to passim.

CHAPTER 2.

1 J. David Singer, 'The Levels-of-Analysis Problem in International Relations', *World Politics XIV*: 1, Oct. 1961, pp. 77–92.

2 Singer, ibid.; Robert C. North, et al., *Content Analysis* (Evanston: Northwestern University Press, 1963) pp. 5–7; Johan Galtung, *Theories of Peace* (Oslo: Univer-sitetsforlaget, forthcoming).

3 Cf. Richard C. Snyder, H. W. Bruck, and Burton Sapin, *Decision-Making as an Approach to the Study of International Politics* (Princeton: Princeton University Press, 1954); Joseph Frankel, *The Making of Foreign Policy* (London: Oxford University Press, 1963); Roy C. Macridis (ed.), *Foreign Policy in World Politics* (Englewood Cliffs: Prentice-Hall, 1962); George Modelski, *A Theory of Foreign Policy* (New York: Praeger, 1962).

4 Cf. Snyder et al., ibid. and other more recent works relying heavily on conceptualiza-tions in the formation of theory, among them those referred to in the preceding note. It is self-evident that the question of exclusiveness versus inclusiveness should first of all be decided empirically. In our opinion, the very few empirical studies in the Snyder tradition have not been able to prove its fruitfulness.

5 Cf. James N. Rosenau, 'Pre-Theories and Theories of Foreign Policy', in R. Barry Farrell, (ed.) *Approaches to International and Comparative Politics* (Evanston: Northwestern University Press, 1966) pp. 27–92.

6 Cf. J. David Singer, 'Man and World Politics'. Singer stresses the need to combine psychological and societal phenomena for the purpose of explanation. And we have to combine macro and micro phenomena in order to answer the question what degree of latitude individual men, decision-makers and others, enjoy in world politics.

7 We are thinking of e.g. the so called 'national interest' school in international relations, or the man-centered approach of certain psychological and social-psychological traditions (cf. The UNESCO proclamation that peace starts with the single individual).

8 One example of this is the world federalist focus on supra-national factors. For an interesting, quantitative study of the different 'schools' in international relations, see Bruce M. Russett. 'Methodological and Theoretical Schools in International Relations', Monograph No. 2 of the American Academy of Political and Social Science Philadelphia (Oct. 1970) pp. 87–105.

9 Rosenau, in Farrell (ed.), op. cit. calls his contribution a 'pre-theory' of foreign policy-making: it is less than a full-fledged theory; it is tentative. Rosenau defines it '– an early step forward explanation of specific empirical events, a point of view of philosophy about the way the world is. –' Cf. note 41, p. 41.

10 On this point, Rosenau seems to confuse two different axes or dimensions as one. The five levels he is proposing in fact are not found along one single continuum, but are both logically and methodologically to be seen in the context of at least two dimensions: the public vs. private, and the intra-national vs. inter-national. Thus, instead of the linear continuum, a four-fold or an eight-fold table seems to offer a more correct presentation of the categories.

11 Ibid., p. 43. The *idiosyncratic* variables are particular to the individual (his talents, prior experiences, his values); *role* variables are peculiar to the policy-maker's role, and are working irrespective of or independent of idiosyncratic variables; *governmental* variables are peculiar to the governmental structure (executive versus legislative relations, etc.); *social* or non-governmental variables are e.g. the major value orientations of a society, the degree of national unity, the extent of industrialization, etc.; and *systemic* variables are 'any non-human aspects of a society's external environment or any actions occuring abroad that condition or otherwise influence the choices made by its officials . . .'.

12 Cf. footnote 45 on p. 47, ibid. The author criticizes, on pp. 34–35, that many attempts at theory-formation do not make explicit the rationale behind hypotheses on causal relations and that they are rather unsystematic on this point. It seems to us that Rosenau to a large extent is subject to his own criticisms.

13 Cf. p. 48, ibid.; the list of hypotheses is exhaustive in that all categories of variables (representing potentially influencing factors) are related to every one of the eight classes of actors. A further elaboration of the list, including the fourth dichotomy of penetration-nonpenetration and thus making the number of classes 16, is made at the end of his article, see pp. 90–91.

14 As far as we know, a team of political scientists from several American research institutions are presently carrying out a world-wide comparative study based on the Rosenau pre-theory. On the basis of voting patterns in the UN, Bruce Russett offers a validation of the pre-theory, cf. Bruce M. Russett, *International Regions and the International System: A Study in Political Ecology*, (Chicago: Rand McNally, 1967) p. 94. He concludes that while idiosyncratic and role variables on the major issues in the UN seemed to be of a slight significance, the type of governmental system occasionally but not often had a discernible effect. Societal and systemic influences, however, appeared either of them or both to be more important than the others. The limitation of this validation lies in the fact that Russett makes no discrimination between different types of actors.

315

[15] We are particularly referring to his use of the dichotomy *open* vs. *closed* polities, which is not operationalized, but seems to follow a rather conventional use of the concepts, i.e. a Western, 'ideologized' one. To take two examples of the debatable consequences of this: Kenya is classified as 'open', Ghana as 'closed'; to us it seems that even precoup, Nkrumah's Ghana was not particularly less 'open' (in the meaning that participation opportunities, tolerated opposition, etc. existed) than Kenya.

Another weak point is probably the example of Czechoslovakia. For one thing, subsequent events showed that this country, by definition a closed one, was 'open under a cover of closedness': the January 1968 revolution in fact was a manifestation of the latent openness of the Czechoslovakian society. Another thing is that later events again have 'closed' this society from the top through systemic influence, which should be accredited much more weight than it is in the Rosenau scheme: in fact only the short 'Czechoslovakian 1968 Spring' gave credit to his strong emphasis on intra-national factors, while the systemic influences clearly both prior to and after this period have played a paramount role.

[16] Rosenau, op. cit. p. 65. Cf. also Fred W. Riggs, 'International Relations as a Prismatic System', *World Politics XIV*: 1 October 1961, pp. 144–81.

[17] Rosenau, ibid. distinguishes between four different issue-areas: the territorial, the status, the human resources and the nonhuman resources areas, '– each of which encompasses the distinctive motives, actions, and interactions evoked by the clusters of values that are linked to, respectively, the allocation of territorial jurisdiction, the allocation of status within horizontal political systems or within nonpolitical systems, the development and allocation of human resources, and the development and allocation of nonhuman resources.' pp. 82–83.

[18] Dahl in his community study found an overlap among 'leaders' and 'subleaders' in the three issue-areas involved in the study of only 3 % of his sample, while only 1.5 % were leaders in all three areas. (Dahl, op. cit., p. 175.) Similar findings have been reported by Miller and Stokes: they found statistically highly significant differences between the operation of representation processes in three major issue-areas – social welfare, foreign involvment, and civil rights – among congressmen. (Warren E. Miller and Donald E. Stokes, 'Constituency Influence in Congress', *American Political Science Review LVII*: 1, March 1963, pp. 45–56). In our opinion, their findings are compatible with what we have proposed ourselves, as they do not necessarily, nor logically, support the thesis that there are several issue-areas with distinctly separate processes of policy-making *within* the area of foreign policy.

[19] Michael Brecher, Blema Steinberg, and Janice Stein, 'A Framework for Research on Foreign Policy Behavior', *Journal of Conflict Resolution XII*, 1, 1969 pp. 75–101.

[20] Rosenau uses the Netherlands as an example of an actor falling into this class.

[21] Our objections to his theory are both theoretical and methodological. First, we find that the dimensions he has chosen, although representing basic traits of the international society, do not tap the interesting and important aspects of that society relevant in this context. Especially his use of the penetrated – nonpenetrated dichotomy leaves much to be desired.

Methodologically, his scheme – when all four dichotomies are included, plus three or four issue-areas – is too detailed, too overloaded: as long as the universe consists of less than 150 formally independent national actors, the number of units falling into each of the classes may be too small for empirical analysis. More important, instead of the use of dichotomies we think that an index would be the appropriate thing, as it would also escape the difficulty just mentioned, and as it would give a more reliable picture of the international society and its complexity. While we may have to dichotomize each single variable going into the index, we may arrive at a more refined classification by using the 'end result' of the additive index for ranking, etc. By such an operation, we shall get a flexible measure of inter-actor differences, which shows *degrees* or shades of properties characteristic of the different classes, not the clear-cut (and unrealistic) 0,1 classification of the method Rosenau employs.

22 Galtung, 'Foreign Policy Opinion as a Function of Social Position'. His index employed the following variables: *Age*; *Income*; *Occupation by position* (leading or subordinate, employer or employee); *Occupation by sector* (primary, secondary, tertiary); *Place of residence* (as by geographical location); *Place of residence* (in towns or in rural, sparsely populated areas); *Education*; and *Sex*. All variables were dichotomized according to certain standards.

23 These problems are taken up in more detail in Nils P. Gleditsch and Helge Hveem, 'On an International Center-Periphery Index' (forthcoming).

24 We are referring to e.g. the socio-metric study by J. David Singer and Melvin Small, 'The Composition and the Status Ordering of the International System, 1815–1940', *World Politics* 1966, pp. 236–282, where the authors determine the rank of states by means of the rank and the number of diplomatic legations a state receives from other states. Cf. also Simon Schwartzmann and Manuel Mora y Arauja, 'The Images of International Stratification in Latin America', *JPR*, 3, 1966, pp. 225–243; and Helge Hveem, 'Images of International Stratification: The Ranking of African States', paper presented to the University Social Science Conference, Nairobi, 8–13 December, 1969.

25 Johan Galtung, 'Small Group Theory and the Theory of International Relations: A Study in Isomorphism', in Morton A. Kaplan, ed., *New Approaches in International Relations* (New York: St. Martin's Press, 1968) pp. 270–303.

26 Apart from those cited in footnote 24 above, we may mention Per Olav Reinton, 'International Structure and International Integration: The Case of Latin America', *JPR*, 4, 1967, pp. 234–265; and Kurt Jacobsen, 'Voting Behavior of the Nordic Countries in the General Assembly', *Cooperation and Conflict*, 1967, pp. 139–157.

27 Cf. Galtung, 'Foreign Policy attitudes as a Function of Social Position'.

28 Some of the variables in the national index which have not been 'matched' in our index might of course have been represented in the latter as well, e.g. place of residence: urban or rural at the international level may be represented by urbanization; sex (more or less) by predominant race.

29 The number of memberships in international organizations, global and 'regional', governmental and non-governmental, of African states correlates (1965 figures) by .75 (Spearman's rank correlation) with the ranking of African states made by a sample of African students, cf. Hveem, op. cit. note 24 above. Population, which was selected as one of the size variables, to some extent may be seen as a potential for interaction or for 'exporting' the values, attitudes and images etc. of a nation-state; as such it is related to the relational dimension.

30 I am indebted to Kurt Jacobsen of the International Peace Research Institute, Oslo for the use of his data on UN behavior.

31 In the case of the national center-periphery index, indicators used for validation of

the index included degree of knowledge (in general), political participation, and the degree to which people expressed an opinion on an issue.

32 An outstanding example of this tradition is Richard A. Snyder and James A. Robinson, *National and International Decision-Making* (New York: Institute for International Order, 1961). The opposite school is represented by e.g. Kenneth Waltz, *Man, the State, and War* (New York: Columbia University Press, 1959), and John Herz, *International Politics in the Atomic Age* (N. Y.: Columbia Paperbacks, 1959).

33 Bruce M. Russett, *Community and Contention: Britain and America in the Twentieth Century* (Cambridge, Mass.: M.I.T. Press, 1963).

34 On theories of disequilibrium, see Johan Galtung, 'A Structural Theory of Aggression', *JPR*, 2, 1964, pp. 95–119; and Nils P. Gleditsch, 'Rank and Interaction: A General Theory with some Applications to the International System', *Proceedings of the IPRA Third General Conference II* (Assen: Van Gorcum, 1970) pp. 1–21.

35 Russett, *International Regions and the International System*, p. 219.

36 These two propositions may seem to contradict each other, as wider range and consequently wider dispersion logically would lead to less pronounced tendencies. However, it is believed that the wider range makes itself felt over a number of variables on a certain issue area, and thus single-variable central tendencies may be maintained.

37 Symmetric penetration means practically equally much penetration of each other's communities or polities by both partners in a relationship of two (dyad).

38 Cf. Russett, *Community and Contention*.

39 In this case there is little or no interaction between the two actors, or little action by the better-placed toward the ill-placed (in terms of international position).

40 In fact, this is the impression held by most observers of East-West relations in the 60s when they use the concept *detente*; it may even be related to United States – France relationship under Gaullism.

41 Cf. Galtung, 'Foreign Policy Attitudes as a Function of Social Position'; Nils H. Halle, 'Social Position and Foreign Policy Attitudes', *JPR*, 1, 1966, pp. 46–74.

42 An already classical and strongly critical account of this process of penetration is Frantz Fanon, *Les damnes de la terre* (Paris: Maspero, 1961) (also in English translation, Penguin Books).

43 Cf. Robert Michels, *Political Parties* (Glencoe: The Free Press, 1958).

44 Cf. James Rosenau, *The Attentive Public and Foreign Policy* (Center for International Studies, Princeton University, 1968) mimeo. Rosenau shows that public interest and participation in foreign policy matters in the US has increased during the last few years. This most probably is true even with Norway, although the Vietnam debate may make it particularly true of the United States.

45 Karl W. Deutsch and Richard L. Merritt, 'Effects of Events on National and International Images', in Kelman (ed.), *International Political Behavior*, show that external events may mobilize the general public into strong involvement and affect, but that this involvement tends to fluctuate, to drop after some time down to a 'natural' level and then rise again with some new dramatic external event, with similar shifts in attitudes held.

46 Cf. James N. Rosenau, 'Private Preferences and Public Responsibilities', in J. David Singer, *Quantitative International Politics: Insights and Evidence* (New York: Free Press, 1968). Rosenau here provides empirical support for the proposition that role

variables are more potent than individual, idiosyncratic variables. This is done by analyzing Congressmen's behavior toward the former US Secretary of State, John Foster Dulles and his policies. What Rosenau shows is that the role of a partisan, i.e. member of one of the parties in the Congress, is more determinant to a person's behavior than his personality or his personal preferences. To us, it seems that Rosenau goes too far in generalizing on the relative potency of the factors mentioned from such findings only. Dulles probably was not the Secretary of State who would be most inclined to create the type of bipartisan backing of the foreign policy which is so often found in U.S. politics. On the other hand, these findings are in accordance with what we shall propose ourselves: that party affiliation is important in explaining intra-milieu variances in foreign policy attitudes.

47 Rosenau and we are probably more in agreement when the concept of penetration is brought in. For an evaluation of the relative importance of inter- and intra-national factors on foreign policy making, see Deutsch and Edinger, op. cit. They conclude on the basis of their empirical material, that international or extranational factors were the more important up to the mid-50s, intra-national factors from that time on.

48 This would be true in the case when e.g. minority groups in actor A 'belong to', or is of the same nationality as, actor B.

49 Cf. Deutsch, *The Nerves of Government*: and Herbert C. Kelman, 'Social-Psychological Approaches: the Question of Relevance', in Kelman (ed.), *International Political Behavior*, pp. 565–605.

50 See references in note 34 above, as well as Hveem, 'Images of International Stratification'.

51 Russett, op. cit., p. 92.

52 Cf. Ørvik, op. cit., and Halvdan Koht, *Norsk utanrikspolitikk fram til 9. april 1940* (Oslo: Tiden, 1947).

53 This is indicated, among other things, by the frequency of official top-level meetings between these states in the period, and by trade data, particularly as far as Nordic cooperation is concerned. The small state interaction – to some extent keeping Great Britain out – was also seen at League of Nations conferences.

54 Philip M. Burgess, *Elite Images and Foreign Policy Outcomes: A Study of Norway* (Ohio State University Press, 1968) is one of the latest and most detailed accounts of this period.

55 What we call 'structural changes' is a reference to the fact that a great part of the Norwegian elite and the policy-makers went into exile, mostly to Great Britain and the United States, at the beginning of the war. Some of the elite members, however, exiled to Sweden and they to a large extent seemed to be the old, 'neutralist' guard, while the emerging Atlantic-oriented part of the elite to a large extent was found in London or Washington. This geographical split of course was largely instrumental in widening pre-war differences in outlook, in that people at the various places were influenced by the images and attitudes prevalent or developing in their respective milieu and environments.

56 Cf. the writings of some of the leading Atlanticists from that time, e.g. Trygve Lie, *Hjemover* (Oslo, 1958); Edvard Hambro, 'Demokrati og nøitralitet', *Fritt Ord* 1939, pp. 107–116; (same author) 'Small States and a New League: From the Point of View of Norway', *American Political Science Review*, October 1943, pp. 902–909; and Arnold Raestad, 'Nøitralitet og nøitralitetspolitikk', *Tidsskrift for rettsviden-*

skap 1940, pp. 43–58.

[57] The aim of strengthening the United Nations and of strongly supporting it is traditionally mentioned at the beginning (among foreign policy statements) in the King's yearly report to the Norwegian Parliament.

[58] The period 1945–49 has by several authors (see note 35 for Chapt. 1 above) been named as the 'bridge-building' period of Norwegian foreign policy, i.e. a period where Norway actively pursued a neutralist policy. We find, on the basis of much evidence some of which has been referred to in the text, that this characterization is somewhat inappropriate. At most, it may be used as a description of some surface tendencies of neutralism, first of all due to the former Norwegian foreign minister Trygve Lie at that time being Secretary General of the United Nations. Cf. Ørvik, opera cit., Lie, op. cit.

[59] Authentic expressions and systematic use of terms as 'small power policy' and 'trade union of small powers' are found e.g. in Halvdan Koht, 'Neutrality and Peace. The View of a Small Power, *Foreign Affairs*, January 1937, and in *Norsk utanrikspolitikk fram til 9. april 1940.*

[60] Haskel in a comment to Burgess, op. cit. contends that role theory or role variables are more efficient in explaining the policy shift which took place than image theory. To support this, she mentions that former Foreign Minister Koht, who after the World War II had *not* changed his preference for neutrality, still defended the pro-NATO position of the government in 1949, as a member of the Labour party. Another example is Mr. Lie, who as Secretary-General of the United Nations, although he had since long a pro-Western alliance image, hesitated to extend his support for NATO membership because of his new position as 'bridge-builder'. In our opinion, these examples do not suffice to establish role, variables as the more important, if not 'role variables' do also include the major structural changes of the Norwegian elite during the war and the role they played as exiles, being exposed to new environments. The two men mentioned as examples, moreover, were not the decisive ones at that time. See Barbara Haskel, 'A Mirror for Princes? Elite Images', *Cooperation and Conflict*, 4, 1968, pp. 240–246.

[61] Exceptions from recent years are Johan Jørgen Holst, *Norsk sikkerhetspolitikk* (Oslo: Norsk Utenrikspolitisk Institutt, 1968) and Arne Olav Brundtland, *Sikkerhetspolitisk omprøvning?* (Oslo: Tidens Ekko 1968); research done at the International Peace Research Institute, Oslo and reported in a number of articles by Johan Galtung, Ingrid Eide and others; and recent studies (not yet publicized) by Philip Burgess and Matth. Bonham.

[62] These values, on the other hand, should probably be seen as in fact very much 'Westernized', or of 'Western' origin.

[63] Norway not only is a member of the NATO; after the Second World War she received 460 million dollars under the socalled Marshall plan (OEEC). Moreover, she is a member of the OECD. Source: Löchen, op. cit. p. 40.

[64] Herbert C. Kelman, 'Compliance, Identification, and Internalization', in J. David Singer (ed.), *Human Behavior and International Politics* (Chicago: Rand McNally, 1966) distinguishes between three different processes of influence: *compliance* which occurs when an individual accepts influence because it hopes to achieve a favorable respons from the influencing source; *identification*, which occurs when an individual accepts influence because it wants to conform with another individual, wants to maintain a selfdefined satisfactory relationship with that other one; and *inter-*

nalization which occurs when an individual accepts the behavior – and thus also the attitudes – which is performed by another individual because that behavior (or set of attitudes) is congruent with its own value system.

All these three processes may have acted or may act, separately or in conjunction, on the Norwegian foreign policy milieu – permanently, at some decisive stage, or in several concrete instances or issues.

65 These are 1967 figures. Another important 'piece of reality' is Norway's strong dependence on the international service market for its big shipping business. Such 'external realities' would still remain as *another* constant, at least for a considerable time period, even if the present leaders and elite were shifted out.

If this constant either changed 'by itself' or if a new foreign policy elite would like to change it, this would probably have major repercussions on e.g. the ability of Norway to maintain her high level of achievement, repercussions for which the elite would have to answer.

66 The trade figures for 1963 and 1966 show the following ranking of partners, for imports and exports respectively (figures in percentage of total import and export):

	1963		1966	
	Export	Import	Export	Import
United Kingdom	18.7	17.8	18.8	13.7
Sweden	14.1	17.6	15.3	18.8
Western Germany	14.8	17.9	13.3	16.1
United States	9.4	9.6	8.9	17.5
Denmark	8.8	5.1	7.1	5.8

One of the trends to be seen from these figures is that Sweden has been catching up with Great Britain and is at present virtually competing with it for the first place as Norway's trading partner. Source: Johan Galtung, 'Norge i verdenssamfunnet', in Ramsøy (ed.) op. cit. p. 485.

67 Cf. figures for 1966 in the note above.

68 In 1963, more than 65% of Norway's exports and imports were with NATO countries, while the percentage was somewhat, but not much lower in 1966.

If Sweden, Switzerland and Finland are included, as EFTA or 'Western' countries as well, the percentage increases to a total of more than 80%.

69 Great Britain and the United States ranked as number 2 and 3, respectively, as the country with which Norwegian parliamentarians thought it was natural to compare Norway with, cf. Galtung, 'Norge i verdenssamfunnet', in Ramsøy, op. cit., pp. 446–447. According to a nation-wide survey made in 1966, 24% of all Norwegians mentioned the United States as the one foreign country in which they could wish to settle; this country clearly ranked on top of the list, which moreover was very much dominated by 'Western' countries. Great Britain on this question, on the other hand, ranked as number 8 only, after countries like Italy, Australia, Canada and Spain, and the two Scandinavian 'colleagues'. Cf. Galtung, ibid. p. 448.

70 Sweden has by far topped the list of countries which the parliamentarians (in the period 1962–68, according to content analysis of their speeches) thought Norway should be compared with; it was mentioned by 27% against approximately 13% for Great Britain and the United States, each of them. Denmark as number 4 was

referred to by 9%. Sweden emerged as the second most preferred country for immigration or settlement abroad: it was mentioned by 17%, while 7% preferred Denmark. That pro-Nordic feelings are increasing, is evidenced e.g. by a survey made in 1969 by the Norwegian Gallup Institute.

[71] For an account of the inter-Nordic and intra-Norwegian discussions and decision-making over these questions, see Barbara Haskel, 'Regionalism without Politics', *Cooperation and Conflict*, 3, 1968, pp. 195–198; and Arne Olav Brundtland, 'Hvorfor ikke skandinavisk forsvarsforbund?', *Internasjonal Politikk* nr. 2, 1964

[72] This happened throughout the 1950, when plans for a customs union ran into nothing, due largely to fears, particularly in Norway, that it would be contrary to her Atlantic policies and Anglo-American affiliations. It happened again in the 60s when the European Economic Community attracted more attention in Norway and Denmark, at least, than any Nordic scheme; and to some extent the Nordic-EEC dualism or conflict has even been felt recently during discussions of the socalled Nordec plans of a customs union, in particular in Denmark and Norway.

Cf. e.g. Amitai Etzioni, *Political Unification* (New York: Holt, Rinehart & Winston, 1965); Raymond Lindgren, 'International Cooperation in Scandinavia', *Yearbook of World Affairs*, 1959; and Nils Andrén, 'Nordic Integration', *Cooperation and Conflict*, 1967 pp. 1–25.

[73] Knut Frydenlund, op. cit.

[74] Jacobsen, op. cit.

[75] Russett in 'International Regions and the International System' shows that the same closeness to the Commonwealth holds for trade data as well.

[76] The reason why the United States does not score 16, i.e. fall within the very top center category, is that they receive only medium rank on geographical centrality, a factor which gives Europe a preeminent position. This factor has been used by Gleditsch, 'The Structure of the International Airline Network' (Oslo: unpublished magister thesis, 1968).

[77] Cf. Galtung, 'Norge i verdenssamfunnet', in Ramsøy, op. cit. pp. 450–451. Over a number of 71 different variables, data on which are taken from Bruce Russett et al., *World Handbook of Social and Political Indicators* (New Haven: Yale University Press, 1964), Norway shows an extremely uneven rank profile, measured by her position in a decile group on any one variable. Compared with Great Britain and Sweden, the two top-ranking countries in Norway's reference group, her profile is extremely uneven: while Sweden and Great Britain tend towards the extreme deciles (i.e. the highest and the lowest ones) Norway distributes herself very evenly on all deciles.

[78] Galtung, ibid. p. 470 ff. sees aggressiveness as an attempt to change (one's environment, in the case of an over-achieved). He contends that Norway makes this attempt, and thus spells out her aggressiveness, through international cooperation and organization, while she probably had been more aggressive in a physical or violent meaning of the concept, had she been more powerful, higher on size, more resourceful.

[79] In Hveem, 'Images of International Stratification', the argument that interaction gives prestige is given an empirical backing. It is shown that those countries which rank low on development (achievement), high on size are the ones which tend to be interacting particularly much, i.e. seeking increased rank through interaction with others (and with those which rank higher than oneself).

322

That this holds true e.g. for trade data, may be seen from the fact that the eight countries ranking on top, both in 1963 and 1966, as Norway's principal trading partners, are all ranking higher than Norway on the international position index four of them in fact belonging to the top score group.

80 For attempts at clarifying it, see Herbert McCloskey, in James Rosenau, (ed.) *Domestic Sources of Foreign Policy;* and Kenneth W. Terhune, 'Nationalistic Aspiration, Loyalty, and Internationalism', *JPR*, 3, 1965, pp. 277–287.

81 Johan Galtung, 'On the Future of the International System', *JPR*, 4, 1967, pp. 303–333. Other categories of attitude sets along this dimension is nationalism sub-nationalism, and *extra-nationalism*, the latter representing the case where an individual feels stronger loyalty to an actor outside his own country than to this country itself.

82 In 1968, Norway's shipping in terms of total size of her shipping fleet (in tons dead weight) was the third highest ranking in the world, only 'convenience flag' Liberia and Japan ranking higher. In the last years Norway has always been among the four or five largest shipping countries in the world.

83 For the period 1960–66, Norway had an average annual % growth rate (for growth in GDP per capita, real GDP at market prices) of 4.2, while countries like the United States (3.5), Canada (3.7) and Sweden (3.9) scored lower. The highest achieving countries, on the other hand, are Japan (8.7), Greece (7.4), Trinidad and Tobago (7.3), and Taiwan (6.7). Source: *Yearbook of National Accounts Statistics*, 1967.

84 In the period 1946–49, e.g. Norway's average annual percentage growth rate (real GDP per capita) was 10.7%, which of course to a large extent is due to the 'necessary' strong achievements after a major war.

Schwartzmann and Mora y Araujo, op. cit. report that Norwegian students, when evaluating criteria of international stratification of Latin America, stressed *achieved* development as of particular importance.

85 Among the achieved, resourceful opponents, Western Germany and France may be mentioned (at least pre-Brandtian Western Germany and Gaullist France). That opposition and support of this measure of course will be due to other factors as well, e.g. ideological, strategic, and technological-economic, is evident, but do not necessarily reject the value of our argument.

CHAPTER 3.

1 Edward Shils, 'The Concept of Consensus', in *International Encyclopedia of the Social Sciences 3*, pp. 260–266.

2 This may actually not be an English dictionary word, according to the dictionaries we have consulted, but it is used in the meaning it is employed here, by several American authors.

3 Robert Zajonc, 'Conformity', *International Encyclopedia*, pp. 253–259.

4 James W. Prothro and C. W. Grigg, 'Fundamental Principles of Democracy: Bases of Agreement and Disagreement', *Journal of Politics 22*, 1960, pp. 276–294.

5 Herbert McClosky, 'Consensus and Ideology in American Politics', *American Political Science Review 58*, 1964, pp. 361–382.

6 A 2/3 consensus seems too little, i.e. 2/3 of those who given a specific answer, other than NA or DK. Our limit, however, is close to 2/3 of the total (NA's and DK's included) i.e. to 66.7%.

7 Exactly in what sense this is so may be discussed: the former may be seen as more 'serious', in that a nearly 100 % consensus in one group (e.g. the elite) receives only a 55 % or a little more than half the total, support from another (e.g. the public opinion). On the other hand, in the case of a 75 % to 35 % disagreement, the former is above, the latter *below* the simple majority level, which may be seen as more serious in some cases.

8 Cf. Lewis Coser, *The Functions of Social Conflict* (Glencoe: Free Press, 1956) and Johan Galtung, *Theories of Conflict* (forthcoming).

9 Shils, op. cit.

10 This has been maintained to be true at the international level in the case of e.g. Mainland China, by one of the 'China schools'. See also Coser, op. cit. p. 146, who holds that 'common values and norms develop in the course of struggling together ..'.

11 Norway is no. 1 among 66 countries according to the percentage of the total population who speaks the dominant language of the country, and it is among the top-ranking countries when it comes to the percentage of the population who is registered with the dominant church (the Lutheran, the percentage being 96 %) As the number of immigrants is comparatively low and the number of immigrants from not-white areas of the world is very low, ethnically it is close to 100 % white. Cf. Russett et al., *World Handbook of Political and Social Indicators.*

12 There is only one nation-wide trade union organization, one broadcasting company etc. Moreover, the number of private schools is very low: only 3.1 % of the secondary school attendants go to private schools, while the corresponding percentage for the primary school is 0.4 %. See Galtung, 'Norge i verdenssamfunnet', in Ramsøy (ed.), op. cit., p. 456 ff.

13 Shils, op. cit., p. 265.

14 Harry Eckstein, *Division and Cohesion in Democracy. A Study of Norway* (Princeton, Princeton University Press, 1966).

15 See Ulf Torgersen's and Erik Allardt's comments to Eckstein's work in *Tidsskrift for samfunnsforskning* (Oslo: Universitetsforlaget) no. 2/3, 1967, pp. 232–256.

16 Stanley Milgram, 'Nationality and Conformity', *Scientific American*, Dec. 1961, 205 (6), pp. 45–51 found in a comparative study that a French sample was significantly more resistant to social pressures (leading e.g. to distortion of perception) than a matched Norwegian sample.

17 Robert K. Merton, *Social Theory and Social Structure* (Glencoe: Free Press, 1957) p. 121.

18 Cf. Galtung, 'Foreign Policy Opinion as a Function of Social Position', and Katz, op. cit.

19 Arnold Wolfers, in Kelman (ed.), *International Political Behavior* p. 589 makes the point that consensus is generally highest in questions of 'national survival', i.e. in fundamental live-or-die questions.

20 Cf. Johanne Åmlid, *Ut av kurs* (Oslo: Pax, 1966) who gives a first-hand report on how and why this event had a great impact on the ruling party, Labor, when it discussed security policy matters and NATO membership for Norway.

21 This has been shown by Willy Martinussen, 'Velgerne og de politiske stridsspørsmål', *Tidsskrift for samfunnsforskning*, 2/3, 1967, pp. 163–186.

22 The importance of consensus vis-a-vis other groups is stressed in relation to small group theory by Homans when he says that 'a decline in interaction in the external system engaged in by the group leads to a decline in interaction in the internal

system, hence to a decline in agreement on norms, and, through the descending cycle, to the disintegration of the group. Thus common action vis a vis the outside world is a crucial variable.' Cf. George C. Homans, *The Human Group* (New York: Harcourt, Brace, 1950) pp. 449–450.

23 Moreover, before this happens the former majority may have changed its position, redefined the Establishment in the direction of the dissenters in order to maintain its power. The very raison d'etre of the ruling (majority of the) elite is that it always *is* on the side of public opinion.

24 Kenneth W. Boulding, *The Image*, p. 64 holds that '– The basic bond of any society, culture, sub-culture, or organization is a 'public image', that is, an image the essential characteristics of which is shared by the individuals participating in the group'.

25 Shils, op. cit. p. 262.

26 For a collection and some comments on Norwegian public survey data from the post-World War II period, see Johan Galtung', in Bjørn Alstad (ed.), *Norske meninger* (Oslo: Pax, 1969).

27 Hveem, 'Foreign Policy Opinion in the Elite and the General Public'.

28 Cf. Singer, 'Man and World Politics', pp. 151–152.

29 William Eckhardt and Theo F. Lentz, 'Factors of War/Peace Attitudes', *Peace Research Review I*, 5, Oct. 1967, p. 20.

30 Hveem, op. cit. p. 266.

31 William A. Scott, 'Social-Psychological Approaches', in Kelman (ed.), op. cit. pp. 70–103.

32 We might even add a fifth type, 'the autocratic dictatorship of the proletariat' system, where a few persons or one single person 'on behalf of the public', assumes power. Thus, the typology seems to approach the famous 'full circle': the latter, fifth type evidently will approach the first one, the autocratic system.

Which system is the more legitimate probably is a question of values and norms: 'Western culture' will see type *c* as the most legitimate *by definition*, whereas 'Communist culture' will see type *d*. (at least officially) as the more legitimate system.

33 'The dictatorship of the proletariat' has been left out, because it does not apply to the class of actors we are focusing on, but also because it probably does not exist or have not existed in real life (while the three others do).

34 Cf. Edinger and Searing, op. cit.; Daniel Lerner, ' French Business Leaders Look at EDC: A Preliminary Report', *Public Opinion Quarterly XX*, 1, Spring 1956, p. 220.

35 James Robinson and Richard A. Snyder, in Kelman, (ed.) op. cit. p. 457.

36 The most salient issues in the opinion of our two samples were found to be:

	Elite	Opinion-makers
NATO membership	32%	27%
EEC membership	10%	7%
Technical assistance	2%	6%
UN policy	2%	3%
Policy towards the East	2%	2%
Disarmament policy	1%	3%
Others	4%	3%
NA/DK	47%	49%
	100%	100%

37 Ottar Hellevik, *Stortinget – en sosial elite?* (Oslo: Pax, 1969) or (same author) 'Recruitment to the Position of Foreign Policy Specialist in the Norwegian Parliament', *Proceedings of the International Peace Research Association*, Second Conference (Assen: Van Gorcum, 1968).

38 Cf. Almond, op. cit.

39 The 'neutral administrator' does not exist, although members of administrative groups or organizations often *believe* so themselves and make others believe it. For a 'de-formalization' or de-mystification of the role of the administrative man, see Herbert A. Simon, *Administrative Behavior* (New York: Free Press, 1965).

40 An example of a study which employs the Galtung index on a very limited and non-representative sample of the population at large is Håkan Wiberg, 'Social Position and Peace Philosophy', *JPR* 3, 1968, pp. 277–292. This study however, is careful in not inferring falsely from the results obtained from interviewing a group of students to society as a whole, and is able to provide some fruitful hypotheses on peace-thinking differences.

41 Galtung, 'Foreign Policy Opinion as a Function of Social Position', pp. 214–216.

42 Hveem, op. cit.

43 Halle, op. cit.

44 This is e.g. seen from two nation-wide surveys made in Norway by the Norwegian Gallup Institute in 1968 and covering two of the 'hottest' issues on the international – the Vietnam war – and on the foreign policy scenes – Norway's membership in the NATO. In April 1968, people were asked if they approved of the participation of a Swedish Cabinet member, now Prime Minister, Olof Palme, in a big Stockholm demonstration together with North Vietnamese representatives, against the US Vietnam policy. In October, people were asked whether they were for or against Norwegian membership in NATO. (The latter question was asked only a few weeks after the Czechoslovakia invasion, which means that the favorable response is particularly high.) The distribution of the responses according to age categories was:

	Opinion on Palme's action:		Opinion on Norwegian membership in NATO	
	Favor it:	Against it:	Favor it:	Against it:
Age:				
15–29 years:	43 %	34 %	74 %	14 %
30–59 – :	40 %	44 %	71 %	20 %
60– – :	36 %	40 %	73 %	15 %

45 About the early socialization of political opinion, relatively little is known yet, and it seems that this particular field should be made subject to far more interest from the part of political scientists or social research at large. Some such studies, however, have appeared in the last few years, e.g. Trond Ålvik, 'The Development of Views on Conflict, War, and Peace among School Children. A Norwegian Case Study', *JPR* 2, 1968, pp. 171–195; and Magnus Haavelsrud, 'Views on War and Peace Among Students in West Berlin Public Schools', *JPR*, 2, 1970, pp. 99–120.

46 This age – the period of 'maturing' and of fundamental political socialization – most probably is lowered over time, as people in general seem to be involved in

326

politics or social affairs at an ever earlier stage. At least, this seems to hold for a society like the Norwegian.

Deutsch and Edinger, op. cit. p. 126 ff. discuss age variations from a rather similar point of view.

47 Although East-West problems have dominated the world scene in the post World War II period, cf. Hayward Alker Jr. and Bruce M. Russett, *World Politics in the General Assembly* (New Haven: Yale University Press, 1965) it is believed that these problems will not be particularly prominent in the minds of the younger. They probably are more in accordance with the images and perspectives of the elder. Issues or cognitive cues which compete for the attention of individuals, particularly the younger, are de-colonization, the 'North-South problems', etc.

48 Kenneth W. Gergen and Kurt W. Back, 'Aging, Time Perspective, and Preferred Solutions to International Conflicts', *Journal of Conflict Resolution IX*, 2, June 1965, pp. 177–186.

49 Henry Valen, unpublished material.

50 Henry Valen and Daniel Katz, *Political Parties in Norway* (Oslo: Universitetsforlaget, 1967).

51 These two party groups provided the most consensual (intra-party) support for Norwegian application for EEC membership in 1967. This was also true in 1970 when the application for membership was upheld in the parliament.

52 Theo Koritzinsky, *Partiene og utenrikspolitikken* (Oslo: Pax, 1970).

PART II: THE DATA

INTRODUCTION

1 Deutsch and Edinger, *Germany Rejoins the Powers.*

2 Deutsch, et al., *France, Germany and the Western Alliance.*

3 Gorden and Lerner, *Euratlantica.*

4 Nasatir, op. cit.; Rosenau, *National Leadership and Foreign Policy*; and Jerome Laulicht et al's various studies published by the Canadian Peace Research Institute.

5 J. David Singer, 'Soviet and American Foreign Policy Attitudes', *J. Confl. Res. VIII*, 4, pp. 424–485.

6 For an excellent discussion of such problems, see Erwin K. Scheuch, 'The Cross-cultural Use of Sample Surveys: Problems of Comparability', in Stein Rokkan (ed.), *Comparative Research across Cultures and Nations* (Paris: Mouton, 1968) pp. 176–209.

7 A collection and partial analysis of Norwegian polls since the World War II, conducted by the Norwegian Gallup Inst., is found in Galtung's articles in Alstad, (ed.) op. cit.

8 They represent studies made in France, Great Britain, West Germany, Canada, the United States. Recently, elite studies have been undertaken in India, cf. Krishan Nanda, 'Elite Nuclear Policy Thinking in India', in *Bulletin of Peace Proposals*, Autumn 1969 pp. 125–135.

CHAPTER 4

1 Kenneth A. Boulding, 'Integrative Aspects of the International System', *Proceedings of the International Peace Research Association, Inaugural Conference* (Assen: Van

Gorcum, 1966) pp. 27–37. Boulding seems to conceive of the three relations as constituting one continuum, an ordinal scale, whereas it is evident that the integrative relation operates or is found at a level above the two others.

2 Johan Galtung and Mari Holmboe Ruge, 'Patterns of Diplomacy', *JPR*, 2, 1965, pp. 101–135.

3 The fourth and last category no doubt may be criticized from the point of view of exhaustiveness: it may well be seen as part of any one of the other three. This being so, on the other hand, is an argument for treating it as something separate, in the same way as the threat and the exchange relations, in fact sub-types of the integrative relation, are treated separately.

   Another argument for including the fourth relation of socio-economic development is that the other three seem to represent the horizontal dimension of international relations, and that this fourth one may represent the vertical dimension (of status, hierarchy, wealth, etc.).

4 In their study, Gorden and Lerner asked specifically whether or not the respondents thought that the 'Russian threat in general, is still a major factor in international life?' In another question, they asked 'Are the most important problems facing the Western world in the years ahead most likely to come from *within* the Western system of alliances, from the Communist bloc, or from the uncommitted areas?'

5 As the questions used by Gorden and Lerner clearly are more specific and probably somewhat leading, the actor-orientation to some extent may be methodologically determined. On the other hand, China emerges (according to the 1965 responses) as the greatest threat in the eyes of the West German and the British elites.

6 ibid. p. 106.

7 loc. cit.

8 Cf. Galtung, op. cit.

9 Majorities of 88 % in the Soviet Union sample, 63 % in the United States sample mentioned 'One state's aggressiveness' as the major cause of war, in general. Cf. Singer, op. cit.

10 The zero-sum assumption, i.e. the assumption that the amount of power in a system is constant, is made inter alia by Lasswell and Kaplan, op. cit. Parsons on the other hand makes the point that the zero-sum argument does apply under certain conditions, but that these specific conditions do not hold for power systems in general; under different conditions one actor may extend its power without 'the sacrifice of the power of other units', cf. Talcott Parsons, 'On the Concept of Political Power', *Proceeding's of the American Philosophical Society 107*, 3, June 1963, p. 261.

11 In our analysis, we employed a three-point scale: when an actor was ranked by a respondent in the top category, i.e. Rank 1, it received 3 points, when it was ranked in Rank category 2, it received 2 points, etc. Leaving out the two super powers, the rank sums for the countries mentioned in the case of the Norwegian sample were: China 211, France 161, Great Britain 158, West Germany 116, Japan 96, India 83.

12 No doubt, there has been a certain increase in the number of 'Anti-Communists' after the 1968 Czechoslovakian events probably coupled with a slight reducement in the number of 'Anti-Americans'. Such changes, however, are believed to be only temporal and marginal: the main pattern of hegemonism is not reversed or changed.

13 In a private communication to the author.

14 These opinions may also have been somewhat affected by the invasion of Czecho-

slovakia, but again it is thought that they will move towards their 'normal' position over some time.

15 Karl W. Deutsch, et al., *Political Community and the North Atlantic Area* (Princeton: Princeton University Press, 1957).

16 Cf. Alker and Russett, op. cit. who show by means of voting analysis that East-West issues have been steadily increasing in importance. Russett in his *Trends in World Politics* (New York: Macmillan, 1965) comments on this finding as 'most disquieting'.

17 Jacobsen, op. cit. shows that Norway during this period has moved somewhat closer to the Northern cluster in the world assembly, but is still found in the midst of that cluster.

18 Cf. Deutsch et al., *France, Germany, and the Western Alliance*; the French elite perceives multipolarity as increasing and finds it to the same degree as the West German elite finds bipolarity, positive. The authors contend that these differences in emotional ties 'may continue for some time to raise difficulties for any closer French German cooperation in European affairs, and generally in international politics', p. 266.

19 Gorden and Lerner, op. cit., p. 110.

20 One outstanding member of parliament makes the point that a Sino-Soviet split most probably is not in the interest of Norway or the West, in the same way as a split in other existing constellations is not.

21 Cf. *Euratlantica*, the first mimeographed draft of the Gorden–Lerner report where these data were given on p. 12.

22 This corresponds to the attitudes expressed in 1961 by the French and the West German elites, which by clear majorities went against the idea of a disengaged demilitarized zone on the continent. Only the British elite were interested in this disarmament measure, a fact which might be explained by Great Britain's geographical-strategical position. Cf. ibid., p. III-14.

23 Ibid. p. III-14; the three samples felt almost unanimously, that mutual inspection systems were essential. The authors contend that this is a sign of 'tough-mindedness'.

24 *Euratlantica*, p. 142.

25 Norwegian elite members' attitudes toward supra-national institutions, with particular reference to Western Europe have been studied by Trygve Ramberg, who was able to show a not inconsiderable disagreement among *in casu* parliamentarians as to changing the Norwegian constitution (specifically its Para 93) to open possibilities for membership in and delegation of authority to international, supranational bodies. Ramberg makes the point that the disagreement over the question on the whole may be described as a conflict between the 'open' and the 'closed' Norway, which is probably an over-statement, as at least some of the leaders opposing the amendment of the Para 93 in 1962, clearly are openly 'internationalistic', but direct their internationalism toward bodies other than the Western European ones, which were clearly in the minds of all when the amendment were debated. Cf. Trygve Ramberg, 'Stortingsdebatten om § 93' (Oslo 1967), mimeo.

26 Several respondents made the point that candidates for such posts would not be well known to the electorate, and that there would be a danger of candidates being elected on PR campaigns primarily, not on quality or policy.

27 The correlations were (correlations for the opinion-maker sample in brackets):
International democracy – Weighted voting: .36   (.18)
Weighted voting – Supranationality: .24   (.14)

Abolish veto – Supranationality:	.27	(.11)
Abolish veto – International dem.:	.26	(.02)

[28] Morton Kaplan, *System and Process in International Politics* (New York: Wiley, 1957).

[29] On the other hand, the bilateral approach of course may be subject to, or its content may be determined by, multilateral decision-making and consultation. And its aims or at least its consequences, may be a fragmentation of the 'other bloc' which in the long run may be rather assymmetric and thus lead to counteractions and possibly breakdown of contacts amounting to polarization from the part which feels that it is the object of a fragmentation policy. Elite interviewing in Eastern European countries has shown that this is exactly the feeling many elites on that 'side' have toward attempts from Western Europe, at least up to recently coordinated through the European Common Market, to establish contacts with the East. See Johan Galtung (ed.) *Cooperation in Europe* (Oslo: Universitetsforlaget, 1970).

[30] Gorden and Lerner, op. cit., p. 104 ff.

[31] Jerome Laulicht, 'Public Opinion and Foreign Policy Decisions', *JPR*, 2, 1965 pp. 147–160 shows that 77 % of a Canadian elite sample, made up of business leaders, labor leaders, and politicians, were for a policy of coexistence toward the East, while 18 % were ambivalent on the question and 5 % were against it.

[32] Op. cit., p. III-12. The question in the Gorden-Lerner study was: 'Which method of conducting negotiations on arms control is more likely to produce useful results-bilateral negotiations between America and Russia, multilateral negotiations among nuclear nations outside the United Nations, or generalized negotiations within the United Nations?' In 1965, West Germany preferred the bilateral, France the multilateral approach, while Great Britain was equally divided between the two. These responses seem to be well in accordance with the nuclear, and in general political position of the three countries.

[33] This is proposed by e.g. the so called Rapacki and Gomulka plans, put forth by the Polish government.

[34] Op. cit.; 27 % of the sample (see note 31) was of the opinion that Canadian development assistance should remain on its present level, while 4 % wanted to decrease it.

[35] Gorden and Lerner, The mimeographed report, p. IV-17.

[36] Cf. the report of the OECD Development Assistance Committee (DAC) of 1968, which shows that Canada and Norway ranked lowest among the countries compared here when it comes to total transfers to developing countries in 1968. The figures are total transfers, public and private, to LDC's as a percentage of the BNP):

West Germany	1.26 %
France	1.17 %
United Kingdom	0.75 %
United States	0.66 %
Norway	0.64 %
Canada	0.49 %

[37] This was particularly true of perceptions of the French elite under President de Gaulle. To what extent these perceptions may have changed with his demise and the succession of President Pompidou *and* subsequent French consent to negotiations for British and possibly Danish and Norwegian entry into the European Common Market is difficult to say, but there may have been a certain change

toward a more positive evaluation of French attitudes after those events.

38 According to the DaC report, op. cit., only a small percent of France's development assistance was channeled through multilateral organs (in 1967) while the same percentage for Norway was 51 % (1969 figure).

39 In a number of cases from the last years, Norway together with most or all its Western allies, abstained from voting on concrete issues involving Portuguese colonialism and the Southern Africa. Most often, the Norwegian stand has been explained by the government's reluctance to vote for measures proposed (by African and/or other countries) to deal with those issues, because these measures could not be implemented. It has, however, expressed its 'sympathy' with the cause of de-colonization and liberation of the minority-controlled areas.

40 *Euratlantica*, p. 217 ff.

41 The three samples in the Gorden-Lerner study were asked to state which one single relationship (with other states or multi-state bodies) they thought was the most important one to their country.

42 op. cit.

43 Nasatir et al., op. cit.

44 A proposal to consider the possibility of setting up UN jurisdiction or some kind of regime over the seas and the ocean floor was put forth by the representative of Malta in the UN General Assembly in 1967.

45 A survey involving a small sample of American elite people is in the process of being carried out on the request of the World Law Fund. This survey will touch related issues and problem-areas.

46 Gorden and Lerner, op. cit., p. 220.

47 In the British survey from 1961, the question was: 'Do you approve of the integration of a major part of the British armed forces into a permament supra-national army under European Command? NATO Command? UN command?' The question asked about a 'major part' of the forces, while that in the Norwegian case only asked for 'parts of' the armed forces. It may be noted that the British sample was most positive toward integration under NATO command, least positive to a European command of its forces.

48 There may have been a certain, but probably not great decrease in the support for UN forces after the withdrawal of the UNEF from the Gaza strip in May 1967, just after our survey was completed. The withdrawal by some of the elite members, who in fact signed a petition which was published in several Norwegian newspapers expressing their disappointment of the withdrawal, was negatively evaluated.

49 Gorden and Lerner, op. cit. p. 124.

50 While all the three samples in the Gorden–Lerner survey from 1965 by majorities reject the conception, which is Gaullist, of Western Europe as a counterpoise to the United States (as well as to the Soviet Union) the majorities in the French and West German samples were only 51 % and 52 %, respectively, while it was 79 % in the British sample. Ibid., p. 130 ff.

51 *ibid.*, p. 120 ff.

52 In June 1971, 37 of a total 150 Norwegian members of Parliament voted for the withdrawal of the application for full membership. A corresponding vote in 1967 showed only 13 MP's against applying for full membership.

53 Norway among the three Scandinavian countries, according to a survey made among parliamentarians in these countries in 1967, is the one which is least inter-

ested in joining the EEC *without* Great Britain also joining it. Cf. Matth. Bonham, 'Scandinavian Parliamentarians: Attitudes toward Political Integration', *Cooperation and Conflict*, 3, 1969, pp. 149–161. The Norwegian 'Europeanism' then is strongly dependent on the British one.

54 I am indebted to Kjell Skjelsbæk of the International Peace Research Institute, Oslo for this information.

55 Cf. Peter Willetts, 'The Behavior of the African Group in the General Assembly, University of Strathclyde, M. Sc. Dissertation, 1968/69.

56 Nils P. Gleditsch, *Norge i verdenssamfunnet* (Oslo: Pax, 1970) pp. 58–60.

57 I am indebted to Kurt Jacobsen of the International Peace Research Institute, Oslo for these data, made available by the Inter-University Consortium for Political Research.

58 Again I am indebted to Kurt Jacobsen.

59 Cf. Kurt Jacobsen, 'Sponsorships in the United Nations – A System Analysis', *JPR*, 3, 1969, pp. 235–266.

60 These cases represent both Left *and* Right outsiders. The former obviously resent the close affiliation and what they term as total dependecy on the United States and the NATO. The latter seem to put the blame on the more 'ideal' ties we maintain to actors such as the United Nations, UNCTAD, but also EFTA, making the point that Norway is too loyal towards them e. g. in the question of sanctions against Rhodesia, which they maintain other states obstruct. But one of these Right outsider criticis even put the blame on the United States, which he says gets her allies, like tiny Norway, to behave e. g. imposing embargo on trade with certain countries (Cuba, Eastern Europe formerly, etc.) without sticking very strictly to the same rules herself in other cases.

61 One outstanding civil servant makes the point that Norway has had a lot to say within the NATO, but that she particularly towards her home public opinion, has refrained from showing that or saying so because of a too strong and consistent loyalty towards the organization and the collective decision-making. Another respondent makes the point that the Norwegian leaders very often have been able to, and in fact have used Norway's participation in and obligations toward greater units, as an excuse for impopular decisions at home, and he cites the case of the OEEC (now OECD) as an example.

CHAPTER 5

1 These variables are: NATO membership; EEC membership; Rapid vs. step-wise disarmament; Multilateral vs. bilateral development assistance; Multilateral vs. bilateral disarmament or arms control negotiations; Whether *detente* will continue or not; Whether disarmament will be realized in the future, or not; Whether or not a World War III is likely in the future; Whether or not bipolarity will remain; Supranationalism; Global vs. regional preference; and Whether or not own country's development assistance should be increased.

2 They were: Attitudes to the European Coal and Steel Community (1952); to the European Defence Community (1952); to the Western European Union (1955); to the Paris Agreements (1955); and to NATO (1955). The source employed by Deutsch and Edinger is Suzanne Keller, 'Attitudes toward European Integration

of the German Elite', M.I.T. Center for International Studies, multigraphed, October 1957.

3 This holds only when modal values are used as parameter: the acceptance of NATO in 1955 was 74 % in the West German elite (against 86 % in the Norwegian) and 29 % in the West German public opinion (against 52 % in the Norwegian). When ratios of positive to negative responses are considered, the West Germans are more in agreement, but again the very high NA score in the West German public, 60 %, makes comparison difficult if not impossible.

4 The other spheres of governmental activity were: Housing; taxation, economic development, and employment policies. While the public was slightly more satisfied with the employment policy of the government in 1968 than with its foreign policy, in 1969 the latter was clearly the most popular (82 % expressed general satisfaction, against 70 % for economic development policies as the next ranking) Source: Norwegian Gallup Institute. The figures were first published in the newspaper *Aftenposten*, 25 March 1969.

5 Cf. Hveem, 'Foreign Policy Thinking in the Elite and the General Population', pp. 164–65.

6 Two of the elite, four of the opinion-maker respondents are rejecting or being ambivalent to three of the four items, thus lying rather close to the category of 'Anti-Establishmentarians'.

7 For measuring 'Westwardness', four items were employed: Loyalty to West (Euroamerica and the Nordic), Maintain alliances is important to peace, Supranationalism, and Strengthen regional organizations is important to peace.

8 Hveem, 'Foreign Policy Thinking', p. 164: the rank correlations between the three groups, according to their ranking of the peace proposals (totalling 12 items) as important to peace, were:

Elite – Opinion-makers: .89
Opinion-makers – Youth: .80
Elite – Youth: .63

9 All items mentioned in note 1 above, except: Whether disarmament or arms control negotiations should be multilateral or bilateral; Whether or not bipolarity will remain, and Supranationalism, but (in the case of the British sample only) with the inclusion of Attitude toward integration of armed forces in a UN standing force.

10 The other side of the coin *is* the position of the publics in the various countries. Several authors have pointed to the fact that public opinion tends to put restrictions on the foreign policy actually pursued, i.e.: the elites cannot implement all their attitudes, opinions etc. *because* of public resistance. Cf. Almond, op. cit. Thus obviously, agreement on the attitudinal and cognitive level between certain elites does not necessarily mean that their policies will be equally in agreement. To assess the probability of this happening, we have to analyze the attitudes of the respective public opinions and look for international agreement also at that level.

11 Bernard Berelson and Gary A. Steiner, *Human Behavior: An Inventory of Scientific Findings* (New York: Harcourt, Brace & World, 1964).

12 Correlations are (for opinion-makers in parentheses):

	Problem	Trend	Threat
Trend	.12		
	(.33)		
Threat	.16	.20	
	(.49)	(.21)	
Hoped 2000	.12	−.06	.06
	(.26)	(.16)	(.19)

[13] For a thorough analysis of the public opinion responses, employing the individual social position index, and for the data used here, see Johan Galtung, 'Attitudes toward Different Forms of Disarmament. A Study of Norwegian Public Opinion', *Proceedings of the International Peace Research Association Inaugural Conference*, pp. 210–238.

[14] Source: Norwegian Gallup Institute.

[15] ibid.

[16] Cf. Galtung, in Alstad (ed.), op. cit.

[17] ibid.

[18] Cf. Ingrid Eide Galtung, 'Attitudes to Technical Assistance: A Study based on Norwegian Public Opinion Data', *Proceedings of the International Peace Research Association, Second Conference* Vol. II, pp. 342–368.

[19] Galtung, op. cit.

[20] Cf. Ramberg, op. cit.

[21] One indication of this is the obvious increased opposition among parrlamentarians, notably from the Center party, against membership. The opposition is based on explicit references to these perspectives.

[22] Cf. Norwegian Gallup.

[23] For a review of trends in Norwegian public attituder toward EEC. See Tord Høivik, Nils P. Gleditsch and Ottar Hellevik 'Folkeopinion og EEC', in Susan Høivik (ed.), *10 innlegg om EEC* (Oslo: Universitetsforlaget, 1971) pp. 97–130.

[24] Cf. Norwegian Gallup.

[25] Galtung, in Alstad (ed.), op. cit.

[26] ibid.

CHAPTER 6.

[1] The ten variables employed are: NATO membership; Whether or not Norwegian development assistance should be increased; Multilateral vs. bilateral development assistance; EEC membership; Global vs. regional policies primarily; Weighted voting in the United Nations; Supranationalism; Role of non-aligned countries positive or negative; Whether or not any value of aim is great enough to justify a major war; and Economic sanctions.

[2] Galtung, *Theory and Methods of Social Research,* p. 399.

[3] All the Christian/Center party elite members are found in the periphery category; 3/4 of the Socialist People's Party/Communists in the same. This periphery position is coinciding with what has been reported in Johan Galtung, 'Social Position, Party Identification, and Foreign Policy Orientation: A Norwegian Case Study', in Rosenau (ed.) *Domestic Sources of Foreign Policy* pp. 161–193.

[4] Keller, op. cit.

5 The corresponding correlation in the case of the opinion-makers is considerably lower, .16, which seems to back the contention of high exposure as being relatively crucial in this context, as it may be expected that exposure is even lower at the level of opinion-makers.

6 Cf. Karl W. Deutsch, *Arms Control and the Atlantic Alliance* (New York: John Wiley, 1967) p. 53.

7 In the case of the opinion-makers, the verification of the hypothesis is in doubt, because of great variances in NA or DK scores among the four age categories. The average (mean) percentage scores of acceptance *and* NA/DK responses are as follows:

	Y	MY	M	O
Acceptance	64.2	68.8	61.2	62.4
NA/DK	8.2	12.6	26.6	23.6

When the variances in NA/DK scores are controlled for, it seems that the hypothesis is fairly well backed, possibly with the exception that the Middle category is at least as positive or as concerned with cooperation, as the Old category.

8 Deutsch et al., *France, Germany, and the Western Alliance* p. 23.

9 loc. cit.

10 Galtung, 'Attitudes toward Different Forms of Disarmament', *Proceedings*, Inaugural Conference; and Eide Galtung, op. cit.

11 To control for arbitrariness in the definition of the center and periphery categories, Galtung defined them in two ways, in both cases using the 8 variable additive index, so that the only difference is in the cutting points. His definitions are as follows:
Definition I: Center = 6–8, Periphery = 0–2
Definition II: Center = 8, Periphery = 0–1.
See Galtung, op. cit. in preceding note, p. 214.

12 Valen and Katz conclude 'The national leaders in the Labour government represent a program of defence and foreign policy which Labour party members have difficulty in understanding and following'. Cf. Valen and Katz, op. cit. p. 258.

13 The Labor party probably has the strongest and most effective party machinery among Norwegian political parties, being able to maintain a relatively strong central leadership of the party.

14 The six 'Establishment-related' items were: Global vs. regional policies; Merchant marine assistance for less developed countries; Unilateral vs. mutual disarmament; Value or aim justifying major war; Maintain alliances important to peace; Maintain balance important to peace.

CHAPTER 7.

1 Festinger, op. cit.

2 Galtung, *Theory and Methods* p. 301.

3 L. L. Mc Quitty, 'Elementary Linkage Analysis for Isolating Orthogonal and Oblique Types and Typal Relevancies', *Educational and Psychological Measurement 1965*, pp. 207–229.

4 Factor analysis by Åke Hartmann at the International Peace Research Institute. Oslo.

5 In the youth study from 1967, the respondents besides giving their preference for several peace proposals were asked to state which of the proposals they believed most likely would lead to peace. This of course is not quite the same as being asked about the 'realism' of the proposals, but we think that the responses would at least give an indication of the perceptions of the respondents. Unfortunately, data on this question do not lend themselves easily to comparative purposes. Responses were given to one single question only in the form of a multiple choice question with only one response. Moreover, NA/DK responses were very high. On the basis of the responses available, however, the suggestion that the dissonance is greatest among the public opinion (youth) sample, seems justified.

6 An article which deals with related problems is Hans and Shulamith Kreitler, 'Crucial Dimensions of the Attitude towards National and Supra-national Ideals', *JPR*, 2, 1967, pp. 107–124.

7 Unpublished material from a study made by Herman Schmid at the Institute of Sociology, Lund University, Sweden, in 1966–67. Members of such organizations were asked what would be more important in creating peace: that we get more peace-oriented leaders, or that the international system is changed. 51 % thought that more peace-oriented leaders was most important, while 34 % believed in system changes, a result which clearly contrasts with the thoughts of the Norwegian elite. On a question which asked if peace could be better secured if or when the political leaders were changed or educated to peace, 29 % of the elite sample was in favor of the idea, 44 % against it. The respective percentages in the opinion-maker sample were 49 % and 20 % (while the two Norwegian samples were in nearly complete agreement as to the idea of raising individuals generally to peace). This seems to indicate some differences *due* to stratification or different social position.

The British sample of peace activists on the other hand is far more anomic than the Norwegian samples; it favors extra-parliamentary action to promote its policies, ideas that are not represented (in the same form, at least) among the elite members, and hardly so among the opinion makers.

CHAPTER 8.

1 Johan Galtung, 'Images of the World in the Year 2000', European Coordination Centre for Research and Documentation in Social Sciences, Vienna, 1970.

2 Deutsch et al., *France, Germany, and the Western Alliance* p. 107.

3 Deutsch et al. obviously do not take such factors explicitly into consideration when they make the point that 'current opinions about domestic and world politics, even if they deal with what is desirable, will necessarily have a bearing upon future developments. How much is hard to say. Between those who claim that the knowledge of such opinions cannot help us see ahead into the future and those who rely almost exclusively upon them in predicting trends, there is a middle ground. Elite opinions we feel, give us a basis for careful and qualified 'guessing' ---', loc. cit.

Although we in principle share the point made, we would warn against employing it as generally and undiscriminatingly as they seem to propose.

4 A similar conclusion is made in a report on a study of Norwegian elites from recent years on the basis of other, but not unrelated variables. See G. Lowell Field and John Higley, 'Elite-konsensus i et utviklet politisk samfunn', *Tidsskrift for samfunnsforskning*, 1, 1971, pp. 1–28.